DECENTRALISATION

Need for

REFORMS

About the Author

Mr D.N.GUPTA joined Indian Administrative Service (IAS) in 1989. For the last decade and a half, he has been closely associated with development planning, and management of implementation of social and rural development programmes.

He has worked in various capacities in the state of Orissa. He has held posts of Sub-collector, Malkangiri sub-division; Project Director, Tribal Development Project, Koraput; Managing Director, Orissa Textiles Mills, Cuttack; District Collector, Sonepur district; and Joint Secretary, Department of Welfare, Govt. of Orissa. He was Deputy Secretary, Ministry of Rural Development, Govt. of India.

He has extensively worked in the field of watershed development, participatory planning, and training. His specialisation is in the field of micro-planning, project design and management of programmes. Besides, his areas of interest pertain to development administration, governance and decentralisation.

Presently, he is working as Fellow, Institute of Social Sciences (ISS), New Delhi.

DECENTRALISATION
Need for
REFORMS

D.N. GUPTA, IAS

CONCEPT PUBLISHING COMPANY, NEW DELHI-110059

Cataloging in Publication Data--DK
Courtesy: D.K. Agencies (P) Ltd. <docinfo@dkagencies.com>

Gupta, D. N. (Devendra Nath), 1966-
Decentralisation : need for reforms / D.N. Gupta.
p. cm.
In Indian context.
Includes bibliographical references (p.)
Includes index.
ISBN 8180691411

1. Decentralization in government--India. 2. India --Politics and government. I. Title.

DDC 352.283 095 4 21

ISBN 81-8069-141-1

First Published 2004

Published and Printed by
Ashok Kumar Mittal
Concept Publishing Company
A/15-16, Commercial Block, Mohan Garden,
NEW DELHI-110059
Phones : 25351460, 25351794
Fax : 091-11-25357103
Email : publishing@conceptpub.com

Dedicated to my Parents
Smt. Sharda Devi Gupta and Shri R.N.S. Gupta
as a mark of respect for their exceptional
Quality of Perseverance and Hard Work

Dedicated to my Parents

Smt. Sharda Devi Gupta and Shri R.V.S. Gupta

as a mark of respect for their exceptional

Qualities of Perseverance and Hard Work

PREFACE

Since the early 1990s, distinctly pronounced moves towards decentralisation are found in all parts of the world, which get more rooted into the constitutional systems beyond the rhetoric of day-to-day politics. From 1930s to 1980s, it was a period of decentralisation in many ways. Since 1980s, there has been disillusionment with big government everywhere leading to a variety of changes. The world has passed through cycles of centralisation and decentralisation and has always been in a dilemma (Kueck, 1998). During the independence and revolutionary movements in the countries like France, USA and India, the writings and sayings of the leaders were strongly in favour of decentralised political system (Kueck, 1998). Now, nearly all countries world-wide are experimenting with decentralisation (Manor, 1999). In India there have been forces since independence urging the political system within the country to be decentralised, to have a structure of local governments where local decisions are taken by the people as near the point as possible. This has led to 73rd Constitution Amendment Act with an aim to provide the structure of the local institutions and to empower them.

With this Act, a very large responsibility of overall development of the villages has been placed in the hands of PRIs. But, earlier in most states, PRIs were not effective for long and excessive government control and direction have crept in. In the process, the PRIs now in place find it difficult to cope with the new roles. Keeping this in mind, it is vital to assess how the PRIs can come up to the level of operating from 'within' to carry out developmental activities for the village development in general and the poverty alleviation in particular. In this backdrop, the book examines critically the provisions enshrined in the 73rd Constitution Amendment Act, socio-political processes at the village level, the existing state of functioning of PR institutions and their capacity to meet the people's needs at the local level; and recommends measures for initiating reforms in order to meet the growing need of good governance.

The book has been organised in two parts. The first part dwells on present state of decentralisation while the second part deals with the capacity building of local institutions and sets the agenda for reforms.

Chapter one explains the need for the study of decentralisation. It has stressed the necessity of covering all the dimensions—political, functional, administrative and financial—in order to get a complete view about the status of decentralisation. Specifically, the issues covered are environment building, people's participation, administrative and financial powers of panchayats, taxation, support system, transparency and accountability. The objectives of the study are: to study the present status of decentralisation and examine the problems therein;

to assess how decentralisation has helped in the socio-economic development of rural areas; and to explore measures that are necessary to strengthen the process of decentralisation and in meeting the norms of good governance.

Chapter two examines the emergence of decentralisation world over, and the evolution of panchayati raj system in India. It also provides an overview of the Central Amendment Act. To begin with, we take the case of the gram sabha. Article 243A prescribes that the gram sabha may exercise the powers and perform such functions at the village level as the state legislatures may provide. The states have made necessary provisions for the role of gram sabha in the village development. Articles 243B and 243C deal with the formation of panchayats and territorial constituencies respectively. The direct election for members at all the three tiers are provided by Article 243C, and with this the elections for the local bodies have been made mandatory once in five years. With the aim to broaden the base for the representation in the panchayat bodies, Article 243C specifies that the states may provide representation to MPs and MLAs in the panchayat bodies. For giving representation to the weaker sections, Article 243D makes provision for the reservation of women, SCs and STs, and such reservation should be rotated.

Article 243G defines that the states may endow the panchayats with the necessary powers and responsibilities for certain functions in order to enable them to function as institutions of self-governance. To improve the internal resources of panchayats, under Article 243H, the states may authorise the panchayats to impose and collect taxes. And for enhancing the financial autonomy, as per Article 243I, the states may devolve funds upon panchayats based on the recommendations of SFC. For observing financial discipline, Article 243J provides that the states may make provisions for the maintenance of accounts by panchayats and the auditing of such accounts. In order to facilitate the preparation of district plan, Article 243ZD (of 74th Constitution Amendment Act) stipulates for setting up of district planning committee (DPC). And, the 11th Schedule provides the subjects that are to be transferred to the panchayats at the three tiers.

While examining the evolution of panchayati raj system in India, it states that it has been influenced by centralisad approach of decision-making without giving due regards (in operational terms) to people's participation, transparency, accountability, save responsiveness to people's problems. It further adds that the focus of the evolution of PRIs has been more on election, powers and control than on the development role of local institutions in meeting basic services of people.

Chapter three analyses the states' legislations and the measures initiated by the states for operationalising the Act. It examines all the dimensions viz., political, functional, administrative and financial that are essential for decentralisation.

Under political decentralisation the political status has been given to local institutions and elected members. Some steps have been taken for encouraging people's participation and ensuring accountability. Kerala has taken wide-ranging initiatives for enhancing people's participation and for accountability through social audit. The functional decentralisation has not been adequately attended to, and only partially some functions have given. While in the state of Kerala suitable measures have been taken for transfer of functions and for inter-tier demarcation of functions

As regards the administrative decentralisation, it is still in infancy stage. It is only in the state of Kerala the institutional mechanisms for planning, implementation, coordination and monitoring have been placed. And the steps have been taken for placement of officers and staff of line departments with PRIs. Also, in the states of Gujarat, Karnataka, Madhya Pradesh, Maharashtra, Uttar Pradesh and West Bengal some measures have been initiated for providing administrative responsibilities and powers to PRIs. The financial devolution has not taken the desired shape. Collection of taxes is poor, devolution of funds has not taken place and the sources of funds are inadequate in all the states, except in Kerala.

Chapter four provides an account of the critical observations made from the field studies. It is evident from the studies that the functioning of gram sabha, which is a fulcrum of participatory development, is far from satisfactory, rather it is something that needs immediate attention. The poor attendance, lack of visible people's participation and the discussion on narrow agenda in the gram sabha present a poor account of functioning of panchayats at the grassroots level. The PR members are more concerned with the devolution of funds, transfer of functions, and control over officers and staff for the transfer and postings, rather than the involvement of people at every stage of development. Similarly, the studies indicate that participatory planning at the gram panchayat level is hampered by a number of factors such as lack of awareness among people at the village level, indifferent attitude of people about the capacity of the panchayats to deliver, lack of capabilities in elected members at panchayat level, influence of individuals in the gram sabha meeting, poor women participation and so on.

The gram panchayats do not find adequate representation in the higher tiers, as the views of the chairpersons of gram panchayats are not duly attended to by the higher tiers. While, in the gram sabha, which is the forum of accountability, it is the chairperson of the gram panchayat who has to answer to the questions of people. Thus, in a way, the members who have to answer in the gram sabha do not have much say in the proceedings of the higher tiers.

Article 243B deals with the formation of gram panchayats. It is on the concerned states to decide about the size of the gram panchayat. The states have formed the gram panchayats based on the population criterion. If we look into the average size of the population of one gram panchayat, it is normally in the vicinity of 2000 in most of the states (only a few states like Assam, Kerala and West Bengal have population more than 10,000). Now, if we examine critically, the small size of gram panchayats has caused some practical problems for the panchayats to function effectively, as the states are not able to provide necessary manpower, infrastructural and logistics support. It is rendering panchayats un-viable units of development.

The Act makes provision for the reservation of the weaker sections and such reservation should be rotated. The states have construed that the rotation can be for every five years. As observed, one term is not sufficient for carrying out sufficient development activities if long term view is taken. Also, it discourages members from taking innovative projects as they feel that they have less chance to become members again.

In certain states an interesting feature has come out that the duration of chairpersons of panchayats has been fixed for certain period. For instance, in Karnataka, it is fixed for twenty months for chairpersons of taluk (intermediate) and zilla panchayats, and thirty months for chairpersons of gram panchayats. Similarly, in Maharashtra, for intermediate and zilla panchayats, earlier (in 1999-2000) the term was fixed for one year, which has been raised to two and a half years. By any account, these are retrograde steps. Now, in this process, chairpersons hardly find sufficient time to perform and members are more occupied in identifying suitable substitutes (for future) for most of the time.

As enshrined in the Act, the states may authorise the panchayats to impose and collect taxes. States have made provisions for the collection of taxes. However, the present status of panchayat finances is marked with low tax-base and poor institutional arrangements. If we examine carefully the poor state of collection of taxes, it reveals that it is due to combination of various factors such as lack of political will in PR members, lack of confidence of people in the present set-up of PR institutions to deliver, lack of conducive environment at the village level for the people to pay taxes in order to avail services, the low income level of people to pay taxes and low income-base of panchayats, coupled with high cost of collection of taxes at local levels.

As per Article 243I the states may devolve funds upon panchayats based on the recommendations of state finance commission (SFC). The SFCs of almost all the states have submitted reports, still not much has been done to address the problems of panchayat finances. And no serious attempt has been made to devolve funds upon panchayats and to augment their own income. Here, one important observation is about the recommendations of SFCs. That they have not looked into certain vital points such as requirement of development funds for panchayats, how the resources of panchayats be raised to meet their development needs, user charges, cross-subsidy, tax collection mechanism and so on. Though some recommendations have been made, but they are not comprehensive.

For setting up of district planning committee (DPC), some steps have been taken by the states for its formation, but there are certain shortcomings. *First*, the chairperson of DPC is not an elected member from panchayats or municipalities in most of the states. *Second*, DPC does not have adequate experts as its member. *Third*, DPC is formed but the supporting wing in the form of planning unit is not adequately placed. *Finally*, no planning committee or unit exists at the block or GP level in order to carry out local level planning and also to provide vital inputs on local needs and resources to DPC. And, even after the constitution of DPCs in some states, there appears to be no qualitative improvement in the planning process at the district level.

If we closely examine, it would appear that the measures (taken by states) such as conducting panchayat elections, formulating guidelines for organising gram sabhas, transfer of functions and setting up of state finance commission (SFC), basically emanate from the statutory provisions of the Act rather than the necessity for empowering the people and improving the capacity of PRIs. Similarly, it appears that the role of PR members is more on contesting elections, taking control of funds, identifying beneficiaries or works (mainly construction type) and executing works by their choice than on people's participation and improving the effectiveness of panchayats to deliver. And field studies have revealed that their decisions are mainly guided by immediate gains and political considerations.

There are certain lessons that can be drawn from Kerala's experience of 'People's Plan Campaign'. Under this, in 1996-97 state government had initiated massive programme of awareness building, making information available to people, setting up of planning units at all the three tiers and training of all elected representatives and development functionaries at each tier. Besides, the locally available technical experts are also tapped in order to augment the capacity of the gram panchayats. Such efforts, in Kerala, have paid high dividends to panchayats at all the three tiers in enhancing their capacities and in enabling them to take up the task of participatory planning. While other states, due to their lack of initiatives for empowering people and improving the capacities of panchayats, have not been successful in local level planning. Thus, to conclude, that the explanation of Kerala's success in participatory village development planning, and by contrast that of other states' failure, combines in its own way four major elements in the following order: *first*, high awareness level among people; *second*, database and information system at the village level for empowering people with knowledge; *third*, improved capabilities of PR members and development functionaries; and *fourth*, availability of technical people at local level.

Chapter five summarises the present state of decentralisation. The Act came into effect in April, 1993 and well over ten years have now elapsed, but much progress has not been made as regards the operational part of the Act. The implementation of the Act varies in content and degree from state to state. Kerala has moved much ahead of others in the process of decentralisation. Some other states like Karnataka, Gujarat, Madhya Pradesh, Maharashtra, Uttar Pradesh and West Bengal have taken some measures to strengthen the PR institutions; and a few ones like Andhra Pradesh, Assam, Haryana, Orissa and Punjab are struggling to make definite impact on decentralisation. Though there is a consensus among states as far as the strengthening of PR institutions is concerned, yet wide differences persist among them with regard to the approach for various fundamental issues such as capacity building (in terms of institutional capabilities), transfer of functions and devolution of funds upon panchayats, raising of income level of panchayats through taxes, and support system (manpower, administrative and infrastructural) to panchayats.

The findings of the study have categorically revealed that under the given state of decentralisation, the panchayats are not in a position of meeting the basic needs of people at the grassroots level. The reasons attributed for poor state of local institutions are poor people's participation, meagre financial resources and lack of requisite institutional capabilities for undertaking the task of development planning and implementation. Also, the small size of gram panchayats has raised the question of their administrative and financial viability. The transparency and accountability system is not adequately placed. People do not have access to information, and decision-making is marked with lack of openness. In a way, panchayats lack proper environment in terms of proper value system with regard to transparency, responsiveness for people's concern and accountability; of opportunities for people to participate, especially for the weaker sections; and of capabilities to perform. The panchayat leadership is more synonymous with the number of people one can organise and what one can speak. There is a little emphasis on values and substance. Values like people's participation in development, collective decision-making, respect for rules and norms, and responsiveness for grievances do not get much attention. There is a lack of culture of discussion. People do not feel that they matter in the decision-making process.

Further, it adds that the lack of success of implementation of the Act is as much due to lack of devolution of funds as is due to low people's participation, poor capacities of PR institutions, and non-placement of systems of transparency, monitoring and social audit. But, presently, it is the devolution of funds that is where the focus is, while other important issues that are very vital for strengthening the PRIs have not been adequately thought of. But Kerala stands apart. As in order to strengthen the PR institutions, it has placed specific components for environment building, transfer of functions, devolution of funds, training, planning, implementation, transparency and accountability in the right perspective.

The analysis also brings out that the panchayats at all the three tiers are not in a position to perform as expected. And the pace and the direction of decentralisation are not upto a satisfactory level. Neither are people empowered to participate meaningfully, nor are their needs addressed, nor do panchayats have the capacity to deliver as per the local needs. Moreover, there are no organic linkages among the three tiers. Also, the Central Act is not in a position to address these issues. Moreover, most of the provisions in the Act are indicative and not mandatory in nature. All these point towards having a re-look at the Constitution Amendment Act, and for effecting necessary amendmens.

For good governance at the grassroots level, **chapter six** suggests the measures for augmenting the capacity of local institutions. It should enable them to take up the task of planning and implementation of programmes and to deliver basic services as per the local needs. It emphasises the need to explore as to where the problem lies and whether the fundamentals (people's participation, capacity of panchayats, transparency and accountability) are placed in their right perspective for operationalising the Act.

The Act has provided framework for decentralisation. States have made attempts to give the Act an operational shape. But, in order to achieve the desired objectives of decentralisation, it should pass certain conditions for success. Now, what constitute the vital conditions are: political will; environment building and capabilities in elected members; sufficient financial resources to accomplish important tasks; adequate capacity to accomplish those tasks; and reliable accountability mechanism. Against this backdrop, it would, therefore, necessitate that the states should adopt an integrative approach keeping in view the whole spectrum of issues concerning the process of decentralisation and need to initiate the following measures:

Creating enabling environment: It would include taking steps for providing security and peace at the village level; secured status for local bodies; empowerment of people; political will for providing autonomy to panchayats; and training of PR members and development functionaries to understand, appreciate and then perform their jobs.

Improving capabilities of PR members is of high importance due to their enhanced roles and responsibilities in the process of development. It should also be appreciated that planning will require certain knowledge and skills before a meaningful village plan can be developed. All these will demand that concerted efforts should be made to have training programmes on a continuous basis for PR members, especially for the women and members of the weaker sections. Also of importance is the need of bringing attitudinal changes for good value system.

Optimal and rational allocation of sectoral funds, both for inter- and intra-panchayat, will call for developing suitable planning methodology that should include planning process, tools and techniques, and integration of plans of each tier. With the increasing responsibilities of PR members and devolution of large funds upon panchayats, the transparency and accountability assume a new dimension. PR members are expected to be accountable for the administrative and financial decisions that would be taken by them. This calls for establishing proper procedure and guidelines along with certain statutory provisions for transparency and social audit.

Another area that needs urgent attention is how the internal resources of panchayats can be augmented. It will call for bringing some more items under tax-basket, fixation of certain minimum service charges, creating conducive political environment for generating awareness among people about the need for paying taxes that are vital for the continuation of services for them, and providing institutional support to panchayats for the collection of taxes. Besides, the panchayats should deliver effectively and efficiently, so that people would have confidence in the local institutions and feel that what they would pay is worth paying. Further, SFC requires revitalisation. It needs to be given more teeth with mandatory provisions for suggesting not only devolution package but also user charges and norms for cross-subsidy for various services, and for reducing the horizontal and vertical distortions in the panchayat finances.

The functional viability of gram panchayats is very important in order to provide people the basic services such as primary education, health services, drinking water, availability of agricultural inputs, veterinary services, land settlement, irrigation management and so on, at one point and also at GP level. Accordingly, the required delivery mechanism should be set up for each gram panchayat, and from the point of view of administrative and financial viability, minimum size of one gram panchayat assumes high significance. Rightly so, also keeping in view the principle of making basic services available to people as close to them as possible, the optimal size of the gram panchayat should be determined.

Keeping in view that people should be able to participate in the socio-politico-economic process of development at the village level and that the panchayats should become the units of development, the chapter suggests about bringing amendments in the Central Act (also thereafter in the state panchayat Acts). The areas that require urgent attention are timely election of panchayat bodies, people's participation, capacity of panchayats to function, constitution of various bodies such as DPC, SFC, organic linkages, transparency and accountability. It also recommends for incorporating clauses for people's watch committees, constitution of tribunal and strengthening planning unit and delivery system.

In essence, the chapter emphasises if good governance is to be ensured at the village level, building enabling environment should precede every other effort and the institution building should move much more rapidly (and in any case not later) than any devolution of funds or transfer of functions.

Chapter seven sets the issues for further reforms. The Amendment Act has been an attempt for strengthening the democracy at the grassroots level, but the findings have indicated that the Act has not been any effective in meeting the fundamental requirements of involvement of people, especially the weaker sections and of the availability of basic services at the village level. It has been assumed that the panchayat Acts, though vital, would automatically lead to greater institutional capability. Under the given environment of lack of responsiveness, transparency and accountability of panchayats, the elections have become the ultimate test of the performance of panchayats that come every five years. The lack of opportunities to people and poor capacity of panchayats to deliver basic services have raised the questions about good governance. And such a state does not inspire confidence in people about the panchayat system at the grassroots level. In this context, it becomes important to re-examine the various provisions in the Act from the point of view their effectiveness in improving the capacity of PR system. Though, keeping in view the spirit of the Constitution Amendment Act, the states should take initiatives, however, in order to provide a definite direction, there is a need for bringing the amendments in the Central Act in order to bring mandatory nature in the Act.

The panchayats should address the bigger issue of development by making a definite shift from the present state of control and command of resources. It must make endeavour for addressing the development issues that matter people the most in every stage starting from election, to conducting gram sabha, to planning, to implementation, to monitoring and to accountability. Panchayats should provide forum for people's participation, for convergence of resources and services, for synergy at the local level, for improving performance of availability of basic services, and for accountability to people. Panchayats must become the units of development. Even if the funds are not devolved upon panchayats, panchayats should (and can) play vital role in the areas like: hundred percent enrolment of children in the schools, immunisation, sanitation, clean environment including plantation, mobilising resources for innovative projects and so on. The success of this system would, however, depend on how the people are empowered and how the institutions are built at the local levels.

Now, in the backdrop of above, it is crucial that people have to be at the centre of the process of decentralisation. And human resources development (HRD) must be a central concern. The underlying need of HRD is necessitated, if the vital objectives of decentralisation —people's participation, collective action and improved opportunities to people—are to be achieved. The development of local institutions like the progress of any organisation can only be a slow process, as changeover from one system to another can't change people and their varying attitudes in short time. Therefore, a well-conceived capacitation programme assumes great significance for all those from villagers who would vote, participate in the development process to those who would have to operate it at every level and in every position for having greater understanding of the system and for increasing access to opportunities. Of particular importance is to bring in healthy culture of participation and the values such as transparency, accountability, respect for rules and norms and responsiveness (in all stakeholders) through a process of attitudinal changes. The improved culture should add to social capital.

Secondly, of crucial importance is institution building. Institutional underpinnings are vital without which the very purpose of the decentralisation would be defeated. The capacity of panchayats should be built to enable them to deliver basic services at the village level and to operate successfully for meeting people's aspirations. Also, in the context of globalisation, the changes taking place in the economic activities at the national and international levels, especially with regard to agriculture and allied sectors, are directly impinging on the rural economy. It further necessitates that the capacity of local institutions needs to be enhanced in order to enable them to take up the challenges of liberalisation, international trade and so on. *Thirdly*, of necessity is bringing policy reforms. The policies are critical that will give panchayats the right options for village development and in meeting the aspirations of people. It is evident from the field visits that the policies have direct impact on the ability of panchayats to function. And the success of programme output will depend upon how the policy measures are initiated. So, if the right development policies are formulated, the panchayats can deliver better and the process of decentralisation will find acceptance among people. The needed reforms should be such that would facilitate in creating the productive assets and investment in HRD in order to provide capital gains to people on a sustained basis. It would require taking measures for comprehensive development, rather than piece-meal approach through wage employment or sectoral programmes without linkages, and calls for integrating the activities of agriculture and allied fields, natural resources management, infrastructural development, food-processing industries and so on for holistic development of a village.

Finally, it stresses that changes cannot be brought about merely by regulations and legislations. It will call for having a definite programme of reforms that will facilitate in evolving sound decentralised development system at the grassroots level. The reforms should focus on fundamentals: how the decentralisation can contribute to achieving broad objective of mobilising the people in the development process; how the decentralisation can improve economic and managerial efficiency through institution building; and how the decentralisation can increase the government responsiveness to the needs and demands of various interest groups and can be a sustainable process to enable people in rural areas a good quality life. And, for good governance, reforms have to be a focal concern.

The book concludes with laying stress on primacy of human resources development, institution building and initiating right development policies for successful decentralisation.

CONTENTS

LIST OF TABLES

LIST OF FIGURES

LIST OF BOXES

ABBREVIATIONS

ABDO	:	Additional Block Development Officer
AP	:	Andhra Pradesh
APD	:	Additional Project Director
BDO	:	Block Development Officer
BPL	:	Below Poverty Line
CMP	:	Centre for Micro Planning
CQT	:	Centre for Quantitative Techniques
CSED	:	Centre for Sustainable Economic Development
DDC	:	District Development Commissioner
DDP	:	Desert Development Programme
DIC	:	District Industries Centre
DPAP	:	Drought Prone Areas Programme
DP	:	District Panchayat
DPC	:	District Planning Committee
DRDA	:	District Rural Development Agency
DS	:	Delivery System
DWCRA	:	Development of Women and Children in Rural Areas
EAS	:	Employment Assurance Scheme
F & A	:	Finance and Accounts
GKY	:	Ganga Kalyan Yojana
GOI	:	Government of India
GP	:	Gram Panchayat
HDI	:	Human Development Index
IAS	:	Indian Administrative Service
IAY	:	Indira Awas Yojana
IDP	:	Infrastructure Development Programme
IGS	:	Income Generating Scheme
IP	:	Intermediate Panchayat
IRDP	:	Integrated Rural Development Programme
ITI	:	Industrial Training Institute
JE	:	Junior Engineer
JRY	:	Jawahar Rozgar Yojana
JGSY	:	Jawahar Gram Samridhi Yojana
LVLW	:	Lady Village Level Worker

M & E	:	Monitoring and Evaluation
MIS	:	Management Information System
MLA	:	Member of Legislative Assembly
MLALADP	:	Member of Legislative Assembly Local Area Development Programme
MP	:	Member of Parliament
MPLADP	:	Member of Parliament Local Area Development Programme
MWS	:	Million Wells Scheme
NFBS	:	National Family Benefit Scheme
NMBS	:	National Maternity Benefit Scheme
NOAPS	:	National Old Age Pension Scheme
NRM	:	Natural Resources Management
OBB	:	Operation Black Board
PR	:	Panchayati Raj
PRIs	:	Panchayati Raj Institutions
PS	:	Panchayat Samiti
R & B	:	Roads and Buildings
SHG	:	Self-help Group
SIRD	:	State Institute of Rural Development
SITRA	:	Supply of Improved Toolkits of Rural Artisans
SSP	:	Social Security Programme
TN	:	Tamil Nadu
TRYSEM	:	Training of Rural Youth for Self Employment
VLW	:	Village Level Worker
ZP	:	Zilla Parishad / Zilla Panchayat

PART 1

Status of Decentralisation in India

1

INTRODUCTION: Need of Study of Decentralisation

1.1 Background

World over the twentieth century has witnessed the emergence of decentralisation in the development system. What has been striking is that in many countries, decentralisation as a means of achieving socio-economic goals has got constitutional mandate (Kueck, 1998). In India, since independence, there have been strong voices in favour of decentralisation and to have a structure of local governments where local decisions are taken by the people as near the point as possible. This has led to 73rd Constitution Amendment Act with an aim to provide the structure of the local institutions and to empower them.

The Act has opened avenues for facilitating social mobilisation process at the grassroots level. The first five-year plan categorically declared its belief in the necessity of strong panchayati raj institutions. As early as in 1953, S.K. Dey advocated (Dayal, 1965) 'parallel people' organisations be dovetailed with government agencies at all the levels to implement rural development policies. Subsequently, therefore, the gram sabha, comprising the assembly of all people living in a village, has been especially enshrined in the Act, so as to enable the people to manage their affairs as a collectivity.

It is only the gram sabha, the general assembly of the people, which can function as the institution of participative democracy. The canvas of their functions and powers has to be wide enough for real self-governance. It is an indefensible fact that even after fifty years of independence an average villager has to depend on some authority or the other outside the panchayat for everything small or big. What should comprise the minimal package to give self-governance at the panchayat level a real content has to be considered seriously at this juncture. The package, among other measures, must include management of local resources, devolution of funds as well as powers and capacity building of PR institutions.

While it will be naive to expect panchayati raj to transform rural economic and social scenario into egalitarian direction, it does provide a basis for participation by the people. However, participation cannot occur unless the participants share control of scarce resources, technology and knowledge. In this paradigm, new initiatives in rural development should focus on people driven strategies on a self sustaining basis by blending local human resources with natural resources, in combination with the resources from state, village organisations and also individuals.

The Act has placed a very large responsibility of overall development of the villages in the hands of PRIs. But, earlier in most states, PRIs were not effective for long and excessive government control and direction have crept in. In the process, the PRIs now in place find it difficult to cope with the new roles. Keeping this in mind, this study on 'decentralisation' has been undertaken with a view to find a suitable strategy to strengthen the panchayats to come up to the level of operating from 'within' to carry out developmental activities at local levels.

1.2 Why Study

The 73rd Constitution Amendment Act has provided framework for decentralisation at three levels viz., district, block and gram panchayat. As panchayat being the state subject, the onus of implementation of the Act has been entrusted to states. The states have made attempts to give the Act an operational shape. They have initiated measures for giving representation to weaker sections, conduct of elections, transfer of subjects to panchayats, constitution of SFC, devolution of funds and so on. These measures have been taken keeping in view the need of addressing the local needs, utilisation of local resources and involving the people in development. In this backdrop, it was felt vital to study how the states have initiated the measures for operationalising the Act; how decentralisation has helped in meeting the local needs and aspirations of people; and measures that are necessary for building the local institutions. It has necessitated to study all the dimensions viz., political, administrative, functional and financial, as only then would it provide a comprehensive view about the status of decentralisation.

Before attempting to study the process of decentralisation in India, it was felt necessary to give a look to the enabling conditions that would facilitate the successful process of decentralisation at the grassroots level and to achieve its desired objectives. What constitute the vital conditions or prerequisites for the success of the process of decentralisation are indicated below (Manor, 1999):

- Environment building: suitable behavioural and psychological factors;
- Sufficient powers to exercise substantial influence within the political system and over significant development activities;
- Sufficient financial resources to accomplish important tasks;
- Adequate administrative capacity to accomplish those tasks; and
- Reliable accountability mechanisms — to ensure both the accountability of elected members to citizens and the accountability of government officials to elected members.

In the context of above conditions, it was felt necessary to study the present status of the implementation of the Act, to examine the factors that are crucial in the process of decentralisation, as also suggest measures for operationalising the Act.

Specific Objectives

Decentralisation involves issues related to political, functional, administrative and financial aspects, which require extensive as well as intensive study. So for a comprehensive and focused study, the specific objectives that were identified are outlined below:

- Present status of decentralisation and problems
  - How have the state governments initiated the measures for operationalising the 73rd Constitution Amendment Act?
  - Which are the factors that are vital in the process of decentralisation at the village level?
  - How has the capacity of PRIs improved and to what extent have these institutions been able to meet the constitutional mandate?
- How decentralisation has helped in socio-economic development
  - How have the people been involved in the planning and implementation of programmes?
  - How has the process of decentralisation contributed towards qualitative improvement in the socio-economic life of people in rural areas, and in providing good governance at the village level?
- Measures that are necessary to strengthen the decentralisation and to provide good governance at the grassroots level
  - How should the capacity of PRIs and the capabilities of PR members be improved for undertaking the task of village development in general and for making basic services available to people in particular?

1.3 Methodology of Study

Decentralisation has got many dimensions. These include political decentralisation, functional decentralisation, administrative decentralisation and financial decentralisation. And the vital issues, under these dimensions, range from environment in the panchayat area, to people's participation, to capabilities of PR members, to capacity of local institutions to deliver, to financial devolution, to fiscal management, and to accountability. Under the present dispensation of decentralisation, the states have to attend to these issues and to provide operational shape to decentralisation process.

Now, in the context of the complex and multidimensional matter of decentralisation system, a systematic methodology is required to reduce subjectivity in the analysis and bringing objectivity as much as possible (Saxena, 1995). The system approach offers one such possibility. System approach focuses on output and integrates the various administrative processes in a logical way, or it can be defined as logical problem-solving process, which is applied to identifying and resolving important development problems. The focal point of this approach is the 'system'. Here, the system is assumed to be having elements or parts which have dynamic relationships among themselves and with the whole, and each of these parts affect independently or in relation with other (one or more than one) influence the outcome (Kaufman, 1972).

In decentralisation process, various components such as environment building, capacity building, transfer of functions and devolution of funds, fiscal management, planning, delivery mechanism and accountability are very closely linked to each other and the one affects the outcome of the other. It necessitates that an integrative approach for the study of the whole spectrum of issues concerning the process of decentralisation is to be adopted. Therefore, in this backdrop, the system approach has been applied for the purpose of study of decentralisation system.

1.4 Specific Areas of Study

Decentralisation is a process through which authority and responsibilities for some substantial government functions are transferred from central government to intermediate and local governments, and often also to communities. It involves devolving political power, defining people's role in the decision-making, transfer of functions, devolution of funds, making administrative arrangement for planning and implementation, taxation powers and financial autonomy upon panchayats and so on. We need to look at all these issues from the system's point of view, as the issues are inter-related and affect the total outcome of the system.

The focus of study has been on the issue of governance vis-a-vis the process of decentralisation. Good governance is in essence about being able to provide equal opportunities to people in socio-economic and political life, being responsive to people's need, being able to meet basic needs of people, and fair and accountable in dealings.

Therefore, in the backdrop of above, under the present study (see table 1.1) on decentralisation, all the four dimensions viz., political, functional, administrative and financial have been covered from the system point of view in order to cover issues in totality and to present a comprehensive status of decentralisation in different states, and also to provide a framework for initiating future course of action for a meaningful process of decentralisation.

1.4.1 Political Decentralisation

Under political decentralisation people are drawn into decision-making process through empowerment. Political or democratic decentralisation thus signifies the quest for a

TABLE 1.1: **Political, Functional, Administrative and Financial Indicators under the Study of Decentralisation System**

S. N.	Dimensions	Definitions	Broad indicators	Specific indicators for assessing the process of decentralisation
1.	Political Decentralisation	Transferring powers and responsibilities from central/state government to autonomous/local bodies that have been elected by their respective local constituencies.	• Election • Political status • Autonomy • Participation • Accountability	• Mode of election • Fairness of election process • Representation to weaker sections • Political status of elected members • Role of woman members and chairpersons, and that of weaker sections • Conflicts among PR members and officials • People's participation in gram sabha • The category of people participating in the discussion • The response of PR members in the gram sabha at the GP level • Type of issues discussed in the gram sabha • Mode of identification of works in the gram sabha • Factors influencing discussions and the decisions in the gram sabha • Gram sabha functioning and action plan preparation at the GP level • Discussion in the gram sabha about the implementation of works at the GP level • Membership of gram panchayats in higher tier • Membership of MLAs and MPs in PRIs • Size of panchayats • Procedure of social audit and financial accountability
2.	Functional Decentralisation	Transferring the functions to local bodies	• Transfer of functions	• Transfer of functions to each tier under 29 subjects • Demarcation of functions among three tiers

(Contd.)

TABLE 1.1 *(Contd.)*

S. N.	Dimensions	Definitions	Broad indicators	Specific indicators for assessing the process of decentralisation
3.	Administrative Decentralisation	Placing planning and implementation responsibilities with local units.	• Planning • Implementation • Monitoring and MIS • Support system • Defining roles and responsibilities • Transparency	• Participatory planning • Planning unit at each tier • Planning methodology • DPC • Beneficiaries' participation in the implementation • Implementation procedure of programmes • Manpower position at each tier • Administrative powers of PR members • Training of PR members • Infrastructural position at each tier • Transparency in functioning • Roles and responsibilities of PR members and development functionaries • Capacity of PRIs to deliver services to people • Constraints in the functioning of PR system
4.	Financial Decentralisation	Devolving taxation, funds and expenditure powers upon local bodies.	• Power of taxation • Sharing of taxes • Devolution of funds • Autonomy in the expenditure	• Own income of panchayats • Important items in total taxes of panchayats • Payment of user charges • Devolution of funds and grants upon panchayats • Own income vis-a-vis plan outlay and devolved funds • Collection of taxes vis-a-vis per capita state domestic product • Financial autonomy • Horizontal and vertical imbalances • Role of SFC in augmenting panchayat finances

participative and community approach. It entails the transfer of authorities from central government to autonomous and local tiers that have been democratically elected by their constituencies.

The issues that are studied are conduct of election, socio-political environment, political status of local bodies, autonomy, people's participation and accountability. Also, issues like capacity and responsiveness of PR members, conflicts, size of the panchayats and the representation of gram panchayats in the higher tiers have been examined. In a way, an attempt is made to address the following questions:

- Are panchayats constitutionally recognised?
- Have the members of district, block and village panchayats been elected through a democratic, free and fair electoral process?
- Do the panchayats have functional autonomy?
- What is mechanism for people's participation? And, how is that effective in giving opportunities to people in their participation?
- How is the accountability of elected members to people is ensured?

1.4.2 Functional Decentralisation

It refers to transferring subject specific functions to local tiers.

Issues that are studied are transfer of functions and inter-tier demarcation of functions in order to enable them to discharge their functional roles. It is attempted to assess the following questions:

- Whether the major functions have been formally transferred to PRIs?
- Whether the inter-tier demarcation of functions under each subject is carried out?

1.4.3 Administrative Decentralisation

It involves placing planning and implementation responsibilities with the local bodies and assigning the roles and responsibilities to functionaries and elected members.

Issues that are studied are participatory planning; institutional mechanism for planning, implementation, coordination, monitoring, transparency; support system; roles and responsibilities; and mechanism for resolving conflicts, settling disputes and arbitration. Also, the performance aspect is examined. More precisely, the following questions are studied:

- Whether the panchayats have been provided with the mechanism for planning?
- Have the services of field officers and staff of line departments been placed with the panchayats?
- Do the panchayats have administrative and technical control over programmes implemented locally?

- What are the measures taken to enhance the capabilities of elected members?
- Whether the specific functional roles and responsibilities (planning, implementation, monitoring, supervision, control) under each subject have been given to each tier?
- Whether specific demarcation of roles and responsibilities has been made between PR members and development functionaries?
- Whether the panchayats have sufficient infrastructural and logistics support in order to carry out their development works?
- How is the transparency in the panchayat functioning observed?

1.4.4 Financial Decentralisation

It involves devolving powers with regard to taxation, funds and expenditure upon local bodies in order to first improve the financial position then giving them the financial autonomy for planning and implementation as per local needs.

Issues that are studied are collection of taxes by local bodies, own income of panchayats, devolution of funds by state, criteria for inter-panchayat devolution of funds and expenditure by panchayats as per local needs (financial autonomy). Besides, horizontal and vertical imbalances and the role of SFC are also examined. And specifically, the following questions are addressed:

- What is the level of panchayat income?
- What is the status of their own tax and non-tax revenues?
- How is the financial autonomy of panchayats?
- What has been the role of SFC in the financial management of panchayats?
- What share of grants from government is tied to a particular scheme or project?
- What share of the plan budget is devolved upon PRIs?

Socio-cultural Factors and Development Policy

Besides the issues such as socio-cultural factors and development policy are also examined. Under this, the following issues have been covered:

- How do the socio-cultural factors affect the process of decentralisation, and more specifically the decision-making, the allocation of funds, interest of weaker sections and so on?
- How does the HRD level influence the functioning of panchayats?
- How do the policies influence the development process and affect the decentralisation and vice-versa?

1.5 Definitions of Terms

The important terms as mentioned above are further elaborated which are as follows:

Under Political Decentralisation

Election of local bodies in a free manner is a vital part in the process of decentralisation. Issues that are crucial are fairness of election process, the external factors that influence the election, role of political parties, etc. There are various problems like money and physical power, consumption of liquor, etc. during the process of elections that affect outcome of the election. Also of significance is the representation of weaker sections in the panchayat bodies.

Socio-political and cultural environment affects the working environment of panchayats. Good social relation among people and proper functional understanding among various groups will add to harmonious functioning, while on the other hand, warring groups or divisions on party lines may vitiate the atmosphere of working at panchayat level. The cultural factors like caste (discrimination), role of village elites, decision-making process, prestige for winning elections, exercising control over village panchayat and role (in terms of importance given) of poor and other weaker sections in the panchayat functioning, influence the environment in the villages.

Political status is important to ensure the functional autonomy of the local body and to give executive position to elected representatives. The *people's participation* in the decision-making of village development planning and implementation is crucial and is one of the ultimate objectives of decentralisation. It can be measured in terms of participation by people in election, the category of people participating in the discussion, the response of PR members in the gram sabha at the GP level, relationship of people with elected representatives, type of issues discussed in the gram sabha and mode of identification of works in the gram sabha and so on.

And, *accountability* will require the system or procedure of making elected representative responsible for their duties and answerable to people, and to ensure fairness in the panchayat functioning so that the decisions are taken on merit and the members (elected) take steps to rectify their improper or wrong decisions. Understanding the causes of *conflicts* and then resolving them is important. These conflicts may be in the form of inter-personal or intra-personal in nature, or among elected representatives, or between officials and elected representatives, or intra-tier or inter-tier.

The *size of the panchayats* also assumes importance in order to enable them to deliver services to people keeping in view of physical reach and also from the point of view of administrative and financial viability.

Capacity of PR members is crucial for their abilities to deliver. Here, the factors that are crucial are dummy candidates, background (educational and financial) of PR members and their capabilities. It would be useful to know, as it would facilitate in initiating measures for capacity building programme for the members.

Responsiveness of PR members assumes high significance in the process of decentralisation. It is one of the important factors that will determine how the panchayats will attend to people's grievances and their needs. It can be assessed by: how PR members attend to the development priorities, how they address people's grievances at the GP level and how they attend to the problems of weaker sections like landless people and the poor.

Representation of gram panchayats in higher tiers is important to assess how the gram panchayats are given role and voice in the decision-making process of higher tier. Also of importance is the role of MLAs and MPs in the functioning of panchayats.

Under Functional Decentralisation

The *functions* under 29 subjects, as identified in 11th Schedule, are to be transferred to panchayats. Also, *inter-tier demarcation* of functions for each subject is important in order to clearly specify the functions that are to be handled by a particular tier. For example, under agriculture, which tier (district, block and gram panchayat) will handle cropping pattern or supply of inputs or marketing of produce should be clearly demarcated.

Under Administrative Decentralisation

Participatory planning is important for eliciting people's knowledge about local problems, needs and resources during the process of planning so that the plans so prepared will reflect the people's needs and aspirations in a more meaningful way.

Planning is important for rational allocation of resources at the local level. Planning methodology, people's participation, supporting unit at each tier and database preparation are vital for the success of participatory local level planning. Implementation of works should involve procedure for work execution, beneficiaries participation and their contribution.

Monitoring of programmes and *MIS* are essential for keeping supervision and control over development works, finance and accounts. Of equal importance is to define subject specific roles and responsibilities of PR members, development functionaries, people and NGOs / CBOs, in order to avoid overlap and conflicts. Also, role under each subject and financial limits of administrative and technical sanction need to be specified for each tier for assigning responsibilities to panchayats.

Transparency will require the system or procedure of making people aware about their rights and the details of panchayat functioning. It could be through compulsory display of accounts, details of panchayat activities, proceedings of panchayat and gram sabha meetings and so on and also through providing certified copies of documents to people.

Support system in terms of manpower, infrastructure and logistics is vital for having planning and implementation system at panchayat levels viz., district, block and gram panchayat. Under manpower support placement of officers and staff of line department with PRIs and control over them is important; infrastructural support will include building for office and conducting meetings; and logistics will include equipments for execution of works in the villages and accessories for carrying out various office works.

Mechanism for resolving conflicts, settling disputes and arbitration is important for two reasons. *First*, to have a forum for settling conflicts for harmonious functioning, and *second*, to instil confidence in people that there is an impartial body to arbitrate about the conflicting or wrong decisions, and that can give direction for rectification.

Performance of the local bodies need to be assessed in order to know the direction of

TABLE 1.2: **Performance-oriented Indicators under the Study of Decentralisation**

S. N.	Broad indicators	Specific indicators
1.	Capacity of PR members	How the following affect the functioning of panchayats: • Background of PR members at the GP level • Dummy candidates • Capabilities of PR members
2.	Political environment	• Socio-political environment • How local problems during elections are taken care of
3.	Planning system	• How far the people's participation is successful • How effective are the local planning units in local plan preparation
4.	Effectiveness of PRIs and implementation quality	• Inter-tier linkages • How the problems of gram panchayats are attended to by higher tiers • Attending to the problems of landless and poor • How the beneficiaries are involved in the implementation of programmes • How effectively the projects are implemented by the panchayats • Construction quality • Advantages to people through PR system • Timeliness of availability of services
5.	Responsiveness of PR members	• How PR members attend to the development priorities • Addressing people's grievances at the GP level
6.	Attitudinal issues	How the following are attended to and resolved: • Intra-tier conflicts • Inter-tier conflicts • Conflicts between PRIs and departmental functionaries
7.	Transparency and accountability system	• Whether the information is made available to people in time • Whether decision-making in the gram sabha is transparent • How effective is the social audit at the panchayat level • Whether the line departments are accountable to panchayats • Whether the PR members are accountable to people

process of decentralisation and to have clear idea whether the objectives of the decentralisation are achieved. It can be measured (see table 1.2) in terms of quality of works, timeliness of availability of services and tangible advantages to people through these bodies. The indicators of performance have been broadly grouped as indicated below:

- Capacity of PR members;
- Political environment;
- Planning system;
- Effectiveness of PRIs and implementation quality;
- Responsiveness of PR members;
- Attitudinal issues; and
- Transparency and accountability system.

Under Financial Decentralisation

Power of *taxation* is important for augmenting the internal resources of panchayats. The own income of the panchayat broadly includes tax and non-tax revenue. The tax revenue includes property tax, profession tax, etc. and non-tax revenue includes water taxes, user charges, etc. *Sharing of taxes* is for those items that are normally collected by the state government and allocated to panchayats. *Devolution of funds* upon panchayats by the state is important in order to augment financial capacity of panchayats. *Financial autonomy* is important in order to provide panchayats scope to prepare plans as per local needs, and then to make expenditure.

The study of *horizontal and vertical imbalances* is important for assessing the relative financial strength of the panchayats. Fiscal imbalance is measured by

$Ii = Ei - Ri$
where
I = the extent of imbalance
E = expenditure incurred
R = revenues raised by the concerned unit of government itself.
Subscript 'i' represents the unit of government.

Normalising we get,

$Fi = Ei - Ri / Ei = 1 - Ri / Ei$; where Fi: Fiscal imbalance index

The imbalances at different levels of government (inter-governmental) are known as vertical fiscal imbalances, while those at different units of the same level of government (inter-jurisdictional) are known as horizontal fiscal imbalances. If the distribution of revenue sources and expenditure responsibilities between the centre and the states is such that the centre raises more than it spends while the states spend more than they raise it is called vertical imbalance.

Horizontal imbalances occur when the ability to raise revenues or the unit cost of providing public services vary widely among different jurisdictions. This can cause significant differences in the standard of public services provided unless those with lower ability to raise revenue or higher unit cost of public services levy taxes at higher rates. These imbalances are going to pose serious problems (as it may cause imbalances in development) if there are large inter-tier and intra-tier differences in the income.

The *role of SFC* has been examined to assess its present impact on augmenting the panchayat finances and also how its role can be widened for efficient management of panchayat finances.

Other Terms

Institutional Development (ID): It refers to the process of improving the ability of institutions to make effective use of human and financial resources available. It includes the following components:

- Organisational structure;
- Support system;
- Management system, including monitoring and evaluation;
- Financial management (budgeting, accounting, auditing procedures) and planning systems;
- Personnel management, staff development and training;
- Inter-institutional relationships;
- Legal framework; and
- Government regulations and procedures.

Why Institutional Development: The studies by World Bank (1989 and 1995) have explicitly shown that the implementation of projects have chances of success when ID is rightly attended to. Israel (1987) suggests that policy changes that ignore the institutional underpinnings are unlikely to last and may even have pervasive outcomes.

ID is vital for giving operational shape to policy or action plan or programme or any project. Its basic objective is:

- To facilitate the implementation process;
- To support the inter-sectoral linkages; and
- To contribute to the sustainability of the process of development.

Institutional Development for Sustainability: The study by World Bank (1995) shows that the institutional development and sustainability of the development process are correlated as indicated by figure 1.1.

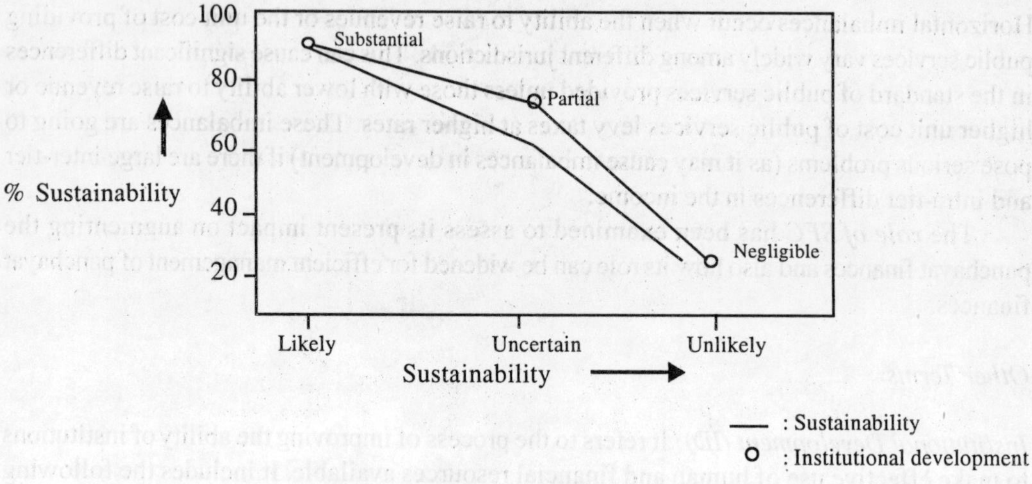

Fig. 1.1: **Institutional Development and Sustainability**

Cultural Factors: In the functioning of panchayats the role of people in general and that of PR members in particular is crucial, so the cultural factors are going to play their role and influence the outcomes (see table 1.3). The factors that have been examined are indicated below:

- Caste;
- Role of village elites;
- Capabilities of people in development;
- Decision-making process;
- Prestige for winning elections;
- Exercising control over village panchayat, as a matter of right; and
- Importance given to poor and other weaker sections in the panchayat functioning.

Policy Issues: Policies have definite impact on the outcome of development process or in other words the results of development efforts are policy specific (see table 1.3). Specific items, that will have impact on rural development and decentralisation, are given as under:

- Rural development policy;
- Policy on HRD;
- Policy on development of weaker sections;
- Inter-sectoral development; and
- Policy on institution building.

TABLE 1.3: **Other important Indicators under the Study of Decentralisation**

S.N.	Issues	Indicators
1.	Institutional Development	• Organisational structure; • Support system; • Management system, including monitoring and evaluation; • Financial management (budgeting, accounting, auditing procedures) and planning systems; • Personnel management, staff development and training; • Inter-institutional relationships; • Legal framework; and • Government regulations and procedures.
2.	Cultural factors	• Caste • Role of village elites • Capabilities of people in development • Decision-making process • Prestige for winning elections • Exercising control over village panchayat by elites, as a matter of right • Importance given to poor and other weaker sections in the panchayat functioning
3.	Policy Issues	• Rural development policy • Policy on HRD • Policy on development of weaker sections • Inter-sectoral development • Policy on institution building

In the light of above, it was also felt important to suggest measures that may be necessary for strengthening the process of decentralisation. The important aspects that were considered for recommendations have been:

- The impact of constitutional amendment on the status and the functioning of PR institutions;
- The strategy for environment building;
- The present level of capacity of PR institutions and the measures that are required for strengthening them;
- Measures for transfer of functions to and devolution of funds upon panchayats;
- Measures for effective administrative arrangement at each tier;
- To devise methodology for planing and implementation in order to facilitate the gram panchayats in the preparation of their action plans and then their implementation; and
- To suggest the system of accountability.

Governance: The governance is a process encompassing of decision-making and delivery of services with norms and values determining it. The norms and values, among others, will include responsiveness to people's needs, fairness and consistency, transparency, performance matching capacity, and accountability to people. And the good governance means achieving the desired goals and delivering through a system of adequate capacity to perform with sound norms and values. To judge good governance the issues examined are participatory development, availability of basic services at the village level, gender equality and equity in development, and institutional capacity (including norms and values) to deliver.

Or in sum, as outlined above, the study has specifically looked into social, political, cultural and economic factors influencing the process of decentralisation, the role of state in strengthening the local institutions and the role of panchayats in involving people in the participative process as well as delivery of services. Besides, the inter-relationship of various variables and how the one is influencing the other was primarily taken into account while studying the process of decentralisation. Institutional performance with specific reference to people's participation, quality of work, responsiveness of PR members, efficiency and effectiveness of implementation of programmes, and accountability of PR members has been examined in order to evaluate whether the objectives of decentralisation are achieved. And, lastly, the efforts have been made for addressing the issues of reforms in the areas of HRD, development policies and institution building that will strengthen the process of decentralisation.

2

DECENTRALISATION: Evolution and Constitutional Amendment

In the decade of 1990s, the third world countries have increasingly adopted decentralisation policies and programmes as a part of their mandate for national development (Sundaram, 1997). The thinking that has led for having decentralised system is based on certain fundamental factors: *first*, decentralisation is seen as a way of mobilising support for national development priorities by interacting with people at the local level and taking their feedback (Amatya, 1988 and Kueck, *et al.*, 1998). *Second*, local institutions can be effective channels of communication between the central government and local communities. And, *third*, greater people's participation in local development planning and management not only promotes national integration by giving people in different regions of a country the scope to participate in decision-making and their community development, but also to have their support for political stability. In India, 73rd Constitution Amendment Act has heralded a new chapter in the process of decentralisation. The Act has tried to strengthen the panchayati raj system for establishing decentralised form of development at the grassroots level. The panchayati raj system in India has roots since historical times, and its evolution has origin, which dates back to the period of British Raj.

2.1 Emergence of Decentralisation

The decades of 1950s and 1960s saw the demands (Kueck, *et al.*, 1998) coming from the people and a number of civil society groups for a variety of development needs ranging from health to poverty alleviation to marketing of agricultural produce to civic amenities. The central governments in several countries felt the pressure for addressing these problems. Thus, it was a period that was marked with the setting up of local governments in a number of countries. A new thinking and approach on local governments that could meet the challenges of local development got favourable response. The expert writings (Maddick, 1970) further promoted and exemplified this trend. They dwelt at length on the needs and the limitations of decentralised system of government. The discussion focused on various forms of decentralisation, planning, organisational structure and management of basic services. The decade of 70s saw the emergence of decentralisation as a development alternative, and got the focused attention when the debate picked up momentum in 1980s. Many countries in Asia and Africa emphasised the role of decentralisation as a means of national development and for achieving a variety of development objectives, ranging from people's participation to meeting their aspirations to political stability. This period saw paradigm shift in the approach for development, and led to shift in orientation from structured development planning to planning from below and from growth to redistribution of income with the objectives of equality, improved quality of life and reduction in poverty.

2.1.1 Causes of Decentralisation in South Asian Countries

In the last two decades many South Asian countries have adopted decentralisation with varying degree of success in public participation (Aziz and Arnold, 1996). The multiple factors have contributed towards the emergence of decentralisation in these countries, and the prominent among them are summed up as follows:

- What has led to the emergence of decentralisation for the governance at the local level in Asian countries including Bangladesh, India, Nepal, Sri Lanka, etc. is based on several historical, social, political and economic factors. And one of the important factors has been the traditional form of village councils (panchayats) in the olden times. The belief in these councils has led to opinion building for setting up of local institutions as near to people as could be in some of these countries.
- Another important factor of the political demands for democracy in countries previously governed by authoritarian regimes has played an important role. This has been the case in Nepal, Bangladesh, Malaysia and Philippines, where each of which has undergone the transition from autocratic to democratic. The adoption of representative form of democracy at the national level is often seen as the first step towards giving role to people in national development. In these countries, decentralisation can be seen as the 'second wave' of democratic reform (Manor, 1999), depending and building on the democratisation process taking place at the national level. Also, oil shocks of 1970s gave signals to many Asian countries having over-centralised form of government to have a system that can withstand pressures at different levels.
- The ethnic diversity in some of the countries and the different groups within Asian societies have spurred the demand for greater political autonomy. This has been noticed in India, China, Sri Lanka, Indonesia and also in a number of south and south-east Asian countries. In India, for example, various regions such as North East, Kashmir and backward states are asking for more political devolution. Similarly, in China, many provinces, especially the southern parts, have been demanding for autonomy, and in case of Sri Lanka, it is with regards to north-eastern region. There is gradual emergence of consensus in these countries for recognising the essential need for political decentralisation to manage the stresses and strains of ethnic and regional

diversity.

- Besides historical and political reasons, there are some very fundamental reasons as to why decentralisation has been accepted in a number of countries. It is sheer impossibility of the centralised form of development to reach intended beneficiaries and deliver tangible benefits to rural communities. For instance, China's experiment with local democracy is based on the premise of promoting rural development and providing employment to people through small enterprises governed in a decentralised way. The 1987 Village Committee Organisation Law and subsequent experiments with democratically elected village councils are the results of the grassroots demands for greater participation in the village development.

  The new constitutional amendment in India seeks to work in the direction of people's participation in the village development, which is difficult to come by through state controlled resources and distant institutions. Similarly, in Nepal it has been felt that it is a difficult task to reach remote mountain hamlets and the rural development can't proceed by the centralised approach. Likewise in Philippines, the major emphasis has been on local development, which envisages role for people in the development planning and implementation. In sum, from the development perspective, the following points have been guiding factors for decentralisation:
  - Not meeting the local aspirations through the central planning and control of development activities;
  - The implicit need for participatory development programmes with the objective of 'growth with equity'; and
  - Local units need to be strengthened in order to meet the basic needs of people, which are difficult to come by from centrally controlled system.

- With the introduction of economic liberalisation policies in several Asian countries, the process of decentralisation has picked up momentum. Conceptually, there is a logical connection between privatisation and decentralisation, if the primary objective is to reduce the control of central-state structures over economic decision-making. Besides, some international donor agencies have strongly encouraged decentralisation as part of an overall structural adjustment package. Though economic liberalisation can't be a predominant factor in the decentralisation process, but it has definitely contributed towards favourable policy climate for the promotion of local institution building.
- The concepts of nationally planned development, adopted in developing world, were followed vigorously in East European bloc. The economic failure of East European countries, which were evidenced by poverty and inequality, inefficiency, irresponsiveness of the centralised administration led to rethinking in the Asian countries and generated a favourable climate for decentralisation.

Presently, many developing countries are engaged in restructuring and re-inventing their governments. The challenge is to find the right balance between centralised and decentralised form and to link them in ways that promote development most effectively as well as efficiently. The need is to determine the optimal mix of these two approaches, which is not easily determined. It requires identifying functions that can be handled under centralised and those that can be by decentralised way. Worldover, the decentralisation and local planning have become the topics of intense discussion among development practitioners.

2.1.2 Why Decentralisation : World View

The studies (Vajpeyi, 1990 and Tordoff, 1994) have shown that the causes, that have led to decentralisation of development system, differ substantially from country to country. The causes have ranged from historical, political and economic conditions to the policies of government to welfare of people, to efficiency of delivery of services and to political compulsions. The historical and cultural values have an impact on the extent and pattern of decentralisation in any country, or for that matter, the political and administrative structures even at the national level (Meenakshisundaram, 1994). The theories and experiences suggest the probable validity of the following propositions (Manor,1998):

- No single factor is sufficient to explain decisions to decentralise in all countries or in a single country.
- No single factor is necessary to decisions to decentralise in all countries.
- Decentralisation in each country is the result of a combination of causes.
- The combination of causes producing decentralisation varies from country to country.

The decentralisation has been adopted by a number of countries irrespective of their political thinking — left, right and centre; economic conditions, rich or poor or under debt-trap; and practising autocracies and democracies. It makes it clear that a diversity of influences has been at work, and that decentralisation has been undertaken for a variety of reasons and with a variety of objectives in mind.

Factors leading to decentralisation

- Historically many developing countries followed the system of central command and traditional control by elites, which flourished under the guise of patronage. With the time, the degeneration of patronage system took place that played a vital role in opening up of opportunities for people to express their grievances, in building pressure.
- Many countries over-centralised power so much that it undermined the autonomy, resources, effectiveness and responsiveness of institutions. People at the lower level started becoming impatient with the failure of governments to deliver. The governments faced mounting demands from organised groups, which got compounded

by the sluggish economic growth and increasing corruption by elites at all levels that undermined their ability to respond to the demands of various groups.

- Colonial Period — not meeting people's aspirations. Several developing countries, that saw the central rule without giving regard to local problems and their needs, preferred to have decentralised form of development system in order to involve the people in the development process and also to empower them.
- The industrial development in a decentralised way, which promoted flexible and small units, also influenced the thinking. By the late 1970s, many industries taking technological advantages did well due to their flexibility and their capacity to react quickly to changing conditions and consumer demands. Subsequently, in the developing countries the process of liberalisation has contributed towards decentralised thinking. Likewise, the development also required to be responsive to people's needs and to address the problems in the fast socio-economic scenario. This drove the policy makers towards greater decentralisation.
- During the 1980s, some donor agencies also began to shift their emphasis away from large-scale development programmes to more small, micro-level projects into which grassroots communities could be drawn as participants, in the hope of making development more sustainable (Manor, 1980).
- The failure of centralised institutions in the East European countries generated a favourable climate for decentralisation in the developing world .
- The democratisation of numerous formerly autocratic regimes, especially in Africa, led to thinking of more role for civil society, and that facilitated the creation of local government because of its proximity to people and for bridging the gap between the state and marginalised groups (Tordoff, 1994).
- Cultural factors like traditional role of village councils (or panchayats), community action, consensus approach and so on have contributed towards decentralisation. For instance, in the developing countries like India and Bangladesh, the functioning of village panchayats (since historical times) in the village affairs influenced the decision for establishing local government system.

2.1.3 Considerations Underlying Decentralisation

Against the widespread notion that centralised governance has not succeeded, many countries facing a variety of problems — political, social or economic — have adopted the path of decentralisation. It also provided opportunity to political leadership with diverse considerations and compulsions to have decentralised form of governance.

Also, there is little or no empirical evidence to indicate what decentralisation could and could not achieve or how specific types of decentralisation would produce specific results (Manor, 1998). Though the unease with commandism was very perceptible in East European, African and other developing countries, yet it offered few clear and specific indicators to help leaders choose particular form of decentralisation. Countries like Nepal, India, Bangladesh,

Nigeria, China, Sri Lanka, Brazil and Chile, which have adopted decentralisation more vigorously in the last two decades, do not have any similarity of either the cause or the objective or the form. It has emerged due to their socio-economic and politico-cultural factors that are more country-specific than represent any general trend.

Notwithstanding above, some evidence (Smith, 1985 and Sundaram, 1997) suggests that the development concern has its share in adopting the course of decentralisation as it would facilitate in addressing local problems, in improving administrative efficiency and in meeting needs of diverse groups.

Decentralisation for Welfare and Development Concerns

Most countries have gone for decentralisation with a variety of goals in mind. Some of them have often proceeded on the basis of genuine considerations of empowering the people at the grassroots level.

- Providing opportunities to people for their socio-economic development;
- Enhancing people's participation at lower level by providing them opportunities in the decisions-making;
- Utilising the local knowledge in the development planning;
- Raising the competence level of development functionaries and the capacity of local institutions for more sustained development;
- By equitable distribution of resources;
- Empowering the weaker sections through improvement in their capabilities and by giving them voice in the decision-making;
- Facilitating socio-economic development including alleviation of poverty by way of tapping individual potential and the services of social groups at local levels;
- Enhancing the transparency of functioning and responsiveness as well as accountability of departments, elected representatives and political institutions to people, and thus improving the efficiency of functioning; and
- Also providing opportunities to people at the lower level for future political role.

Decentralisation with Narrow Focus and Political Gains

Similarly, there have been considerations having more inclination towards narrow or partisan political advantages, such as:

- Providing a feeling of democratisation without giving adequate functions and responsibilities;
- Giving responsibility to local institutions of raising resources, but giving no financial and institutional support;
- Providing patronage to the inconvenient political figures by way of giving some powers;

- Entrusting tasks which the central government finds costly or inconvenient, or both, onto lower level authorities;
- Providing funds and powers at the lower levels, and facilitating the ruling party in building its political base at the local level, and thus to get votes through this strategy;
- Divert the attention of countrymen and outside observers from other coercive actions of the central government; and
- Appealing donor agencies who favour decentralisation (Manor, 1998).

2.1.4 Objectives of Decentralisation

Decentralisation refers to a process of assigning the public functions and responsibilities of planning and implementation from central government to sub-district level in order to carry out specific tasks at the local level. As indicated by this definition, the public affairs are to be managed at the local level and there are certainly specific objectives for the need to choose the path of decentralisation. The prominent among them are:

- *Firstly*, to handle promptly the local-specific development needs:
  There are functions, which have only or predominantly local significance, along with functions which depend substantially for their performance upon information and resources available locally, can be better managed by the local bodies. For example, community roads, local water supply, schools and markets can be better handled by the local administration.
- *Secondly*, to improve the efficiency of programme implementation:
  Considering the issues from the point of view of administrative efficiency, we need to divide up and disperse the workload to the organisations in the field to benefit from local knowledge for their efficient implementation. Decentralisation of functions gives dividends in terms of speed and efficiency in service and performance. It helps in achieving better coordination of related functions assigned to a variety of local officers, and it takes lesser time in taking decisions at the local level than the time taken in centralised planning system.
- *Thirdly*, to reach the distant locations effectively:
  Through decentralisation the benefits of development can be extended to people in distant localities more equitably and to meet the different needs of a diverse population.
- *Fourthly*, to increase the responsiveness of local administration to people's needs:
  The actions of local level development functionaries can be best monitored by the local population, and through their regular feedback an effective control is possible, which will help in making the local administration more responsive.

2.1.5 Prerequisites for Successful Decentralisation

The effective and responsible performance of decentralised development system depend upon the several indispensable conditions. There are conditions of utmost importance and are prerequisites for successful decentralisation and require assurance from the central as well as state governments. These are:

- *First*, political will and the confidence of the higher levels at the central and the state governments to devolve powers, resources and functions at the local level; and adequate safeguards against the arbitrary dissolution of local bodies.
- *Second*, an environment of stability assured by the preservation of law and order.
- *Third*, adequate administrative arrangements for harmonious functioning between PR members and departments. It will call for clearly defined roles and responsibilities of PR functionaries and development agencies at different tiers viz., district, block and gram panchayat.
- *Fourth*, of overriding importance is the local organisation's capacity to perform job, to deliver results in the performance of assigned functions. The organisation's capacity includes: resources, infrastructure, qualified personnel with adequate skills and knowledge, and an operating organisational structure. In the absence of organisation's proper capacity, the decentralised planning will be of little significance and use.
- *Fifth*, the availability of a reliable database, planning methodology and information and reporting system which help the local functionaries to act with confidence and to take appropriate action for planning and implementation of programmes.
- *Sixth*, the system of accountability. It is essential for maintaining public confidence in governance, justifying development activities and ensuring the overall legitimacy of the local body. The accountability (Zaffarullah, 1997 and UNDP, 1997) has administrative, political and economic dimensions. In terms of 'administrative significance', the local bodies should be accountable for various administrative actions for undertaking different programmes such as building rural infrastructure, maintaining local schools, providing agricultural inputs and maintaining sanitation facilities. In addition to these basic responsibilities carried out at the local level, the massive development programmes, as envisaged in the constitutional amendment, need people's participation and human resource mobilisation at the local level, which together constitute a basis for the cooperation at local institutions. However, in order to ascertain maximum initiatives and the cooperation of local institutions to ensure people's participation and mobilisation, it is necessary to make these institutions accountable for such a task. In other words, with the increasing developmental role of local institutions, there is a further need to maintain their accountability.

  In terms of political significance, the local institutions should be accountable for their various 'political responsibilities'. For instance, in order to avoid politicisation and monopolisation by rural elites, the local institution should be made accountable for a fair distribution of goods and services among various target groups, especially landless, marginal farmers, women, SCs and STs. So, it is expected when the local institutions are accountable to local residents, they would be more responsive to the people's needs. Local level accountability is politically significant to local people because they have more direct contact with access to and influence over the elected members of local institutions than the national-level political representatives such as parliamentarians and ministers. In other words, in the case of local government institutions, people have a better opportunity to make these institutions directly accountable (Zaffarullah, 1997).

Lastly, in terms of 'economic significance' of local level accountability, it is necessary to ensure that the economic programmes and responsibilities assumed by local authorities are properly carried out. Local authorities have various public sources of revenue, including local taxes, proceeds from goods and services and government grants, for which they must be held accountable. There are a variety of economic activities performed by local authorities, including utilities, infrastructure, low cost housing and market facilities, which involve financial transactions, and thus, require strict measures of accountability because there is always a potential for impropriety in the process of raising and spending public money. Thus, local authorities dealing with public funds and assets have to be accountable for any use of resources.

In addition, local authorities have to be accountable not only for the quality of services expected by local residents, but also for satisfying the diverse needs of various social groups or communities. Local authorities should be accountable for fair or equitable distribution of goods and services, which is often a problem in the present context due to dominance of elite groups in the local bodies.

- Seventh is electoral reforms, including the framing of standards for the entry of PR functionaries in local bodies. As clearly pointed out by Mishra (Yugandhar, 1991) "that recruiting local leaders often with dubious credentials is not people's participation, it often amounts to curbing participation of the common man and woman".

Variants of Decentralisation

The variants of decentralisation are de-concentration, delegation, devolution and privatisation. These are defined as:

De-concentration implies handing over limited central government powers, functions and resources to its field units.
Delegation implies transferring responsibility for specifically defined functions to lower level organisations.
Devolution implies transfer of functions and authority with a greater autonomy in respect of certain defined functions, including decision-making authority. The authority handed over to

local institutions through devolution can be taken back only after making amendments in the law.

Privatisation refers to a form of decentralisation in which the government may transfer functions to voluntary organisations or private enterprises and allow them to perform certain functions.

2.2 Evolution of Panchayati Raj System in India

2.2.1 Pre-independence Period

Panchayats in olden times: In the olden days, there was caste and village panchayat system in India. Caste panchayats mainly carried out the functions related to social customs, marriage and rituals. Village panchayats consisted of elders of prominent households in a village (from family of original owners of the land or family of superior caste). They were primarily concerned with adjudicating civil disputes of residents related to rights in land and administering criminal justice. They also performed regulatory functions related to village common land (grazing land, forest and ponds).

The old village panchayats in India (Maddick, 1970) functioned as little village republics. These were not based on legislative enactments but were custom-based and tradition-bound institutions. These institutions were sustained by a reciprocity of interests between landowners bound together by ties of kinship on one hand and the farm tillers and labourers on the other.

Ambedkar (Dayal, 1965) has been critical of the then existing form of village panchayats, which were highly discriminatory against the weaker sections, and served basically the interest of only a few i.e. village elites, and opined that the village panchayats should be formed on the premise of equality to all the sections and opportunities to everyone at the panchayat level. Also, the voice of concern was raised by Jayprakash Narayan (Amatya, 1988) that the village panchayats existed physically but did little to find the solutions for the village problems.

British Period

After the British rule the role of panchayats as institutions administering justice was abolished and replaced by legislations in 1860 such as the Indian Penal Code (IPC), Criminal Procedure Code (Cr.P.C.), Contract Act, etc., along with land revenue settlements. These new laws supplanted the customary / traditional law. Collectorates and courts took the powers of caste / village panchayats to establish the rule of law.

In the early stages of British rule the demand for democratic decentralisation came from the elites who wanted share in the power and patronage. It was envisaged that the local bodies and municipalities must meet their local needs through local taxation. This principle was incorporated by Lord Mayo in a decentralisation scheme formulated by the Government in 1870 which made provision for taxes being raised locally by municipal and rural bodies to meet their local needs.

The objective of Lord Mayo's scheme was to relieve the finances of British raj from the management of local needs. Further, Lord Ripon extended a decentralised system of finance by transferring certain items of finances from the centre to local and municipal taxation to enhance their financial position and for uniform development throughout the country.

Lord Ripon's Resolution: Arguing for budgetary freedom for development functions to be performed by local bodies, Lord Ripon's Resolution of 1880 stressed the need of training of elected representative in particular and the people in general, and that the educative principle of training of people to participate in representative institutions of government should not be subordinated to demands for development activities. Finally, Lord Ripon's famous Resolution that came in 1882 has been regarded as the Magna Carta of local self-government in India. The Resolution's emphasis was mainly on the political and popular training of educated Indians through these local representative institutions. The resolution categorically stated that the measure was "chiefly designed as an instrument of political and popular education" and utilise the "rapidly growing class of intelligent and public spirited men." The resolution created several rural local boards in all the states.

The Bengal Municipal Act of 1884 and Bengal Local Self Government Act, 1885 were formed by this philosophy.

In 1919 (Montagu-Chelmsford Reforms), in order to bring local supervision and monitoring of development activities, local bodies were constituted under the new Act. The taluka / tehsil served as the basic unit for local boards, and dealt with the subjects such as sanitation, education and health. These local bodies were also given powers to collect taxes.

Under the Government of India Act, 1935, the provincial governments enacted legislations on local self-government. The local government Acts were passed by the provincial governments to devolve powers of local development administration upon panchayats. All these provided for panchayats by and large co-terminus with administrative units like Patwari Circle, Tehsil/Taluka and District. But the provincial governments jealously guarded their interests by providing powers to the Collector to supersede the decisions of apex level district bodies.

2.2.2 Post-independence Scenario

At the time of formation of the constitution, initially the inclusion of panchayats was not considered in the first draft, in the context of historical caste and class dominated structure in the villages. But it was modified during the discussion in the Constituent Assembly. And so a provision was included in Part IV of the Constitution (in the Directive Principles of State Policy), which is not mandatory. Article 40 reads, 'The state should take steps to organise village panchayats and endow them with such power and authority as may be necessary to enable them to function as units of self-government'. Also, in the Constitution 'local government' is mentioned in Schedule seven, List II (State List) item, which reads: 'Local government that is to say the constitution and power of municipal corporation, improvement trusts, district boards, mining settlement authorities and other local authorities for the purpose of local self-government or village administration.' Thus it may be inferred that the panchayats' role was envisaged from the consideration of taking democracy to the villages and bringing powers to the village.

The Gandhians considered the panchayats to meet the village needs, and they focused on democratic decentralisation and for devolving power upon people. However, Ambedkar expressed concern about the caste-ridden village society in India that had been detrimental to millions of people of weaker sections and he was very much for the concept of giving power to people. His perception was also well appreciated by others. There were quite a good number of people (Dube, 1958) who looked at panchayats for handling the problems of meeting the aspirations of the peasantry, large land holdings by a few, the traditions of discrimination and domination based on religion and caste.

While distributing powers between the Union and the States, the Constitution of India, Article 40 (Directive Principles of State Policy), vested local bodies and panchayati raj as a subject with the states. Since independence, states have taken various measures for establishing panchayati raj system. There have been cases of successes and failures. In this context, in order to examine the role of PRIs in development, various committees and experts groups were constituted. The first of them was the Balwantrai Mehta Commission in 1957 with an objective to study and report on the status of panchayati raj institutions.

Balwantrai Mehta Committee in 1957

Panchayati Raj was given important role in the context of community development projects launched in 1952. The Balwantrai Mehta Committee in 1957 was set up with an objective to study and report on the Community Development Projects and National Extension Service. It made the following vital recommendations:

- The committee emphasised that community development would only be effective when the community was involved in the planning, decision and implementation process.
- Community development can be real only when the community understands its problems, realises its responsibilities, exercises the necessary powers through its chosen representatives and maintains a constant and intelligent vigilance on local administration. With this objective the committee recommended an early establishment of statutory elective bodies and devolution upon them of necessary resources, power and authority.
- The report underlined the role of elected panchayat samitis at the community development block / tehsil level as the basic unit of democratic decentralisation. The advisory role was contemplated for the zilla parishads.
- The committee focused on the rural sector and recommended that the functions of PRIs should cover the development of agriculture in all its aspects, the promotion of local industries and other services such as drinking water, road building, etc.
- The panchayat samiti should have a life of 5 years.

- The panchayat samiti will have two sets of officers, i.e. those at the block level and those at the village level. All of these officers will be drawn from the corresponding state cadres and will be sent to the panchayat samiti by the state government.
- It may be necessary to have standing committees of the zilla parishad to ensure rapid disposal of work.

The PRI structure was introduced in most parts of the country as a result of the Balwantrai Mehta Report. However, the legislation that followed the Committee's Report basically continued the three-tier structure and provided for overriding powers of the state government through the district Collector. What followed was not very encouraging for the promotion of local institutions. The new form of Acts did not develop the requisite democratic momentum and failed to cater to the needs of rural development. As analysed, the prominent reasons for this were: *first*, political resistance at the state level of sharing of power and resources with the local level institutions; *second*, the control over local institutions by the rural elites; *third*, the lack of capabilities (for planning and implementation of programmes) in the elected representatives at the local level; *fourth*, lack of accountability of elected representatives; and, *finally*, the absence of political will of the grassroots leaders.

K. Santhanam Committee

The Mehta Committee was followed by the K. Santhanam Committee (1963) to examine the issues of PRI finances. Its recommendations covered a wide range of issues, the prominent among them were: the panchayats should have more items that can be brought under tax-net; the grants from the state level should be in the nature of untied; and a Panchayat Raj Finance Corporation should be set up which would look into the financial resources of PRIs at all three levels, provide loans and financial assistance to these local institutions.

Since 1957, the functioning of the panchayati raj institutions was marked with various shortcomings and the desired results could not be achieved. The people's participation in the activities of the PRIs was limited. They did not identify themselves with these institutions, and even the panchayats did not make attempts to ensure their involvement in decision-making process. Many panchayats were superseded and elections were not held for many years. Rather, the whole process of development through panchayats gave an opportunity to the rural elites to emerge as centres of power, and there usually was an alliance between local representatives and government functionaries at local levels. It further discouraged the rural poor and disadvantaged groups for meaningful participation in the decision-making and implementation process. Also, the state governments and the local political elites did not make positive steps to strengthen the local institutions.

Apart from above, as the funding for community development projects reduced considerably by the mid-1960s, panchayats did not get enough funds for local development. They remained financially weak for decades without funds, superseded by decisions of district collectors, without elections being held to re-constitute them and could not provide representation for women, scheduled castes and tribes.

Ashok Mehta Committee in 1978

Having realised the poor state of local institutions, in 1978, the Ashok Mehta Committee was constituted to review the functioning of PRIs and to make recommendations in order to revive the local institutions.

The committee reviewed the structural and operational aspects of panchayati raj institutions since 1959. It outlined three phases of panchayati raj system: the first was the phase of ascendancy (1959-1964); second, the phase of stagnation (1965-69); and the third that of decline (1969-77) (Government of India, 1978). It made the following observations:

- The PRIs were not given the opportunities to take up planning or implementation work on a sizeable scale. The essential idea that all developmental activities should flow only through the block level organisation was not given focus. Rather, there were steps in the opposite direction.
- The state governments were not fully supportive of panchayati raj system. Panchayat elections were postponed or they were superseded for some or the other reasons. The attitude of the political elites at higher level towards strengthening of local institutions was not encouraging.
- Of particular significance was the lack of enthusiasm shown by MPs and MLAs in some states towards panchayats, as they would perceive a threat from the panchayat leadership to their position in their respective constituencies.
- The field officers and staff were not positive about the role of panchayats in development.
- PRIs were dominated by economically or socially privileged sections of society.
- The performance of PRIs had also been vitiated by political factionalism, rendering developmental thrusts, either warped or diluted.
- Inefficiency, corruption, lack of appreciation for procedures, undesirable interference in day-to-day administration, parochial loyalties, ego-clashes, etc. seriously hampered the functioning of panchayati raj for the village development.

In the light of the above findings, in order to strengthen the PRIs, the committee made the following recommendations:

- This committee recommended grouping of a number of villages to constitute a mandal panchayat covering a population of 15,000 to 20,000 for keeping the balance between technological requirements and possibilities for meaningful participation by the people. It would ensure administrative and economic viability and also facilitate the necessary linkages with the villages and gram panchayats.
- The committee suggested that the block level panchayat samitis would become

non-statutory executive committees of zilla parishads, and the mandal panchayats would carry out the development programmes.

- The committee suggested that in the elections, the scheduled castes / scheduled tribes should get representation on the basis of their population.
- PRIs should be empowered with the powers to take their own decisions and prepare plans according to local needs. The planning should be an important function to be discharged by the zilla parishads exclusively.
- The mandal panchayats would be responsible for implementation of the schemes and projects assigned by the zilla parishad. They would play the role in activating community action, project formulation and implementation of programmes.
- As regards the planning, there should be a team with experts at the district level for preparation of district plans.

In a few states efforts were made to revive them after the Ashok Mehta Committee Report was submitted in 1978, and Andhra Pradesh and Karnataka tried out the system of mandal panchayats.

G.V.K. Rao Committee 1985 (CAARD)

The periods of 1970s and early part of 1980s were not encouraging for the panchayati raj system. In view of this, in 1985 G.V.K. Rao Committee was constituted to examine various aspects of PRIs. After evaluating the functioning of local bodies, the committee made the following important observations:

- It suggested for integrated rural development. It has to encompass all economic and social development activities handled by different agencies at the field level.
- PRIs should be activated and given the necessary support so that they can become effective organisations for handling local development.
- Elections to local bodies should be held regularly.
- The block development officer should be given pivotal role in the rural development process. But the district should be the basic unit for policy planning and programme implementation.
- Restructuring of planning and implementation machinery at the district level was also suggested.

Singhvi Committee

The Rao committee was followed by the L.M. Singhvi Committee. It was constituted by the Government of India, Department of Rural Development in 1986 and made the following recommendations:

- It considered the constitution of gram sabha for encouraging democracy at the grassroots level.
- It recommended that the PRIs have to be viewed as institutions of self-government which would naturally facilitate the participation of the people in the process of planning and development and as a part of the concept of self-government.
- The committee was of the view that the panchayati raj should be directed to achieve community and social mobilisation, transcending the barriers of caste, religion, sex and disparities of wealth and surmounting social disabilities and disadvantages.
- The committee envisaged and recommended that the panchayati raj bodies should be constitutionally recognised.

The 73rd and 74th Constitutional Amendments

Though Constitutional status for PRIs was opposed by the Sarkaria Commission, but the idea gained momentum in the late 1980s and was recognised in the 64th Constitutional Amendment Bill in 1989.

The 73rd and 74th Constitutional Amendments in 1992-93 have ushered in the present phase where panchayats are described as institutions of local self-government, and are expected to prepare plans for economic development and social justice. The Act stipulates some very vital measures for strengthening PR institutions, and besides constitutional status, the prominent among them are: time-bound elections, powers to gram sabha, devolution of powers and funds, constitution of SFC, transfer of functions. There are now approximately 2,25,000 gram panchayats, 6000 panchayat samitis and 550 zilla parishads duly elected and governed by state legislation in different states and union territories.

2.3 Salient Points of 73rd Constitution Amendment Act, 1992

Constitutional status to panchayati raj system was a step in the direction of speeding up the process of decentralisation and giving strength as well as stability to local institutions. In this perspective the need for conferring constitutional status to Panchayati Raj Institutions (PRIs) has validated the constitutional intention of Article 40, as envisaged at the time of formulation of Constitution.

The 73rd Constitution Amendment Act, 1992 came into force in 1993 with the assent of the President of India. The Act provides for the establishment of panchayats in every state with the following features (see appendix 6):

Gram Sabha: The Article 243A envisages for the constitution of gram sabha with the objective of providing participation to people in the decision-making process. The gram sabha means a body consisting of persons registered in the electoral rolls relating to a village comprised within the area of panchayat at the village level. The gram sabha may exercise such powers and perform such functions at the village level as the legislature of a state may by law provide.

Constitution of Panchayats: For having uniformity in the pattern of panchayat structure, the Article 243B provides that there shall be constituted, in every state, panchayats at the village level, intermediate and district levels in accordance with the provisions of this part. But for a low population state, notwithstanding anything in Clause (1), panchayats at the intermediate level may not be constituted in a state having a population not exceeding 20 lakhs.

Composition of Panchayats: As per the Article 243C, the legislature of a state may, by law, make provisions with respect to the composition of panchayats. As regards the representation in the panchayat, it has been left to the state legislature to provide for the representation of:

- the chairpersons of the panchayats at the village level, in the panchayats at the intermediate level;
- the chairperson of the panchayats at the intermediate level, in the panchayats at the district level;
- the members of the House of people and the members of the Legislative Assembly of the state;
- the members of the Council of States and the members of the Legislative Council of the state.

The chairperson and other members of a panchayat whether or not chosen by direct election from territorial constituencies in the panchayat area shall have the right to vote in the meetings of the panchayat. The Act further provides that the chairperson of a panchayat at the village level shall be elected in such a manner as the legislature of a state may, by law, provide; and a panchayat at the intermediate level or district level shall be elected by, and from amongst, the elected members thereof.

Reservation of Seats for Weaker Sections: In order to give representation to weaker sections in the panchayats, the Article 243D prescribes that the seats shall be reserved for the SCs and STs in every panchayat and the number of seats so reserved shall bear, as nearly as may be, the same proportion to the total number of seats to be filled by direct election in that panchayat as the population of the STs in that panchayat area bears to the total population of that area and such seats may be allotted by rotation to different constituencies in a panchayat. Not less than one-third of the total number of seats reserved under Clause (1) shall be reserved for women belonging to the SCs or the STs as the case may be.

Not less than one-third (including the number of seats reserved for women belonging to SCs and the STs) of the total number of seats to be filled by direct election in every panchayat shall be reserved for women and such seats may be allotted by rotation to different constituencies in a panchayat. The offices of the chairpersons in the panchayat at the village or any other shall be reserved for the SC/STs and women in such a manner as the legislature of the state may provide by law.

The state legislatures can make provisions for reservation of seats in any panchayat or offices of chairpersons in panchayats at any level in favour of backward class of citizens.

Duration of Panchayat: In order to provide stability to the panchayats, the Article 243E stipulates that every panchayat, unless sooner dissolved under any law for the time being in force, shall continue for five years from the date appointed for its first meeting and no longer. No amendment of any law for the time being in force shall have the effect of causing dissolution of a panchayat at any level.

Disqualification for Membership: The Article 243F has provided that a person shall be disqualified for being chosen as and for being a member of panchayat if he is so disqualified by or under any laws for the time being in force for the purpose of elections for the legislature of the state concerned, provided that no person shall be disqualified on the ground that he is less than 25 years of age, if he has attained the age of 21 years; if he is disqualified by or under any law made by the legislature of the state.

Powers, Authority and Responsibilities of Panchayats: In order to enable the panchayats to take up the task of the preparation of plans for economic development and social justice; and the implementation of schemes for economic development and social justice, the legislature (as per Article 243G) of a state may, by law, endow the panchayats with such powers and authority as may be necessary to enable them to function as institution of self-government.

Powers to Impose Taxes by and Funds of the Panchayats: Enhancing the own income of panchayats has been duly recognised by the Act, and so the Article 243H envisages that the legislature of a state may by law authorise a panchayat to levy, collect and appropriate such taxes, duties, tolls and fees in accordance with such procedure and subject to such limits. It may also make provisions for making such grants-in-aid to the panchayats from the consolidated fund of the state.

Constitution of Finance Commission: The Article 243I envisages the constitution of State Finance Commission to review the financial position of the panchayats and to make recommendations as to the principles which should govern: (i) the distribution between the state and the panchayats of the net proceeds of the taxes, duties, tolls and fees leviable by the state; (ii) the determination of the taxes, duties, tolls and fees which may be assigned to, or appropriated by the panchayats; and (iii) the grants-in-aid to the panchayats from the consolidated fund of the state, the measures needed to improve the financial position of the panchayats.

Audit of Accounts of Panchayats: As contained in the Article 243J, the legislature of a state may, by law, make provisions with respect to the maintenance of accounts by the panchayats and the auditing of such accounts.

Constitution of State Election Commission: For ensuring the fairness of the election process, as per Article 243K, State Election Commission will look after the superintendence, direction and control of the preparation of electoral rolls for, and the conduct of, all elections to the panchayats. It also envisages that the legislature of a state may by law make provision with respect to all matters relating to, or in connection with, elections to the panchayats.

Application to Union Territories: The provisions of this part shall apply to the Union Territories and shall, in their application to a Union Territory, have effect as if the references to the Governor of a state were references to the administrator of the Union Territory appointed under Article 239 and references to the Legislature or the Legislative Assembly of a State were references, in relation to a Union Territory having a Legislative Assembly, to that Legislative Assembly. The President may, by public notification, direct that the provisions of this part shall apply to any Union Territory or part thereof subject to such exceptions and modifications as he may specify in the notification.

Part not to Apply to Certain Areas: The Article 243M stipulates that nothing in this part shall apply to the Scheduled Areas and the tribal areas, the states of Nagaland, Meghalaya and Mizoram, the hill areas in the state of Manipur for which District Councils exist under any law for the time being in force.

The Act further stipulates that nothing in this part relating to panchayats at the district level shall apply to the hill areas of the District of Darjeeling in the state of West Bengal for which Darjeeling Gorkha Hill Council exists under any law for the time being in force.

However, Parliament may, by law, extend the provisions of this part to the Scheduled Areas and the tribal areas referred to in Clause (I), subject to such exceptions and modifications as may be specified in such law, and no such law shall be deemed to be an amendment of this Constitution for the purposes of Article 368.

Bar to Interference by Courts in Electoral Matters: The Article 243O provides for the bar to interference by courts in electoral matters for certain specific matters concerning and the conduct of election. It lays down that notwithstanding anything in this constitution: (a) the validity of any law relating to the delimitation of constituencies or the allotment of state to such constituencies made or purporting to be made under Article 234K, shall not be called in question in any court, and (b) no election to any panchayat shall be called in question except by an election petition presented to such authority and in such manner as is provided for by or under any law made by the legislature of a state.

Amendment of Article 280: It prescribes that in Clause (3) of the Article 280 of the constitution, after sub-clause (b) the following sub-clause shall be inserted, namely :

(bb) The measures needed to augment the consolidated fund of a state to supplement the resources of panchayats in the state on the basis of the recommendations made by the Finance Commission of the State.

2.4 Constitutional Provisions for Fifth and Sixth Scheduled Areas

The scheduled areas, as identified, are part of the states in which they are situated. The Governor is given specific powers for the administration of scheduled areas. These powers are: (a) to modify central or state laws in their application to them, (b) to frame regulations for their peace and good governance and particularly for the protection of the rights of tribals in land, (c) allotment of land, and (d) their protection from money-lenders. However, in framing these regulations, the Governor is required to consult the Tribes Advisory Council (TAC). Further, the Governor is required to submit to the President a report annually or whenever required regarding the administration of the Scheduled Areas in his state.

Part B, Para 4 of the Fifth Schedule envisages setting up of a Tribes Advisory Council (TAC). It is an advisory body meant to act as an instrument for prevention of exploitation and discrimination. It facilitates governance of the scheduled areas in the larger interest of the tribes.

Fifth Schedule: For the Fifth Scheduled Areas (see table 2.1 for the list of states and their tribal population), there is a division of responsibility between the state governments and the union government to screen legislation unsuitable for extension to the Scheduled Areas. The state government is responsible for framing regulations relating to such items. The state government has also to implement special schemes pertaining to welfare and general development of Scheduled Tribes in the state. The union government extends guidance with regard to administration and provides additional funds for the betterment of the tribal community. Further, Article 339(2) of the constitution provides:

"The executive power of the Union shall extend to the giving of directions to a state as to the drawing up and execution of schemes specified in the direction to be essential for the welfare of the Scheduled Tribes in the state".

TABLE 2.1: **Tribal Population in Fifth Scheduled Area**

Sl. No.	State	Percentage of ST population to total population	Percentage of total ST population living in rural areas
1.	Andhra Pradesh	6.31	92.40
2.	Bihar	7.66	93.00
3.	Gujarat	14.92	91.91
4.	Himachal Pradesh	4.22	97.52
5.	Madhya Pradesh	23.27	95.15
6.	Maharashtra	9.27	87.53
7.	Orissa	22.21	94.86
8.	Rajasthan	12.44	95.35

Source: Panchayati Raj Directorate of the concerned state and Census of India, 1991.

Sixth Schedule: In each autonomous district and region, District Councils (DC) and Regional Councils (RC) are envisaged under Paragraph 2 of the Sixth Schedule. The DC will have not more than thirty members, of whom the Governor shall nominate not more than four persons. A simple majority elects members on the basis of adult suffrage from a single member constituency. The elected members of DC shall have a term of five years. The District Councils have been assigned with the powers of the legislature, the executive and the judiciary. The Regional Council for an autonomous region will be constituted separately in respect of all areas within such region notified by the Governor.

2.4.1 Panchayats (Extension to the Scheduled Areas) Act, 1996 (for Fifth Scheduled Areas) (CENTRAL ACT NO. 40)

The Central Act 40 provides the scope of the state legislation regarding extending the provisions of Part IX of the Constitution to the Scheduled Areas. It emphasises, 'A state legislation on the panchayats shall be in consonance with the customary law, social and religious practices and traditional management practices of community resources'.

The Central Act has defined the functions and powers of gram sabha in the scheduled areas. A careful examination reveals that these can be grouped in the following categories:

- Development functions
- Consultative role
- Recommendatory functions
- Statutory powers of the gram sabha

The important features are summarised below:

Development Functions

The development functions and powers assigned to the gram sabha are as follows:

- to approve the plans, programmes and projects for social and economic development before they are taken up for implementation by the village panchayat;
- to identify or select the persons as beneficiaries of poverty alleviation and other programmes;
- to give certification of utilisation of funds by the panchayat for the above programmes.

These powers make the gram sabha a powerful body with regard to implementation of projects for social and economic development of tribals;

- the power to exercise control over institutions and functionaries in all social sectors; and
- the power to control over local plans and resources for such plans including tribal sub-plans.

Consultative Role

Regarding the acquisition of land, the Act has assigned consultative power to the gram sabha. It says, before making acquisition of land in the Scheduled Areas by the authorities concerned for development of projects and before resettling or rehabilitating persons affected by such projects in Scheduled Areas, the gram sabha or the panchayats at the appropriate level (i.e. intermediate and district levels) will be consulted.

Recommendatory Functions

The Central Act has stipulated that the prior recommendations of the gram sabha or the panchayats at the appropriate level will be compulsory in the following matters:

- for grant of prospecting license or mining lease for minor minerals in the Scheduled Areas; and
- for grant of concession for the exploitation of minor minerals by auction.

Statutory Powers of the Gram Sabha

The Act has prescribed that the State Governments will endow panchayats in the Scheduled Areas with such powers and authorities as considered necessary to enable them to function as institutions of self-governance. With a view to ensuring this, the Act specifies that a state legislature will ensure that the panchayats at the appropriate level and gram sabha in the Scheduled Areas are endowed specifically with following powers:

- the power to enforce prohibition or to regulate or restrict the sale and consumption of any intoxicant;
- the ownership of minor forest produce;
- the power to prevent alienation of land in the Scheduled Areas and to take appropriate action to restore any unlawfully alienated land of a Scheduled Tribe;
- the power to manage village markets by whatever name called; and
- the power to exercise control over money lending to the Scheduled Tribes.

2.5 Critical Analysis of Evolution of Panchayati Raj System in India

In the backdrop of the discussion about the evolution of panchayati raj system since olden times till 73rd Amendment Act, some distinct observations have been made that are based on the studies made by experts. Some of them are summarised below:

In the analysis of the functioning of village panchayats of pre-British period, H. Tinker (1954) has commented,

> 'The panchayats of the past were rarely representative of the village as a whole: they might be drawn from the members of the founding families or from the brahmins and

> the superior cultivators. The menials and the landless had almost no say in its affairs, except perhaps in South India.'

While discussing the initiatives taken by British government, Maddick (1970) mentioned, 'From 1887 to 1900 district boards and taluk boards were set up all over India, at least all over British India. They consisted mainly of nominated members and of almost as many officials; and mainly their functions were roads, health and primary education.'

Regarding the role of chairmen of the elected bodies before independence, Maddick (1970) has reflected that they fell broadly in two categories. The first, in small number, desired to serve the community. The second looked on the post as providing lucrative advantages for himself, his family and his friends. Neither of these was conducive to a higher standard of efficiency or to the development of political participation. Furthermore, only a few chairmen could depend upon a stable majority, the rest depended on factions. These problems apart, there was the question of income of panchayats, which was far too small for the proper discharge of their full responsibilities.

Similarly, in the analysis of the pattern of village panchayats around the period of independence, Tinker (1954) points out the problems of local institutions and mentions that the philosophy behind these institutions is no longer in touch with the reality. In support, he quotes Shri Tarlok Singh:

> 'For several decades, as a well-knit social organisation the village community has been slowly but steadily declining. As the pursuit of individual interest within and outside the village has become more common, the influence of the community over its members has diminished. The growth of inequality in the ownership of land, land transfers to non-cultivators and migration to towns are evidence of these trends. The old leadership in the village has been losing its position and influence without substantial signs of a new leadership stepping into its place. In this situation conflicts of interest within the village community have sharpened and the process continues. There are now few values which can be said to be common to the whole community and certainly there is no common purpose which inspires all sections equally.'

Besides, the panchayat system, whether be in the olden times or be during British period or be after independence, is controlled by elites in the villages. And even after amendment Act, the local institutions are handicapped by poor capacity of institutions, low capabilities of elected members, lack of poor participation by the people and centralised form of democratic system (Montgomery, 1980; Yugandhar, 1991; NIRD, 1997; Jha and Mathur, 1999; and Isaac, 2000).

If we closely examine the circumstances leading to the inclusion of panchayati raj system in constitution, it is based on the concept of giving 'voice to people', 'taking democracy to villages', and 'giving powers' to villages for their self-governance (Dube, 1958). From the conceptual point of view, these were desirable, but what actually a person in a village needs is: whether he has access to basic services like education, health; whether he has access to the economic opportunities; and whether he can get justice near to his village and in time. These are the issues and the concerns not duly recognised in the panchayati raj system.

The analysis of the recommendations of subsequent committees and measures for the promotion of local institutions also point towards more on control and powers to panchayats than on addressing the fundamental issues like, *first*, providing opportunities to people, and *second*, the need for building capacities of local institutions to deliver basic services to people. These issues are not dealt in depth and are rather overlooked from the operational point of view. Although some references have been made but concrete measures or action plans have not been suggested or attempted for addressing these two vital aspects.

2.5.1 Comments on 73rd Constitution Amendment Act

As regards the Constitutional Act, references are more on statutory powers for elections, reservation for the weaker sections, devolution of funds and so on. These are important, but what about developing human capabilities that will determine the people's participation, delivery mechanism for providing services to people and meeting development needs in the villages, system of transparency and accountability. And these issues are not covered in right perspective in order to empower the people and to give strength to institutions to manage local affairs of development.

Though the panchayati raj was a strategy for rural development in the context of centralism, yet its evolution has been influenced by historical factors. At the time of independence there were problems of meeting the aspirations of the peasantry for better conditions, land reforms and institutional change to do away with the traditions of discrimination and domination based on religion and caste. This required the strong Central and State governments to handle the local elites, whether 'landlords' or 'superior castes'. These constraints along with others related to the legacy of the British raj, partition of the country and the inclination for a planned economy, shaped centralism. This centralism was not conducive to the growth in the status of local bodies. But, while having the design of panchayati raj system, the thinking that has gone into is to look from the centralisad approach of decision-making. And, so the same thinking has percolated down from centre to state to district to block and gram panchayats, without giving due regards to people's participation, transparency, accountability, save responsiveness to people's problems. Historical reasons, with strong bias towards centralism and power, have blurred the focus of development role (though assumed, but has remained in assumption) of panchayats in the Acts.

Thus, there has been very little attempt to look into operational aspects such as people's involvement in the decision-making and the efficacy of local institutions to deliver basic services. In sum, it appears that the focus of the evolution of panchayati raj system has been more on elections, powers and control, and still rooted in the historical tradition of central decision-making, than on the developmental and welfare role of the local institutions.

> '.....while having the design of panchayati raj system, the thinking that has gone into is to look from the centralisad approach of decision-making. And, so the same has percolated down from Centre to state to district to block and gram panchayats, without giving due regards to people's participation, transparency, accountability, save responsiveness to people's problems. Historical reasons, with strong bias towards centralism and power, have blurred the focus of development role (though assumed, but has remained in assumption) of panchayats. Thus, there has been very little attempt to look into operational aspects such as people's involvement in the decision-making and the efficacy of local institutions to deliver basic services. In sum, it appears that the focus of the evolution of panchayati raj system has been more on election, powers and control, and still rooted in the historical tradition of central decision-making, than on the developmental and welfare role of the local institutions.'

2.5.2 Comments on Scheduled Areas Act

From the provisions provided in the Scheduled Areas Act it is amply clear that the gram sabha has been given both development and regulatory roles. Besides, it is assumed that, in future, the panchayats would function as self-government with the devolution of powers upon panchayats in the scheduled areas.

Envisaging the self-governance role is too big a issue: It is envisaged that the panchayats should function as units of self-governance. By assigning this role it enlarges their functions enormously. If we examine this aspect carefully, it will require handling of political, fiscal and administrative subjects[1] besides legislative roles. Now this aspect should be looked in the light of two important points, *first*, what is the present capacity of the institutions, whether they are in a position to manage such responsibility, and *second*, what is the core responsibility of panchayats, which is undoubtedly the development. So by assigning panchayats the role of self-governance, this way we will be asking them to look into too many functions, which may not be politically or economically desirable.

It appears that the present Scheduled Areas Act envisages too large a responsibility for the panchayats starting from village planning to implementation of plan to management of MFP and village markets to regulation of illicit liquor and money lending. With this kind of approach there is no focused approach. Rather development, which should be at the centre of the panchayat system in the tribal areas, has lost prominence. And it is likely that at the functional level, when the panchayats will start devoting their time and resources on regulation, the development of local areas is further going to suffer. Moreover, experience shows that development and regulation can't go hand in hand, and the efficiency of functioning, especially

1. Self-government exists when a level of government has dominion over substantial, clearly defined functions, and can pass / enact laws with regard to these functions within its area of jurisdiction — state, district, village, etc. For self-government to exist there must be unambiguous roles and functions.

in respect of development, is bound to come down. Besides, the following two questions remain unanswered:

First, what is not logical is as to why to give the dual responsibility (of regulation and development) to panchayats while both the functions require altogether different approach, and

Second, why the primacy of development has not been realised while the tribal areas with low HRD and infrastructural level require more focus on these issues.

Like 73rd Amendment Act, the Scheduled Areas Act looks more into regulation, control and powers than development and service role. Rather, it lacks focus and tries to cover as many issues as can be, without looking into the capacity of the panchayats to handle and also the viability of such a proposition.

2.6 Limitations and Opportunities for Future

Limitations of Decentralisation

If we examine the system at the macro-level, it entails a substantive and extensive analysis of, first, the implications of various macro-economic, sectoral and trade policies, and second, alternative policy options that explicitly take into account the resource constraints. Also, at the macro-level, it calls for the operationalisation of regional, economic development-cum-environmental planning and management. While, at the micro-level, it calls for local resources planning, management of eco-system with participatory action and making services to people. Thus, by the very nature of the functions under decentralisation, it may not be possible and also prudent to handle all the subjects by the local institutions. In this context, there are certain limitations of decentralisation, which as follows:

- *Resource mobilisation:* Mobilising resources for big projects or for running services may be a major constraint for local institutions.
- *Food security:* Ensuring the availability of food in remote areas will require macro-planning (though at the operational level the panchayats can manage the distribution of commodities).
- *Strategic programmes of development:* There are certain programmes like immunisation, special programmes for oilseeds or pulses development, etc., that have national priorities, need policy and programme support from the Centre.
- *Industrialisation:* Industries, especially the large and medium scale, can be handled suitably by the central and state governments.
- *R&D:* It requires specialised technical and investment interventions, which can be suitably addressed by governments at higher level.
- *Marketing network:* Network for inter-district or region, inter-state marketing, export-import can be provided by Centre and state.
- *Big infrastructural development:* The infrastructure like power, telecommunication, highways, transport, etc. require the support of the central government.

Notwithstanding above, the overall policies and programmes are to be determined by the central and state governments, but at the operational level some functions, with decision-making, can be given to local levels.

Opportunities for Future

In spite of limitations of decentralisation, the present Act offers the following opportunities for future for people and local institutions:

- *Forum for People's Participation:* The gram sabha can be a forum for people to express their problems and needs. The gram sabhas can be a forum for educating people about various development programmes, and eliciting valuable views on the problems arising out of the implementation of programmes. And the feedback can be suitably used for mid-course correction wherever necessary. Also, the panchayat system provides an opportunity to people to participate in their village development planning and implementation, and to be a partner in the process of development.
- *Convergence of Resources and Services, and Synergy at the Local Level:* The panchayats can be very effective in meeting the objective of convergence of resources and services at the local level. This convergence can be achieved both at the planning stage — by way of resource matching and linkages of programmes of various sectors, and at the implementation stage — by way of be integrating the development efforts of line departments. The panchayats can facilitate in coordinating the works of various other institutions like cooperatives, voluntary and community based organisations (CBOs) in order to bring synergy at the village level and improving the reach of deliver mechanism. These CBOs include the watershed development committees, water user associations, the user groups under the water supply and sanitation programmes, the parents committees, the joint forest management committees, etc.
- *Improving Performance of Basic Services:* Nearness of panchayats with people provides an opportunity to better appreciate the problems of people and to timely attend to their basic services. For example, to name a few, the attendance of children in the school can be increased, the absenteeism of teachers can be checked, health services like immunisation can be provided in time and the availability of essential commodities can be managed efficiently by the panchayats.
- *Accountability of Local Institutions:* The gram sabha together with the social audit provides an opportunity for ensuring the accountability of panchayats to people. The gram sabhas, if regularly conducted can definitely achieve the purpose for which they have now been created by providing a ready and effective forum of accountability of elected members. This would add strength to the grassroots democracy.

Summing up

Decentralisation should be seen as a means of mobilising people for development work, giving them opportunities and encouraging them in the decision-making for local area development, and also facilitating the implementation of national development policies. Importance of decentralisation, particularly in a democratic system of governance, need not be over-emphasised. Local development units can be effective links between the central government and local communities. Greater participation in development planning and management may not only promote national integration by giving people in different regions of a country a greater ability to participate in planning and decision-making, but also increase their share in managing the local needs and meeting their aspirations. And the panchayat Acts should focus on these very fundamentals.

3

MEASURES BY STATES FOR DECENTRALISATION

With the emergence of trend towards decentralisation in many parts of the world, especially in the third world, India also moved in the direction of decentralising the political system and to have a structure of local governments where local decisions are taken by the people at the village level. This led to 73rd Constitution Amendment Act with an aim to provide the structure of the local institutions and to empower them.

The Act provides certain provisions of mandatory nature that have added considerable strength to panchayati raj institutions. The prominent among them include: statutory provisions for timely elections; reservation for weaker sections viz., SCs, STs, OBCs and women; forum for people's participation; opportunities for local level planning; and framework for devolution of funds and transfer of functions. These provisions have provided a great deal of stability to PR institutions. In this chapter attempts are made to examine various stages of decentralisation in different states. Under this, the discussion is classified under the following categories:

Political Decentralisation
- Election to local bodies
- Representation to chairmen of intermediate and gram panchayats in the higher tiers
- Representation to MLAs and MPs in PRIs
- Accountability

Functional Decentralisation
- Transfer of functions

Administrative Decentralisation
- Placement of officers and staff of line department with PRIs and their functional relationship
- Assigning subject specific responsibilities
- District planning committee
- Chairperson of various bodies at district level

- Training to PR members
- Transparency

Financial Decentralisation

- Collection of taxes
- Devolution of funds
- Expenditure as per local needs

Note: In this particular section only the above issues in each of the dimensions of decentralisation are covered, while other issues are covered in the subsequent chapters four and five.

The description on each of the above issues is outlined below:

3.1 Political Decentralisation

Election of Local Bodies

In the context of elections to local bodies, the following important features are observed:

- *Delay in the conduct of elections:* In several states like Andhra Pradesh, Bihar, Karnataka, Gujarat, Madhya Pradesh and Punjab, either the elections for all the three tiers or for one / two tiers were delayed or have been postponed (see table 3.1). And, in the state of Bihar the elections were held after a period of 23 years, and in Assam the elections have been held in Jan., 2002, after a gap of nine years.
- *Elections not held simultaneously for all the three tiers:* In certain states like Gujarat, Maharashtra and Punjab the elections for all the three tiers were not held at a time. To be more specific, in Gujarat, the elections for intermediate and district panchayats were held in September, 2000, leaving the elections for gram panchayats for a separate date (and finally conducted in Dec., 2001), and in case of Maharashtra, there was a gap of six months. Similarly, in Punjab the elections for the gram panchayats were conducted in January, 1998 but not for other two tiers.

  This particular pattern (of elections not held simultaneously, in which the period of all the panchayats does not begin and end simultaneously) is not going to be in the functional interest of panchayats if we look from the point of view of organic linkages. This is particularly important where one or two tiers are in position and the other tier (tiers) is (are) in position.

As regards the delay in the conduct of elections in many states and admittance of petitions regarding the elections in the court, there is a need to have a fresh look into the provisions viz., Articles 243E and 243O (bar to interference by courts in electoral matters) and

TABLE 3.1: **Status of Panchayat Elections in Different States**

S. N.	Name of the state	Status (when last elections held)	Remarks
1.	Andhra Pradesh	Election for intermediate and zilla panchayats held in July, 2001, and for gram panchayats in August, 2001	Elections to gram, intermediate and zilla panchayats delayed
2.	Assam	Elections held in Jan., 2002	Elections held after the gap of 9 years
3.	Bihar	Elections held in April, 2001	Elections held after the gap of 23 years
4.	Gujarat	Election for intermediate and zilla panchayats held in Sept., 2000, and for gram panchayats in Dec., 2001	Elections to gram, intermediate and zilla panchayats delayed and also not held simultaneously
5.	Himachal Pradesh	Elections held in Dec., 2000	-
6.	Haryana	Elections held in March, 2000	-
7.	Karnataka	Elections held in Feb, 2000 in GP and in July, 2000 for IP and ZP	Conduct of last elections were delayed by two years
8.	Kerala	Elections held in Sept. 2000	-
9.	Madhya Pradesh	Elections held in Jan., 2000	Conduct of last elections were delayed by one year
10.	Maharashtra	Elections held in March, 1997 for IP* and ZP, and Oct., 1997 for GP	Elections for all the tiers not held simultaneously
11.	Orissa	Elections held in Jan., 1997	-
12.	Punjab	Elections held for gram panchayats in 1998, and for for IP and ZP in June 2002	Elections to intermediate and zilla panchayats delayed and also not held simultaneously for all the three tiers
13.	Rajasthan	Elections held in Jan., 2000	-
14.	Tamil Nadu	Elections held in Oct., 2001	-
15.	Tripura	Elections held in July, 1999	-
16.	Uttar Pradesh	Elections held in June, 2000	-
17.	West Bengal	Elections held in Sept., 1998	Elections held on time since last five consecutive terms

Source: Panchayati Raj Directorate of the concerned state (till July, 2002).
*IP : Intermediate Panchayat.

to have prompt actions by the both state and the Central governments.

Membership of Intermediate Panchayat and Zilla Parishad

In some states, the chairpersons of gram panchayats are not the members of intermediate panchayat (block / panchayat samiti). These states are Andhra Pradesh, Gujarat, Haryana, Maharashtra and Tamil Nadu. In the case of Himachal Pradesh and Madhya Pradesh, at a time only one-fifth of the total members become members of intermediate panchayat by rotation. Besides, in some states like Madhya Pradesh, Uttar Pradesh, though chairpersons of gram panchayats are the members of block panchayat but they do not have voting rights (see table 3.2).

While in none of the states, chairpersons of the gram panchayats have representation in zilla panchayat except in Bihar and Rajasthan.

Chairpersons of intermediate panchayats are the members of zilla panchayat in most of the states except in Andhra Pradesh, Gujarat, Rajasthan and Tamil Nadu. In certain states, even if they are the members of zilla panchayat, they do not have voting rights. These states are Kerala, Madhya Pradesh and Uttar Pradesh.

In a way by not giving representation to gram and intermediate panchayats in the higher tiers, the lower panchayats in the concerned states are deprived of putting forth their problems. And thus, the organic linkages among these tiers are not established.

Membership and Voting Rights of MLAs and MPs in Intermediate Panchayat and ZP Meetings

In most of the states MLAs and MPs are the members of intermediate (block) panchayats and zilla parishads and also they have voting rights in the meetings of the concerned panchayats. While in Madhya Pradesh they do not have voting rights in the zilla parishad (but have in intermediate panchayat) but are the members in both the tiers. Kerala, Maharashtra and Rajasthan do not provide representation to MLAs and MPs in the intermediate and zilla panchayats, while Tamil Nadu provides representation only in zilla panchayat. In the state of Gujarat, only MLAs are permanent invitees in block panchayat, and MLAs and MPs are permanent invitees in the zilla panchayat but they do not have voting rights. Similarly, in Uttar Pradesh they are the members but do not have voting rights in both the tiers (see table 3.3).

Accountability

As per the central Act, for the financial audit, all the states have provisions and it has been ensured by the necessary provisions in the Act (see table 3.4).

With regard to social audit necessary provisions have been made by most of the states except Haryana, Punjab, Tripura and Uttar Pradesh. Regarding the *modus operandi*, it is basically ensured through gram sabha where the PR members are expected to answer to the

TABLE 3.2: **Membership of Lower Tiers in the Intermediate Panchayat and Zilla Parishad**

S. N.	Name of the state	Whether GP Chairperson				Chairperson intermediate panchayat	
		member of intermediate panchayat (IP)	has voting rights in IP (Y/N)	member of ZP (Y/N)	has voting rights in ZP (Y/N)	member of ZP (Y/N)	has voting rights (Y/N)
1	2	3	4	5	6	7	8
1.	Andhra Pradesh	N	N	N	N	N	N
2.	Assam	Y	Y	N	N	Y	Y
3.	Bihar	Y	Y	Y	Y	Y	Y
4.	Gujarat	N	N	N	N	N	N
5.	Himachal Pradesh	Yes, one-fifth of the chairpersons in the intermediate panchayat by rotation every year	Yes, but except in the election or removal of the chairperson or vice-chairperson	N	N	Y	Yes, but except in the election and removal of the chairperson or vice-chairperson
6.	Haryana	N	N	N	N	Yes, chair-person ex-officio member	Yes, except for the election and removal of chairperson / vice chair-person
7.	Karnataka	Y	Y	N	N	Y	Y
8.	Kerala	Y	Y	N	N	Y	N
9.	Madhya Pradesh	Yes, as ex-officio member, one-fifth by rotation	N	N	N	Y	N
10.	Maharashtra	N	N	N	N	Y	Where specifically provided by the Act
11.	Orissa	Y	Y	N	N	Y	Y
12.	Punjab	Y	Y	N	N	Y	Y
13.	Rajasthan	Y	Y	Y	Y	N	N

(Contd.)

TABLE 3.2 *(Contd.)*

1	2	3	4	5	6	7	8
14.	Tamil Nadu	N	N	N	N	N	N
15.	Tripura	Y	Yes, except in the meetings for election of chairperson or vice-chairperson, and for their removal	N	N	Y	Yes, except in the meetings for election of chairperson or vice-chairperson and for their removal
16.	Uttar Pradesh	Y	N	N	N	Y	N
17.	West Bengal	Y	Yes, except in cases of elections to, or removal from, the post of chair-person or vice-chairperson	N	N	Y	Yes, except in cases of elections to or removal from the post of chairperson or vice-chairperson

Source: Panchayati Raj Directorate of the concerned state (till July, 2001).

TABLE 3.3: **Membership and Voting Rights of MLAs and MPs in Intermediate Panchayat and ZP Meetings**

S. N.	Name of the state	Whether MLAs and MPs are members of		Whether they have voting rights in the meetings of	
		intermediate panchayat (Y/N)	zilla parishad (Y/N)	intermediate panchayat (Y/N)	zilla parishad (Y/N)
1	2	3	4	5	6
1.	Andhra Pradesh	Y	Y	Y	Y
2.	Assam	Y	Y	Y	Y
3.	Bihar	Y	Y	Y	Y
4.	Gujarat	Yes, MLAs are permanent invitees	Yes, permanent invitees	N	N
5.	Himachal Pradesh	Y	Y	Yes, except in the election or removal of the chairperson or vice-chairperson	Yes, except in the election or removal of the chairperson or vice-chairperson
6.	Haryana	Yes, MLAs, as ex-officio members	Yes, MLAs & MPs, as ex-officio members	Yes, except in the election and removal of chairperson / vice chairperson	Yes, except in the election and removal of chairperson / vice-chairperson of ZP
7.	Karnataka	Y	Y	Y	Y
8.	Kerala	N	N	N	N
9.	Madhya Pradesh	Y	Y	Y	N
10.	Maharashtra	N	N	N	N
11.	Orissa	Y	Y	Y	Y
12.	Punjab	Yes, only MLAs	Y	Y	Y
13.	Rajasthan	N	N	N	N
14.	Tamil Nadu	N	Y	N	Y

(Contd.)

TABLE 3.3 *(Contd.)*

1	2	3	4	5	6
15.	Tripura	Y	Y	Yes, except in the meeting for election of chairperson and vice-chairperson, and for their removal	Yes, except in the meeting for election of chairperson and vice-chairperson and for their removal
16.	Uttar Pradesh	Y	Y	N	N
17.	West Bengal	Y	Y	Yes, except in cases of elections to, or removal from the posts of chairperson or vice-chairperson	Yes, except in cases of elections to, or removal from the posts of chairperson or vice-chairperson

Source: Panchayati Raj Directorate of the concerned state (till July, 2001).

queries of people. In the state of Kerala, the monitoring samitis have been formed for supervising various development works and to report to gram sabha about their findings.

3.2 Functional Decentralisation

Specific Functions given to Three Tiers for Various Subjects

In the states of Andhra Pradesh, Assam, Bihar, Haryana, Himachal Pradesh, Punjab, Rajasthan, Tamil Nadu and Tripura, at all the three tiers, only specific functions related to anti-poverty programmes have been given. But no other specific function for other subjects has been transferred (see table 3.5). At all the three tiers, only subjects have been defined in general (without specific item) in the state Act.

In the states of Gujarat, Karnataka, Madhya Pradesh, Maharashtra, Orissa and West Bengal, the functions for the subjects of departments as mentioned (against a particular state) in table 3.7 are transferred to zilla parishad, but for all practical purposes, these functions are tied to pre-defined budget. As regards the block and gram panchayats, no specific functions, except for anti-poverty programmes, are transferred (see table 3.5).

In Kerala, the functions for the subjects of departments as mentioned in table 3.7 are transferred to zilla parishad. Design of programmes and schemes is prepared as per local needs for the devolved funds. As regards the block and gram panchayats, clearly defined functions for the subjects, as mentioned in the table 3.7, are assigned to these tiers.

In Uttar Pradesh, functions have been given (as per appendix 4.2 of chapter four) without any earmarked funds, but funds are given for anti-poverty programmes under centrally sponsored schemes.

The information collected from the states reveal that none of the tiers viz., district, block and gram panchayat have been given specific functions under various subjects. But to a reasonable extent, in the state of Kerala certain functions have been given to three tiers under various subjects.

3.3 Administrative Decentralisation

Posting of Field Staff at Gram Panchayats

Most of the states have made no provisions for the postings of field staff of line departments at the gram panchayat level, except Kerala, Madhya Pradesh and Uttar Pradesh. In these states the postings of field staff of a number of departments like agriculture, animal husbandry, health, ICDS, etc. have been made to gram panchayats (see table 3.6).

As regards the own staff of gram panchayat only in the states of Kerala and Madhya Pradesh there is one secretary for each GP, while others have one for 3-5 GPs. Similarly, gram panchayats in many states either have no staff or have very limited staff except in the states

TABLE 3.4: **System of Transparency and Accountability**

S. N.	Name of the state	Transparency in the panchayat functioning incorporated			Financial audit in the panchayat functioning incorporated		Social audit in the panchayat functioning incorporated	
		Yes/No	Mode /Necessary provisions in the Act	Certified copy of documents can be taken (Y/N)	Yes/No	Mode /Necessary provisions in the Act	Yes/No	Mode /Necessary provisions in the Act
1	2	3	4	5	6	7	8	9
1.	Andhra Pradesh	Y	Gram Sabha	Y	Y	Local Fund Audit	Y	Gram sabha
2.	Assam	NA	-	-	Y	NA	NA	-
3.	Bihar	NA	-	-	NA	-	NA	-
4.	Gujarat	Y	By Laws 108,109, 110,111,112,113	Y	Y	Local Fund Audit Act	Y	Yes, put before gram sabha all audit reports as per rules
5.	Himachal Pradesh	Y	By way of directions	Y	Y	Under the provision of section 118 of Himachal Pradesh Panchayati Raj Act, 1994	Y	By issue of notifi-cation under section 7(4) of Himachal Pradesh Panchayati Raj Act, 1994.
6.	Haryana	Y	Yes, Sec.20,72 & 132 of the Hr.Panchayati Raj Act, 1994	Yes on payment of prescribed amount provided under rule 19 of the Hr.Panchayati Raj Rules,1996	Y	Yes, Sec.43,105 and 154 of the said Act , 1994	N	N
7.	Karnataka	Y	Jamabandi	Y	Y	Act	Y	Gram sabha
8.	Kerala	Y	S.2714 of KPR Act, 1994	-	-	a. Local Fund Audit Deptt. b. Performance Audit Team		Gram sabha (Monitoring samitis)

(Contd.)

TABLE 3.4 *(Contd.)*

1	2	3	4	5	6	7	8	9
9.	Madhya Pradesh	Y	Y	Y	Y	Y	Y	Panchayat rules
10.	Maharashtra	Y	NA	NA	Y	Panchayat Act	Y	Administrative instructions are issued
11.	Orissa	N	Executive Instructions	Y	Y	Local Fund Audit Act	Y	Section 5(3) of OGP Act
12.	Punjab	Y	By instructions	Y	Y	Y	N	N
13.	Rajasthan	Y	Right to information	Y	Y	Necessary provisions in the Act	Y	Necessary provisions in the Act
14.	Tamil Nadu	Y	N	Y	Y	As per Sec.193 of the Tamil Nadu Panchayat Act, 1994	Y	Rules provided
15.	Tripura	Y	Y	Y	Y	Y	N	N
16.	Uttar Pradesh	Y	Y	Y	Y	Y	N	N
17.	West Bengal	Y	NA	N	Y	NA	Y	NA

Source: Panchayati Raj Directorate of the concerned state (till July, 2001).
N.A.: Not Available.

TABLE 3.5: **Specific Functions given to Three Tiers for Various Subjects**

S. N.	Name of the state	Specific functions given to ZP for various subjects	Specific functions given to IP for various subjects	Specific functions given to GP for various subjects
1	2	3	4	5
1.	Andhra Pradesh	Specific functions related to anti-poverty programmes. No other specific functions given, only subjects defined in the Act	Specific functions related to anti-poverty programmes. No other specific functions given, only subjects defined in the Act	Specific functions related to anti-poverty programmes. No other specific functions given, only subjects defined in the Act
2.	Assam	-do-	-do-	-do-
3.	Bihar	-do-	-do-	-do-
4.	Gujarat	Functions for the subjects of departments as mentioned in table 3.7*	No specific functions, except for anti-poverty programmes	No specific functions, except for anti-poverty programmes
5.	Himachal Pradesh	Specific functions related to anti-poverty programmes. No other specific functions given, only subjects defined in the Act	Specific functions related to anti-poverty programmes. No other specific functions given, only subjects defined in the Act	Specific functions related to anti-poverty programmes. No other specific functions given, only subjects defined in the Act
6.	Haryana	-do-	-do-	-do-
7.	Karnataka	Functions for the subjects of departments as mentioned in table 3.7*	No specific functions, except for anti-poverty programmes	No specific functions, except for anti-poverty programmes
8.	Kerala	Functions for the subjects as mentioned in table 3.7. Also functions are clearly defined for each tier. Design of programmes and schemes as per local needs for the devolved funds	Clearly defined functions for the subjects as mentioned in table 3.7	Clearly defined functions for the subjects as mentioned in table 3.7
9.	Madhya Pradesh	Functions for the subjects of departments as mentioned in table 3.7*	No specific functions, except for anti-poverty programmes	No specific functions, except for anti-poverty programmes
10.	Maharashtra	Functions for the subjects of departments as mentioned in table 3.7*	No specific functions, except for anti-poverty programmes	No specific functions, except for anti-poverty programmes
11.	Orissa	Functions for the subjects of departments as mentioned in table 3.7*	No specific functions, except for anti-poverty programmes	No specific functions, except for anti-poverty programmes

(Contd.)

TABLE 3.5 *(Contd.)*

1	2	3	4	5
12.	Punjab	Specific functions related to anti-poverty programmes. No other specific functions given, only subjects defined in the Act	Specific functions related to anti-poverty programmes. No other specific functions given, only subjects defined in the Act	Specific functions related to anti-poverty programmes. No other specific functions given, only subjects defined in the Act
13.	Rajasthan	-do-	-do-	-do-
14.	Tamil Nadu	-do-	-do-	-do-
15.	Tripura	-do-	-do-	-do-
16.	Uttar Pradesh	Functions (as per appendix 4.2 of chapter four) given without any earmarked funds, except for anti-poverty programmes	Functions (as per appendix 4.2 of chapter four) given without any ear-marked funds, except for anti-poverty programmes	Functions (as per appendix 4.2 of chapter four) given without any ear-marked funds, except for anti-poverty programmes
17.	West Bengal	Specific functions related to anti-poverty programmes. No other specific functions given, only subjects defined in the Act*	Specific functions related to anti-poverty programmes. No other specific functions given, only subjects defined in the Act	Specific functions related to anti-poverty programmes. No other specific functions given, only subjects defined in the Act

Source: Panchayati Raj Directorate of the concerned state (till July, 2001).

* In these states, state sector programmes are implemented as per the specific direction of their respective state governments.

TABLE 3.6: **Posting of Field Staff to Gram Panchayats**

S. N.	Name of the state	Whether the field staff of departments transferred to gram panchayat and reporting to GPs (Y/N)											Own staff of GP	
		Primary schools	Health centre	ICDS	Water supply	Agril.	Soil cons.	Animal hus.	Fisheries	Irrig.	VLW	Revenue inspector/ patwari	GP Secretary (Y/N) (or in-charge of more than one GP)	Other staff (number)
1	2	3	4	5	6	7	8	9	10	11	12	13	14	15
1.	Andhra Pradesh	N	N	N	N	N	N	N	N	N	N	N	Executive officer for 4-5 GPs	N
2.	Assam	N	N	N	N	N	N	N	N	N	N	N	Y, one for 3-5 GPs	2
3.	Bihar	N	N	N	N	N	N	N	N	N	N	N	-do-	N
4.	Gujarat	N	N	N	N	N	N	N	N	N	N	N	-do-	-
5.	Himachal Pradesh	N	N	N	N	N	N	N	N	N	N	N	-do-	1 (GP sahayak)
6.	Haryana	N	N	N	N	N	N	N	N	N	N	N	-do-	N
7.	Karnataka	N	N	N	N	N	N	N	N	N	N	N	-do-	4-5 staff.
8.	Kerala	Y	Y	Y	Y	Y	Y	Y	N	Y	Y	N	Y, for each GP	6-7 staff
9.	Madhya Pradesh	Y	Y	Y	Y	Y	Y	Y	Y	Y	Y	Y	-do-	N
10.	Maharashtra	N	N	N	N	N	N	N	N	N	N	N	Y, one for 3-5 GPs	N
11.	Orissa	N	N	N	N	N	N	N	N	N	N	N	-do-	1 *
12.	Punjab	N	N	N	N	N	N	N	N	N	N	N	-do-	1 *
13.	Rajasthan	Y	N	N	N	N	N	N	N	N	N	N	-do-	I *
14.	Tamil Nadu	N	N	N	N	N	N	N	N	N	N	N	One panchayat assistant / part time panchayat clerk	1 *

(Contd.)

TABLE 3.6 (*Contd.*)

1	2	3	4	5	6	7	8	9	10	11	12	13	14	15
15.	Tripura	N	N	N	N	N	N	N	N	N	N	N	Y, one for 3-5 GPs	N
16.	Uttar Pradesh	N	Y	Y	N	Y	Y	N	N	Y	Y	N	-do-	N
17.	West Bengal	N	N	N	N	N	N	N	N	N	N	N	-do-	4 to 5

Source: Panchayati Raj Directorate of the concerned state (till July, 2001).

* One temporary peon or scavenger can be hired by the panchayat.

of Karnataka, Kerala and West Bengal

Relationship of Line Department Officials and Staff with ZP

In none of the states, the line department officers at the district level are under the administrative control of zilla parishad (ZP). However, in some states some partial control (through review meetings and standing committees) is exercised by CEO and chairperson of ZP for ensuring their accountability to zilla parishad. For example, in states like Madhya Pradesh, Orissa and Uttar Pradesh, the officers of line departments have been designated as additional CEO, ZP, but zilla parishad does not exercise any control over other officers and staff of line departments. The states of Gujarat, Karnataka, Kerala, Madhya Pradesh, Maharashtra, Orissa and West Bengal have taken some administrative measures for control of ZP over the line departments as indicated by table 3.7.

Relationship of Line Department Officials and Staff with Intermediate and Gram Panchayats

In none of the states (see table 3.8) there is administrative control of intermediate and gram panchayats over the officers and staff of line departments. While in the states of Gujarat, Karnataka, Madhya Pradesh, Maharashtra, Uttar Pradesh and West Bengal there is some control by the standing committees for the review of works undertaken by the departments. While in Kerala the officers and staff report to concerned panchayats for their respective works. And in case of Madhya Pradesh, only at the gram panchayat level the field staff report to it, and in case of Uttar Pradesh one multi-purpose (in-charge of eight departments) is placed with the gram panchayats. As regards the salary of the officers and staff, it is provided by the concerned departments.

DPC Formation

In a number of states, DPC has not been constituted, while in the states of Haryana and Orissa it is in the process of formation (see table 3.9). The states where the DPC has been formed are Karnataka, Kerala, Madhya Pradesh, Maharashtra, Rajasthan, Tamil Nadu, Uttar Pradesh and West Bengal. Wherever the DPC has been formed, the chairpersons of GPs and block panchayats are not the members of the planning committee with the exception of Tamil Nadu where one-fifth of total block chairpersons in the district are the members of DPC by rotation. While except in Kerala, in all the other states MLAs and MPs are either the members or special invitees of DPC, and in the states of Rajasthan, Tamil Nadu and Uttar Pradesh they have been given voting rights. In case of West Bengal, the chairpersons of Panchayat Samitis, MLAs and MPs can become the members of the DPC and have voting rights by the special government order.

TABLE 3.7: **Relationship of Officials and Staff of Line Departments with ZP**

S N.	Name of the state	Whether line-deptt. officers under ZP or under its admn. control (Y/N)	Nature of arrangement (line deptts. officers as addl. CEO or any other arrangement)	Whether the line deptt. are the staff of ZP or under its admn. control (Y/N)	Which are the deptts. under ZP	Whether the salary of such line deptt. officers and staff given by ZP (Y/N)
1	2	3	4	5	6	7
1.	Andhra Pradesh	N	NA	N	NA	N
2.	Assam	N	NA	N	NA	N
3.	Bihar	N	NA	N	NA	N
4.	Gujarat	N	Officers report to CEO, ZP and ZP standing committee	Some administrative control through review and standing committees	Control over the departments: Primary Edu., Animal Husbandry, Agri., PWD, Health & Family Welfare Irrigation, Co-operation, Social Welfare	N
5.	Himachal Pradesh	N	NA	N	NA	N
6.	Haryana	N	NA	N	NA	N
7.	Karnataka	N	Officers report to CEO, ZP and ZP standing committee	Some administrative control through review and standind committees	Control over the departments: Agriculture, Animal Husbandry, Fisheries, Small Scale Industries, Industries, Rural Dev., Primary Edu., Tech. Edu., Cooperatives, Pub. Works, Health, Woman & Child Dev.	N
8.	Kerala	N	Officers dealing with transferred subjects are under the control and supervision of Panchayat	Administrative control	Control over the departments: Agriculture, Animal Husbandry, Fisheries, Small Scale Industries, Industries, Rural Dev., Primary Edu., Tech. Edu., Cooperatives, Pub. Works, Health.	N

(Contd.)

TABLE 3.7 *(Contd.)*

1	2	3	4	5	6	7
9.	Madhya Pradesh	N	Designated as Addl. CEO, and report to CEO, ZP and ZP standing committee	Some administrative control through review and standing committees	Control over the departments: Health, Edu., Social Welfare, Woman & Child Dev., R.D. Agriculture, Rural Dev., Primary Edu., Tech. Edu., Cooperatives, Pub. Works, Health	N
10.	Maharashtra	N (Only there are some officers and staff under ZP)	Officers report to CEO, ZP and ZP standing committee	In some cases (of deptts. with the ZP)	Control over the departments: Agriculture, Animal Husbandry, Fisheries, Small Scale Industries, Industries, Rural Dev., Primary Edu., Tech. Edu., Cooperatives, Pub. Works, Health, Woman & Child Dev.	To some officers and staff, who are under its admn. control
11.	Orissa	N	Designated as Addl. CEO, and report to CEO, ZP and ZP standing committee	N	Control over the departments: Agriculture, Animal Husbandry, Fisheries, Industries, Rural Dev., Primary Edu., Tech. Edu., Cooperatives, Pub. Works, Health, Woman & Child Dev.	N
12.	Punjab	N	NA	N	NA	N
13.	Rajasthan	N	NA	N	NA	N
14.	Tamil Nadu	N	NA	N	NA	N
15.	Tripura	N	To be designated as Addl. CEO	N	NA	N

(Contd.)

TABLE 3.7 (*Contd.*)

1	2	3	4	5	6	7
16.	Uttar Pradesh	N	Designated as Addl. CEO, and report to CEO, ZP and ZP standing committee	N	Control over the departments: Agriculture, Animal Husbandry, Fisheries, Industries, Rural Dev., Primary Edu., Health, Woman & Child Dev.	N
17.	West Bengal	N	Officers report to CEO, ZP and ZP standing committee	Some administrative control through review and standing committees	Control over the departments: Agriculture, Animal Husbandry, Fisheries, Industries, Rural Dev., Primary Edu., Pub. Works, Health, Woman & Child Dev.	N

Source: Panchayati Raj Directorate of the concerned state (till July, 2001)
NA: Not applicable.

TABLE 3.8: **Relationship of Officials and Staff of Line Departments with Intermediate and Gram Panchayats**

S. N.	Name of the state	Whether the line deptts. are the staff of intermediate panchayat (IP) or under its administrative control (Y/N)	Which are the deptts. under intermediate panchayat (IP)	Whether the salary of such line deptts. officers and staff given by IP (Y/N)	Whether the line deptts. are the staff of GP or under its administrative control (Y/N)	Which are the deptts. under GP	Whether the salary of officers and staff of line deptts. given by GP (Y/N)
1	2	3	4	5	6	7	8
1.	Andhra Pradesh	N	NA	N	N	NA	N
2.	Assam	N	NA	N	N	NA	N
3.	Bihar	N	NA	N	N	NA	N
4.	Gujarat	N (control through standing committees)	NA	N	N (control through standing committees)	NA	N
5.	Himachal Pradesh	N	NA	N	N	NA	N
6.	Haryana	N	NA	N	N	NA	N
7.	Karnataka	N (control through standing committees)	NA	N	N (control through standing committees)	NA	N
8.	Kerala	N (but services of field staff transferred in some cases)	Reporting by the field staff of the following departments: Agricul-ture, Industries, Rural Dev., Social Welfare, S.C.Dev., S.T. Dev., Health, Ayurveda, Homoeopathy	N	N (but services of field staff transferred in some cases)	Reporting by the field staff of the following departments: Agriculture, Animal Husbandry, Dairy Dev., Fisheries, Rural Dev., Social Welfare, S.C.Dev. S.T. Dev., Health, Ayurveda, Homoeopathy, Primary Edu., Pub. Works	N

(Contd.)

TABLE 3.8 *(Contd.)*

1	2	3	4	5	6	7	8
9.	Madhya Pradesh	N (control through standing committees)	NA	N	N (but services of field staff transferred in some cases)	Reporting by the field staff of the following departments: Agriculture, Animal Husbandry, Dairy Dev., Fisheries, Rural Dev., Social Welfare, Health, Primary Edu., Drinking Water, Land revenue	N
10.	Maharashtra	N (control through standing committees)	NA	N	N (control through standing committees)	NA	N
11.	Orissa	N	NA	N	N	NA	N
12.	Punjab	N	NA	N	N	NA	N
13.	Rajasthan	N	NA	N	N	NA	N
14.	Tamil Nadu	N	NA	N	N	NA	N
15.	Tripura	N	NA	N	N	NA	N
16.	Uttar Pradesh	N (control through standing committees)	NA	N	N (control through standing committees)	N (One multi-purpose worker is transferred to GP)	N
17.	West Bengal	N (control through standing committees)	NA	N	N (control through standing committees)	NA	N

Source: Panchayati Raj Directorate of the concerned state (till July, 2001)
Note 1: Intermediate and gram panchayats have administrative control over officers and staff of rural development department in all the states.
Note 2: Notwithstanding the above information, there is some partial control of intermediate and gram panchayats over field staff, through review meetings.
NA: Not applicable.

TABLE 3.9: **Constitution of DPC**

S. N.	Name of the state	Whether DPC formed (Y/N)	Total members	Whether chairpersons of GPs members of		chairpersons of intermediate panchayats members of		MLAs and MPs members of	
				DPC (Y/N)	Voting rights (Y/N)	DPC (Y/N)	Voting rights (Y/N)	DPC (Y/N)	Voting rights (Y/N)
1	2	3	4	5	6	7	8	9	10
1.	Andhra Pradesh	N	-	-	-	-	-	-	-
2.	Assam	N	-	-	-	-	-	-	-
3.	Bihar	N	-	-	-	-	-	-	-
4.	Gujarat	N	-	-	-	-	-	-	-
5.	Himachal Pradesh	N	-	-	-	-	-	-	-
6.	Haryana	Y, in four districts	20 - 25	N	N	N	N	Special invitees	N
7.	Karnataka	Y	36	N	N	N	N	Special invitees	N
8.	Kerala	Y	16	N	N	N	N	N	N
9.	Madhya Pradesh	Y	15-25	N	N	N	N	Y	N
10.	Maharashtra	Y	30 -50	N	N	N	N	Special invitees	N
11.	Orissa	N	-	-	-	-	-	-	-
12.	Punjab	N	-	-	-	-	-	-	-
13.	Rajasthan	Y	25	N	N	N	N	Y	Y

(Contd.)

TABLE 3.9 *(Contd.)*

1	2	3	4	5	6	7	8	9	10
14.	Tamil Nadu	Y	NA	N	N	One-fifth of the total number of chairpersons of intermediate panchayats annually	Y	Y	Y
15.	Tripura	N	-	-	-	-	-	-	-
16.	Uttar Pradesh	Y	NA	N	N	N	N	Y	Y
17.	West Bengal	Y	Depending upon population	N	N	N (unless appointed by the state government)	Y, if appointed	Same as in cases of chair-persons of panchayat samiti	Same as in cases of chairpersons of panchayat samitis

Source: Panchayati Raj Directorate of the concerned state (till July, 2001)

NA: Not applicable

Chairpersons of various bodies

Chairperson of DRDA: In many states, the chairperson of the zilla parishad has been appointed as the chairperson of DRDA. But there are certain states like Andhra Pradesh, Assam, Bihar, Gujarat, Haryana, Punjab, Tamil Nadu and Tripura where the chairperson of DRDA is district Collector or Dy. Commissioner or Addl. Collector. In case of Maharashtra, CEO, ZP is a chairperson, DRDA (see table 3.10).

CEO of ZP: In certain states like Andhra Pradesh, Karnataka, Kerala, Madhya Pradesh, Maharashtra, Punjab, Rajasthan and Tamil Nadu, a special officer either called CEO or secretary has been appointed. In other states either district collector or DDC or DDO or Addl. DC or CDO is the CEO of ZP (see table 3.10).

Chairperson of DPC: In some states like Madhya Pradesh, Maharashtra and Uttar Pradesh, the chairperson of DPC is minister-in-charge of the district. While in some states like Karnataka, Kerala, Rajasthan and West Bengal, the chairperon or zilla parishad is the chairperson DPC. In the state of Haryana, the chairperson is chosen by the state government from among the nominated members, and in Tamil Nadu, the district collector is the chairperson (see table 3.10).

Administrative Approval of Department Funds by ZP

In majority of the states, the departmental funds are not approved by the zilla parishad. Only in the cases of Gujarat, Karnataka, Kerala, Madhya Pradesh and Maharashtra, and partially in the states of Orissa and West Bengal, the funds are approved by the zilla parishad as per the following procedure (see table 3.11):

In the states of Gujarat and Karnataka, the funds are approved through ZP budget. In case of Madhya Pradesh, the approval is made by the general administration of the zilla parishad.

In case of Kerala, administrative sanction is given by the zilla panchayat. The plans and schemes have to be approved and authorised by the zilla panchayat, supported by a resolution, then the implementing officers of the line departments shall implement the scheme.

In the case of Orissa, there are two ways, first, resources can be provided to ZP for implementation of the identified schemes by ZP or through ZP with the transfer of schemes budgetary provision for these schemes will have to be placed with the ZP. And second, alternatively funds available under the scheme in the budget of the departments shall be placed with the concerned district level offices. The district level officer shall before utilisation of such funds obtain the approval of concerned standing committee or of zilla parishad.

In all the aforementioned states, the state sector programmes are implemented as per the direction of the respective state governments.

In case of West Bengal, zilla parishad places fund with the district level officers of the line departments for execution of earmarked schemes. In other cases, line departments execute

TABLE 3.10: **Chairperson of various Bodies**

S.N.	Name of the state	Chairperson of DRDA	CEO of ZP	Chairperson of DPC if formed	Remarks
1.	Andhra Pradesh	Distt. Collector	CEO	Not constituted	-
2.	Assam	Dy. Commissioner	-	Not constituted	-
3.	Bihar	Distt. Collector	DDC	Not constituted	-
4.	Gujarat	DDO	DDO	Not constituted	-
5.	Himachal Pradesh	Chairperson of zila parishad	Addl. DC of the Distt.	Not constituted	-
6.	Haryana	Dy. Commissioner	Addl. DC	Chosen by state Govt. from amongst nominated members	-
7.	Karnataka	-	CEO	President of zilla parishad	DRDA merged with ZP
8.	Kerala	President of zilla parishad	Secretary	President of zilla parishad	-
9.	Madhya Pradesh	Chairperson of zilla parishad	Secretary	Minister-in-charge	-
10.	Maharashtra	CEO, zilla parishad	CEO	Minister-in-charge of the district	-
11.	Orissa	President, zilla parishad	Collector	Not constituted	-
12.	Punjab	Distt. Collector	Secretary	Not constituted	-
13.	Rajasthan	Zilla Pramukh	Secretary	Zila pramukh	-
14.	Tamil Nadu	Distt. Collector	Secretary	Distt. Collector	-
15.	Tripura	Collector	Collector	Not constituted	-
16.	Uttar Pradesh	Chairperson of zilla parishad	CDO	Minister concerned	-
17.	West Bengal	Sabhadhipati of the ZP	Distt. Collector	Sabhadhipati of zilla parishad	-

Source: Panchayati Raj Directorate of the concerned state (till July, 2001)

schemes out of the fund received from the state government directly on the basis of the decision of the zilla parishad on selection of sites, target group or beneficiaries and prioritisation.

Training of PR Members

The states have taken steps for organising training for PR members. Based on the information available (see table 3.12) from the states, the following points are observed:

- In all the states, except in Kerala, training has been organised for a period of about three to five days and the frequency of such training is once in five years. Besides, the subjects covered during the training are basically related to constitution amendment Act, PRI administration, anti-poverty programmes. As regards Bihar and Assam, the panchayats have been constituted late so the training would be organised later on.
- In case of Kerala the training has been organised for two-five days depending upon the subject. Training has been given to each member. The frequency is once in a year (unlike once in five years for other states). Besides, the training inputs related to all the subjects as per constitution amendment Act have been covered during the training. Also, the training on decentralised planning has been organised successfully.

System of Transparency

The states have taken measures for transparency in the panchayat functioning (see table 3.4). The mode of transparency varies from state to state. In certain states like Gujarat, Haryana, Kerala and West Bengal specific provisions have been made in the act. In some states like Himachal Pradesh and Orissa provisions of transparency are made through executive instructions. In case of Rajasthan it is through provisions under right to information.

3.4 Financial Decentralisation

Devolution of Funds

- *Devolution of funds upon panchayats:* In none of the states the funds are devolved upon panchayats (see table 3.13). While in the state of Kerala, since 1996-97, the Government has taken bold steps for devolving funds upon ZP in the lumpsum with a formula to further allocate them to three tiers. Funds under this category are quite large and the value is Rs. 516.0 cr. (in 1997-98).
- *Untied Funds:* As regards the untied funds, various states have taken measures for providing them in the lumpsum to zilla parishad. These funds are allocated for different projects in the district planning board as per the advice of MLAs. Also, in the states of Karnataka, Madhya Pradesh, Maharashtra, Rajasthan and West Bengal, the funds are given to ZP even department-wise in order to enable them to have programmes of their own choice. These funds to the departments are normally quite

TABLE 3.11: **Administrative Approval of Funds of Line Departments by ZP**

S N.	Name of the state	Whether the funds of line deptts. are approved by ZP (Y/N)	Mode of approval
1	2	3	4
1.	Andhra Pradesh	N	NA
2.	Assam	N	NA
3.	Bihar	N	NA
4.	Gujarat	Y	Provided by deptt. sanctions and operated by ZP committees
5.	Himachal Pradesh	N	NA
6.	Haryana	N	NA
7.	Karnataka	Y	Through ZP budget
8.	Kerala	Y	Administrative sanction is given by zilla panchayat. The plans and schemes have to be approved and authorised by the zilla panchayat, supported by a resolution, then the implementing officers of the line department shall implement the scheme
9.	Madhya Pradesh	Y	In Gen. adm. of panchayat
10.	Maharashtra	Y	Powers delegated to CEO; chairperson; subject committee; standing committees and zilla parishad, depending upon the financial limit
11.	Orissa	In some cases	There are two ways: i. Resources can be provided to ZP for implementation of the identified schemes by ZP or through ZP with the transfer of schemes budgetary provision for these schemes will have to be placed with the ZP. ii. Alternatively funds available under the scheme in the budget of the departments shall be placed with the concerned district level offices. The district level officer shall before utilisation of such funds obtain the approval of the concerned standing committee or of zilla parishad

(Contd.)

TABLE 3.11 *(Contd.)*

1	2	3	4
12.	Punjab	N	NA
13.	Rajasthan	N	NA
14.	Tamil Nadu	N	NA
15.	Tripura	N	NA
16.	Uttar Pradesh	N	NA
17.	West Bengal	In some cases	i. Zilla parishad places fund with the district level officers of the line departments for execution of only earmarked schemes ii. In other cases, line departments execute schemes out of the fund received from the state government directly on the basis of the decision of the zilla parishad on selection of sites, target group of beneficiaries and prioritisation

Source: Panchayati Raj Directorate of the concerned state (till July, 2001).

TABLE 3.12: **Training of PR Members**

S.N.	Name of the state	Tier	Functionaries	Place of training (Days)	Duration of	Subjects/Items covered during training	Frequency of training (No. of times in five years/one term)
1	2	3	4	5	6	7	8
1.	Andhra Pradesh, Gujarat, Himachal Pradesh, Haryana, Karnataka, Madhya Pradesh, Maharashtra, Orissa, Punjab, Rajasthan, Tripura, Uttar Pradesh, West Bengal	Zilla Parishad	i. Chairperson ii. Members	SIRD level	(3-5 days)	Mainly on Panchayat Act and rules, about their functions and duties and about statutory provisions. In some cases on: Accounts, Development works and social sector schemes	Once in a term (5-year)
		Intermediate Panchayat	iii. Chairperson iv. Members	SIRD level / District level District level	(3-5 days)	-do-	Once in a term (5-year)
		Gram Panchayat	v. Chairperson vi. Ward Members	District level / Block level Block level	(1-2 days)	-do-	Once in a term (5-year)
2.	Assam, Bihar	NA (Not applicable)	NA	NA	NA	NA	
3.	Kerala	Zilla Parishad	i. Chairperson ii. Members	KILA, SIRD, IMG -do-	(2 to 5 days on each subject)	i. Panchayat raj system, ii. Decentralised planning, iii. Training on SC/ST, on SCP and TSP schemes. iv. Training to woman members on different subjects	Almost all members were given training on various subjects. (once in a year)

(Contd.)

TABLE 3.12 *(Contd.)*

1	2	3	4	5	6	7	8
		Intermediate Panchayat	iii. Chairperson iv. Members	SIRD level / District level District level	-do-	-do-	-do-
		Gram Panchayat	v. Chairperson vi. Ward Members	District level / Block level Block level	-do-	-do-	-do-

Source: Panchayati Raj Directorate of the concerned state (till July, 2001).
KILA : Kerala Institute of Local Administration, IMG: Institute of Management in Government.

small in comparison to total funds given to districts under various development programmes (see table 3.13).

- *Tied Funds:* The tied funds have been provided directly by the state governments to zilla parishad in some states. Among them, Gujarat, Karnataka, Madhya Pradesh and Maharashtra have shown considerable lead over others, and during 1999-2000 the allocations made to these states were Rs.101.33 cr, 2707.95 cr, 757.57 cr. and 5942.10 cr. respectively. In the states of Orissa, Rajasthan and West Bengal, some steps have been taken to provide tied funds to ZP (see table 3.13). These funds are placed with ZP, as per specific programme or scheme of a department.

Expenditure as per its Own Needs

The funds given to PRIs are mainly in the tied form or in other words the local institutions get funds for a particular scheme, thus their financial autonomy is restricted. Only in the state of Kerala there is a large degree of autonomy as 40 per cent of funds under general sector (1997-98) were in the untied form. Even the states like Gujarat, Karnataka, Madhya Pradesh and Maharashtra, which provide substantial funds to zilla parishad, do not give much scope to panchayats in terms of autonomy, as funds are invariably tied to a particular programme or scheme.

3.5 Status of Scheduled Areas Act (Act 40 of 1996)

The Scheduled Areas Act provides the provisions for extending the provisions for setting up panchayati raj institutions in the fifth scheduled areas (see table 3.14 and appendix 3.1). The Central Act has defined the functions and powers of gram sabha in the scheduled areas regarding development functions, consultative role, recommendatory functions and regulatory powers of the gram sabha. A brief note about the status is given below :

- *The acquisition of land in the Scheduled Areas*

  The action at the government of India level is pending. Orissa and Gujarat have taken measures, while others have yet to initiate the action.

- *Planning and management of minor water bodies in the Scheduled Areas shall be entrusted to Panchayats at the appropriate level*
  All the states have taken measures in this regard.

- *The grant of prospecting license or mining lease for minor minerals in the Scheduled Areas and for grant of concession for the exploitation of minor minerals by auction*
  The actions have been taken by all the states in this direction, except in Andhra

TABLE 3.13: **Devolution of Funds**

S. N.	Name of the state	Whether the funds are devolved upon panchayats			Whether the untied funds are given to panchayats Y / N	Funds given to zilla parishad as tied-funds
		Y/N	Year of placement of funds	Value		
1	2	3	4	5	6	7
1.	Andhra Pradesh	N	NA	NA	Y, the allocation of funds is decided in the DPB as per the advice of MLAs	-
2.	Assam	N	NA	NA	-do-	-
3.	Bihar	N	NA	NA	-do-	-
4.	Gujarat	N	NA	NA	-do-	Funds are given to ZP for the earmarked schemes. Its value was Rs.101.33 cr. in 1999-2000
5.	Himachal Pradesh	N	NA	NA	-do-	-
6.	Haryana	N	NA	NA	-do-	-
7.	Karnataka	N	NA	NA	Y, the allocation of funds is decided in the DPB as per the advice of MLAs. Also some untied funds* are given department-wise	Funds are given to ZP for the earmarked schemes. Its value was Rs. 2707.95 cr. in 1999-2000
8.	Kerala	Y	1997-98	516.00 cr (under general sector)	Plan funds given as untied funds.	-
9.	Madhya Pradesh	N	NA	NA	Y, the allocation of funds is decided in the DPB as per the advice of MLAs. Also some untied funds* are given department-wise	Funds are given to ZP for the earmarked schemes. Its value was Rs. 757.57 cr. in 1999-2000
10.	Maharashtra	N	NA	NA	-do-	Funds are given to ZP for the earmarked schemes. Its value was Rs.5942.10 cr. in 1999-2000

(Contd.)

TABLE 3.13 *(Contd.)*

1	2	3	4	5	6	7
11.	Orissa	N	NA	NA	Y, the allocation is decided in the DPB as per the advice of MLAs	Some funds are given to ZP
12.	Punjab	N	NA	NA	-do-	-
13.	Rajasthan	N	NA	NA	Y, the allocation of funds is decided in the DPB as per the advice of MLAs. Also some untied funds* are given department-wise	Some funds are given to ZP
14.	Tamil Nadu	N	NA	NA	Y, the allocation of funds is decided in the DPB as per the advice of MLAs	-
15.	Tripura	N	NA	NA	-do-	-
16.	Uttar Pradesh	N	NA	NA	-do-	-
17.	West Bengal	N	NA	NA	Y, the allocation of funds is decided in the DPB as per the advice of MLAs. Also some untied funds * are given department-wise	Some funds are given to ZP

Source: Panchayati Raj Directorate of the concerned state (till July, 2001).
Note I : Untied funds means the amount given in lumpsum to the local tiers for planning at their level, either deptt.-wise or for general development programme.
* Normally, untied funds are less than 5% of the total plan funds.
DPB: District Planning Board.

TABLE 3.14: **Status of Subject Laws amended / to be amended for Panchayats in 5th Scheduled Areas**

S. N.	Subject Laws	AP	Chhatisgarh	Gujarat	HP	Jharlkhand	M.P.	Maharashtra	Orissa	Rajasthan
1.	Acquisition of land	The action is to be taken by the GOI. Orissa and Gujarat have taken measures. Other states have yet to work on it								
2.	Grant of prospecting licence or mining for minor minerals	In the process	Yes	Yes	Yes	Yes	Yes	Yes	Yes	In the process
3.	Power to enforce prohibition	Yes	Yes	No	Yes	Yes	NA	Yes	Yes	In the process
4.	Ownership of minor forest produce	Yes	Yes	Yes	Yes	Yes	NA	Yes	Yes	In the process
5.	Land alienation	In the process	Yes	In the process	In the process	In the process	NA	Yes	Yes	In the process
6.	Management of village markets	In the process	Yes	In the process	Yes	In the process	NA	In the process	Yes	In the process
7.	Control over money lending	Yes	Yes	Yes	Yes	Yes	Yes	Yes	Yes	In the process
8.	Control over institutions and functionaries in all social sectors	Not yet done in any state								

Source: Panchayati Raj Directorate of the concerned state (till July, 2001) and MORD (2001b).

Pradesh and Rajasthan where it is under process.

- *The power to enforce prohibition or to regulate or restrict the sale and consumption of any intoxicant*
  All the states have taken actions in this direction and necessary provisions in the Excise Act have been changed, except Rajasthan.
- *The ownership of minor forest produce*
  All the states have taklen measures as per Central Act, except Rajasthan.
- *The power to prevent alienation of land in the Scheduled Areas*
  Chhatisgarh, Maharashtra and Orissa have taken appropriate measures, and others are in the process of doing so.
- *The power to manage village markets by whatever name called*
  Himachal Pradesh, Chhatisgarh and Orissa have taken measures as per the central Act, and other states are in different stages of doing so.
- *The power to exercise control over money lending to the Scheduled Tribes*
  It has been ensured through the Act in all the states, except Rajasthan.
- *The power to exercise control over institutions and functionaries in all social sectors*
  It has not been done in any state, but is under consideration in all the states.
- *The power to control over local plans and resources for such plans including tribal sub-plans*
  It has not yet been done.

Note 1 : All the states have initiated measures and are in the various stages of implementation.
Note 2 : The above findings are based on the available information from the states by July, 2001.

3.6 Panchayats in North-eastern States

The status of panchayats in north-eastern states is summarised as under:

Arunachal Pradesh

In Arunachal Pradesh, a 3-tier system of Panchayati Raj, consisting of gram panchayat at the village level, anchal samiti at the block level and zilla parishad at the district level has been functioning since 1967. The elections for panchayats were first held in 1969 and thereafter at an interval of every three years under the North Eastern Frontier Panchayat Raj Regulation, 1967. The last elections were held in 1992 and the tenure of these bodies continued upto 1997 when it was allowed to expire. The Arunachal Pradesh Panchayati Raj Bill has been accorded President's assent, following on the passage of the 86th Constitution Amendment Act, 2000, whereby Arunachal Pradesh has been exempted from the requirement of providing reservation for scheduled castes. Although, due to low state population, Arunachal Pradesh could have had a 2-tier system {Article 243B (2)}, the state has opted to retain the intermediate tier also, in view of the importance it attaches to this level.

Assam

In Assam, the Panchayati Raj System has been in place since 1919. Subsequently, it passed new Acts in 1959, 1972, 1986 and 1994. Under the 1994 Act, the 3-tier system, as prescribed by the 73rd Constitution Amendment Act, has been introduced. As the panchayat elections were held in 1992 under the 1986 law, these were allowed to continue till October, 1997. Under the new Act, the state government has held elections in January, 2002.

Autonomous District Councils: The 73rd Constitution Amendment Act does not apply to the entire state of Assam. The two hill districts, Karbi Anglong and North Cachar Hills are covered by the Sixth Schedule of the Constitution with Autonomous District Councils (ADCs.). Although, technically sixteen departments are transferred to ADCs, but practically very little devolution of powers and functions have taken place, resulting in considerable discontent. Subsequently, a Memorandum of Understanding was signed between the Government of Assam and representatives of Autonomous State Demand Committee (ASDC) in April, 1995, granting more autonomy to the district councils. Under this agreement, the state government has consented to transfer thirty departments to autonomous council. The working of these autonomous councils, however, clearly indicates that the councils do not favour any decentralisation of powers and functions to the village or block level local bodies. It has also been reported that the functioning of ADCs, is characterised by absence of administrative skills and financial prudence.

Manipur

Manipur has two forms of local self-government — 73rd Amendment Act in the valley and Autonomous Hills in the hill areas (see table 3.15). The hills have a 2-tier system comprising Autonomous District Councils and Village Authority. The district councils and the village authorities are not inter-connected in as much as the village authorities are not under the control of the district councils. The district councils were introduced under the Manipur Hill Areas District Council Act, 1971, passed by the Parliament in 1972. The district councils do not enjoy legislative and judicial powers that are vested in the district councils in the Sixth Scheduled Areas.

The village authority comprises the village chief as chairman and elected or nominated members. The village authority has been created primarily by extending legal status to the transitional village self-governing institutions under the 'Manipur State Hill People's Regulation 1947' and 'Manipur State Courts Act 1947'. The sub-divisional magistrate has, however, been given the powers of superintendence over the village authorities. The village authorities enjoy administrative and financial powers. There is considerable social acceptance partly because of the powers that village authorities enjoy and partly also because of the connection that these authorities have with the traditional modes of self-governance. In fact, village authorities are quite capable of assuming the role that has been contemplated for

TABLE 3.15: **Number of Districts Under 5th and 6th Scheduled Areas in North Eastern and Sikkim States**

S.N.	Name of the state	Total no. of districts	No. of districts under 5th Schedule	No. of districts under 6th Schedule	No. of districts under 73rd CAA	Name of the of districts under 6th Schedule
1.	Arunachal Pradesh	12	-	-	12	Nil
2.	Assam	23	-	2	21	Karbi Anglong, North Cachar Hills
3.	Manipur	9	-	5	4	Chandel, Churachandpur, Senapati, Tamenglong, Ukhrul
4.	Meghalaya	7	-	7	-	East Garo Hills, East Khasi Hills, Jaintia Hills, West Garo Hills, West Khasi Hills, South Garo Hills, Ri Bhoi (New districts South Garo Hills from East Garo Hills, and Ri Bhoi from East Khasi Hills created)
5.	Mizoram	7	-	7	-	Aizawl, Chhimtuipui, Lunglei, Mamit, Kolasib, Serchhip, Champhai, Lawngtlai (New districts Mamit, Kolasib, Serchhip and Champhai created from Aizawl; and Lawngtlai from Chhimtuipui created)
6.	Nagaland	8	-	8	-	Kohima, Mokokchung, Mon, Phek, Tuensang, Wokha, Zunheboto, Dimapur (New district Dimapur created from Kohima)
7.	Tripura *	4	-	4	4	North Tripura, South Tripura, West Tripura, Dhalai (new district Dhalai created from North and South Tripura)
8.	Sikkim	4	-	-	4	Nil

Source: Panchayati Raj Directorate of the concerned State and ISS (2000).
* In the same district there are areas of overlap for 6th Schedule and 73rd CAA.

panchayats under the 73rd Constitution Amendment with regard to economic development, social justice and prioritisation of development needs.

In the valley the 73rd Constitution Amendment Act is applicable. Although the valley districts account for only 10 per cent of the area, they have 54 per cent of the state's population. The Manipur Panchayati Raj Act allocates thirty two subjects to gram panchayats, but the functioning of panchayats is not satisfactory, as no real devolution of powers has taken place.

Meghalaya

The local government system in Meghalaya is a mix of traditional and elected representatives. The entire state has self-governing institutions at the village, intermediate and district levels. The Sixth Schedule districts are indicated by table 3.15.

Each of these districts has an Autonomous District Council. At the village, there is a village head and there are clan leaders who are the members. In Garo community, the village head is the husband of the traditional heiress of the clan land called Nokma. Among the Khasis and Jaintias, there is a traditional village Darbar (council) presided over by an elected headman. This headman is assisted by executive members who are nominated by him. Since the land belongs to the community and the clans, the darbars and the clan councils play an important role in managing the lands and forests.

In spite of considerable vesting of administrative and legislative powers and functions, only some funds are available to the autonomous district councils (ADCs). At the village level also, the local bodies can't function well as the state government is directly handling all the local developmental activities. There is considerable demand by the ADCs for the transfer of functions and devolution of funds

Mizoram

Under Sixth Schedule, Mizoram has three districts. At the village level, village council is constituted, which is headed by a president, chosen either unanimously or by a majority of the elected members of the council. Each village council consists of 4 to 15 members depending on the number of houses in the village. Village councils enjoy administrative and judicial powers and functions. The entire land, other than homesteads, belongs to the village council. The village council has the responsibility of collecting taxes, supply of water, construction of approach roads, etc., apart from deciding the new jhum sites and allotment of land to families. Each village council also maintains a court for the dispensation of justice.

Nagaland

Nagaland has had traditionally organised village governments which exercised both regulatory and judicial functions. In 1978, the government of Nagaland enacted the Nagaland village and

Area Council Act. The Act provides for the constitution of village councils in all the recognised villages of Nagaland, comprising members chosen by all prominent residents of the village. The hereditary village chiefs i.e. the gaon Burahs and Ahngs are ex-officio members of the village council. The village council elects a member as the chairman of the council.

Wide ranging powers have been vested in the village council. One of the functions of the village council is to constitute the village development board (VDB) as an executive wing of the council. Detailed rules have been prescribed for functioning of the council and model rules have been prescribed for functioning of the VDB. VDBs have been provided certain powers of judicial and development functions. Presently, VDBs have three sources of funds as given under:

- The matching cash grant is equivalent to the fund raised by the village from out of the proceeds of its common property resources.
- Grant-in-aid is given from the state rural development department.
- Grants under the centrally sponsored schemes, such as EAS, JGSY, etc., the whole or most of which comes to the VDB.

Sikkim

After the Amendment Act, 1992, under the Sikkim Panchayati Raj Act, 1993 the panchayat elections were held in 1997. At the district level, there is zilla parishad and the deputy commissioner is its secretary. The zilla parishad also has sabhapatis of the village panchayats, MPs and MLAs as ex-officio members. The gram panchayats are associated with almost all the development works in the rural areas and the zilla panchayats play the role of coordinating agencies at the district level and also supervise the big projects. Traditional institutions of tribals (dzumsas) in Lachen and Lachung villages have been protected by incorporating specific provisions in the new Panchayati Raj Act of 1993. The state government has undertaken programmes for capacity building, and measures for transfer of functions and devolution of funds, but these are not sufficient to add to the strength of the panchayats.

Tripura

Tripura has a dual system of local governance. In the non-tribal plains areas the panchayati raj system is applicable to and the autonomous district council works in the sixth scheduled area in the tribal hilly areas of the state.

In Tripura, the system of panchayati raj in the non-tribal plains areas is similar to that of West Bengal where standing committees at the panchayat samiti and zilla parishad levels have been given a prominent role in planning and implementation. Tripura has not shown much political commitment for transfer of functions and devolution of powers upon PRIs.

The Tripura Tribal Areas Autonomous District Councils are functional in the four districts, comprising the tribal majority areas of the state. This council consists of thirty members, of which twenty eight are directly elected and two are nominated by the Governor.

Of the twenty eight elected members, twenty four are ST and four are non-ST members. One of the elected members is elected as chairman of the Council to act as speaker of the council. There is an executive committee of seven members constituting of a kind of Cabinet. One of the members is selected as leader, designated as Chief Executive Member. The autonomous district council is assisted by CEO. The ADC has at each district headquarters a zonal development officer and twenty sub-zonal officers at the block headquarters. The ADC has been vested with substantial administrative, legal and financial powers and is allocated wide ranging functions, but devolution of funds is meagre to carry out development activities.

3.7 Panchayat Finances

The panchayats at the three levels have certain, though limited, own means of tax collection, but they have to largely depend upon the state budget for either transfer of tax collected by the state or development grants. Presently, there are broadly three sources of funds for panchayats (see table 3.16):

- first, own resources through direct taxation;
- second, shared taxes; and
- third, grants-in-aids.

• *Own Resources Through Direct Taxation*

The article 243H of amendment Act empowers the states to assign collection of taxes by the panchayats to augment their income. These taxes are covered under two categories, *first*, tax revenue, and *second*, non-tax revenue (see table 3.16).

TABLE 3.16: **Major Sources of Income for Panchayats**

S.N.	Source	Items
1.	Tax collection (own income)	
	i. Internal Cources taxes	Property tax, tax on vehicles, animals, trade and profession, theatre / show tax, tax on advertisements, boats, etc.
	ii. Non-tax revenue	Rents from panchayat assets (including panchayat land), user charges, fee and fines, income from municipal investments, etc.
2.	Shared taxes	Entertainment tax, motor vehicle tax, land revenue, stamp duty, forest revenue.
3.	External sources grants-in-aid	General purpose, specific purpose

TABLE 3.17: **Panchayats with Overlapping Tax Assignments**

S.N.	Name of the state	Tax	GP	IP	ZP
1.	Andhra Pradesh	Transfer of property	Yes	Yes	Yes
2.	Assam	Profession	Yes	Yes	Yes
		Water rate	Yes		Yes
3.	Bihar	Toll	-	Yes	Yes
		Lighting	-	Yes	Yes
		Registration of vehicles	-	Yes	Yes
		License fee for market, etc.	-	Yes	Yes
4.	Madhya Pradesh	Land revenue	Yes	Yes	Yes
		Stamp duty	-	Yes	Yes
5.	Maharashtra	Pilgrims	Yes	-	Yes
6.	Sikkim	Fairs	Yes	-	Yes
		Sanitation	Yes	-	Yes
		Special work on utilities	Yes	-	Yes
7.	Tamil Nadu	Water rate	Yes	-	Yes
8.	Tripura	Water rate	-	Yes	Yes
		Toll tax	-	Yes	Yes
		Lighting	-	Yes	Yes
9.	Uttar Pradesh	Water rate	Yes	Yes	-
10.	Haryana	Hospitals	-	Yes	Yes
		Schools	-	Yes	Yes
		Water	-	Yes	Yes
11.	West Bengal	Toll levy on ferry	-	Yes	Yes
		Water	-	Yes	Yes
		Lighting	-	Yes	Yes
		Registration fee	-	Yes	Yes

Source: KAF (1998)

- *Tax Assignment at the Village Level :* The village panchayats are entrusted with a number of taxes. The important amongst them are building tax, profession tax, tax on advertisements, show tax, service tax, surcharge on buildings tax, land conversion cess, land cess, surcharge on panchayat taxes for district and block panchayats, fees for temporary occupation of village sites, roads and other public places. The GPs also collect user charges. These include water rate, lighting fee / rate, street cleaning fee, conservancy fee, drainage fee, sanitary fee for public latrines and pilgrimage fee.
- *Tax Assignment at the Intermediate Level :* At the intermediate level the tax items that are assigned are: tolls on vehicles, animals, ferries; water rate, lighting rate, fee on registration of vehicles, fee for providing sanitary arrangements; license fee for a market, etc. (see appendix 3.2). In some states, viz. Himachal Pradesh, Karnataka and Orissa, the intermediate panchayats do not collect taxes (MORD, 2001b).

- Tax Assignment at the District Level : The items that are assigned to district level are: tax on property, water tax, electricity tax, tolls and fees under lease of property or road place, school fee, library fee, fee on exhibitions, registration of animals and meals, license fee and tolls in markets, etc. But these items vary from state to state (see appendix 3.3). In some states viz., Himachal Pradesh, Madhya Pradesh and Orissa, the district panchayats do not collect taxes (MORD, 2001b).

Note 1: There are certain tax items that are collected by more than one tier as indicated by table 3.17.
Note 2: Among these taxes there are certain mandatory taxes to be imposed by the panchayats, and there are some that are to be levied with the approval of state government (see appendix 3.2).

- *Shared Taxes*

The states also compensate the panchayats for certain items of tax collection such as entertainment tax, motor vehicle tax, land revenue, stamp duty, forest revenue. These items are indicated in appendix 3.3.

- *Provision of Grants-in-Aid to Panchayati Raj Institutions*

Due to low base of financial resources at the panchayat levels, the states have to provide grants-in-aid. These are either general purpose like untied fund, or specific purpose like funds under centrally sponsored schemes (CSS), Tenth Finance Commission (TFC).

3.8 State Control

Though Constitution Amendment Act envisages self-government role of panchayats, the states in their discretions have been overcautious in checking the malpractices and misuse of powers by panchayats. All state governments have provided necessary legislative provisions in their panchayati raj Acts in this regard. These controls are exercised either by the panchayati raj department (or rural development) or District Collector, depending upon the state Act. These state controls over the PRIs are categorised (see table 3.18) as follows:

- power to cancel / suspend resolution;
- power to take action in default of gram panchayat;
- power to remove elected representatives;
- power to dissolve the PRIs;
- power to give direction to PRIs;
- power to call for records and inspection; and
- power to conduct enquiry.

In this regard the official version is that these are to be applied only in situations like unlawful activities or financial irregularities. However, wide powers of suspension and dismissal vested in the state administration have straightaway placed PRIs in a position of disadvantage vis-a-vis even middle rung functionaries of the state governments. It is an issue that requires debate between giving autonomy to PRIs and control by state. But such matters, if arise, need to be resolved by independent agency like tribunal or ombudsman.

TABLE 3.18: **State Control over the PRIs**

S. N.	Items	States
1.	Power to cancel / suspend direction	Andhra Pradesh, Himachal Pradesh, Kerala, Madhya Pradesh, Manipur, Orissa, Rajasthan, Sikkim, Tamil Nadu
2.	Power to take action in default of gram panchayat	Andhra Pradesh, Orissa
3.	Power to remove elected representatives	Andhra Pradesh, Orissa, Sikkim, Tamil Nadu, Uttar Pradesh
4.	Power to dissolve PRIs	Andhra Pradesh, Arunachal Pradesh, Assam, Gujarat, Himachal Pradesh, Kerala, Madhya Pradesh, Maharashtra, Orissa, Rajasthan, Sikkim, Tamil Nadu, Tripura, West Bengal
5.	Power to give direction to PRIs	Arunachal Pradesh, Bihar, Himachal Pradesh, Sikkim.
6.	Power to call for records and inspection	Arunachal Pradesh, Assam, Gujarat, Himachal Pradesh, Karnataka, Kerala, Madhya Pradesh, Maharashtra, Orissa, Rajasthan, Tripura, Uttar Pradesh, West Bengal
7.	Power to conduct enquiry	Assam, Bihar, Gujarat, Himachal Pradesh, Karnataka, Madhya Pradesh, Maharashtra, Manipur, Orissa.

Source: Planning Commission (2001).

APPENDIX 3.1

Status of PR Extension to Scheduled Areas Act (PESA) in different States

S.N.	Subject Laws	Status							
		AP	Chattisgarh	Gujarat	HP	MH	MP	Orissa	Rajasthan
1.	Traditional rights of tribals	Gram Sabha	Gram Sabha	Gram Sabha	Gram Sabha	Gram Sabha	Gram Sabha	Gram Sabha	Gram Sabha
2.	Approval of plans, programmes and projects	Gram Sabha shall approve	Provisions are made subject to the rules which the State government may make	Provisions made	Gram Sabha shall approve	Gram Sabha is competent	Provisions are made subject to the rules which the State government may make	Provisions made	Provisions made
3.	Acquisition of land	With Mandal Parishad	With Gram Sabha	With Taluka Panchayats	Gram Sabha	Gram Sabha, Panchayat Samiti or Zilla Panchayat	With Gram Sabha	With Zilla Parishad	The Gram Sabha or the PRIs at such level as the case may be
4.	Management of minor water bodies	Gram Panchayat, Mandal Parishad or Zilla Panchayat as the case may be	Gram Sabha, Janpad Panchayat or Zilla Panchayat	Gram Panchayat	Gram Sabha is to advise Gram Panchayat	Gram Panchayat, Panchayat Samiti or Zilla Panchayat as the case may be	Gram Sabha, Janpad Panchayat or Zilla Panchayat	Zilla Panchayat	As may be specified by the state government

(Contd.)

APPENDIX 3.1 *(Contd.)*.

S.N.	Subject Laws	Status							
		AP	Chattisgarh	Gujarat	HP	MH	MP	Orissa	Rajasthan
5.	Grant of prospecting licence or mining lease for minor minerals	Gram Panchayat	Gram Panchayat (Amendment made)	Gram Panchayat	Gram Sabha	Gram Panchayat	Gram Panchayat (Amendment made)	Zilla Parishad	By the Gram Sabha or the PRIs at such level and in such manner as may be prescribed
6.	Power to enforce prohibition	Gram Sabha or the Gram Panchayat as the case may be	Gram Sabha (Amendment made)	Gram Panchayat	Gram Sabha or the Gram Panchayat as the case may be	Gram Sabha	Gram Sabha (Amendment made)	Gram Sabha to control and supervise and Gram Panchayat to execute	PRIs at appropriate level or Gram Sabha as may be prescribed
7.	Ownership of minor forest produce	Gram Sabha or the Gram Panchayat as the case may be	Not mentioned	Gram Panchayat	Gram Sabha or the Gram Panchayat as the case may be	Gram Panchayat	Not mentioned	Gram Sabha to control and supervise and Gram Panchayat to execute	PRIs at appropriate level or Gram Sabha as may be prescribed
8.	Preventing alienation of land	Gram Sabha or the Gram Panchayat as the case may be	Gram Sabha*	Not mentioned	Not mentioned	Gram Sabha (make recom-mendations through panchayat)	Gram Sabha*	Gram Sabha to control and supervise and Gram Panchayat to execute	PRIs at appropriate level or Gram Sabha as may be prescribed

(Contd.)

APPENDIX 3.1 *(Contd.)*

S.N.	Subject Laws	Status							
		AP	Chattisgarh	Gujarat	HP	MH	MP	Orissa	Rajasthan
9.	Managing village markets	Gram Sabha or the Gram Panchayat as the case may be	Gram Sabha	Not mentioned	Gram Sabha or the Gram Panchayat as the case may be	Not mentioned	Gram Sabha	Gram Sabha to control and supervise and Gram Panchayat to execute	PRIs at appropriate level or Gram Sabha as may be prescribed
10.	Control over money lending	Gram Sabha or the Gram Panchayat as the case may be	Gram Sabha (make recom-mendations through Gram Panchayat)	Gram Panchayat	Gram Sabha or the Gram Panchayat as the case may be	Gram Sabha (make recom-mendations through Gram Panchayat)	Gram Sabha (make recom-mendations through Gram Panchayat)	Gram Sabha to control and supervise and Gram Panchayat to execute	PRIs at appropriate level or Gram Sabha as may be prescribed
11.	Control over institutions and functionaries	Mandal Parishad	Gram Sabha or Janpad Panchayat	Gram Panchayat	Panchayat Samiti	Gram Panchayat or Panchayat Samiti	Gram Sabha or Janpad Panchayat	Panchayat Samiti (in consultation with Gram Sabha)	PRIs at appropriate level or Gram Sabha as may be prescribed
12.	Control over local plans and resources	Mandal Parishad	Gram Sabha	Taluka Panchayat	Panchayat Samiti	Gram Sabha	Gram Sabha	Gram Sabha (to be consulted while preparing plans) and Panchayat Samiti (prepare plan and exercise control)	NA

(Contd.)

APPENDIX 3.1 *(Contd.)*

S.N. Subject Laws	Status							
	AP	Chattisgarh	Gujarat	HP	MH	MP	Orissa	Rajasthan
13. Panchayats as self-governing institutions	No specific provision	No specific provision	No specific provision	No specific provision	No specific provision	No specific provision	No specific provision	No specific provision

*Not mentioned but provision giving such power to Gram Sabha exists in MP Land Revenue Code, 1959.
NA: Not Available
Note : For Jharkhand, information not available.
Sources : MORD, 2001a and Planning Commission 2001.

APPENDIX 3.2

A Sample List of Items of Tax Collection Assigned to Panchayats by Some Selected States

S.N.	Level	Andhra Pradesh	Kerala	Punjab	Uttar Pradesh
1	Village Panchayats	- House tax* - Kolagarum or - Katarusum* - Special tax on houses for civic purposes* - Vehicle tax - Tax on agri. land for a specified purpose - Land cess at Rs. 0.02% on specified lands - Surcharge on the seigniorage fees on materials other than minerals quarried - Surcharge on land / local cess and education tax - Tolls - Tax on advertisements - Fees for the use of other communal lands - Fees for occupation of buildings - Fees for temporary occupation of village sites, roads & other public places - Fees on public / private markets, brokers, commission agents, weighmen and village fishers	- Building tax* - Profession tax* - Tax on advertisements* - Show tax* - Service tax for civic purposes* - Surcharge on buildings tax - Land conversion cess - Land cess - Surcharge on panchayat taxes for district and block panchayats** - Fees for temporary occupation of village sites, roads and other public places. - Fees from beneficiaries of institutions run on or financed wholly or partly by the panchayats	- Tax on lands and buildings - Profession tax* - Addl. stamp duty on entertainments* - Water rate - Lighting rate - Conservancy rate - Special tax on construction of any public work of general utility** - Fee on registration of vehicles - Fee for providing sanitary arrangements - Advertisement tax - Leasing fee for common property - Market fee - Tax/fee on non-domestic property	- Surcharge on land revenue* - Entertainment tax - Tax on animals and vehicles - Tax on persons - Tax on goods for sale - Water rate - Tax on latrines - Tax for sanitation - Lighting tax - Irrigation rate - Fees on registration of animals sold and on the use of slaughter houses

(Contd.)

APPENDIX 3.2 *(Contd.)*

S.N.	Level	Andhra Pradesh	Kerala	Punjab	Uttar Pradesh
2	Intermediate Panchayats	Nil	- Fee from the beneficiaries of the institutions run or financed wholly or partly by them	- Tolls on persons, - vehicles, animals, ferries. - Water rate - Lighting rate - Fee on registration of vehicles - Fee for providing sanitary arrangements. - License fee for a market	- Water tax - Electricity tax - School fee, library fee, fee on sarai, service bulls, exhibitions, registration of animals and melas. - License fee and tolls in markets
3.	District Panchayats	Nil	- Fee from the beneficiaries of the institutions run or financed wholly or partly by them	- Can levy any tax or fee if VPs or IPs default	- Tax on property - Water tax - Electricity tax - Tolls and fee under lease of property or road place - School fee, library fee, fee on sarai, service bulls, exhibitions, registration of animals and melas - License fee and tolls in markets

* Mandatory taxes to be imposed
** To be levied with the approval of state government

Sources: State Panchayat Acts and MORD (2001b).

APPENDIX 3.3

Taxes, Duties, Tolls and Fee Levied and Collected by State Government whose Proceeds are Assigned to Panchayats

S. N.	Level	Andhra Pradesh	Assam	Arunachal Pradesh	Bihar	Goa
1	2	3	4	5	6	7
1.	Village Panchayats	- Land cess - Entertainment tax - Surcharge on stamp duty - Mineral cess - Profession tax - Seigniorage fees	- Land revenue - Local rate	NA	Nil	Nil
2.	Intermediate Panchayats	- Land cess - Mineral cess - Surcharge on stamp duty - Land revenue	Nil	NA	Nil	(Intermediate Panchayats not existing)
3.	District Panchayats	- Land cess - Surcharge on stamp duty - Mineral cess	Nil	NA	Nil	Nil

(Contd.)

APPENDIX 3.3 *(Contd.)*

S. N.	Level	Gujarat	Haryana	Himachal Pradesh	Jammu & Kashmir	Karnataka
1	2	8	9	10	11	12
1.	Village Panchayats	- Land Revenue - Forest revenue	- Sale proceeds of country liquor - Stamp duty - Registration fee	- Local rate - Additional duty - Land revenue	Nil	33.92% of the non-loan gross own revenue receipts transferred to PRIs
2.	Intermediate Panchayats	- Land revenue - Local cess leviable on water rate	- Stamp duty & Registration fee - Revenue from cattle fairs	- Local rate	Not existing	Nil
3.	District Panchayats	- Land revenue - Local cess leviable on lands	- Stamp duty & Registration fee - Revenue from cattle fairs	Nil	Nil	Nil

(Contd.)

APPENDIX 3.3 *(Contd.)*

S. N.	Level	Kerala	Madhya Pradesh	Maharashtra	Manipur	Orissa
1	2	13	14	15	16	17
1.	Village Panchayats	- Basic tax - Duty on transfers of property - Motor vehicles tax	- 2.91% of the gross tax and non-tax revenue receipts of state govt. transferred to PRIs	- Land revenue - Additional stamp duty - Entertainment tax - Motor vehicle tax - Royalty on minor irrigation - Royalty on minor forest - Land revenue cess	Nil	- Cess on land revenue - Kendu leaf grant - Minor forest produce - Sairat revenue - Entertainment tax
2.	Intermediate Panchayats	Nil	Nil	Nil	NA	- Land revenue cess - Kendu leaf grant - Minor forest produce
3.	District Panchayats	Nil	Nil	- Forest revenue - Water rate - Cess on land revenue - Cess on royalty in respect of minerals - Additional stamp duty	Nil	- Land revenue cess - Kendu leaf grant

(Contd.)

APPENDIX 3.3 *(Contd.)*

S. N.	Level	Punjab	Rajasthan	Sikkim	Tamil Nadu
1	2	18	19	20	21
1.	Village Panchayats	- Land revenue - Surcharge on stamp duty	- Entertainment tax - Charges on conversion of agricultural land to non-agricultural use	- Land revenue	- Profession tax - Duty on transfer of immovable property
2.	Intermediate	Nil	- Cess on land revenue	- NA	- Local cess
3.	District Panchayats	Nil	- Surcharge on stamp duty - Mandi tax	Nil	Nil

(Contd.)

APPENDIX 3.3 *(Contd.)*

S. N.	Level	Tripura	Uttar Pradesh	West Bengal
1	2	22	23	24
1.	Village Panchayats	Nil	- 4% of the State taxes	- Entertainment tax transferred to PRIs.
2.	Intermediate Panchayats	Nil	Nil	Nil
3.	District Panchayats	Nil	Nil	- Land revenue - Road cess - Public works cess

NA : Not available

Sources: State Panchayat Acts and MORD (2001b).

4

FIELD STUDY AND SURVEY OF PROCESS OF DECENTRALISATION

Why Field Study and Survey

The need of the field study was felt to have assessment of the impact of the measures initiated by various states for improving the functioning of panchayats and their ability to address the development concerns as per the felt-need and aspirations of people at the grassroots level. The aspects that have been specifically studied are how the panchayati raj institutions have been able to take up the local level planning and development, how the people have been benefited under the new panchayat setup and which are the areas that need to be further addressed for strengthening the panchayats. Likewise, the survey of process of decentralisation has been undertaken to elicit views of people (selected through random sampling) about various issues such as role of panchayat members, functioning of gram sabha, people's participation, local level planning, responsiveness of PR members, functioning of panchayats in meeting local development needs and so on.

4.1 Field Study

For the study of panchayati raj institutions, the field studies were conducted in fifteen states. During the visits, discussions were held with the respective director and secretary, panchayati raj department. It was followed by field visits to districts. During the field visits, the discussions were held with the officials and field staff of district, blocks and gram panchayats, PR members at each tier and people in the villages. Village meetings were also conducted to study the group dynamics, people's participation in the discussion, role of PR members in conducting village meetings, role of women and weaker sections, the kind of issues discussed in the gram sabha and so on. Discussions were also held about the devolution of administrative and financial powers upon panchayats and so on.

The visits to states were made between June, 1998 and January, 2001. Based on field visits, state-specific points are indicated below:

TABLE 4.1: **The Districts, Blocks and Gram Panchayats of the Study Area**

S.N.	Name of the state	Name of the district	Name of the block	Name of the GP
1	Andhra Pradesh	i. Nalgonda	i. Thirumalgiri	i. Tatpamla
			ii. Chotupal	i. Pipalpahar
				ii. Narkedapally
				iii. Chirkonda
2	Assam	i. Kamrup	i. Hajo	i. Kulhati
3	Gujarat	i. Anand	i. Anand	i. Vasad
				ii. Napad
4	Haryana	i. Kurukshetra	i. Thanesar	i. Umri
				ii. Jirbari
5	Karnataka	i. Mysore	i. Mysore	i. Coorgally
				ii. Yelawala
6	Kerala	i. Kollam	i. Kottarakara	i. Pooyapalli
7	Madhya Pradesh	i. Hoshangabad	i. Kasala	i. Kasala
				ii. Saheli
		ii. Vidisha	NA	i. Puakhedi
				ii. Hirnai
		iii. Raysen	NA	i. Tejapur
				ii. Dhahua-Chapua
8	Maharashtra	i. Pune	i. Bhiwandi	i. Chidaki
				ii. Kosapur
			ii. Maval	i. Badeshwar
				ii. Kasauli
9	Meghalaya	i. Ri-bhoi	i. Urnsing	i. Nongster
		ii. East-Khasi	ii. Mylliem	i. Mawiong-rin
10	Orissa	i. Ganjam	i. Kukudakhandi	i. Baulajholi
		ii. Dhenkanal	i. Govindpur	i. Govindpur
				ii. Khadagparsad
				iii. Manipur
		iii. Keonjhar	i. Padampur	i. Padampur
11	Punjab	i. Hoshiarpur	i. Hoshiarpur-I	i. Lasrala
			ii. Hoshiarpur-II	i. Mahana
				ii. Chharikalan
			iii. Mahilpur	i. Hariziana
				ii. Buddowal

(Contd.)

TABLE 4.1 *(Contd.)*

S.N.	Name of the state	Name of the district	Name of the block	Name of the GP
12	Rajasthan	i. Tonk	i. Newai	i. Gunsi
				ii. Luhara
		ii. Sawai Madhopur	i. Sawai Madhopur	i. Kusthala
				ii. Mori
		iii. Jaipur	i. Sanganer	i. Mohanpura
13	Tamil Nadu	i. Kancheepuram	i. Wallajabad	i. Vellivallam
14	Uttar Pradesh	i. Faizabad	i. Sohawal	i. Seikhpur Zafar
				ii. Magasil
		ii. Gonda	i. Nawabganj	i. Tulsipur Majha
			ii. Bazirganj	i. Bazirganj
		iii. Barabanki	i. Masoli	i. Masoli
15	West Bengal	i. Midnapur	i. Garbheta	i. Banachapada
			ii. Panasguda-I	i. Panasguda
			iii. Panasguda-II	i. Kola-I
		ii. Howrah	i. Bagnan-I	i. Bagnan-I
			ii. Bagnan-II	i. Sharat Chandra

Note: In Meghalaya the provisions of Scheduled Area Act (6th Schedule) are applied.

NA: Not Available.

4.1.1 Observations in Andhra Pradesh

As per the recommendations of Balwantrai Mehta Committee, the Andhra Pradesh brought forward legislation to create a 3-tier system of panchayati raj and Andhra Pradesh Panchayat Samiti and Zilla Parishad Act, 1959 was enacted. Thereafter in 1964, the Andhra Pradesh GP Act, 1964, superseded the earlier Act. Under this new Act, which set the pattern for the future panchayati raj structure in the state, every village had to have a gram sabha consisting of all the eligible voters. The gram sabhas met at least twice a year to consider the annual statement of accounts and audit, the report of the administration for the previous year, the programme of works for the year ahead and the proposals for fresh taxation or for

Notes:

1. During the field visits, the village meetings were organised, and based on the discussions with PR members, people and field officers and staff, the observations are presented.
2. The names of districts, blocks and gram panchayats that were visited are indicated in table 4.1.
3. The reports of the visits were prepared immediately after the visit to each state and the reports have been taken as such without any change in the 'tense form'.
4. The names of panchayats, as mentioned above, are as existed at the time of writing the book.

enhancement of existing taxes. The *sarpanch*, or in his absence, the *up-sarpanch* of the gram panchayat, presided over the meeting.

Now, to conform with the constitution (73rd Amendment) Act, 1992 Andhra Pradesh has enacted the Andhra Pradesh Panchayati Raj Act, 1994.

Field Visits

Visit to Tatpamla GP in Nalgonda District

i. The *sarpanch* is a woman. Before being elected she was a housewife. Her husband has his business. The people informed that she has to depend upon her husband for day to day functioning of panchayat and is accompanied by her husband during the panchayat meetings.

ii. As per the Panchayat Act, gram sabha is to be called minimum twice in a year. During the first time in gram sabha, 1/3rd members should be present for maintaining the quorum and if quorum is not maintained first time then there is no need of quorum when the meeting is called second time. It was pointed by the people that during the first meeting in gram sabha hardly forty people participated. So, second meeting was called where only a few members participated (about 8-10). And the gram sabha meeting was completed with less number of people. With the launch of *Janmabhoomi* programme, gram sabhas are being conducted regularly once in two months on an average even then the attendance in the gram sabha has not improved substantially.

iii. Money-lending is widely prevalent in the village. Most of the people have taken loan for various purposes, especially for consumption purpose during rainy season. The interest charged varies from Rs. 3 to 4 per month for Rs.100, which means 36 to 48 per cent annual interest rate. People hesitate to tell about the amount taken from money-lender, the interest rate charged by him and also the year during which loan was availed, but as per the version of people in the village meeting, about 60 per cent people take loan in a year. When the people were asked to take loan from banks, they mentioned that they were not able to get loan from the banks because they would ask for the security and moreover banks would not be able to provide loan as and when required.

iv. On the issue of handling of problems of weaker sections (SCs and women), some members expressed that there is no special attention given to their problems. One of them said that *sarpanch* and panchayat members are occupied in routine matters and attending to the problems of their groups. The woman and SC panchayat members get elected mainly for the purpose of elections. These members hardly involve themselves in the panchayat functioning.

Visit to Pipalpahar GP in Nalgonda District

i. The panchayat *sarpanch* is a woman. She is just literate and is able to sign. She has to depend upon her husband for the day-to-day functioning of the panchayat. The executive officer (EO) of the mandal does the necessary supervision of works and the maintenance of accounts.

ii. The people's participation, as informed in the meeting is poor and only a few people speak during the meeting. It was pointed out that about hundred people participated in the last gram sabha meeting. Further, it also came out during the discussion that people mainly discuss about the selection of beneficiaries and identification of works such as road formation or maintenance of drainage or tank. It was mentioned that the people have to identify mainly works related to maintenance or *kutcha* type, as the funds available with the panchayat are very small in comparison to requirements. For example, under JRY (now JGSY) the panchayat gets about Rs.50,000 per year and with this amount the panchayat is not able to take up asset works. Moreover, there is a tendency on the part of ward members to take up works in each ward as far as possible so that people in their wards are satisfied. So, firstly, due to low allocations and then thinly spread of funds for many works, no substantial work is done in the panchayat and the funds are not effectively utilised, which was admitted by people and the panchayat members.

iii. The own income of panchayat is very small. This was about Rs.1600 during 1997-98 and it came from house and water taxes. This is a fraction of the grants received by the panchayats. It was also informed that the tax collection is less than 20 per cent of the demand. People are normally not keen to pay the taxes and the panchayat does not take desired initiative for collection of taxes.

iv. One woman member in the meeting raised the issue of her non-inclusion in the list of beneficiaries for Indira Awas, while it was included during the last gram sabha meeting. At this the *sarpanch* told that she would be considered in the next year. Some others also complained of such instances of change of names after the gram sabha.

v. People spoke in negative, when the issue of elections was raised. They mentioned how in the last elections, many candidates fought but were not concerned about their village problem of drinking water, while they spent good amount of money for campaigning. On being asked why some of you did not contest. One of them said that it was beyond their capacity and they could not win elections. Some of them expressed that neither the women nor SCs and STs benefit form the elections. And even after the elections they do not get any benefits. The *sarpanch* and his supporters do work as per their own choice.

Visit to Narkedpally GP in Nalgonda District

i. The *sarpanch* of the panchayat is having basic knowledge about the functioning of panchayat. As per his version, he is more concerned with the maintenance of accounts and registers and fulfilling the statutory responsibility as prescribed by the government. He seems to be least concerned about people's participation in the decision-making process and the role of gram sabha in village planning.

ii. As far as the implementation is concerned, it is virtually done by the *sarpanch* with the assistance of junior engineer (JE) of mandal. People are not involved in the identification of site, in the arrangement of building materials and in the monitoring and supervision of works.

Visit to Chirkonda GP in Nalgonda District

The *sarpanch* is a woman and is just literate (able to sign). As per her version, she has to depend upon her husband for necessary official works. At this, someone in the meeting commented that it has become husband *karobar*. The *sarpanch* is not well-versed with the functioning of panchayat and has very limited understanding of people's participation. These observations may be true, but one important points needs to be appreciated that very little effort has been made in the last four years to train the *sarpanch* and also to make people aware about their rights. This is where there is a lack of direction and due to this the capacity of *sarpanchas* not only in this panchayat but also in other panchayats (where the study was conducted) is poor and comes very much in their way to function successfully.

On the discussion regarding the issues raised during the election campaign, people expressed their empathy and opined that the candidates are more bothered for proving their supremacy over the others, while development issues are overlooked, even the crucial issue of drinking water like fluoride content, which is causing serious health problem, was not discussed during the last election campaign.

Common Observations

The performance of functioning of gram sabhas is an area of concern and it was informed that in the earlier gram sabhas less than 2 per cent people have participated. Besides, the participation is confined to a few people, and the issues discussed in the meetings are only concerning with the selection of beneficiaries and identification of works related to maintenance of roads or tanks or drainage.

The infrastructural position at the gram panchayat level is poor. Normally, the panchayat offices have two rooms, but do not have enough space for conducting gram sabha meetings. The school buildings do not have enough rooms (available 3-4 for 300 children) to accommodate all the children. Similarly, the health and veterinary centres are about 25 to 40 km. from the GP headquarters.

As regards the own-income of panchayats, it is poor in comparison to funds that are received by the panchayats. The main sources of panchayat income are water and house taxes. And the amount paid by the people is normally less than 25 per cent of the demand.

Measures taken by the State Government

The state government has taken the following steps for improving the capacities of local bodies:

i. The 16 subjects have been transferred to PR Institutions. These are: a) Agriculture; b) Animal Husbandry; c) Rural Water Supply; d) PR M.I. Tanks; e) Social Forestry and Farm Forestry; f) Small Scale Industries and Food Processing; g) Khadi and Village Industries; h) Fuel and Fodder; j) Roads, Culverts, Bridges, Ferries, Water Ways; k) Non-conventional Energy; l) Technical Training, Vocational Education; m) Adult and Non-Formal Education; n) Libraries; o) Cultural Activities; p) Markets, Fairs and Sandies (excepting market yard); and q) Maintenance of Community Assets.
ii. Sand auctions / leases will be conducted and decided by a district committee headed by chairman, zilla parishad.
iii. The 50 per cent of the honorarium to *sarpanchas* will be paid by the government.
iv. The grants under profession tax, seigniorage fee and salary grant will be released in full to local bodies.
v. Certain taxes like cable tax and irrigation tax will be collected by the local bodies.
vi. The maintenance of tanks and canal systems would be done by the panchayats.

Discussion with District-level Officers and President of Zilla Parishad

The discussion was held with the district level officers and president, ZP about the state of decentralisation, the problems therein and the likely solutions that are necessary for smooth implementation of 73rd Constitution Amendment Act. The salient features are given below:

Functioning of Gram Sabha: There was unanimity about the fact that the gram sabhas are not organised properly and their functioning is far from satisfactory. The reasons cited are: the lack of initiative on the part of *sarpanch*, lack of awareness among people and lack of funds with the panchayats that leave little option for the people to discuss the development issues.

Transfer of Functions and Devolution of Funds: The state government has not taken measures to transfer functions upon panchayats and so far no funds have been devolved. It seems that there is a very little urgency in this direction. The president, ZP was very vociferous in asking for devolving more funds so that the panchayats can perform their legitimate duties.

Functioning of DRDA: The chairman of DRDA continues to be district collector. Though, ZP discusses the functioning of DRDA but effectively it has no administrative control over DRDA. DRDA has its own programme of rural development that is separate from ZP action plan.

MLAs and MPs as Members of ZP: MLAs and MPs are the members of ZP. It was informed that they have voting rights too. It was highly resented by ZP president, as he mentioned that no one other than the ZP member should be the part of ZP in order to maintain its sanctity.

Also, sometimes the elected representatives (MLAs and MPs) want certain names to be included in the beneficiaries list for IAY or SGSY.

Training of PR Members: The training is confined only to presidents of ZP and mandals, and *sarpanchas*. The ward members are not covered so far. The training was given only on the basic issues which are necessary but planning and implementation aspects were overlooked.

Janmabhoomi Programme: Janmabhoomi programme is a people's campaign and covers all the development aspects of the village. This programme is organised normally four times in a year and is for seven days at a time. Generally, each occasion is earmarked for a special drive that could be health check-ups, or enrolment in the primary school or immunisation. For the purpose of this programme, self-help groups (SHGs) and village committees participate very actively and these are the ones who are entrusted with some responsibilities for the implementation of works. No doubt, the programme is well appreciated by the people and has been able to reach people in providing basic services to them. But, if we look from the point of view of organisational sustainability, we need to give serious thought to it. As in future, panchayat or mandal or district level institutions should be able to shoulder the responsibility and carry out the programmes on their own in future.

Here, it is worth mentioning that the panchayats at each tier should be effectively involved in this programme and the SHGs and village committees should provide necessary support to the panchayats in augmenting their capacities. Or, in a way, there is a need for strong partnership between panchayats on the one hand and SHGs and village committees on the other hand, so that their efforts are complementary and lead to convergence of resources.

Standing Committees : The Zilla Parishad is functioning with seven standing committees (SCs). These are:

S.C. No. I	:	Finance and Planning
S.C. No. II	:	Rural Development
S.C. No. III	:	Agriculture
S.C. No. IV	:	Education and Medical Services
S.C. No. V	:	Women Welfare
S.C. No. VI	:	Social Welfare
S.C. No. VII	:	Works

The standing committees so constituted are specialised bodies intended to deal with specific matters entrusted to them. These standing committees meet once in sixty days. The zilla parishad meets once in ninety days regularly and discharge duties of approval of proceedings of all the standing committees. The main reviews of the zilla parishad relate to agriculture, irrigation, electricity, rural development, education and welfare programmes of various departments.

Tax Collection: The collection of taxes by the panchayats is another area of concern due to existing poor state of finances of panchayats and low level of collection. The per capita collection is about Rs.1.12, which is hardly any amount to maintain any service. The poor state of tax collection is due to various reasons, the prominent among them are: *first*, lack of political will as there is a fear of losing popularity in the event of imposing taxes; *second*, lack of confidence of people in the present setup of PR institutions as people are skeptical about their abilities to provide services effectively to them; and *third*, lack of conducive environment in terms of educating and motivating the people for giving taxes for availing legitimate services.

Minimum Size of GP: It was also discussed whether there is any need for minimum size of GP as the present size of the GPs varies from 1000 to 10,000 with an average of 2000. It was mentioned that such small units of development, the necessary vital support systems (manpower, infrastructural and logistics) are not made available to each panchayat in order to make it a viable functional unit. As otherwise, it would require heavy investment, if all the panchayats were to be given all the support system. Thus, from the point of view of economic and administrative viability, it is important to have minimum size of GP and the GP should be provided with the necessary support system in order to enable it to provide basic services (to people) such as primary education, health, drinking water, irrigation, veterinary, agricultural inputs and certificates for land, caste, etc.

Election for Intermediate and District Level Members: This issue was also discussed and it came out that the members so elected for mandal panchayat and zilla parishad do not have much role except in attending meetings and passing the budget. Also there are too many members in this process that leads to conflicting situations with the GP *sarpanchas* in the mandal panchayat meetings. They were also of the opinion that only the gram panchayat *sarpanchas* should be the members of mandal panchayat and they should elect their presidents who, in turn, should be the members of the ZP. And, the ZP president should be elected by these members. This will provide true representation to grassroots members in each tier of the district, which is not a case presently.

District Plan: DPC is not formed, so the district plan is formulated by the ZP. The concerned standing committees prepare the plans of their respective subjects. Finally, the ZP gives the approval. After detailed examination, it was found that the plans so prepared are generally the compilation of schemes given by the departments (with certain modifications like 10 per cent addition on the previous year's budget). No detailed inter-sectoral planning or backward-forward linkages analysis is carried out, or no innovative programmes are incorporated to meet the local needs like eradicating poverty or solving the water crisis or improving the health system.

4.1.2 Observations in Assam

Field Visits

Visit to Kulhati GP in Kamrup District

i. As the elections have not been held for panchayats, so the BDO of the block is officiating as an administrator.
ii. During the discussion it was found that the development works are executed by the block and the involvement of people is very less.
iii. As regards the own income, the gram panchayat does not collect any tax, while it is done by *anchalik* (intermediate) panchayat or zilla panchayat.
iv. The panchayat does not have much infrastructure except for office building and schools. Also, manpower support is very thin at the gram panchayat level and the line departments work independently with very little coordination with block or GP.

Some Important Issues

i. In the state of Assam the panchayat elections have been held in 2002, after a gap of nine years.
ii. District Autonomous Councils: These councils are in place in the districts of Karbi Anglong and North Cachar (NC) Hills. The council at the district level is headed by the Chief Executive Member (CEM). The council has normally 25-30 members. The CEM allocates the works to the members. All the line departments are accountable to district council. In the council area, the Dy. Commissioner officiates as District Judge.
iii. Existing Traditional Village Committees: In Assam each village generally has village committee in the form of either Namghar Unnayan Committee or Supa Unnati Committee or Masjit Unnayan Committee. These committees exercise their traditional control over the resources of the villages and their development activities.

4.1.3 Observations in Gujarat

Field Visits

Visit to Vasad GP in Anand District

i. This gram panchayat has male *sarpanch* who is well-educated (diploma in Mechanical Engineering); he is very confidant and articulate about the panchayat functioning.
ii. During the discussion in the village meeting it was found that the panchayat *sarpanch* was mainly speaking during the discussion while others were keeping quiet and were

answering as and when asked purposefully. It was also informed that during the earlier gram sabhas about 5-7 per cent (300-400) people had participated. The *sarpanch* mentioned that in such a large gathering (in terms of number) it becomes difficult to organise the gram sabha meeting properly as most of them do not find opportunity to speak and moreover, the discussion does not follow a desired sequence because people start raising issues as per their convenience. The issues that are mainly discussed pertain to selection of beneficiaries and construction of a few items such as village roads, drainage, repair of school buildings, etc. Besides, some discussion also takes place on panchayat accounts and budget (which is more of a ritual than any meaningful discussion).

iii. The own income of this gram panchayat is substantially high as it is near to a big business town and is able to collect good amount of octroi. The total income from internal sources was about Rs. 20.30 lakhs during 1999-2000. Taxes are paid for house, water and street light. It was informed by the *sarpanch* that the water tax is paid by one donor* (rice mill owner) on behalf of people in the village. Further, it also came out during the discussion that such a custom (of giving donations) is very much prevalent in many gram panchayats in the district. In a way it is good, but it curtails the people's participation for paying their dues for what they are utilising.

Visit to Napad GP in Anand District

i. This gram panchayat also has male *sarpanch* who is a graduate and is well-versed with the functioning of panchayat. He takes keen interest in the panchayat functioning.
ii. In this panchayat also, as in the case of aforementioned GP, the people's participation is less in the gram sabhas as about 6 per cent of the members have attended in the past meetings. During the gram sabhas, normally people come late and leave during the course of discussion as they have several other works to attend. Women in the villages do not attend the meetings as they find the gram sabhas to be of little use for them due to focus of discussion mainly on a very few subjects like construction works such as roads, drainage, and selection of beneficiaries. Besides, only a few vocal people dominate during the discussion.
iii. The own income of the panchayat was about Rs. 4.08 lakhs (during 1999-2000), which comes mainly from octroi, property tax, water tax and lighting tax and the contribution of the octroi is maximum (more than 50 per cent of the total).
iv. With regard to implementation of work, it is mainly implemented by the panchayat and it is the *sarpanch* who does practically all the work pertaining to activities involved in the implementation, and the involvement of beneficiaries is very less.

* Perhaps, better option could be that the donations may be taken for meeting infrastructural cost but user charges should be paid by the people in order to instill the feeling of responsibility for the maintenance and upkeep of panchayat's assets.

Critical Issues

- During the discussion with the officials it was informed that the elections for zilla parishad and taluka (block) panchayats have been held, but the elections for gram panchayats have not been completed due to drought. Besides, a peculiar point came out that earlier the elections for gram panchayats were not held at a time in all the gram panchayats in the state.
- The chairman of DRDA is DDO. The DPC has not yet been constituted and the planning work is looked after by district planning board whose chairman is Minister-in-charge of the district. The district level officers of line departments such as primary education, health, agriculture, veterinary, minor irrigation and PWD are under the administrative control of DDO (while the line departments at the block level work directly under district level officers of concerned departments and block has no administrative control over them).
- The zilla parishad functions through nine standing committees.
- Though the funds are devolved upon the zilla parishad directly by the state government but these are basically meant for a specified scheme in a particular sector. And the ZP has little say in the allocation of funds. As regards the preparation of ZP plan, it is basically a compilation of plans received from various departments.

4.1.4 Observations in Haryana

Field Visits

Visit to Umri GP in Kurukshetra District

i. The gram panchayat *sarpanch* is a woman who has passed primary school. Though she is not very active in the panchayat functioning but she is making efforts to learn the day-to-day working of panchayat.
ii. The people's participation is encouraging but mainly vocal people participate in the discussion. Similarly, it was informed that in the gram sabhas the people attending them is not large and the discussion is confined to activities pertaining to construction of roads, drainage, etc. During the meeting some people tried to raise the issue of poor quality of road constructed during the last year. At this people of other group started raising voice against such objection. The *sarpanch* found herself in a difficult position and was non-committal to the problem raised.
iii. When we discussed about how the gram sabha attends to the problems of weaker sections (women and SCs), at this people could not mention any issue that was raised in the previous gram sabhas for addressing their problems in particular.
iv. In this GP the own income has been astronomically high and it was about Rs. 2.06 cr. during 1999-2000. This is mainly due to receipt of compensation from the housing board for the acquisition of panchayat land.

v. Due to high income of gram panchayat and higher awareness among PR members and the people, the GP has taken initiative for starting computer training for women.

Visit to Jirbari GP in Kurukshetra District

i. The GP *sarpanch* is a male and has passed class ten. He is very active in the panchayat functioning. During the meeting it was evident that he was able to answer questions promptly and was able to defend his actions.
ii. In this panchayat, though awareness level is high and people understand the functioning of panchayat, the participation level is still low and the attendance in the gram sabha is not encouraging.
iii. The panchayat is taking initiative for the construction of school buildings, village roads and community centre, and it has been possible as the GP is able to utilise own funds (which is significantly high and was about Rs. 2.75 lakhs, during 1999-2000) for creation of infrastructure.

Common Observations

It was noticed in both the gram panchayats that the awareness level is quite high among people, the PR members are well aware about their roles in the panchayat functioning, the infrastructural position is good and the own income of the panchayats is high. The functioning of the gram sabha remains a gray area as far as the selection of beneficiaries is concerned. It was brought to the notice that the list of beneficiaries for various programmes undergoes changes after the gram sabha meetings.

The major contributor in the own income is the income from the agricultural land (except for income from land acquisition in case of Umri GP), while the income from other sources like property tax, users charges, license fee, etc. is insignificant. Another important point that came out during the discussion was that in some cases the dummy candidates have filed nominations on behalf of earlier *sarpanch* (now having no chance for contesting election due to reservation) or some influential person. These nominations are mainly under women or SCs or STs or OBCs category. Also, on the issue of the nomination of candidates for the panchayats, people expressed that these are basically from the influential and political families.

On the issue of elections, many people expressed that the elections are mainly for political parties. They have high stakes involved. So they spend large money. They take the help of party workers and mobilise people in their favour. As huge expenditure is involved, a common man has very little scope for participation in the elections. Women will contest if there is a reserved seat, otherwise not. They also expressed that in many cases if seats are reserved, the woman members from the ex-*sarpanch* or some political family will contest. Similarly, in the case of SCs, they do not normally contest if the seat is not reserved for them. On the issue of consumption of liquor during elections, people expressed that the liquor is served (sometimes in a large quantity) one day before the elections.

4.1.5 Observations in Karnataka

Field Visits

Visit to Coorgally GP of Mysore District

i. The panchayat *sarpanch* is a male and well-educated (up to intermediate). He is well-versed with the panchayat functioning, though it is confined to a few activities like conducting gram sabhas, implementation of construction works, maintenance of accounts, etc.
ii. During the discussion it was amply clear that the villagers were not participating in the discussion (during the village meeting). It was also informed that during the gram sabhas the percentage of members attending them is quite low and it is around 4-5 per cent. Besides, the discussion mainly revolves around construction activities, PDS and election of beneficiaries.
iii. The own income is significantly high in this gram panchayat and was about Rs. 4.12 lakhs during 1999-2000. The income is mainly from the collection of royalty from the mining activities.
iv. As regards the implementation of works, it is mainly executed by the *sarpanch* of the gram panchayat with the support of panchayat secretary and the JE of the block, and there is no involvement of beneficiaries at the implementation stage.
v. On the issue of addressal of grievances of weaker sections, some people mentioned that during elections panchayat members go to their houses, but after that they do not attend to their problems. The panchayats are only for elections and thereafter members are more concerned in their affairs.

Visit to Yelawala GP of Mysore District

i. The gram panchayat *sarpanch* is a woman and scheduled tribe. She has modest educational background and has passed primary school. She has basic understanding about the panchayat functioning.
ii. Similar to the above GP, the people's participation and the functioning of gram sabhas are not very satisfactory. Here, some people complained that the names of the beneficiaries are changed after the gram sabha meeting and the different list is sent to block. Even they mentioned that some ward members try to fix target for the number of beneficiaries for their respective wards. Sometimes other elected representatives (MLAs) also want certain names to be included as reported by the *sarpanch* and BDO.
iii. In this gram panchayat also the own income is high and was about Rs. 2.10 lakhs during 1999-2000 and this is mainly in the form of collection of royalty from mining.
iv. While discussing about the payment of taxes for street light and sanitation, people

were not interested in paying taxes. They said that GP cannot manage such activities, and it has been our experience in the last many years. The *sarpanch* replied that though in the past such attempts have not succeeded and it is difficult to try due to various interest groups, however it is worth trying.

Critical Issues

Devolution of Funds: The state government is giving funds directly to zilla parishad under various departmental heads. The funds are given under two sectors viz., state sector and district sector. The state sector funds are planned exclusively by the state government and zilla parishad looks after the planning for district sector. Under district sector, the funds are tied to certain programmes or schemes and zilla parishad has practically no flexibility in the allocation of funds for the activities that may be suitable for the local areas. These funds are to be utilised as per the guidelines given by the concerned state department, while the guidelines may not be suitable as per the local conditions. In this very context, during the discussion with the district officials it was informed by the district agriculture officer that certain centrally-sponsored programmes like OSDP (for oil seed), PDDP (pulse development), ICDP (for coconut) are not so much suitable for the local area, but the funds are given to the district and these are not utilised fully for want of demands in the district.

Size of Gram Panchayats: In the newly constituted gram panchayats, the size of the gram panchayat in terms of population and area has come down significantly. Presently, the population is about 5000 against the earlier average population of 12,000. With these smaller gram panchayats, the panchayats have become compact but it has caused certain practical problems for the development works. These problems are: *first*, reduced availability of funds with the panchayats due to lower population, which has left lesser options for the gram panchayats to have infrastructural-oriented (or *pucca* type) works; *second*, increased number of members for intermediate tier as the number of gram panchayats has increased and it makes it difficult to conduct the meetings of intermediate panchayat due to large number, and also monitoring of programmes and accounts becomes a difficult exercise; and *third*, difficulty in placing field staff of line departments with the increased number of gram panchayats.

Term of Chairperson of Panchayats: The state government has taken steps for reducing the term of chairperson of all the tiers. It is thirty months for the *sarpanchas* of gram panchayats and twenty months for the chairpersons of intermediate and zilla panchayats.

Training of PR Members: The PR members have been given training regarding the issues pertaining to panchayati raj and anti-poverty programmes. The training has been given to members only once (and normally given once in five years) and that too only for 3-4 days. The field observations have revealed that the knowledge and skills level of members is very limited and also narrow. That is the reason why the members confine their discussions and the programme design limited to a few items such as construction activities, PDS or selection of beneficiaries.

District Plan Formulation: The discussion with the district level officers revealed that the preparation of district plan is almost an extension of previous year's plan and normally the same schemes are carried forward by adding 10-15 per cent to the budgetary allocation of the previous year. Also, no innovative schemes are prepared which may suit the local conditions, besides, no inter-sectoral analysis is carried out. So, the preparation of the district plan remains an exercise of compilation of programmes submitted by various departments.

Election of Intermediate and Zilla Panchayats: It came out during the discussion that the elected members of the higher tiers need not be from the same constituency wherefrom they are contesting (and may contest from anywhere in the panchayat area) but they should be in the electoral list of the intermediate and zilla panchayats as the case may be. In this process, as discussed with the people, the members for the intermediate and zilla panchayats mainly contest more from the consideration of caste or political influence.

While discussing about the elections, people mentioned about the lobbying that takes place for the election of chairperson of zilla parishad. They even mentioned that by manipulations the candidates (for chairperson) come to know who is casting for whom.

4.1.6 Observations in Kerala

In 1960, Kerala Panchayat Act 1960, was enacted. Under the Act the panchayats were given very little functions and no responsibilities were entrusted to them. Later on in 1964, Kerala Panchayat Union Councils and Zilla Parishad Bill was introduced on the lines of the recommendations of Balwantrai Mehta Committee but it could also not make much progress and so the new Kerala Panchayati Raj Bill, 1967 was introduced. But it also lapsed in 1970. Thereafter, the Kerala District Administration Bill was enacted in 1979. But, not many functions were given to the panchayat union, as envisaged in the Act. After the 73rd Constitution Amendment Act, Kerala Panchayati Raj Act, 1994 was enacted.

Field Visits

Visit to Pooyapalli GP in Kollam District

i. GP president is a woman, who has completed graduation. She takes very active part in the GP activities. She has good understanding about the functioning of gram sabha and the preparation of action plan, implementation and monitoring of works. The people's campaign plan has contributed in improving her knowledge and skills for development planning and implementation. She has good ability to communicate with the people, to understand their problems and work for the development of the GP. Other ward members are equally good as they have good educational background. All of them have completed high school. They have good understanding about the functioning of GP. They are sensitive about the problems of their GP and are willing to cooperate in the development process.

The participation level of woman elected members is significant and the same is expected from them. Rather, people take it very strongly if any aberration regarding the functioning of woman PR members is noticed.

ii. The gram sabhas in the GP have been activated due to active participation of people. This has been a result of people's plan campaign. In this plan special programmes like audio-visual shows, cultural programmes, etc. were organised to encourage and motivate the people to participate in their respective gram sabhas for the purpose of planning and implementation of village plan. Besides, the systematic training programme at the panchayat level for PR functionaries, government functionaries and resource persons (voluntary workers from the same GP) has contributed a great deal in improving the capacity of the gram panchayat, whereby generating enthusiasm among people. One of the ward members added that there is virtually no discrimination due to caste or class or gender or religion. It is due to higher social awakening as a result of earlier socio-economic reforms (including land reforms).

iii. For improving the human resources of the panchayati raj institutions, various resource persons like retired government servants (from different departments like agriculture, irrigation, health and so on), volunteers from NGOs and local professionals were encouraged to join task forces. This increased the human resources base of the panchayats, which has contributed significantly for their improved capacity.

iv. During the discussion with PR functionaries, it was pointed out that at the gram panchayat level, task forces have been formed. To name a few these are for agriculture, health, education, social welfare and woman development. The task force has one chairman either a subject specialist or ward member. These task forces undertake the planning for their respective sectors. After the preliminary planning exercise (resources analysis, database analysis, inter-spectral analysis, etc.) is completed by the task force then final shape is given to village plan of each sector at gram panchayat level.

v. The state government has devolved upon panchayats substantial funds and transferred several subjects especially in the social and primary sectors. That has helped them in the formulation of plans as per their local needs.

vi. *Implementation and Monitoring:* For implementation, in each sector an implementing committee is formed with one of the ward members as its chairman to look into the details of implementation of programmes. The beneficiaries committee is formed for every project at the ward level that actually looks after the implementation. With regard to monitoring, a committee is formed for each sector at the GP level to monitor the progress of the work in that sector. Supervision of the work at the field level is done by the beneficiaries themselves and is supported by ward member of respective ward where the work is taken up.

Kerala provides a very distinct picture regarding the efficient implementation of the programmes. It is because of the following reasons:

- *Good Organisational Structure at GP Level:* The GP has a good number of staff about four in the office and five as the field staff for various development works related to anti-poverty schemes.
- *Availability of Equipments and Good Logistics Support:* As most of the villages are near to towns, so equipments like road-roller, cement concrete mixture etc. and vehicular support for supply of material are easily available.
- *The Functioning of Beneficiary Committee* is viable due to one important factor that the people take keen interest in the implementation through committee, and the committee members have capacity in terms of knowledge and skills to execute the work.

Finally, the efficient functioning of panchayats, which is very much in contrast with other states, leads to the following conclusions:

- Political will is the first prerequisite for decentralisation and it is the central point where from all the necessary directions emerge.
- Education and access to information are essential for participation of people.
- With the improved education participation rates among women rise considerably.
- From the institutional perspective, improving the capacity of the local institutions is necessary for making services available to people.
- Accountability is crucial for enhancing responsiveness of panchayats towards people's grievances.

Notwithstanding successful cases, as expressed by people, there have been instances when implementation of projects was done by party workers as proxy of president GP, and without the involvement of beneficiaries. Also, there have been cases when the beneficiaries have been chosen for extraneous considerations like political affiliation. As regards, transparency some opposition members expressed that the chairperson of GP did not consult them and the names of beneficiaries were not decided in gram sabha. Though efforts are made for social audit in order to make elected members accountable to panchayats, in some cases it was reported that the members did not look into the objections seriously and tried to avoid discussion in the gram sabha.

There was discussion with officials of SIRD, key resource persons (KRPs) and members of technical corps. They gave some mixed report about the decentralization. They mentioned though there are areas of success, it would be premature to make judgment that panchayats are doing well in all the places in the state. But, there is a definite trend towards strengthening of local institutions and involvement of people in the panchayat functioning.

4.1.7 Observations in Madhya Pradesh

Field Visits

Visit to Kasala GP in Hoshangabad District

i. The *sarpanch* is a tribal and has not got formal education but is able to sign. He finds it difficult to do necessary official work and has to depend on panchayat secretary. It was also informed that some of the other educated ward members assist him in the functioning of panchayat.

ii. The panchayat does not have resources of its own. Though the government has given powers to panchayats for the collection of various taxes, yet the panchayats do not find many avenues. Presently, only source of income is through collection of land revenue that is collected by the *patwari* and deposited with the panchayat. People mentioned that the system of collection of land revenue through *patwaris* is very prompt and also cost effective, as otherwise the panchayat would have to engage additional manpower for the collection. It was informed that the own income of the panchayat was Rs.1700 during 1998-99.

iii. Under the funds that are received by the panchayat, mainly the works related to maintenance and repair are taken. It was also informed that GP has taken up the formation of road without metalling (i.e. without spreading stones). On this, during the discussion it also came out that such type (*kutcha*) of works are not of much use for the village and no permanent asset is created. The villagers also expressed their helplessness, as the funds that are received by the panchayat are too small for any viable work. Besides, as regards the type of works, it is mainly decided by the panchayat *sarpanch* who consults people of his group.

iv. Though this area comes under Scheduled Areas Act, yet the people were not aware about the special provisions made for the tribals in spite of the fact the government has passed an Act in 1997. Even the officers of PR Department were not having full knowledge about the special powers given to gram sabhas in tribal areas.

v. There was an issue of grievance redressal. Some people complained that the GP is not able to address their grievances. On detailed enquiry with *sarpanch* and other members, it was revealed that GP office has only temporary staff who is in-charge of 2-3 GPs and he is unable to record the grievances properly. Besides, the GP does not have field centres of various departments such as agriculture, health, veterinary, etc., that hampers the timely availability of services to people. The people agreed with such argument, but they also said neither panchayat members nor the functionaries take interest in their problems. Further, some of them complained that the handling of grievances takes place selectively—that is those who are close to the group of *sarpanch* get benefits while others do not.

Visit to Saheli GP in Hoshangabad District

i. The *sarpanch* is a woman and has passed fifth class. She has basic understanding about the functioning of the panchayat but during the discussion it was clear that her husband helps her in the day-to-day official work, as during the meeting, he was trying to answer on her behalf. With regard to reservation, the *sarpanch* commented that in the coming elections this GP would be reserved for some other category. So, she would not get another chance to contest. It gave the impression that the present system of keeping reservation for one term does not give incentive to the existing incumbents to show their performance and then contest again.
ii. The people in this panchayat were also not active during the discussion in the meeting and were not much aware about many important aspects like the importance of 73rd Constitutional Amendment, the rural development programmes that are run in the panchayat, how the execution of works should take place and so on.
iii. It came out during the discussion that the *sarpanch* implements the work with the help of panchayat secretary and the village committees do not implement the works in the village. It was commented upon by the people that the *sarpanchas* have become *de facto* contractors under this panchayat system. Not only this, people are not provided the desired information such as cost of materials or number of labourers engaged, physical specifications and also they are not involved in the monitoring and supervision of works.
iv. In this panchayat also the formation of road by spreading morrum (without metalling or spread of stones) was taken up under JRY during 1998-99. It was done as the funds available were small in comparison to requirement for metalled road.
v. The training of PR members has been done partially as only the *sarpanch* has got training and the other ward members have not yet been given even after four years in the office.
vi. The own income of this panchayat is poor as the people are reluctant to pay taxes for lighting, property, etc. and the panchayat does not make serious attempts for the collection of taxes from the people.

Visit to Puakhedi GP in Vidisha District

i. The *sarpanch* is a woman and is very articulate about the problems of panchayats. She has completed primary education. It was informed by the villagers that she does not depend upon her family members. The *sarpanch* also agreed that the education has helped her to have confidence in the panchayat functioning.
ii. It came out during the discussion that the people find gram sabha of little use as the proceedings are dominated by a few people and also under the given state of panchayat funds no significant work can be taken up by the panchayat. Some of the members complained that the gram sabha proceedings are not made available and the panchayat

accounts are not displayed, but it was denied by the *sarpanch*.

iii. The infrastructure position in the panchayat is poor. The condition of school building is very bad and it has only two rooms for five classes, the nearby health centre is not in good shape and lacks many basic equipments, veterinary centre is about 25 km away from the panchayat, etc. The lack of infrastructure is one of the major reasons as to why people find it hard to avail the basic services in time.

iv. Though in this village Nirman Committee is formed to implement the development works under JRY, yet people are not properly involved at the implementation stage. This committee is headed by *sarpanch* and has some members (5-7) chosen in the gram sabha (GS). As in the GS only a few people participate and moreover a handful of people speak, so the selection of members for the committee is a mere formality (which is mainly done by *sarpanch*). Besides, there is no established procedure for maintaining transparency.

v. There is a division in the village on caste as well as party lines. The members of one group try to oppose others. In this process the development activities get hampered. One Scheduled Caste member said that the panchayat does not attend to the problems of their community, and most of the funds are allotted to other community. He also added that due to their (community's) poor education, their community is not able to do much, and the discrimination further erodes their ability to participate in the development process.

Visit to Hiranai GP in Vidisha District

i. The *sarpanch* is a woman. She is just literate and is able to sign. It was informed that she works as a labourer in the house of one landlord-cum-ex-*sarpanch* of the same panchayat. It came out during the discussion that the GP was reserved for woman so the ex-*sarpanch* has nominated her for contesting as *sarpanch*. Regarding the interference of the family members and dependence on panchayat secretary, it came out that the husband does some of the official work and the panchayat secretary maintains the accounts that are blindly signed by the *sarpanch*. The *sarpanch* reluctantly agreed this position.

ii. The discussion was made about the functioning of gram sabha. It was quite shocking to know that some of the earlier GS meetings were held in the premises of ex-*sarpanch*. Some members openly criticised this and even mentioned that during the GS only the people close to *sarpanch* participated, thus disallowing any dissent during the course of discussion. As regards the attendance in the GS, it was poor during the last meeting and about 50 people participated. The discussion that takes place during the GS has very narrow agenda (though the Government has prescribed a format but it is hardly followed and people hardly understand about the panchayat accounts, etc.) as far as the people are concerned because panchayat members like to discuss mainly issues pertaining to selection of beneficiaries for various programmes rather than the problems faced by the people.

Visit to Tejapur GP in Raysen District

i. The *sarpanch* is a graduate and is very active and takes serious interest in the development activities of panchayat. He has been *sarpanch* since 1989. Attempt was made to know how he succeeded to remain *sarpanch* for so long. He replied about his political role that he has been playing for long. On the question of the issues of the discussion during his election campaign, he named a few ones like construction of roads, the problem of drinking water, but could not add further.

ii. Though the *sarpanch* is active, yet the people have not been so. Their level of participation in the meeting was poor and only a few people participated in the discussion. Rather, the *sarpanch* was dominating the discussion. The woman members were not present in the meeting and the *sarpanch* had no genuine answer for their absence.

iii. The *sarpanch* was happy with the availability of funds, as this panchayat has got good amount of money under various schemes including TFC grants. He admitted that the works are undertaken by him and he personally does all the relevant activities related to construction. Thus, he almost agreed that he is working like *de facto* contractor. The involvement of people in the implementation of works is very little. Also, some of the works undertaken by him were from the consideration of pleasing the members of some of his group. It was observed that such a state is inevitable as these people (who have been benefited by his patronage) try to defend him during the gram sabha.

iv. People complained about the non-availability of the essential commodities in the village and the gram panchayat has not been effective in handling this problem. At this the *sarpanch* could not give any satisfactory answer but assured of taking actions in future. It appeared as if he was more occupied with his construction activities than such complaints.

v. The own income of panchayat is poor. It was hardly Rs. 3000 during 1998-99, that too from land-revenue. Income through other sources like taxes from lighting, water, property, etc. is absent. *Sarpanch* also admitted that he is not interested in the collection of taxes, as it is not going to benefit him politically.

Visit to Dhahua-Chapua GP in Raysen District

i. The *sarpanch* has passed high school and is articulate about the functioning of panchayat. As noticed in other panchayats, he is also not well-versed with the planning aspects. Though the action plan of panchayat is prepared, it is merely a collection of proposals from various members. No inter-sectoral analysis or backward-forward linkages analysis is carried out. The *sarpanch* seems to be concerned only with the placement of funds, but not with issues like: whether the people come in the gram sabha or not, whether the people are involved in the planning and implementation stages, whether the transparency is maintained in the development process and so on.

ii. The implementation of works is done by the *sarpanch* and panchayat secretary, and the people are not involved during this process.

iii. The own income of the panchayat is poor, as people are not willing to pay taxes for lighting, property and water. Hardly 20 per cent of the demand is collected under these taxes. Whatever income comes to the panchayat, the major sources are: selling of bamboo trees and royalty from mining. The PR members are not very much inclined to take taxes from the people, for the obvious reason that they might lose popularity among people.

Common Observations

The participation of people in the village meetings (during the field visit) was poor and only a few people participated in the discussion. It was observed, in many cases, that the people from the group of *sarpanch* came for the meeting and mainly the ones who were close to *sarpanch* participated in the discussion.

With regard to the functioning of gram sabhas, only a few people turn up. It was told that in the last gram sabhas hardly 50-60 people have gathered. As far as the discussion in the gram sabha is concerned, people normally discuss very limited issues like construction of roads or drainage, selection of beneficiaries for various schemes, etc. And, the discussion on selection of beneficiaries dominates the proceedings. While other vital issues such as: how the education among tribals can be improved; how the crop yield can be enhanced; how the income of landless people can be increased; and so on, do not find much importance in the discussion during the gram sabha.

The infrastructure position in the GPs is poor. The condition of school buildings is bad and have normally 2-3 rooms for five classes, the health centres are not in good shape and lack many basic equipments, veterinary centres are far away from the villages and so on. The lack of infrastructure is one of the major reasons as to why people find it hard to avail the basic services in time.

As regards the social audit, though the procedure has been given by the government, it is yet to be implemented by the *sarpanchas*, who try to avoid such audits. Moreover, people are not aware about such arrangement in which they have right to ask questions pertaining to development activities of panchayat. It also came out that the higher tiers are not responsive to the problems of gram panchayats and are not subjected to social audit.

Finally, it was observed that the candidates either for the chairmanship or for membership of panchayats were closely linked to the political parties or families. And in some places the cases of dummy candidates came to light.

As for the elections for the chairpersons of zilla parishad and panchayat samiti, some panchayat members mentioned about the lobbying for these positions. They expressed that in the last elections, the candidates came to know who was casting for whom.

Discussion with CEOs ZP and District-level Officers

The discussions were held with the concerned CEOs and the district-level officers of three districts. These were mainly on people's participation and functioning of gram sabha, merger of DRDA with ZP, devolution of funds and transfer of functions, and district government. The salient points are listed below:

i. On the issue of merger of DRDA with zilla parishad, some of the officers mentioned that this merger may be required but is not going to make any qualitative change in the functioning. The officers and staff continue to do their respective works / assignments as before and it is the CEO, ZP who has to look into the day-to-day functioning with regard to planning and implementation of programmes. Even if the merger had not taken place and President, ZP had been made the chairman of DRDA and the DRDA made accountable to ZP, the functioning of DRDA would have remained same. During the discussion, it was amply clear that what really mattered was strengthening the institution by taking concrete measures such as enhancing HRD level of field staff, creating more infrastructure for planning at each tier and strengthening the monitoring and evaluation system.

ii. The district-level officers have been designated as Addl. CEOs of ZP. The specific functions of each department have been assigned to three tiers. ZP has been given powers of transfer and postings of district and lower level functionaries. Besides, the gram panchayat level functionaries (of line departments) would report to the concerned GP where their office is situated. In this context, the two important observations were made after taking the views of the officials. These are:
   - The district-level officers found it difficult to control their lower level functionaries due to multiplicity of control. As the works of field functionaries are now supervised and monitored by various institutions like GP, Block, ZP, besides their own departments. Under such a state, simultaneously all give instructions, which are not in harmony with each other, to field staff and officers. Such situations create confusion in some cases.
   - The panchayat functionaries are reporting to the gram panchayat where they are posted while they are supposed to work for 3-5 GPs. Thus, a particular functionary, who is working for the gram panchayats of his jurisdiction, is not accountable to those panchayats where he is not reporting.

iii. The concept of district government has been introduced by the state government to bring the administration near to the people. Under this the district planning committee (DPC) has been entrusted with certain powers related to transfer and postings, approval of tenders and sanctioning of projects. These powers are such that were earlier exercised by the government or directorate. The chairperson of DPC is minister-in-charge and the secretary is District Collector. During the discussion it came out that there are certain areas of overlap between ZP and DPC and DPC has been given much more power in comparison to ZP. Such an arrangement of district government has raised certain basic questions. These are:

- When the ZP, which is an elected body and constitutionally recognised, why there is a need for another body for doing similar functions such as approval of tenders, sanctioning of projects, transfer and postings of staff and officers, etc. Whereas under district government, if at all there was any such need, the ZP should have been given all the necessary powers. It makes one to feel that another government body has been imposed at the district, while the ZP, which is a constitutional body, also exists.
- The primary purpose of DPC is to look into the planning aspect. This is what the DPC should be doing. Here, it is important to mention that district planning is an important and scientific exercise and should be meticulously followed. This is precisely the reason why such a body was recommended in the constitutional amendment. And, so, DPC should exclusively be devoting to the task of planning.

Measures Taken by State Government

Devolution of funds and transfer of functions upon three tiers: The government has taken the following measures for devolving funds and transfer of functions to the local tiers:

- Transfer of functions to each tier by the concerned departments;
- Declaration of district level officers as additional CEOs of ZP;
- Powers to ZP for transfer and postings of district and lower level functionaries. ZP also approves the budget for line departments; and
- Reporting by GP level functionaries to the gram panchayat.

District Government: The government has taken measures for setting up district government in order to decentralise the administrative system. Under this the DPC, which is headed by district minister, takes decisions with regard to transfer and postings of staff and officers within district, approval of tenders (for some items above certain value), sanction of big projects, etc.

The Scheduled Areas Act: The MP Act, No. 43 of 1997 for Scheduled Areas has been enacted. The gram sabha has been empowered for certain functions. The salient features are: to safeguard and preserve the traditions and customs of the people; to exercise control over institutions and functionaries in all social sectors; to manage natural resources; to manage village markets; to control local plans; and to regulate the use of minor water bodies. But the gram sabha has not been endowed with the following specific powers as per the provisions of the Panchayats (Extension to the Scheduled Areas) Act, 1996 (40 of 1996):

- Power to regulate sale and consumption of any intoxicant;

- Ownership of minor forest produce;
- Alienation of land; and
- Control over money lending.

Also, with regard to the powers and functions that are given to gram sabha (under the new Act), the necessary steps have not been taken by the concerned departments for taking specific steps for empowering the gram sabha.

Training to PR Members: Some measures have been initiated for providing training to presidents and vice-presidents of zilla parishads and presidents and vice-presidents of *janpad* panchayats at the state level. The training was imparted at the administrative institute. Similarly, at the district level, the *sarpanchas* and *nayab-sarpanchas* were also imparted training. The training is given only for issues pertaining to constitutional amendment, but no technical training for action plan preparation is given. But the ward members have not been covered under the training.

Tax Collection by Panchayats: The gram panchayats have been given certain powers to levy taxes like property tax, light tax, water tax, land revenue, income from ponds, royalty from minerals, royalty from granite, etc. With regard to land revenue, it is collected by the patwari but deposited with the gram panchayat subsequently. And for royalty from minerals and granite, it is collected either by patwari or gram panchayat.

With regard to action taken report on the recommendations of SFC, the state government has worked out the necessary details for sharing of taxes between State and the PRIs and also among the three tiers, and the necessary allocations are yet to be made.

Devolution of Funds: So far, no devolution of funds (under state plan) by the government has taken place at the panchayat level. The GPs are getting funds only under JRY, *Moolbhoot* (Fundamental) works and TFC. Under *Moolbhoot* works, the funds are given for certain very crucial works like construction of roads, school buildings, drainage, cleaning of health centres, maintenance of handpumps and so on.

Under TFC the funds are given to the Districts for the specified works as per the recommendations of local MLAs.

Transparency and Social Audit: For improving the transparency and accountability of the actions taken by the PR members, certain measures have been introduced. Under this the panchayats have to display the details of works undertaken by them, the villagers can take the certified copy of any document by paying nominal fees and the members of the gram sabha can raise issues and ask questions from elected members during the meeting of social audit.

4.1.8 Observations in Maharashtra

Field Visits

Visit to Chidaki GP in Pune District

i. The *sarpanch* has passed high school and is well aware about the functioning of panchayat. He is mainly concerned with statutory provisions like conduct of gram sabha meetings, conduct of panchayat meeting and maintenance of registers and accounts. He is least concerned about the people's participation in the development, the ability of panchayat to raise its own income, village development planning, etc.

ii. The functioning of gram sabha (GS) was also discussed. It was informed that in the gram sabha only a few people turn up. Even those who come for the meeting, they do not actively involve themselves during the discussion. In the last gram sabha meeting about 75 people participated. It came out during the village meeting that the DRDA is making efforts to activate the gram sabhas through a number of awareness building programmes. Efforts are also made to ensure that the GS meetings are organised on the specific dates in the entire district so that the officials and staff can attend them. The main issues on which the discussion takes place in the meeting are selection of beneficiaries for various programmes and construction of roads and drainage.

iii. Some panchayat members complained that they are not invited by the *sarpanch* for the gram panchayat meetings, and in some cases the *sarpanch* would prepare the resolutions that are signed by the other panchayat members. It was opposed by the *sarpanch* that led to long session of arguments among members.

iv. During 1998-99, the own-income (Rs. 59,000) of the gram panchayat was sufficiently high due to collection of license fee for the construction of new houses and buildings. Otherwise, in the previous years it used to be low.

v. The infrastructural and manpower support to panchayat is minimal. The school building does not have sufficient rooms; veterinary and health centres are quite far away from the gram panchayat; and condition of roads is poor. Besides, the panchayat does not have any field functionary except the panchayat secretary who is also in-charge of two GPs.

vi. The implementation of development works under JRY, TFC grants, etc. is done by the panchayat, and, in turn, it is the panchayat *sarpanch* and GP secretary who implement the works directly. The beneficiaries' role in the implementation is virtually insignificant and they virtually work as labourers.

vii. Though this panchayat comes under Scheduled Areas Act, yet the people are not aware about the new dispensation under the Act and more specifically about the powers given to gram sabha.

Visit to Kosapur GP in Thane District

i. The *sarpanch* is a woman and is illiterate and is not able to sign. She has very little understanding about the functioning of panchayat, though she tries to make attempts to involve herself in the panchayat functioning. She is not effective in organising gram sabha meetings and is not well-versed with the details of the development programmes.

ii. The gram sabha functioning in this gram panchayat is not satisfactory. As regards the attendance in the last GS meeting, it was just 2.5 per cent.

iii. It was informed by the villagers that one road was constructed by the zilla parishad (ZP) in their gram panchayat about a year back. The villagers were not aware about the length of the road and also about the amount spent. On detailed inquiry, it came out that the ZP has constructed the road by calling the tenders and some contractor has done the work. The villagers were engaged only as labourers. It only shows that even after having people's bodies in the form of ZP, the people are not involved in the development programmes. This example shows that there is a need to do much more in terms of educational and awareness building programmes in order to ensure that the people are meaningfully involved in the development activities of their villages.

iv. During the meeting, it was brought out by the panchayat members that the suggestions of the gram panchayat are not considered by the higher tiers, while there are many projects of importance such as for irrigation, construction of roads, which merit consideration.

v. Generally people were not enthusiastic, when the issue of elections was raised. They mentioned how in the last elections, several political parties fought but they were not concerned about their problems — like school building and health centre, while they spent good amount of money for campaigning.

Visit to Badeshwar GP in Pune District

i. The panchayat *sarpanch* is a tribal and has passed intermediate class. He has some knowledge about the functioning of gram panchayat.

ii. As regards the implementation of work (under JRY), it is done by the panchayat *sarpanch* and the secretary. People's involvement is absent. While the JRY programme was envisaged to involve the people through panchayats in the planning and implementation, but, in practice, this objective is not achieved.

iii. This panchayat comes under Scheduled Areas Act, but the people were not aware about the provisions made in the Act. Even the officials were not having understanding about the special powers given to the gram sabha.

Visit to Kasauli GP in Pune District

i. The *sarpanch* is a woman and has passed class three. She is able to sign, but not proficient in writing. She is not confident about the running of panchayat work. During the discussion it was obvious that she is not able to take initiatives for organising gram sabhas and mobilising people for the village development planning. She was content with the present state of functioning of panchayat in which only some statutory functions such as: convening the meetings, maintenance of records and accounts, etc. are attended to by the panchayat.

ii. As regards the functioning of gram sabha, it is found that it is marked with poor attendance, inadequate participation of the people and lack of proper methodology for village planning. As informed during the discussion, the attendance was less than 15 in the last GS meeting, so in a way the participation by the people was insignificant, and only a few people close to *sarpanch* were the main participants in the discussion, and there was discussion on a few items like construction activities. Though the zilla parishad has prescribed a format, but the discussion follows as per the points raised by some members. As regards the village planning for the preparation of action plan, it was merely a compilation of proposals given by the panchayat members.

iii. The issues that are discussed in the gram sabha mainly pertain to selection of beneficiaries and maintenance of roads and drainage. While many other development issues like improving the income of landless poor, improving the health and education conditions, enhancing agricultural productivity, etc. do not find place during the discussion.

iv. The own income of panchayat has improved due to measures taken by the state government with regard to collection of taxes for houses, lighting and water. During 1998-99, the own income of the panchayat was Rs. 85,345, and the same was less than Rs.15,000 three years back.

v. During the discussion people told that people are divided on party-lines. It starts with the nomination of candidates, which takes place keeping in view mainly the caste and party affiliation. Then it (divide on party-lines) is perceptible during campaigning and also after elections are over. People mentioned such development (leading to groupism, inter-group fighting) hampers the discussion in the gram sabha and no meaningful discussion takes place on any important issue.

Common Observations

During the meetings in all the GPs, the functioning of gram sabhas was discussed. It came out during the discussion that the people do not attend the gram sabha in large number and those who come for the meetings do not participate actively during the discussion. Another important issue pertaining to transparency in the decision-making was raised by the people, who have invariably complained that they are not consulted on the issues related to selection of projects.

As regards the organic linkages among three tiers, it was stressed by the PR members that the higher tiers do not consider the proposals sent by the gram panchayats and they prepare their action plans as per their own priorities.

In spite of some improvement in the tax collection, the own-income of panchayats is low and it is due to lack of tax paying capacity of the people. And, the panchayats do not take any initiative for raising their own income. It seems to be due to, *first*, lack of capacity of panchayat *sarpanch* to activate people for giving taxes; and *second*, poor environment in the gram panchayat for paying taxes.

The infrastructural position in the panchayats is poor as health and veterinary centres are quite far away from the panchayats, school buildings do not have adequate rooms and condition of roads is poor.

With regard to development works in the villages, the funds are received by the panchayats under JRY (now JGSY) and IAY only. The funds received are not sufficient to take up infrastructural development activities. The types of works that are taken under JGSY mainly pertain to repair and maintenance.

Measures taken by State Government

Transfer of Functions and Devolution of Funds: The state government has transferred certain functions to zilla parishad for carrying out various activities under district sector. The funds are devolved upon the zilla parishad for the specific programmes and schemes under various subjects. Besides, the state government continues to provide funds for state plan to respective departments of the district.

The state government has also placed the services of various line department (like agriculture, primary school, rural development, health, water supply, etc.) functionaries with ZP.

There are certain other staff and officers for state plan programmes and these functionaries report to their respective departments in the district. For example, under agriculture, ZP looks after supply of inputs and plant protection equipments and state plan covers national oilseeds, pulses and cereals development programmes. Similarly, under health, state plan covers family planning, malaria and TB control, while the ZP covers immunisation and health services. This system has created dichotomy within the departments, as they have to attend to programmes from two channels, viz., ZP and state government.

Training of PR Members: The chairpersons of zilla parishads and panchayat samitis have been trained at the state-level institute (SIRD). Other members of ZP and PS, and gram panchayat *sarpanchas* and members are trained at the district and block levels. The training is normally given for five days and mainly covers issues related to panchayati raj and decentralisation. No training is given for local level planning and technical aspects of development.

Tax Collection by Panchayats: The taxes are collected by zilla parishad, panchayat samiti and gram panchayat for the items assigned to them. The ZP collects the taxes for general water tax, pilgrim tax, fee on registration of animals sold in the market; panchayat samiti collects for ferries; and the gram panchayat collects taxes through: tax on buildings and land, octroi, tax on pilgrims, tax on fairs, tax on festivals and entertainment, tax on bicycles or vehicles drawn by animals, sanitary tax, general water tax, street lighting tax, markets and weekly markets fee, tax on cart stands, special water tax, fee on water wells and tanks, and fee for erecting sheds, etc. on public places or roads. During 1997-98, the collection of taxes by the panchayat samitis was minimal which was about Rs. 2.25 cr. in the state, while that of ZPs was about Rs. 5.02 cr. and of gram panchayats was Rs. 270.61 cr. The collection position of gram panchayats has improved substantially in the last four years as the panchayats have been entrusted with the collection of house tax, lighting tax and water tax. And the house tax collection has increased substantially since 1997-98. The increase has been of the order of 60 per cent.

Scheduled Areas Act: The state government has enacted Scheduled Areas Act and in consonance with Central Act. The following salient features have been incorporated in the Act: a) selection of beneficiaries by gram sabhas for anti-poverty and other programmes; b) sanctioning projects for socio-economic development; c) utilisation certificate to expenditures incurred by gram panchayat, approval of work; d) regulation on sale of intoxicants; e) regulation on extraction of minor minerals; f) restoration of land illegally transferred to non-Scheduled Tribe; g) to recommend rehabilitation of projects affected people and 'No Objection Certificate' for acquisition of land for public purpose; h) to control money lending; j) minor forest produce returns; k) to recommend management of local resources land, water, forest use, etc.; and l) preserve traditions, cultural heritage, conflict resolution, etc. Accordingly, the necessary changes have been made in the concerned state Acts. These pertain to :

- Maharashtra Minor Forest Produce (Regulation of Trade) Amendment Act, 1997
- Bombay Money-lenders Act of 1946
- Maharashtra Industrial Development Act of 1961
- Maharashtra Housing and Area Development Act of 1976
- Maharashtra Irrigation Act of 1976
- Bombay Prohibition Act of 1949

The state Act has incorporated all the mandatory provisions given in the Central Act, but it has not included power to manage village markets by the gram sabha.

District Planning Committee (DPC): DPC is constituted as per the District Planning Committee (Constitution and Functions) Act, 1998. The chairperson of the committee is the Minister-in-charge of the district. The member-secretary is the District Collector. The MLAs and MPs are also the members. The functions of the DPC are to prepare development plan of the district, to consider the five-year plan and perspective plans prepared by panchayats and municipalities, and to monitor the progress of the district annual plan.

Standing Committees of Zilla Parishad: The Zilla Parishad Act provides the constitution of 9 subject committees for carrying out different functions. These are:

a) Finance Committee
b) Works Committee
c) Agriculture Committee
d) Social Welfare Committee
e) Education Committee
f) Health Committee
g) Animal Husbandry and Dairy Committee
h) Woman and Child Welfare Committee
i) Water Conservation Committee

Critical Issues

Zilla Parishad Functioning — Problem of Dichotomy : Many subjects under various departments (for example, agriculture, horticulture, education, health, etc.) at the district level have been transferred to zilla parishad. The ZP implements the programmes and schemes under district sector. The field officers and staff of the concerned departments report to ZP. Together with district sector, there are programmes under state plan which are implemented by the separate wing of the concerned departments. These wings do not report to ZP. The officers and staff are separate for the two categories of work. This kind of arrangement has created dichotomy at the district level. (Besides, the field level functionaries do not report to panchayat samiti and gram panchayat.)

Tenure of Sarpanchas of Gram Panchayat and Chairperson Block and Zilla Parishad : The tenure of *sarpanchas* of gram panchayat and chairpersons of block and zilla parishad was changed to one year. Besides, the chairpersons of standing committees are also elected only for one year. In this process every year a number of members are elected for the posts of *sarpanchas* or chairpersons as the case may be. As discussed with the district officials, this kind of an arrangement is creating a virtual mess as every year new members are coming and before they are able to come to terms with the functioning, they have to leave the office of *sarpanchas* or chairpersons (but after Jan. 2000 there has been some change in tenure).

Poor Infrastructure at Gram Panchayat Level: The infrastructure position of panchayats is bad (as is the case in other states like U.P. and Orissa). Many of the gram panchayats do not have even panchayat offices with meeting halls; school buildings do not have sufficient rooms; the health and veterinary centres are not available with all the GPs; the offices of tubewells and water supply departments are also not available at the GP level; and infrastructure for marketing of agricultural products is not available in all the GPs. In the absence of these crucial infrastructural items, the gram panchayats find great difficulties in not only delivering the basic services to the people, but also in conducting their office work.

4.1.9 Observations in Meghalaya

Field Visits

Visit to Nongster Village Council in Ri-bhoi District

In this village, the traditional council exists which is headed by village headman who is selected in the village *darbar*. The village council functions through executive committee. During the discussion with the village headman he informed that though the village council looks into the socio-cultural aspects of the village but the development works are basically done by block. He also informed that other elected representative, especially MLAs, have control over the decision-making process of allocation of funds available with the block. This village council did not receive funds from the block as the concerned MLA was not in favour of that. The village council does not raise any tax but for social works the council collects the donations.

Visit to Mawiong- rin Village Council in East-Khasi District

The visit to this council also gave the same impression as in case of above village council. But here the village headman was able to get some funds from the block as the MLA was considerate in providing so.

Note : As per the provisions in the Constitution (Sixth Schedule), the autonomous council have been set up in Meghalaya. These councils have got executive functions and supported by the government of Meghalaya in order to enable them to discharge necessary functions. These functions range from development activities like construction of roads, buildings, etc. to collection of taxes to judicial functions. The details are given in appendix 4.1. Thus, if we closely examine we find that there is dichotomy due to presence of traditional as well as constitutionally recognised councils.

Some Important Issues

The discussions in the two village councils reflected the following important issues:

i. The traditional village councils have little role in development activities of villages.
ii. The elected representatives like MLA have good say in the decision-making process (regarding allocation of funds and execution of works) in the block development activities.
iii. Even the autonomous councils (as indicated by appendix 4.1) have very limited activities that mainly pertain to construction of roads, buildings, repair and maintenance, and they do not look into the holistic village development.

Traditional Village Councils in Meghalaya

The traditional village council in Meghalaya has three tiers. These are:

- Village level — Village headman
- Middle level — Sardar / Syemreid
- State level — Syiem (King)

The heads are nominated from the clan family. These councils look into the traditional socio-cultural activities in the villages.

4.1.10 Observations in Orissa

Field Visits

Visit to Baulajholi GP in Ganjam District

i. The *sarpanch* is a woman. Before being elected she was a housewife. Her husband has business and also does construction work on contract. During the village meeting she was not comfortable to speak to people about the problems of the village. On being asked how she looked after development works, she mentioned that her husband has been managing development works and she is advised by her husband and other panchayat members.

ii. As per GP Act, gram sabha is to be called minimum twice in a year. And during the first time in gram sabha, one-third members should be present for maintaining the quorum and if quorum is not maintained first time then there is no need of quorum when the meeting is called second time. It was highlighted by the people that during the first meeting of gram sabha hardly 50-60 (total members about 3800) people (about 1.5 per cent attendance) had participated in spite of the fact they were informed by the beat of drum. So, second meeting was called where only a few members participated (about 8-10, i.e., 0.25 per cent of total members in gram sabha), and the necessary discussion was completed during that gram sabha. People in the meeting pointed that gram sabha is basically dominated by the influential and vocal people in the village and the participation from the poor is unsatisfactory. People complained about the changes made in the names of beneficiaries after the conduct of gram sabha. At this *sarpanch* avoided making any comment.

iii. Another important point, which came to the fore, was that the PR members are keen about getting funds and the financial power from the government. They want that the funds should be placed with them so that they can utilise it for some development work. On being asked about the planning, implementation, procedure for carrying out the development works, they showed their ignorance. And their priority of development pertains to construction activities, with no emphasis on other development items such as primary education, health, agriculture, etc.

iv. In the panchayat, works under various rural development programmes have been undertaken. Under JRY (in 1998-99), the panchayat took the works for road formation and drainage. Under these a road was planned to connect two villages, in which spread of metal (stone) was a part. But there was no availability of road-roller for doing necessary compaction. Similarly, the drainage work had very little foundation and there was a danger that the drainage structure might get damaged during rainy season. The people mentioned that the funds available under JRY are so thinly spread (about 15 to 20 thousand rupees for one village and 4 to 5 thousand rupees for one work, as the demands of all the villages are to be met) that no meaningful work can be taken up by the panchayat. Moreover, there are problems of availability of equipments like road-roller and also the difference between the actual (market) and the scheduled rates (for cement, sand and stones), so, the actual cost is higher by 20 to 25 per cent if the market rates are paid which is not permissible. Over these problems gram panchayat has little control and these have bearing on the quality of the work.

Visit to Govindpur GP in Dhenkanal District

i. The *sarpanch* is a male member and has completed high school. He is able to explain and understand the functioning of panchayat. But he is not well-versed with planning and implementation of development programmes at the village level. Though he is active yet he is not able to involve the people in the gram panchayat functioning. During the meeting it was evident that the people were sitting idle without making much voice or raising any issue, and were unwilling to speak in spite of persuasion.

ii. The functioning of gram sabha and palli sabha is more of a ritual than a real forum for people's participation. People hardly participate in the meetings and as far as the discussion is concerned, it centres around mainly the selection of beneficiaries for various schemes. A few other development issues like construction of roads and drainage, functioning of schools and health centres are also discussed.

iii. The panchayat's own income is very poor as it was about Rs. 1500 during 1997-98. The panchayat is not willing to impose taxes and the people are also least concerned about the payment of taxes. It could be true that there is a lack of initiative on the part of panchayat to levy taxes but hardly any attempt is made to bring a suitable environment / culture to encourage people to pay taxes in order to meet the expenses for the basic services.

Note: In Orissa the Palli Sabha is organised at the village level and the gram sabha is organised at the GP level.

Visit to Manipur GP in Dhenkanal District

i. The *sarpanch* is a woman and has passed tenth class. She is very articulate and understands the functioning very well. During the discussion it came out that she belongs to a political family. Though she is confident, but as far as functioning of gram sabha and village development planning are concerned, she does not possess much understanding and does not take adequate interest in that.

ii. With regard to the functioning of gram sabha, it is quite unsatisfactory. In the last gram sabha only a few people (about 25) had participated and the participation level was poor.

iii. During the meeting, people complained that the names of beneficiaries are changed after the gram sabha. They mentioned that the names of those close to *sarpanch* or ward members or MLAs find place in the final list. The block staff, present in the meeting, also admitted that the names given by MLAs are also included as they get pressure from them.

iv. The gram panchayat has not been given adequate role in the functioning of activities like mid-day meal (MDM) scheme, running of primary schools and health centres, while people raised issues about the their unsatisfactory functioning.

Visit to Khadagparsad GP in Dhenkanal

i. The GP *sarpanch* is a woman and has passed twelfth class. She is able to understand the basics of panchayat functioning. Though she is educated yet she lacks confidence to organise the gram sabha and conduct it and also does not have good knowledge about the planning and action plan preparation.

ii. The own income of panchayat is significantly large as it is situated near a small business centre where large transactions related to agricultural commodities take place. The income from own sources was about Rs. 65,000 during 1997-98.

iii. In this panchayat, the ward members and the *sarpanch* have not received any training, though the training was organised some time back at block office but they could not attend due to distance factor.

iv. The discussion was also held regarding the linkage between gram panchayat and the higher tiers. It was pointed out by the PR members that the higher tiers do not look into the proposals sent by the gram panchayat. Even the panchayat samiti (block) does not care for the panchayat *sarpanch.* The reason cited for such relationship is due to the fact that the panchayat samiti and the ZP have members who are elected from different constituencies (that are normally the group of GPs), so they do not appreciate the concern of gram panchayats. Though *sarpanchas* are members of PS, but they are not heard properly in the meetings. It was also pointed out by some members that the earlier system was better, in which the *sarpanchas* used to be the members of panchayat samiti and they used to elect chairperson and vice-chairperson of panchayat samiti. And similarly, the chairpersons and vice-chairpersons, panchayat samitis used to be the members of zilla panchayat, and, in turn, they used to elect the chairperson and vice-chairperson of ZP.

v. Some members pointed that the *sarpanch* and his group members generally take the signatures of some members in the attendance register of the gram sabha, even if they have not attended. Similar instances are repeated for gram panchayat meetings. And never the proceedings of and the names of the members attending the gram sabha and panchayat meetings are made public. At this one member pointed out that this has become a norm and similar things were also done during the last term, and whoever becomes *sarpanch*, he wants to avoid discussion.

Visit to Padampur GP in Keonjhar District

i. The *sarpanch* is a tribal woman and has passed tenth class. She has understanding about the functioning of panchayat. The education has helped her a great deal in this regard. Here also, the *sarpanch*'s activities are confined to rituals such as convening gram sabha meetings, maintaining proceedings, records and accounts and preparing monthly statements. She is least concerned or enthusiastic about — how the people should be involved in the planning process. Rather, it is something that is not her concern and the same is true for all the other ward members. Members are simply interested in getting more funds and utilising it as per their wishes (as the people attending gram sabhas do not take part in the decision-making).

ii. As regards Scheduled Areas Act, the people were not aware about the special powers given to the panchayats under the Act. Even the officers and staff of PR department were having vague knowledge about the Act and were not clear about the special powers given to panchayats.

Common Observations

The functioning of gram sabhas, as discussed during the village meetings, is unsatisfactory in all the gram panchayats as only a handful of people (ranging from 30 to 50) have participated in the earlier gram sabhas. The issues that are discussed in the gram sabhas are having very narrow area. The discussion mainly focuses on selection of beneficiaries. It was pointed out by the panchayat *sarpanchas* that the people hesitate to come to gram sabha in case some general discussion other than the selection of beneficiaries is to be carried out.

There was discussion regarding the issues of the discussion during election campaign, people mentioned that issues mainly pertain to political clashes of the candidates and sometimes about road construction or cleaning of village ponds.

The own income of panchayats is very low (except in Khadagparsad GP) and it is about Rs. 3,000 per year. Neither PR members nor people are keen to look into the issue of raising the panchayat income. PR members are scared of losing their popularity in case they impose some taxes and people are sceptical about their (panchayats') ability to utilise the funds judiciously if the taxes are paid to panchayats.

Discussion with President, Zilla Parishad, Dhenkanal

The discussion was held with president and vice-president, zilla parishad, Dhenkanal. At the outset, they mentioned about lack of devolution of funds and transfer of functions to panchayats. They were keen that the panchayats should get more funds, but there was hardly mention about the people's participation and the functioning of gram sabhas. The discussion also touched issues like MPLADP and MLALADP funds, it came out that for this district, the funds under these categories are about Rs.3-4 cr. in a year which is a very significant amount. As far as the decision-making for the utilisation of these funds is concerned, it is solely decided by concerned MPs or MLAs. But the members present in the meeting pointed out that the zilla parishad should also have some say in the decision-making for selecting the projects as per the local needs.

4.1.11 Observations in Punjab

Field Visits

Visit to Mahana GP in Hoshiarpur District

i. The gram panchayat *sarpanch* is a woman and has completed primary school. Though she is not active, yet she is articulate and understands the panchayat functioning. She is not dependent upon her family members for panchayat work. Even the people are critical in case the family members of woman *sarpanch* interfere in the panchayat functioning. It also came out, while discussing, that earlier when the new panchayat was formed, some family members used to interfere but, later on, when the people started raising voice against interference, the woman *sarpanch* took over the functioning completely without depending upon her family members. On the complaints that gram sabha meetings are not held regularly, the members of sarpanch group pointed that such was the position during the last term also.

ii. The panchayat does not have enough resources, as the devolution of funds has not taken place in the state. Only some grant for drainage has been provided by the PR department and the panchayat is able to raise some income through property tax and lease of GP land for raising crops. The property tax levied by the GP is too low (Rs. 10 for big houses, Rs. 5 for medium houses and Rs. 3 for small houses per year) to make any income. Besides, the GP land is not fertile which does not fetch much income. So, the GP has very less income (about Rs. 90,000 from all resources in a year) and is unable to take up many important works like water supply, marketing infrastructure, etc.

iii. The issues that are discussed during the gram sabha mainly pertain to construction of drainage, provision of pipe water supply, etc. It was found that many important issues like how the education standard, especially of SC children, can be improved; how the employment opportunities can be improved; and how the agriculture can be diversified through better marketing system do not find place in the discussion.

iv. During the discussion it was pointed out by some members that the people from scheduled caste (SC) group do not get proper voice in the meetings and also the panchayat is not able to address their problems like education to their children, small land holdings, etc. Besides, the dominance by the upper caste people in the village meeting was visible.

v. On the question of taking up works in all the wards, the *sarpanch* mentioned that they have no option as all the members want that some work should be done in all the wards, otherwise they would oppose and there may be problems.

Visit to Lasrala GP of Hoshiarpur District

i. The GP *sarpanch* is well-educated and is active. The ward members are aware about their roles and participate actively in the meetings. The woman ward members are reasonably educated to understand the panchayat functioning. People in the village have good awareness level and raise questions about the village development during the meeting. In spite of high awareness among people, the people are reluctant to involve themselves in the village development planning. In their opinion, under the given state of panchayat's resources that are very small, the panchayat can do very little.

ii. This GP has been chosen for developing growth centre. Under this, infrastructure for market yards, community centre, health centre, shops and electricity and revenue offices has been constructed. It has provided good infrastructural support not only to this GP but also to nearby GPs. Presently, the panchayat has little control over this infrastructure but once the devolution of administrative powers takes place, the panchayat would be able to provide services to people.

Visit to Chharikalan GP in Hoshiarpur District

i. The GP *sarpanch* is a landlord and is having big orchard. He has good influence over the people due to his higher financial position. Though the people are educated and aware, yet they feel reluctant to participate openly, as once upon a time, the villagers used to work in the agricultural fields of the landlord family of *sarpanch*.

ii. This panchayat has got own land that is about 9 acres. On this land, plantation work has been undertaken in the last five years and the GP is able to get good amount by auctioning the trees. In 1998-99, they got about Rs.64,000, that is many times more than the funds received under any other scheme. In the coming year also, the panchayat is planning to take up plantation in the vacant land and hopes to get good amount in future.

Here, it is pertinent to point out that the plantation schemes have been very much successful not only on panchayat land but also on private land. It is due to three factors, *first*, people are conscious of raising plants and then after maturity taking the advantage by selling trees; *second*, there are a number of timber-based industries which like to utilise the wood; and *finally*, there is less fear of damage of plants by cattle as most of the cattle are stall-fed. Such kind of agro-based approach is quite helpful to people as well as panchayat in raising their income.

iii. In this GP one small bridge is being constructed that will join the adjoining GP in all weather. This bridge is being constructed by the funds from NRIs and the cost of the bridge is Rs. 35 lakhs. This is indeed a good example of mobilising the resources through sources other than the government.

Visit to Hariziana GP of Hoshiarpur District

i. The *sarpanch* is a woman. She is just literate but is able to understand the functioning of GP. She depends on her husband for necessary help in conducting the business of panchayat.
ii. In this GP, one good example of community participation was noticed. The people have constructed pipe water supply system by their own contribution. It has helped people, especially the women and they don't have to go to long distances for fetching water. For water supply they have installed electric motor. Now, they have to pay charges (Rs. 50 to 100) to electricity department which is quite a significant money for the people as they have put in good amount of money (about Rs. 3000-5000) for the installation. The villagers were vociferous in demanding the waiver of charges or at least for reduction.

Visit to Buddowal GP of Hoshiarpur District

i. The GP *sarpanch* is a graduate and is having good understanding of functioning of panchayat. He is very active and articulate. He is from rich family of the village.
ii. In this GP also, the villagers have constructed pipe water supply by their own contribution and were interested for waving the electricity charges. At this they were informed that the PR department would consider their request at the directorate level.
iii. Though the people are educated and aware, yet the people's participation is very little. Only a few people speak during the meeting and the attendance in the gram sabha remains low. In the last gram sabha only 22 (out of about 450 members) people could come for the meeting, which shows that the people are little concerned about the gram sabha. The reason sited for such poor attendance is that it is mainly due to lack of funds with the panchayat and so hardly any meaningful discussion on future action plan is possible.

Common Observations

The people's participation during the meetings in the gram panchayats, though confined to a few people, is well understood by the people. The awareness level is much higher and even the poor make attempts to raise voice. The higher literacy among people has contributed towards more awareness and understanding.

The attendance in the gram sabhas has been poor and, quite often, they were adjourned due to lack of quorum. So, the gram sabhas were convened again, still the turnout was poor but necessary business was transacted with less number of people. It came out during the meeting that people normally do not like to attend gram sabhas for various reasons such as: *first*, people generally have work outside their villages, so they do not like to come for gram sabha; *second*, as the panchayat has very little funds, so there is hardly any scope for taking up big development work; and *third*, the *sarpanch* also does not take much interest in order to avoid embarrassment of facing the questions to be raised by the opposite group.

On the discussion about elections, people expressed that the stakes are high for the candidates, as the prestige for winning elections is involved so the candidates make all possible attempts to mobilise people of their (or a particular) caste, and for winning over them. They also try for large turnout for voting from the section that supports them. And the development issues do not figure in the election campaign.

Discussion with Chairperson, Zilla Parishad, Hoshiarpur District

The discussion was held with chairperson, zilla parishad. The chairperson is a woman and belongs to a political and rich family. She was very unhappy over the lack of response from the government with regard to devolution of funds upon panchayats. She was forthright in mentioning that the MLAs are not at all interested to provide funds to panchayats. It also came out during the discussion that the ZP members, including the chairperson, are not the members of District Planning Board and in the planning board meeting MLAs like to distribute the district funds as per their choice disregarding the views of panchayat members.

Note: In Punjab the zilla parishads and panchayat samitis were superseded by the government in 1998. But in Hoshiarpur district, due to court intervention the chairperson of zilla parishad continued. (It was at the time of field study)

Critical Issues

Women as Sarpanchas and Role of Husbands: It was noticed during the visits to gram panchayats that the family members do not interfere in the functioning of panchayat. It has been due to resistance by the people to disallow the family members to remain away during meetings. It was observed that the woman *sarpanchas* are quite confident and are able to face the meetings without much problem. In this context, it was also felt that the women members are educated and have basic understanding of the functioning of panchayats. It brings to the fore one important aspect that the education has impact on the ability of the members to perform.

GP Income: The gram panchayats are not given funds by the government, except for JGSY and maintenance grants for drainage that are also small in comparison to the requirement of GP, but some panchayats are able to generate their income through own land by giving it on lease. It was informed by the district panchayat officer that some GPs are able to generate income through panchayat land, in the vicinity of Rs.1,00,000 per year and it may be as high as Rs. 4,00,000 per year in some cases, while the income from other sources is meagre. For instance, income from property tax is normally less than Rs. 2,000 per year and no other taxes are levied whereas there is scope for that as the income of people is quite good. Here, it is important to note that both *sarpanch* and people are reluctant to look into this important issue of raising the panchayats' income through taxes. The *sarpanchas* are cautious of losing their popularity in case they impose taxes and the people are least concerned for paying taxes, while there is a good scope for charging taxes on various items like cattle, vehicles, etc.

Infrastructure: Infrastructure with regard to school, health centre, roads, irrigation, marketing godowns and yards is in good shape in all the gram panchayats that were visited. Besides, as informed by the district officials, the other panchayats also have basic infrastructure. It is a very positive sign and may be a catalyst in expediting the process of decentralisation as panchayats would find it easy to provide services to people at their doorsteps.

Staff Position: The field staff is really a constraint as one GP secretary is in-charge of 2-3 GPs and panchayats have no other field staff.

Devolution of Funds: Presently the state government has not taken any measures for devolving funds upon panchayats. Even the zilla parishad members are not the members of District Planning and Development Board, which decides about the allocation of district fund for different projects to various panchayats

Finally, although, the present state of functioning of PR institutions is not satisfactory yet there is considerably good scope for decentralisation due to many favourable factors such as higher educational and awareness level among people and the availability of basic infrastructure at gram panchayat. But in order to fully operationalise the 73rd Constitution Amendment Act, some measures are required to be taken, these are: the programme for capacity building of PR members, devolution of administrative and financial powers upon panchayats and improving the manpower support at each tier.

4.1.12 Observations in Rajasthan

In 1959 the *Rajasthan Panchayat Samitis and Zilla Parishads Act* was enacted. It created

3-tier system. In the Act, an unique feature was the creation of nyaya (Judicial) panchayat for a group of 3-7 gram panchayats to administer civil and criminal cases. With regard to development, although some functions were given to PR bodies but it failed to provide substantial powers to them.

Now to conform with the 73rd Constitution Amendment Act, Rajasthan Panchayati Raj Act 1994 has been enacted.

Field Visits

Visit to Mohanpura GP in Jaipur District

i. The GP *sarpanch* belongs to scheduled tribe and takes active part in the functioning of GP activities. His educational background is under fifth class and he has transport business. He has to depend upon other members of the GP, including ward members and secretary, for understanding various issues like guidelines of different schemes, the procedure for conduct of gram sabha and so on.

ii. It was informed that during earlier gram sabhas, where minimum 1/10th of the members should have participated in the first meeting for maintaining the quorum, only 30-40 (about 2% of total membership) people had participated. So another meeting was called (where there is no need for quorum) and then also very few people participated (about 10, 0.6 per cent of total strength of gram sabha) and the necessary discussion was done for finalisation of GP action plan.

iii. People as well as ward members mentioned that they do not come to know about the date of the gram sabha. Even if they attend meeting, they just put their signature or thumb impression. Often the agenda items are announced, and the meeting concludes without discussions.

iv. During the discussion it was found that people were not aware about their participatory role in planning. It has been mainly due to lack of education and awareness, besides, the people are not organised for such role to be played by them.

v. During the discussion it was also mentioned that the development works were undertaken directly by the gram panchayat through panchayat secretary, while it should have been taken by the beneficiaries committee. On being asked, the people pointed out that it is difficult on the part of beneficiaries committee to take up the work, as beneficiaries did not have experience and the necessary resources (money and equipments) for undertaking works like construction of road, school building, etc.

vi. The woman ward members were not present during the village meeting and they have not participated in the earlier gram sabha meetings as informed by the villagers. They mentioned that most of the woman members have become panchayat members as there is reservation for them but they were very little aware about the panchayat functioning.

vii. It was evident that the panchayat members were not given training and they did not have adequate understanding about the panchayat Act and their role in development.

They were not familiar with 'participatory' way of development and people are not involved in the development process. On the question of involvement of people in action plan preparation and implementation, some panchayat members mentioned that they inform people, if they ask.

viii. On the question of paying taxes both *sarpanch* as well as people were unwilling to consider it. The reasoning given by *sarpanch* was that people would not like to pay taxes and also opposition members would raise issues against him and he would lose chance of winning next time. He further added that it is difficult to collect tax, as panchayat would have to keep an additional person, which would require expenditure for his salary. While people said that they might like to pay provided panchayat would deliver the services properly.

There was some discussion about the educational level of PR members and some people expressed opinion that it is essential that members should have good education, or otherwise, after getting elected necessary training programmes should be organised for them. In this regard, observations by *pradhan*, panchayat samiti, Sanganer in Jaipur, was like this: 'The educational condition is poor in general and is very poor among women and weaker sections. When the education level is so low even among PR functionaries, how can they function without the ability to read and write and there have been cases in which the GP *sarpanchas* have signed measurement books without understanding the content.' He also mentioned that in many cases some candidates among women had contested on behalf of their family members.

Visit to Gunsi and Luhara in Tonk District and Kusthala and Mori Gram Panchayats in Sabai Madhopur District

The field visits (after new bodies constituted) to all these gram panchayats brought out similar observations. The participation level of people is not encouraging, attendance in the gram sabhas is poor, and is normally 3-4 per cent of the total members in a panchayat. As regards the responsiveness of the panchayat, there were some complaints by people in the Kusthala panchayat in Sabai Madhopur district about the quality of work, but the *sarpanch* was not willing to accept such complaints. It also came out during the discussion that the selection of beneficiaries or watershed project is basically the choice of the *sarpanch* and the people are not consulted.

When asked about the conditions of marginalised groups (SCs / STs) in Kusthala and Mori GPs, some people expressed that there is hardly any discussion on them in the gram sabha. Some members from these groups expressed that it is up to *sarpanch*, if he wishes to help them, and they do not get any additional advantage from the panchayat. The allotment of funds for development works is done keeping in view *sarpanch's* caste or the support given by a particular community to the party of *sarpanch*.

While discussing about the participation of weaker sections in panchayati raj system, there were voices that expressed that due to disparities on account of caste people from weaker section do not like to contest in elections. The members from this community remain aloof, and even they do not like to attend the gram sabha meeting. Similarly, women also do not like to participate due to tradition of *purdah* system or inhibitions. Various political parties try to take their votes *en masse*. People also expressed that party workers make attempts to organise them for voting on the previous and the day of elections.

The pattern of own income of the gram panchayats is highly skewed, but, by and large, it is on the lower side. For example, the own income of gram panchayats in case of Tonk district is high (about Rs. 52,000, during 1999-2000) and the same is low (less than Rs. 5,000) in case of Sabai Madhopur district.Even the high own income of gram panchayats in Tonk district is not a representative picture of the district as in most of the other gram panchayats it is low. In these two particular panchayats, the own income is high, as these are located near towns wherefrom they get good income in the form of octroi.

4.1.13 Observations in Tamil Nadu

The Madras Panchayats Act 1958 was passed to bring a 3-tier structure of panchayat administration. It devolved powers upon village and block panchayats. But at the district level, it was left underrepresented. The panchayats had very little functions as most of the schemes were planned by the state. To conform with the Constitutional Amendment, 1992, Tamil Nadu Panchayat Act 1994 was enacted.

Field Visits

Visit to Vellivallam GP in Kancheepuram

i. GP president is a graduate and has good knowledge about the resources and the problems of panchayat. He is very active and articulate. The ward members and the vice-president are also educated but their educational qualification is less than high school level and some ward members are under primary school. In the gram sabha, the people are not very active in the discussion. And, people discuss hardly any matter that concerns the village development. Rather, a few people raise issues and try to ask questions from the president to embarrass him.
ii. It was revealed by the people that the president and the vice-president are having conflicts in certain matters, as the president has taken very keen interest in stopping the production and consumption of liquor, so some people in the village have turned against him. They are trying to create differences between president and vice-president by asking the vice-president not to co-operate with the president. It has led to a situation of conflict and sometimes implementation of some works is getting hampered.
iii. People have taken good interest in one of the community activities, which is the

construction of library building. This building has been constructed by the contribution of people together with some assistance from the government. Now, the president of the GP has taken steps to procure some books through GP fund and Lions Club.

iv. Money-lending is also a problem in the village as most of the people have to depend on money-lenders for consumption purpose, especially during off-season i.e. from January to August (non-agricultural period). With this the control of money-lenders on people is significant as the people hesitate to speak about the amount of loan taken, interest charged and from whom taken. And even they do not speak in the village meetings about these issues.

v. When people were asked to comment about the last elections, they expressed that the use of liquor is found in many places to lure voters. Some members said, 'Liquor is must during elections!' They also added that it is a part of the tactics of candidates to win votes.

4.1.14 Observations in Uttar Pradesh

Field Visits

Visit to Seikhpur Zafar GP in Faizabad District

i. The gram panchayat pradhan is quite active and articulate. He is able to take people and other PR members in confidence with regard to development works in the GP. He is from one of the better off families in the village.

ii. The seminars (for generating awareness) organised at the block level in which the PR members had participated, have helped them in better understanding about the role of panchayats in development. They also got good knowledge about the various aspects related to panchayat development. These seminars have helped partially in achieving the following objectives:
- improved awareness among PR members;
- improved attendance in gram sabha, but marginally;
- clarification of roles and responsibilities of PR members and line department officials and staff; and
- environment building for participatory development.

iii. It was revealed during the discussion that the members mainly deliberate on issues like construction of roads and drainage. Besides, other issues like construction of school building and panchayat *ghar*, and functioning of health centre are also occasionally raised. While many other important issues like improving literacy, especially among poor, enhancing agricultural productivity, marketing of agricultural produce, family planning and sanitation do not find place in the discussion during the gram panchayat or gram sabha meetings. Although, when these issues were raised during the village meeting, they felt a strong need for addressing them.

During the discussion, an attempt was made to know the reasons for confining the discussion around a few items that mainly pertain to construction activities. It came out that the people who mainly raise the voice during the meetings like to concentrate on construction activities and these are the people who are either from the rich families or are the influential groups (or some of them are *de facto* contractors). And the poor hardly get the chance to speak about their problems.

iv. Quite a few number of people raised the issue of damage of mango crop by the fumes of brick-kilns while this panchayat comes under mango-belt. It came out while discussing that the zilla panchayat has given license for establishing brick-kilns without observing the pollution standards. The ZP has been informed by the GP but has remained unwilling to take action for cancelling the license whereas, as per the law, the license should not be given for starting brick-kilns in the mango-belt till the pollution standards are met.

Visit to Magasil GP in Faizabad District

i. The GP *pradhan* is active and keen about the development of the village. He is from a rich family.

ii. The *pradhan* was very critical about the preparation of action plan of *chetra* panchayat (block) and mentioned that normally the suggestions made by the GP are not valued by the *chetra* panchayat. He also cited one example that there was a need for construction of road with the adjoining GP and this proposal was not accepted, as the members (of *chetra* panchayat) did not agree. But what has pinched the *pradhan* was that the GP *pradhans* do not have voting right in the *chetra* panchayat and so the decisions are taken based on the recommendations made by the members of *chetra* panchayat.

Visit to Tulsipur Majha GP in Gonda District

i. The *pradhan* is a woman who is a daughter-in-law of ex-*pradhan*. She is hardly educated and finds it difficult to manage the functioning of panchayat. During the discussion it became evident that she had to depend on her husband for day-to-day functioning. Even, people were asking questions directly to her husband (*pradhanpati* as normally called by the villagers) and it was he who was explaining the details.

ii. During the meeting, people also raised the issue of selection of works under JRY as well as beneficiaries under various schemes. They pointed out that the works are normally decided by the *pradhanpati* and the proper discussion does not take place about the selection of work. Similarly, the beneficiaries are selected by the PR members and *pradhanpati,* without consulting the gram sabha. It also came out during the discussion that the beneficiaries' list for various rural development programmes (SGSY, IAY) is changed after the gram sabha. Some members complained that their *basti* does not get funds and the beneficiaries from there are not selected for IAY. On detailed enquiry it was revealed that people of that have not cast their votes for the *pradhan*.

iii. One specific instance of inappropriate functioning of panchayat was brought to the notice by the people. They raised the objection for changing the sites of tube-wells, which were other than the sites identified during the gram sabha. Here, what was peculiar was that the *pradhan* or PR members have not taken any serious action on the complaint made by people.

iv. People also complained about non-availability of PDS commodities. It was alleged that the retailer is related to *pradhan* and so the gram panchayat is not taking any serious action about the distribution of commodities.

v. On the issue of elections, one of them said, 'As large money is required for the elections and the political parties have enough resources, they can fight elections conveniently. They can engage large number of party workers. He further added, 'Due to likelihood of violence during elections, some people with genuine concern avoid contesting elections'. The people also expressed that the use of liquor is found in many places to induce voters. Some members said 'If liquor and food are not served, how candidates would win votes?'

Visit to Bazirganj GP in Gonda District

i. The *pradhan* is an old lady (about ninety-year old) and is from the politically active family. In this panchayat also she is not able to perform her job actively and has to depend on her grandson who looks after the functioning of GP. Many people were very angry on this kind of arrangement and expressed their feelings strongly about the role of family members of *pradhan*. (It also gave clear impression that the *pradhan* is merely a dummy candidate).

ii. During discussion, people as well as panchayat members told that they do not always get the notice for the meeting. If sometimes they get, they just go to meeting for signing. Sometimes the members of *pradhan's* group put their signatures. More often the *pradhan* would read the agenda items, and it is assumed that decisions are taken by doing so. And no discussion is normally held. People complained that the names of beneficiaries are changed after the gram sabha is over. It was opposed by the group of *pradhan*.

iii. The people in this panchayat are divided very strongly on the party lines and the people of one group seem to be completely against the other group. During the village meeting, one group traded the charges against the group of *pradhan* and made allegations about bad functioning. They pointed out that the *khadanja* (road made by bricks) constructed by the panchayat was of very poor quality. But on inspection it was found that the *khadanja* was constructed quite reasonably well. Likewise, there were serious differences between these groups on many other issues. It gave the impression that the opposite group of *pradhan* was trying to obstruct certain things unnecessarily without much logic. (The District Panchayati Raj Officer told about such type of functioning in other GPs and mentioned that various groups in the gram panchayats keep quarrelling over many issues and in several cases the works get delayed indefinitely.)

Visit to Masoli GP in Barabanki District

i. The *pradhan* is a woman and is well-educated and is from an active political family. She has good knowledge about the functioning of panchayat and takes active part in day-to-day activities. People have regards for her and listen to her. She makes good attempt to attend to the problems of people within her competence and the limited resources.

ii. In this panchayat the multi-purpose worker is from panchayati raj department and so he does not have proper knowledge of other subjects like operating the tube-well. The villagers were very much agitated on account of this problem.

iii. The villagers complained about poor sanitation. At this the *pradhan* intervened and told that the people should make an attempt to clean their drainage and the streets, or otherwise, they should make contribution for engaging sweeper. But the people were not very much in favour of contribution and mentioned that there is no surety that they would get proper service..

Some Common Observations

Invariably in all the GPs, the people's participation is poor. It was brought out that during the earlier gram sabhas, attendance was low and in some cases only ten people participated which is too low a number. As far as the issues for discussion in the gram sabha are concerned, these mainly pertain to construction activities like *khadanja* (brick road) and drainage. Although these are important, but items like infrastructure for irrigation, school building and health centre, problems related to agriculture, animal husbandry, etc. are not adequately considered during the action plan preparation. With regard to women participation, it is very insignificant. It was found that even the woman (panchayat) members did not speak during the village meeting. Besides, there have been cases where the interest (like housing) of weaker sections, including marginalised groups, is not addressed properly in the gram sabha.

In the selection of the candidates for the panchayats, the existing political families have influence over it and in many cases the candidates are relatives of the political people. It is true invariably in the case of woman members.

It was noticed that in all the gram panchayats there are opposition groups with the sole purpose of obstructing the panchayat functioning. These groups are mainly on political lines.

With regard to the role of multi-purpose worker, people raised objections about the ability of the worker to perform all the functions given to him. They pointed that the certain functions under agriculture, health, tube-wells cannot be performed successfully by the worker of other departments, say, panchayati raj or rural development.

There was discussion with some elderly people about the panchayat system. They were somewhat indifferent. They expressed that the way panchayats operate and the political parties play politics, these are something that were not thought. One of them said, 'In the elections so much of money is spent. Not only this, even feasts are organised and liquor is served. After elections, nobody seems to be seriously concerned for the village development. There is politics everywhere and the people and the *bastis* are divided on party-lines.'

Impact of Measures for Decentralisation on Panchayats

In order to strengthen PR institutions, state government has taken various measures. These mainly (see Appendix 4.1) include devolution of administrative and financial powers upon panchayats at three tiers. At each tier, some functions have been given to the concerned panchayats and the services of some staff and officers of line departments have been placed with the panchayats. In content, everything seems to be right, however, based on the field visits, there are certain areas of concern that are placed below:

- During this process of decentralisation, seminars were organised at block level all over the state. In these seminars district officials, including line department officers and PR members, participated. The seminars covered issues pertaining to functions and powers that were to be devolved upon the panchayats. It evoked considerable interest among the PR members and even the officers and staff of all the departments participated with full enthusiasm. No doubt, the seminars helped in creating awareness among PR members, but it remained mostly confined to panchayat *pradhans*. The woman members and the members of weaker sections could not benefit much. It was clearly visible during the village meetings wherein the members of these sections remained aloof and participated little.
- The awareness level among people in the villages remains, by and large, very low. The gram sabhas were organised during May-June, 1999, as per the directive of state government, but the attendance was poor. In several cases meetings were adjourned due to lack of quorum and the fresh meetings were called with the limited number of people as subsequently there was no need for quorum. It also came out during the meeting that the people, including PR members, were not aware about the provisions of 73rd Constitution Amendment Act. Overall, it gave the impression that efforts have not been made to educate the people about the role of panchayat in village development and to actually involve the people in the gram sabha.
- Steps have been taken for improving the staff position at the gram panchayat level. For this purpose one multi-purpose functionary has been posted at each GP. This functionary

could be from one of the eight departments (see appendix 4.1). It is also proposed to provide training to these functionaries in order to enable them to function effectively with respect to twelve subjects that have been given to gram panchayat. With regard to this arrangement, serious reservations have been raised by the *pradhans*, in spite of the fact that each GP has got one full-time functionary who would be completely at the disposal of GP.

The grounds on which the objections have been raised are : *First*, how the functionary from one department would be able to attend to technical items of other departments. For example, how the functionary of gram panchayat department would be able to do the job of agriculture or health or tube-wells. Some of the *pradhans* mentioned that even after imparting the training to multi-purpose functionaries, they would not be able to acquire enough knowledge that would enable them to function effectively. *Second*, the inadequacy of infrastructure at the gram panchayat level. The lack of infrastructure, for instance, for health, veterinary services, agriculture marketing, etc. will come very much in the way of providing services to people. So, the mere posting of staff will not be able to serve the desired purpose of providing services to people at gram panchayat.

- The size of the gram panchayat has been a subject of debate among officials and PR members. The average population of the gram panchayat is about 1200 which is quite a small number. As per the discussion with officials and PR members, broadly two view points have emerged. *First*, the size of gram panchayat should remain small and the present demarcation of panchayats should not be disturbed. Rather, the size may further be reduced for bigger gram panchayats. It would facilitate in better people's participation through large number of elected members. *Second*, others are of the opinion that as they have got very large number of gram panchayats (as many as 58,000), so it is difficult to post the required field functionaries (for health, tube-well, agriculture, veterinary, soil conservation, horticulture and sugarcane) that are crucial for development of a gram panchayat. Moreover, the panchayat secretary, who is a crucial functionary as he is supposed to maintain various important registers and panchayat accounts, cannot be posted to each panchayat due to lack of field staff with the panchayati raj department (there are about 8,500 field staff of PR department against the requirement of 58,000, if one staff is to be posted as panchayat secretary for each GP). Besides, there is also paucity of funds for providing basic infrastructure like panchayat office with meeting hall, centres for agriculture, horticulture, soil conservation, veterinary and godowns as well as yards for marketing. It was pointed out by some PR members and people during the meeting that unless they have the infrastructure for the basic services it would be impossible to provide the desired services to people. And it would be possible only if the field staff of these concerned departments are placed with the gram panchayat and also necessary infrastructure (at the GP level) is created. Under the given circumstances, it is very difficult task to provide both field staff and infrastructure due to fund crunch and it could be possible if the number of gram panchayats are reduced by increasing the average population of the panchayats to 5000-7000.

Besides, with so many number of panchayats, it becomes difficult to organise block level meetings (in which about hundred members participate) and to monitor financial expenditure of GPs and a large number of GPs do not serve practical purpose from the development point of view. So, some people suggested that it would be desirable if the size of the gram panchayat is increased so that they become viable units of development.

Observations regarding Utilisation of Funds under SFC, TFC, MLALADP and MPLADP Funds

During the discussion with presidents, zilla panchayats and district officials, some important features came out that are worth mentioning. These are summed up below:

- The State Finance Commission (SFC) has recommended devolution of 4 per cent of state income from taxes. Accordingly, the funds have been given by the state government to district panchayats and gram panchayats for development works. But the allocation of funds is subject to certain conditions. For example, the 'maintenance' should be given first priority and even in some cases funds come to panchayats only for maintenance work. Under such circumstances, the panchayats have no option but to take up some maintenance activities which may not be the top priority in the area.

  In this context, the president, zilla panchayat, Faizabad district was very critical and mentioned, "The funds released by state government to zilla panchayat are only meant for maintenance and, therefore, it is unable to take up other important development works". He further added, "With this kind of allotment, the panchayats' autonomy gets affected and they are not able to take up the works that are essential for panchayats".
- Regarding Tenth Finance Commission (TFC) award, the funds have been released by the state government to district panchayats and gram panchayats. Here also, certain objections were raised by PR members regarding the modality of allotment of funds by the state government. It was informed by the members that the funds have been allotted by the government for a specific work (as recommended by local MLAs) and so they have no option to decide about the work as per the local priorities. Thus, the panchayat, especially at the district level, finds itself handicapped by such procedure of allotment by the government. Rightly so, the PR members have suggested for not earmarking the funds from the state, instead they should be placed with panchayats for utilisation as per local needs.
- The MLAs and MPs are given funds for the development of their constituencies. During the discussion, it came out clearly that these funds are exclusively decided by MLAs and MPs and the PR bodies do not have any say in that. It was specifically mentioned by some members that the significant portion of these funds are utilised for repair and maintenance of roads (and projects are identified keeping in view the political considerations) and

activities pertaining to assets creation are overlooked. While it would have been prudent to allocate the funds in consultation with local bodies and as per the pre-defined action plan. Such an approach would have helped in convergence of resources and their efficient end-use.

From the above, it becomes evident that the allocation and utilisation of funds for various projects are not done in the rational manner and the local bodies are not involved in the decision-making process.

Critical Issues

Concern for certain Provisions of PR Act: There are a few provisions in the 73rd Constitutional Amendment about which certain points were raised by some members. These are given below:

Reservation of Women, SCs and STs: As per the Act, the seats reserved for women, SCs and STs should be rotated every five years. In principle, it may be desirable but from the practical point of view, it was noticed that the members from these categories take longer time to learn the official work due to their low educational level. So, various PR members made a suggestion that the rotation of these reserved seats may be done for every ten years in order to provide sufficient opportunities to the members of these categories to learn and then perform their duties effectively.

Election of Members of Intermediate and District Panchayats: During the village meetings in Seikhpur Zafar and Magasil gram panchayats, the *pradhans* as well as some members raised their concern about the role of block (*chetra*) panchayat. They pointed out that the *chetra* panchayat does not normally consider their proposals for approval, as the members of *chetra* panchayat do not like to approve them. They pointed out that *chetra* panchayat members have their own agenda and prepare the action plan as per their own priorities without consulting the gram panchayats. Since the pradhans are only invitees having no voting rights, so they find themselves helpless in block meetings. The same is true for the zilla panchayat that also does not consult *chetra* or gram panchayats.

During the discussion it came out that the members of zilla and *chetra* panchayats are elected on different constituencies that are generally the combination of a few panchayats depending on the population. These members, though represent the group of gram panchayats, are not much concerned with the local needs because they do not face the people directly, as is the case with GP *pradhans* (who face in the gram sabha). Now, if we make a close look at the Constitutional Amendment, it basically stresses on two fundamental aspects: *first*, 'people's participation', and *second*, 'planning as per local needs'. These two aspects are well-taken care of during the preparation of gram panchayat action plan, but same is not true in case of intermediate (*chetra*) and district (zilla) panchayats, whose members prepare the action plan as per their own priorities without consulting the gram panchayats or people during the decision-making process. Truly speaking, such a system of panchayati raj is not in the right spirit of the Constitutional Amendment.

There was one issue, which came out during discussion, over which the gram panchayats of the mango-belt had conflict with zilla panchayat. It pertained to giving license to set up kilns in the areas adjoining mango belt by zilla panchayat disregarding the views expressed by the GPs. The people in the mango-belt have raised objections for setting up kilns, as these affect the growth of the mango plants due to pollutants. Rightly so, the matter was reported by the GPs of mango-belt to the zilla panchayat requesting it not to give license. But the zilla panchayat, while it could have denied the license, was least concerned about such concern of people and went ahead with its decision of giving license in order to collect revenue. This example is given to suggest how the higher tier disregards the views of people at lower tier.

Further, this matter was discussed elaborately with PR members and other officials and they all suggested for having GP *pradhans* as the members of *chetra* panchayat and one of the members should be elected as chairperson of *chetra* panchayat. Similarly, all the chairpersons of *chetra* panchayats should be the members of zilla panchayat and they in turn should elect the chairperson of zilla panchayat. This system would not only help in reducing the multiplicity of constituencies, especially those of *chetra* and zilla panchayats, as these are artificial boundaries created by merging the GPs, but also in achieving two major objectives of constitutional amendment. These are:

First, the gram panchayat members will be represented fully in all the three panchayats viz., gram, *chetra* and zilla. Thus, it will give voice to every panchayat in the decision-making process at all the three tiers.

Second, as the members in *chetra* and zilla panchayats will be from the gram panchayats, which are the basic units of development, it will provide opportunities to GP *pradhans* to put forth local problems in the higher tiers. That will provide right projection of people's needs in the development meetings of *chetra* and zilla panchayats and the plans so prepared will reflect the local needs and aspirations. In this way, it will encourage people's participation in a more meaningful way

4.1.15 Observations in West Bengal

Field Visits

Visit to Banachapada GP in Midnapur District

i. The *pradhan* of the gram panchayat is a woman and has passed high school. She is well conversant with the functioning of panchayat and takes keen interest in the working. Her activities are basically confined to organising gram sabha and gram sansad meetings and maintenance of accounts, etc. As devolution of funds and transfer of functions have not taken place, she does not have much scope to work in all the areas other than works related to JRY (now JGSY) or SFC grants.

ii. During the village meeting it was quite evident that the people are very much aware about their rights and take keen interest in the discussion. It seems to be due to the presence of strong PR system since 1978 as supported by the state government. People were vociferous about various issues like functioning of schools, conditions of roads, electricity supply, running of health centre, PDS and so on.

iii. The gram *sansad* meetings are organised at the ward level, thereafter the gram sabha meeting is organised at the gram panchayat level. Normally, the attendance in gram *sansad* meetings is quite high and about 20 per cent people participate in them. While in case of gram sabha meetings less number of people participate which is normally less than 2 per cent. Attendance in the gram sabha could be less due to two reasons, *first*, all the issues are well discussed in the gram *sansad* meetings and so not much is left for discussion in the gram sabha meeting; and *second*, the gram panchayat headquarters is quite far from the villages and the people do not like to come there for the discussion. But the real purpose of participatory development is served as the people actively involve themselves in gram *sansad* meetings.

iv. In this panchayat the people have taken one big project — the construction of wooden bridge by their own contribution. It was really a good achievement on their part and indicates that people are willing to make contributions for their village development.

v. People were critical about the influence of political groups in the decision-making and in the selection of the beneficiaries. Some of the members also expressed that people of a particular group find patronage from the elected members. And further it was mentioned that due to such political preference the initiative for development hampers seriously. It also came out during the discussion that the elected members belong to one or the other political group and the common person has little chance to contest in the midst of battle of political rivalry.

Visit to Panasguda GP in Midnapur District

i. The *pradhan* of the panchayat is a woman and is highly qualified. She is able to handle panchayat functioning very well. She is not dependent upon her family members. Even the people are very much against if the family members interfere.

ii. As regards the functioning of gram *sansad* and gram sabha, it is quite satisfactory as far as the attendance in gram *sansad* is concerned. The attendance in the gram sabha is poor due to reasons mentioned in the above case. Regarding the issues that are discussed in gram *sansads*, these mainly pertain to construction of roads and drainage, PDS, etc. It is often found that the discussions are not having much wider range and are basically confined to limited needs of the people. The reason given for such limited discussion is that the panchayats do not get enough funds so that they can plan for other works (under agriculture or animal husbadry). It is true that the funds received by the gram panchayats are less in comparison to their demands, but if we take a look into their priorities in the last ten years, these normally pertain to construction of roads, repair and maintenance of tanks or drainage. But the vital questions that are not addressed are: whether the people are aware about the development needs in all the sectors, whether the people have been rightly educated and trained for addressing their fundamental development problems and whether the people are able to resolve the conflicting situations and to make their village plan. Here, what is important is that the people should be adequately oriented about other development needs in education, health, agriculture or forestry so that some of these activities find place in the gram *sansad* / gram sabha meetings. And through the educational programmes the public opinion could be mobilised in this direction.

iii. In this gram panchayat people made reference about choosing the beneficiaries from a particular political group. Besides, they also mentioned that the PR members do not respond to such complaints in the gram sabha.

Visit to Kola-1 GP in Midnapur District

i. The panchayat *pradhan* is a graduate and is well conversant with the functioning of panchayat. But his activities remain confined to only conducting gram *sansad* / gram sabha meetings, maintenance of accounts, registers, etc.
ii. The functioning of gram *sansad* and gram sabha is satisfactory from the point of view of attendance in gram *sansad* and involvement of people in the discussion.
iii. The infrastructural position with regard to office building, veterinary centre, health centre, agriculture office and revenue inspector (RI) office is quite good. Though the collection of taxes is not very high but about 60 per cent of the tax demand is collected. It was informed during the meeting that the gram panchayat is not able to take action against the defaulters who are not paying taxes as panchayat has no direct power to take action and it has to file cases in the court for the recovery, which causes inconvenience. Besides, it entails expenditure for paying fees to the lawyers and the panchayat has no funds for that.

Visit to Sharat Chandra GP in Howrah District

The panchayat *pradhan* is a woman and has passed high school. She is well-aware about the functioning of panchayat and takes good interest in the office work, but her activities are confined to those that are mandatory in nature. As regards the functioning of gram *sansad* and gram sabha, people take keen interest in discussing the matters in the meetings. The issues discussed are very limited and pertain to selection of beneficiaries, construction of roads, functioning of PDS, etc. The infrastructural position in the panchayat is good as it has got office building, veterinary centre, RI office, electricity office and bank. It was informed by the people that the execution of work is done by the panchayat and, in fact, it is the job-assistant who maintains the accounts and records and does the implementation of works.

Beneficiaries are not involved, but in some cases they do supervision of works.

Visit to Bagnan GP in Howrah District

The *pradhan* of this panchayat is a graduate and takes keen interest in the work of the gram panchayat. The *pradhan* explained about the process of planning that is undertaken by the gram panchayat. Under this, the panchayat collects the proposals from the members and then these are discussed during the gram *sansad* and gram sabha meetings. Thereafter, as per the suggestions given during the meetings, the gram panchayat compiles the proposals, and thus the action plan is prepared.

As regards the functioning of gram *sansad* and gram sabha, it is informed that the gram *sansad* meetings are attended by a large number of people while the attendance in the gram sabha meetings is far less. The infrastructural position in the gram panchayat for various departments like revenue, agriculture, health, veterinary and bank is quite comfortable and is helpful to the panchayat in providing services to the people.

The *pradhan* made suggestions for providing training to PR members with regards to planning, technical aspects, monitoring and basic legal issues. He mentioned that the panchayat should have staff with some knowledge of legal matters that would be useful for the panchayat in handling various legal matters.

People were quite vociferous about the elections. They told that the stakes are high for the candidates, as the prestige for winning elections is involved. The candidates make vigorous attempts to mobilise people of a particular caste or group (political) or religion, and make all possible attempts for winning over them. They also try for large turnout for voting from the section that supports them. They make door-to-door campaign. While doing so, they are little concerned for development issues. Winning elections is more important than any thing.

Common Observations

The performance of gram *sansad* is reasonably good but that of gram sabhas is far from satisfactory as discussed above and the percentage of members attending the gram sabha is not encouraging.

The infrastructural condition in the gram panchayats is quite satisfactory as they have got office building, veterinary centre, RI office, banks and health centre.

At the gram panchayat level, six committees have been formed under the following heads: education, agriculture, woman and child development, public health, cottage industries and infrastructure development.

The tax collection of the gram panchayats is quite low, and it is in the vicinity of Rs. 2 per capita. The gram panchayat collects house tax, toll tax, etc.

The gram panchayats do not have control over field staff of line departments, but there are review committees for health and education in which necessary discussions take place regarding their functioning in the panchayat area.

There was discussion with local NGO and political party workers on the situation after the elections. One of the them said that the state government has not devolved funds. However, gram panchayats do get some funds under anti-poverty programmes. He also mentioned that the panchayat members need to be given training for managing the planning and implementation of programmes. Further they expressed the concern about the emergence of rival groups after elections, which dampens the village development activities, as each group tries to oppose the other, sometimes just for the sake of it.

Discussion with District Level Officers and ZP Members

During the course of the visit, the discussions were held with officers of ZP, DRDA, DPU, line departments and the PR members, including the president (*sabhadhipati*), zilla parishad. The following were the major points on which the discussion was held:

- *Activation of Gram Sabhas:* The ZP and DRDA have taken certain measures through awareness building programmes to activate the gram sabhas in the district. The district level officers of line departments were instructed to attend the gram sabhas and monitor the people's participation.
- *District Plan Formulation:* The district plan formulation starts with the formulation of plans at the gram panchayat and block levels. Firstly, GPs and blocks prepare their plans and these are then forwarded to District Planning Unit (DPU). Simultaneously, the line departments also prepare their plans and submit them to DPU. Thereafter, the discussions are held in sub-committees/standing committees of ZP. After discussion and incorporating necessary changes, the draft plan is submitted to DPC for its approval.

  If we critically examine the process of preparation of district plan, it is merely a compilation of the proposals given by gram panchayats, blocks and line departments. No attempt is made for database analysis, and analyses for inter-sectoral linkages, backward and forward linkages. Besides, in many cases, the new allocations are made by adding 10 per cent to the previous year's allocations. In a way, such a plan that is prepared does not reflect the critical needs of the sector.
- *Coordination Committee:* The Act provides for the formation of coordination committee in order to coordinate the functioning of various subject committees and also to resolve conflicts among them. It was mentioned that this committee is very useful for the smooth functioning of ZP.
- Some of the PR members made some important suggestions as given below:
  - The PR members at all the three tiers should be given honorarium as the members have to fully involve themselves in the functioning of panchayats and their considerable time is consumed in the panchayat work.
  - Panchayats should be provided with some funds for meeting certain expenses for engagement of advocates, miscellaneous office contingencies, etc., so that the functioning of panchayats is not handicapped by such requirements.
- Some of the ZP members, including the *sabhadhipati* of Howrah district, pointed out that

in many cases the guidelines given under the Central Schemes are not practical. They suggested that the flexibility should be given to the implementing agencies so that the projects can be designed as per the local needs.

- The discussion with members of zilla parishad revealed that they are anxious about the devolution of funds. They expressed that in the absence of funds they are not able to take up projects as per local needs, and also the line departments should work under them. On the issue of participatory planning and the involvement of people in the development process, they were not clear as to how people should be involved. But they mentioned that zilla parishad collects proposal from gram panchayat members and the people are informed by them (members), whenever there is a discussion.

Critical Issues

Issues discussed during the Election Campaign: Though West Bengal has been among leading states, but it appears that when it comes to the discussion at the grassroots level, there is a need to do self-introspection. To be more precise, the issues that find prominence during the election are: settling political scores or the rivalry during the previous period of panchayat functioning, while there is hardly any focus on the issues pertaining to education, health or other economic activities. It shows that the panchayat elections have become the ground for political parties for scoring political points over one another, without having much concern for the development.

Infrastructural Support: The condition of infrastructure at the gram panchayat level is far superior to that in the states like Orissa, Uttar Pradesh, Madhya Pradesh and Maharashtra. Almost all the gram panchayats have good office building, veterinary centre, RI office, health centre, banks, co-operatives and marketing centre.

Manpower Support at the GP Level: Manpower support at the GP level is limited to panchayat secretary, job assistant and panchayat *karmi*, this is comparatively better than that of other states. But the field staff of the line departments are not placed with the gram panchayat. It was felt that in the absence of placement of the services of field staff of departments (of direct importance to people) like education, health, agriculture, veterinary and woman as well as child development, the gram panchayat finds it difficult to work effectively.

Devolution of Funds: The state government has not been successful in devolving the funds upon panchayats, except for rural development and public health and no other department is directly giving funds to panchayats. The departments of PWD, Irrigation and Rural Electrification Departments have been planning to do so from 1999-2000. The untied funds, that are given to the ZP, are very small (about 2-3 per cent of ZP budget) in comparison to local needs.

Organic Linkages among three Tiers

- It was observed that the zilla panchayat and panchayat samiti do not have close linkages with the gram panchayats and the same is true in the case of panchayat samiti vis-a-vis zilla parishad. It seems to be due to the fact that the members of higher tiers are elected on different constituencies and these members work as per their priority. While the members of the lower tier are the members of next higher tier and have voting rights in development matters, it is the higher tier that controls the working, as far as details are concerned with regard to formation of agenda, conduct of meeting, identifying priority projects, recording of proceedings, etc. So, the members of the lower tiers do not find themselves not only neglected but also their views are not respected.
- There is also a growing feeling in the higher tiers to take decisions as per their own priority without looking into the suggestions of lower tiers.
- Another important observation came to the fore that the members of the GP are accountable to people in the gram sabha, while they do not have much role in the decision-making process at the higher tiers. In this process, whatever suggestions that come out during the gram sabha meetings do not find acceptance at higher tiers. In case the proposals are sent by gram panchayats, these are invariably not accepted by higher tiers. And the members of the gram panchayat are not able to provide any cogent answer to the problems (regarding proposals) raised by the people in the gram sabha.

4.2 Survey of Process of Decentralisation

The 73rd Constitution Amendment Act came into being in 1993. Since then the states have been making endeavours to implement it. Its implementation varies in content and degree from state to state. In order to study the factors that have contributed to the success in the implementation, the causes that are hampering the process of decentralisation and the response of the people about the present state of functioning of PRIs, it was felt necessary to conduct the field survey at the gram panchayat level in different states. In total, the study was conducted in fifteen states (see table 4.1). For this, the districts were chosen on a random basis, and within the district, the gram panchayats and the respondents therein were identified randomly (see table 4.2).

Methodology

For the purpose of field survey, the necessary formats were designed to collect the information about the status of PRIs and to ascertain the views of people at the gram panchayat level about the functioning of panchayats. The field information was collected in the formats during the visits to gram panchayats in the respective states. For the purpose of collection of information the help of the panchayat staff and the PR members was taken. Before the collection of information the staff and PR members were explained about the need and the procedure of

TABLE 4.2: **Number of Respondents in different States**

S. N.	Name of the state	No. of GPs under study	No. of GPs near to towns / industrial areas	No. of respondents
1.	Andhra Pradesh	4	-	80
2.	Assam	1	-	-
3.	Gujarat	2	2	40
4.	Haryana	2	2	40
5.	Karnataka	2	2	40
6.	Kerala	1	-	20
7.	Madhya Pradesh	6	-	120
8.	Maharashtra	4	2	80
9.	Meghalaya	2	-	-
10.	Orissa	5	-	100
11.	Punjab	5	-	100
12.	Rajasthan	5	2	100
13.	Tamil Nadu	1	1	20
14.	Uttar Pradesh	5	-	100
15.	West Bengal	5	-	100
	Total	50	11	940

collection of information from the villagers. People (in the villages) were explained in their own language about the questionnaire and also necessary clarifications were made about filling of the information in the survey formats.

Major Findings of the Survey

The findings of the survey are organised in five categories. These are, *first*, socio-political environment; *second*, participation; *third*, responsiveness; *fourth*, support system; and *fifth*, miscellaneous issues. The salient points of the survey are summarised below:

Socio-Political Environment

- *Educational Status at GP Level:* Literacy rate is an indicator of assessing the overall level of education. The status of literacy rate at the gram panchayat level is reflected by the table 4.3, which shows that it is not on the higher side in most of the states. And it is high in the states of Kerala and Punjab, which stands at 92.70 per cent and 91.50 per cent respectively (see table 4.3), while in some states like Andhra Pradesh, Madhya Pradesh, Maharashtra and Uttar Pradesh, it is comparatively much lower.

  Educational status of PR members is presented by table 4.3. It shows that the literacy

TABLE 4.3: **Literacy Rate and Educational Background of PR Members at Gram Panchayat Level**

S.N.	Name of the state	Literacy rate (in %age) (1991 census)	Educational status of PR members (%age of members)					Educational status of woman members (%age of members)				
			Graduate	High school	Primary school	Literate	Illiterate	Graduate	High school	Primary school	Literate	Illiterate
1.	Andhra Pradesh	33.70	2	23	45	22	8	2	6	41	36	15
2.	Assam	48.98	-	-	-	-	-	-	-	-	-	-
3.	Gujarat	70.80	10	45	28	15	2	2	3	38	43	14
4.	Haryana	55.54	1	32	29	28	10	-	5	29	45	21
5.	Karnataka	59.16	5	14	39	31	11	2	7	34	35	22
6.	Kerala	92.70	22	70	8	-	-	15	48	35	2	-
7.	Madhya Pradesh	45.20	2	26	31	32	9	1	6	34	49	10
8.	Maharashtra	43.52	3	34	38	19	6	1	7	37	36	19
9.	Meghalaya	58.90	-	-	-	-	-	-	-	-	-	-
10.	Orissa	54.30	2	11	40	36	11	-	5	33	45	17
11.	Punjab	91.50	4	29	32	25	10	1	11	30	42	16
12.	Rajasthan	65.50	2	20	45	18	15	-	6	33	39	22
13.	Tamil Nadu	55.33	5	20	30	35	10	1	9	40	28	22
14.	Uttar Pradcsh	38.55	1	5	42	40	12	-	2	20	49	29
15.	West Bengal	75.25	10	23	45	20	2	4	10	48	28	10

Note : 'Literate' means just able to sign.

TABLE 4.4: **Background of PR Members at the Gram Panchayat Level**

S.N.	Name of the state	Background of PR members (%age of members)					Background of woman members (%age of members)		
		Political		Financial			From political family	Dummies	Others
		Political families	Others	Rich*	Average	Poor			
1	Andhra Pradesh	64	36	65	20	15	75	15	10
2	Assam	-	-	-	-	-	-	-	-
3	Gujarat	62	38	67	30	3	66	19	15
4	Haryana	60	40	77	17	6	69	26	5
5	Karnataka	55	45	65	29	6	74	20	6
6	Kerala	52	48	73	22	5	68	-	32
7	Madhya Pradesh	70	30	66	28	6	77	19	4
8	Maharashtra	70	30	79	15	6	64	25	11
9	Meghalaya	-	-	-	-	-	-	-	-
10	Orissa	65	35	63	30	7	66	19	15
11	Punjab	63	37	64	29	7	73	15	12
12	Rajasthan	66	34	57	32	11	63	19	18
13	Tamil Nadu	60	40	65	28	7	67	22	11
14	Uttar Pradesh	65	35	67	28	5	68	27	5
15	West Bengal	75	25	60	30	10	75	5	20

NA: Not Applicable.

*Includes the capacity to mobilise resources for elections.

level among the members is not encouraging and majority of them is in the category of primary school or below it. As regards the educational status of woman members, it is rather dismally low and most of the members (about 50 per cent in many states) are either literate (just able to sign) or illiterate.

While Kerala stands apart and the educational level is far above that of other states and a large number (22%) of PR members have crossed graduation. Also, the woman members have significantly good educational background and majority (more than 60 per cent) is above high school.

- *Background of PR Members at GP Level:* The survey has revealed that most of the PR members are from the political families in which at least one member of their families has been in politics. This figure is as high as 75 per cent in West Bengal (see table 4.4). Similarly, majority of the members, upwards of 60 per cent, is from rich families (have the capacity to mobilise resources), whereas only a few percentages are from the poor families. In a way, political background and good financial support have been of great help to members in the panchayats to contest and win the elections.

  As regards the background of woman members, they are mainly from the political families. And in some cases it came out that there are some dummy candidates. These candidates are those who are projected by some ex-chairpersons or some political elites, who cannot contest due to reservation. The percentage of dummy candidates is significantly high in Haryana, Maharashtra and Uttar Pradesh (see table 4.4) and the figures in percentage are 26, 25 and 27 respectively. (This information on dummy candidates was elicited through a process of discussion with the people.)
- *Dependence of Woman Chairpersons:* It was revealed during the survey that the woman chairpersons are largely dependent on their family members and this dependence is mainly on husband. It came out during the survey (see table 4.5) that the dependence of woman chairpersons is high on husbands and also it was informed during the discussions, that the husbands of some of these members accompany them during the meetings. Besides, in certain cases woman chairpersons do not attend the meetings due to some family occupation and their family members informally chair the meetings. But in the state of Kerala the woman chairpersons are not dependent on their family members. It is mainly due to higher education and awareness among people, including woman PR members. An attempt was also made to know reasons for dependence of woman members on others. It came out that it is mainly due to two factors: *first*, dominance by family members; and *second*, low education of woman members.
- *Issues for Discussion during the Election Campaign:* The survey (see table 4.6) has shown that in all the states except in Kerala, where there is some shift, the issues that get focused attention are: issues over political clashes, use of tactics by different parties to win over voters, while other social or economic issues do not find much place during the discussion. Discussion also brought out that the issues like the prestige for winning elections and having control over village panchayat also remain in focus. Even if some issues on economic aspect are discussed, these mainly pertain to construction of roads,

TABLE 4.5: **Dependence of Woman Chairpersons**

S.N.	Name of the state	Dependence	On whom dependence			Reasons for dependence (VH / H / M) *		
		Yes / No	Husband (VH / H / M) *	Other family members (H / M / L) *	Others (H / M / L) *	Low education	Dominance by family members	Any other
1.	Andhra Pradesh	Yes	Very High	Medium	Low	Very High	High	-
2.	Assam	-	-	-	-	-	-	-
3.	Gujarat	Yes	High	Medium	Low	Very High	Very High	-
4.	Haryana	-do-	Very High	-do-	-do-	High	-do-	-
5.	Karnataka	-do-	High	-do-	-do-	-do-	High	-
6.	Kerala	No	No	No	NA	NA	NA	-
7.	Madhya Pradesh	Yes	Very High	Medium	Low	High	High	-
8.	Maharashtra	-do-	High	-do-	-do-	-do-	-do-	-
9.	Meghalaya	-	-	-	-	-	-	-
10.	Orissa	Yes	High	Medium	Low	High	High	-
11.	Punjab	-do-	-do-	-do-	-do-	-do-	-do-	-
12.	Rajasthan	-do-	-do-	-do-	-do-	High	-do-	-
13.	Tamil Nadu	-do-	-do-	-do-	-do-	-do-	-do-	-
14.	Uttar Pradesh	-do-	Very High	-do-	-do-	Very High	Very High	-
15.	West Bengal	-do-	-do-	-do-	-do-	-do-	Low	-

* If respondents are more than 90 per cent in any category, that particular category is selected.

VH : Very high H : High M : Medium L : Low

NA: Not Applicable.

TABLE 4.6: **Issues for the Discussions during Election Campaign**

S. N.	Name of the state	Main issues for discussion during election campaign	Level of discussion		
			Discussion on education and health (High, Moderate, Insignificant)*	Discussion on other economic problems like agriculture, animal husbandry, infrastructure development (High, Moderate, Insignificant)*	Discussion on the problems of weaker sections — landless people, SCs, STs, women, old and disabled, etc. (High, Moderate, Insignificant) *
1	2	3	4	5	6
1.	Andhra Pradesh	Focus on: - Issues over political clashes - Use of tactics by different parties to win over voters - Prestige for winning and having control over village panchayat Other issues: - Construction of roads, drainage, etc.	Insignificant	Insignificant	Insignificant
2.	Assam	-	-	-	-
3.	Gujarat	Same as in the case of Andhra Pradesh	Insignificant	Insignificant	Insignificant
4.	Haryana	-do-	-do-	-do-	-do-
5.	Karnataka	-do-	-do-	-do-	-do-
6.	Kerala	- Education, health and economic activities - Political clashes and their tactics	Moderate	Moderate	-do-
7.	Madhya Pradesh	Same as in the case of Andhra Pradesh	Insignificant	Insignificant	-do-

(Contd.)

TABLE 4.6 (*Contd.*)

1	2	3	4	5	6
8.	Maharashtra	-do-	-do-	-do-	-do-
9.	Meghalaya	-	-	-	-
10.	Orissa	Same as in the case of Andhra Pradesh	Insignificant	Insignificant	Insignificant
11.	Punjab	-do-	-do-	-do-	-do-
12.	Rajasthan	-do-	-do-	-do-	-do-
13.	Tamil Nadu	-do-	-do-	-do-	-do-
14.	Uttar Pradesh	-do-	-do-	-do-	-do-
15.	West Bengal	-do-	-do-	-do-	-do-

* If respondents are more than 90 per cent in any category, that particular category is selected.

drainage, etc. And the issues pertaining to economic problems like agriculture, animal husbandry, infrastructure development and also the problems of weaker sections do not get any attention. Though in the state of Kerala there is some focus on education, health or economic activities, but it is not very profound in terms of level of discussion and also weaker sections do not get much notice of the candidates.

- *Problems during Elections:* In most of the states, during the elections of local bodies, the political climate becomes sensitive (see table 4.7). While in certain states, it becomes highly sensitive and these states are Andhra Pradesh, Uttar Pradesh and West Bengal. Higher sensitivity is due to various reasons like inter-group clashes, political rivalry, intimidation and so on.

  As regards the problems that increase during the elections are: *first*, higher consumption of liquor; *second*, more number of feasts; *third*, increased expenditure of money; and *fourth*, increased intimidation. It was informed during the survey that even in some cases the money is spent to win over the voters. As regards the intimidation, it is high in Andhra Pradesh, Haryana, Tamil Nadu, Uttar Pradesh and West Bengal. In several cases, as reported by people, they are told in advance to vote for a particular candidate otherwise to face some adverse consequences.

Participation

- *People's Participation in Gram Sabha:* While the people's participation is crucial, but the percentage of people participating in the gram sabha is very dismal in all the states except in Kerala (see table 4.8). It shows that it is in the vicinity of 1.5 per cent in all the states and the same is about 33 per cent in Kerala. The improved participation in Kerala is attributed to several reasons: *first*, higher educational level of people; *second*, higher awareness level in the villages; *third*, aware PR members; and *fourth*, active role played by chairperson and ward members of gram panchayat in organising the gram sabha.

  If we examine the categories of participants during the discussion in the gram sabha, these are mainly 'members close to PR members' and 'vocal section of the village'. And normally others do not take active role. It shows the extent to which the people are involved in the decision-making process. Of particular importance is the response of PR members in the gram sabha. The survey showed that the PR members are not prompt in responding to the problems expressed by the people rather they are indifferent in some cases. As regards the case of Kerala, the functioning is relatively better as the involvement of people is higher and the response of PR members is on the positive side.
- *Type of Issues discussed in the Gram Sabha:* A careful examination of the table 4.9 reflects that in all the states, except in Kerala, the issues discussed in the gram sabha mainly pertain to 'selection of beneficiaries' and 'identification of construction works.' While many other vital issues such as agriculture, education, health and problems of poor people do not find prominence during the discussion. It only shows that the discussion in the gram sabha is on a very limited number of issues. But in the state of Kerala, the range

TABLE 4.7: **Problems during Panchayat Elections**

S.N.	Name of the state	Political climate	Type of problems			(H / M / L) *
		Highly Sensitive / Sensitive / Normal	Consumption of liquor	Number of feasts	Expenditure of money	Intimidation
1.	Andhra Pradesh	Highly sensitive	High	High	High	High
2.	Assam	-	-	-	-	-
3.	Gujarat	Sensitive	High	High	High	Low
4.	Haryana	-do-	-do-	-do-	-do-	High
5.	Karnataka	Normal	Medium	Medium	-do-	Low
6.	Kerala	-do-	-do-	-do-	-do-	-do-
7.	Madhya Pradesh	-do-	High	High	-do-	-do-
8.	Maharashtra	Sensitive	-do-	-do-	-do-	-do-
9.	Meghalaya	-	-	-	-	-
10.	Orissa	Sensitive	High	High	High	Low
11.	Punjab	-do-	-do-	-do-	-do-	-do-
12.	Rajasthan	-do-	-do-	-do-	-do-	-do-
13.	Tamil Nadu	-do-	-do-	-do-	-do-	High
14.	Uttar Pradesh	Highly sensitive	-do-	-do-	-do-	-do-
15.	West Bengal	-do-	Medium	Medium	-do-	-do-

* If respondents are more than 90 per cent in any category, that particular category is selected.

H : High M : Medium L : Low

TABLE 4.8: **Percentage of People Participating, the Category of Participants and the Response of PR Members in the Gram Sabha at the GP Level**

S.N.	Name of the state	%age of people participating in the gram sabha	%age of women participating in the gram sabha	Category of participants (H / M / L) *				Response of PR members (No / In a few cases / In some cases / In many cases)		
				PR members	Members close to elected representatives	Vocal section of the village	General public	Very prompt	Prompt	Indifferent
1	Andhra Pradesh	3.1	2.0	Medium	High	High	Low	No	In some cases	In a few cases
2	Assam	-	-	-	-	-	-	-	-	-
3	Gujarat	1.9	1.5	Medium	High	High	Low	No	In some cases	In a few cases
4	Haryana	2.1	0.5	-do-	-do-	-do-	-do-	-do-	-do-	-do-
5	Karnataka	3.6	2.5	-do-	-do-	-do-	-do-	In a few cases	-do-	-do-
6	Kerala	32.5	34.0	-do-	Low	-do-	High	In some cases	-do-	No
7	Madhya Pradesh	1.9	1.0	-do-	High	-do-	Low	No	-do-	In a few cases
8	Maharashtra	1.8	1.0	-do-	-do-	Medium	-do-	-do-	-do-	-do-
9	Meghalaya	-	-	-	-	-	-	-	-	-
10	Orissa	2.5	0.5	Medium	High	Medium	Low	No	In some cases	In a few cases
11	Punjab	2.0	1.0	-do-	Medium	-do-	-do-	-do-	-do-	-do-
12	Rajasthan	1.0	0.5	-do-	-do-	-do-	-do-	-do-	-do-	-do-
13	Tamil Nadu	1.1	0.2	-do-	High	High	-do-	-do-	-do-	-do-
14	Uttar Pradesh	1.0	0.5	-do-	-do-	-do-	-do-	-do-	In a few cases	-do-
15	West Bengal	2.8	2.5	-do-	-do-	-do-	-do-	In a few cases	In some cases	-do-

* If respondents are more than 90 per cent in any category, that particular category is selected.

H : High

M : Medium

L : Low

TABLE 4.9: **Type of Issues Discussed in the Gram Sabha**

S.N.	Name of the state	Type of issues discussed (H / M / L) *				
		Selection of beneficiaries	Identification of construction works	Agriculture, irrigation, etc.	Education and health progs.	Problems of poor people
1.	Andhra Pradesh	High	High	Low	Low	Low
2.	Assam	-	-	-	-	-
3.	Gujarat	High	High	Low	Low	Low
4.	Haryana	-do-	-do-	-do-	-do-	-do-
5.	Karnataka	-do-	-do-	-do-	Medium	-do-
6.	Kerala	Medium	Medium	High	High	Medium
7.	Madhya Pradesh	-do-	High	Low	Low	Low
8.	Maharashtra	-do-	-do-	-do-	-do-	-do-
9.	Meghalaya	-	-	-	-	-
10.	Orissa	Medium	High	Low	Low	Low
11.	Punjab	High	-do-	High	-do-	-do-
12.	Rajasthan	-do-	-do-	Low	-do-	-do-
13.	Tamil Nadu	-do-	-do-	-do-	-do-	-do-
14.	Uttar Pradesh	-do-	-do-	-do-	-do-	-do-
15.	West Bengal	-do-	-do-	-do-	Medium	Medium

*If respondents are more than 90 per cent in any category, that particular category is selected.

H : High

M : Medium

L : Low

of issues discussed is wider and the gram sabha gives high priority to education, health, agriculture, etc.

- *Factors Influencing Discussions and the Decisions in the Gram Sabha—Quality of Participation:* In the context of the discussion in the gram sabha, it was found that the large number of participants in the meeting (see table 4.10) affects the discussion process. As pointed out by the people that in a large gathering of about 100-150 (in some cases 300-350), all of them do not get chance to put forth their viewpoints. Also, the discussion in the gram sabha is influenced by the dominance of certain political groups or individuals. It brings to the fore that the people's participation is still not forthcoming and a few individuals or groups corner the discussion.

  An attempt was made to study the factors influencing the decisions in the gram sabha. It revealed that the factors such as 'political / group influence' and 'personal interest of PR members' mainly guide the decision-making in the gram sabha. 'Decisions based on merit' seems to be distant possibility in all the states except, to some extent, in Kerala.
- *Factors Influencing the Functioning of Gram Sabha and the Plan Preparation:* Factors that are affecting the functioning of gram sabha require some assessment. As reflected by the survey (see table 4.11), the factors such as 'awareness and knowledge level of people', 'initiatives by GP chairperson' and 'political environment' influence greatly the gram sabha functioning. In a way, enlightened people in the villages, active role of gram panchayat chairperson and conducive political environment will lead to healthy functioning of gram sabha. Besides, the factors like 'social environment' and 'initiatives by PR members' also affect the functioning to some extent.

  One of the most important functions of gram panchayats is to prepare local plan through the discussion and approval in gram sabha. It has come out during the survey that knowledge level of chairperson is very crucial for the preparation of action plan. Of significant importance are planning unit at panchayat level and database preparation. In addition, planning methodology and the knowledge level of PR members for the preparation of plan are also of importance.

Responsiveness

- *Responsiveness of PR Members about the People's Grievances:* Responsiveness of the PR members is a vital aspect of the local institutions. It is revealed by the survey (see table 4.12) that while attending to the problems of people, the PR members are more concerned about the problems of their own group. During the survey, people informed that the villages are normally divided into two groups, one supporting the chairperson of the gram panchayat and the other the opposition party. Mostly during the selection of beneficiaries the people are identified from the group of chairperson or identification of work is done in that area which supports the party in power at panchayat level. While, in case of Kerala, due to people's campaign plan, the PR members are more responsive towards the problems of people.

TABLE 4.10: **Factors Influencing the Discussions and Decisions in the Gram Sabha**

S.N.	Name of the state	Issues discussed	Factors influencing the discussions (H / M / L) *			Factors influencing decisions (H / M / L) *		
			Large numbers of participants	Political/Groups/ Individuals dominance	Technical nature of issues	Political/ group influence	Personal interest of PR members	Based on merit
1	2	3	4	5	6	7	8	9
1.	Andhra Pradesh	Main focus on: - Construction activities - Selection of beneficiaries - Complaints regarding PDS or absenteeism of school teacher or health worker - Approval of accounts and budget	High	High	Low	High	High	Low
2.	Assam	-	-	-	-	-	-	-
3.	Gujarat	As in the case of AP	High	High	Low	High	High	Low
4.	Haryana	-do-	-do-	-do-	-do-	-do-	-do-	-do-
5.	Karnataka	-do-	-do-	-do-	-do-	-do-	-do-	Medium
6.	Kerala	Main focus on: - Resources planning - Education and health programmes - Infrastructure development - Approval of village plan, implementation and monitoring of programmes.	Medium	Medium	Medium	Low	Low	Medium to High

(Contd.)

TABLE 4.10 *(Contd.)*

1	2	3	4	5	6	7	8	9
7.	Madhya Pradesh	As in the case of AP	High	High	Low	High	High	Low
8.	Maharashtra	-do-	-do-	-do-	-do-	-do-	-do-	-do-
9.	Meghalaya	-	-	-	-	-	-	-
10.	Orissa	As in the case of AP	High	High	Low	High	High	Low
11.	Punjab	-do-	-do-	-do-	-do-	-do-	-do-	-do-
12.	Rajasthan	-do-	-do-	-do-	-do-	-do-	-do-	-do-
13.	Tamil Nadu	-do-	-do-	-do-	-do-	-do-	-do-	-do-
14.	Uttar Pradesh	-do-	-do-	-do-	-do-	-do-	-do-	-do-
15.	West Bengal	-do-	-do-	-do-	-do-	-do-	-do-	-do-

* If respondents are more than 90 per cent in any category, that particular category is selected.

H : High

M : Medium

L : Low

TABLE 4.11: **Gram Sabha Functioning and Local Plan Preparation at the GP Level**

S.N.	Name of the state	Factors responsible for gram sabha functioning (H / M / L)*					Factors responsible for plan preparation (H / M / L)*				
		Awareness and knowledge level of people	Initiatives by GP chair-person	Initiatives by PR members	Political environ-ment	Social environ-ment	Knowledge level of chairperson	Knowledge level of PR members	Planning unit at GP	Database	Planning methodo-logy
1.	Andhra Pradesh	High	High	Low	High	Medium	High	Low	High	Low	Medium
2.	Assam	-	-	-	-	-	-	-	-	-	-
3.	Gujarat	High	High	Low	High	Medium	High	Low	High	Low	Medium
4.	Haryana	-do-	-do-	-do-	-do-	-do-	-do-	-do-	-do-	-do-	-do-
5.	Karnataka	-do-	-do-	-do-	-do-	-do-	-do-	-do-	-do-	-do-	-do-
6.	Kerala	-do-	-do-	Medium	-do-	Medium	-do-	Medium	-do-	High	High
7.	Madhya Pradesh	-do-	Medium	Low	-do-	Low	-do-	Low	-do-	Low	Low
8.	Maharashtra	-do-	-do-	-do-	-do-	-do-	-do-	-do-	-do-	-do-	-do-
9.	Meghalaya	-	-	-	-	-	-	-	-	-	-
10.	Orissa	High	Medium	Low	High	Low	High	Low	High	Medium	Low
11.	Punjab	-do-	-do-	-do-	-do-	-do-	-do-	-do-	-do-	Low	Medium
12.	Rajasthan	-do-	-do-	Medium	Medium	Medium	Medium	-do-	-do-	-do-	-do-
13.	Tamil Nadu	-do-	High	Low	High	Low	High	Medium	Medium	-do-	-do-
14.	Uttar Pradesh	-do-	-do-	-do-	-do-	-do-	-do-	Low	High	-do-	-do-
15.	West Bengal	-do-	-do-	-do-	-do-	-do-	-do-	-do-	-do-	-do-	-do-

* If respondents are more than 90 per cent in any category, that particular category is selected.

H : High
M : Medium
L : Low

TABLE 4.12: **Responsiveness of PR Members towards the Problems of People**

S. N.	Name of the state	How PR members attend to people's problems (In a few cases / In some cases / In many cases) *		
		Concerned with the problems of all	Indifferent	More concerned with the problems of their own group
1.	Andhra Pradesh	In some cases	In a few cases	In many cases
2.	Assam	-	-	-
3.	Gujarat	In some cases	In a few cases	In many cases
4.	Haryana	-do-	In some cases	-do-
5.	Karnataka	-do-	-do-	-do-
6.	Kerala	In many cases	In a few cases	In some cases
7.	Madhya Pradesh	In some cases	-do-	In many cases
8.	Maharashtra	-do-	-do-	-do-
9.	Meghalaya	-	-	-
10.	Orissa	In some cases	In a few cases	In many cases
11.	Punjab	-do-	-do-	-do-
12.	Rajasthan	-do-	-do-	-do-
13.	Tamil Nadu	-do-	-do-	-do-
14.	Uttar Pradesh	-do-	-do-	In many cases
15.	West Bengal	-do-	-do-	In some cases

* If respondents are more than 90 per cent in any category, that particular category is selected.

- *Responsiveness about the Implementation of Works:* In order to know about the discussion in the gram sabha regarding the implementation of works, it is evident from the table 4.13 that it takes place only in some cases. And what was peculiar in the case of Uttar Pradesh was that the discussion does not take place in the gram sabha, as indicated by the people. In this state, the people mentioned that during gram sabha such issues do not find any prominence and generally the chairpersons try to avoid discussion. Moreover, even if the discussion takes place the PR members avoid giving answers and hardly they provide any satisfactory answer. Besides, when the discussion in the gram sabha is not satisfactory, the follow-up action by the PR members is only in a few cases. Thus in a way, in all the states (except in Kerala), the responsiveness of PR members towards the issues of implementation of works is not ensured in the gram sabha.

  Against the above observation, in Kerala the PR members are accountable to gram sabha and they reply to the questions raised by the members in a satisfactory manner. Also, the PR members take the follow-up action as per the discussion in the gram sabha. In this context, it was observed that the performance in Kerala appeared to be satisfactory due to enlightened people, responsive PR members and strong initiative by the government.

TABLE 4.13: Responsiveness of PR Members in the Gram Sabha about the Implementation of Works at the GP Level
(In a few cases / In some cases / In most of the cases / In all the cases) *

S.N.	Name of the state	Discussion in the gram sabha about the implementation	Answers given by PR members: Satisfactorily	Answers given by PR members: Avoid giving answering	Follow-up action taken by the PR members
1.	Andhra Pradesh	In some cases	In a few cases	In most of the cases	In a few cases
2.	Assam	-	-	-	-
3.	Gujarat	In some cases	In a few cases	In most of the cases	In a few cases
4.	Haryana	-do-	-do-	-do-	-do-
5.	Karnataka	-do-	-do-	-do-	-do-
6.	Kerala	All cases	In most of the cases	In a few cases	In all cases
7.	Madhya Pradesh	In some cases	In a few cases	In most of the cases	In a few cases
8.	Maharashtra	-do-	-do-	-do-	-do-
9.	Meghalaya	-	-	-	-
10.	Orissa	In some cases	In a few cases	In most of the cases	In a few cases
11.	Punjab	-do-	-do-	-do-	-do-
12.	Rajasthan	-do-	-do-	-do-	-do-
13.	Tamil Nadu	-do-	-do-	-do-	-do-
14.	Uttar Pradesh	No	-do-	-do-	-do-
15.	West Bengal	In some cases	-do-	-do-	-do-

* If respondents are more than 90 per cent in any category, that particular category is selected.

- *Advantages to People through PR System:* The basic purpose of the PR system is to attend to the local problems. Now, how these problems are attended to can be seen from table 4.14. It reflects that only to some extent local problems are discussed, partially these problems are solved and in a few cases these are attended to in time.

  What is a cause of concern is that the problems of poor / landless are not given due importance. The panchayats give low attention to their problems. In this context the observations, as given in the table 4.14, may be referred. As regards the quality of work, there is a marginal improvement in all the states. In contrast, in Kerala the response of people is positive about the functioning of panchayats and it appears that the people are able to take advantages through decentralisation.

Support System

- *Infrastructural and manpower position of various line departments at the GP level:* The infrastructural position at the gram panchayat level is poor for most of the line departments (see table 4.15). Only partially some infrastructure exists for primary school, health, anganwadi centre (AWC) and drinking water. Same is true in the case of manpower support, as reflected by table 4.16. In the cases of Punjab and West Bengal, the position is comparatively better. Whereas when we compare with Kerala, the position is very much different and in this state all the departments as per table have basic infrastructural and manpower support.
- *Availability of funds, planning unit and administrative skills of PR members at the GP level:* The existing availability of funds with the gram panchayats (see table 4.17) is in the categories of centrally sponsored programmes, devolved funds from state plan, TFC grants and own source. However, the devolved funds are available in Kerala to a significant level, while the funds are placed with the zilla parishad in the states of Gujarat, Karnataka, Madhya Pradesh, Maharashtra and West Bengal, these funds are earmarked for certain programmes / schemes.

  As regards the planning unit, except in Kerala, it is handicapped by absence of manpower, lack of infrastructure and equipments. The planning methodology, which is crucial for the preparation of village action plan, is not formulated. The administrative skills (for planning and implementation of programmes) of PR members is poor in all the states except in Kerala.
- *Capacity of Gram Panchayats:* The existing status of PR institutions is very poor (see table 4.18). Neither do the institutions have funds to carry out programmes of their importance nor do they have proper infrastructural support nor is there proper manpower and logistics support. Besides, the functioning of PRIs is hampered due to low capabilities of elected members. Moreover, what is equally distressing is that no concrete steps are being taken in this regard. In the state of West Bengal, though some support has been provided, but that is not sufficient to give adequate strength to panchayats. Contrary to this, the local institutions in Kerala have sufficient funds for local area development, good

TABLE 4.14: **Advantages to People through PR System**

S.N.	Name of the State	Attending local problems *			Problems of poor/ landless handled *	Improvement in quality of work *
		Local problems discussed**	Local problems are solved**	Timeliness of attendance***	On priority basis/ In some cases / Low attention given	High/Marginal/ Same
1.	Andhra Pradesh	To some extent	Partially attended to	In a few cases	Low attention given	Marginal to same
2.	Assam	-	-	-	-	-
3.	Gujarat	To some extent	Partially attended to	In a few cases	Low attention given	Marginal to same
4.	Haryana	-do-	-do-	-do-	-do-	-do-
5.	Karnataka	-do-	-do-	-do-	In some cases	-do-
6.	Kerala	To a large extent	To some extent	In some cases	-do-	Marginal to High
7.	Madhya Pradesh	To some extent	Partially attended to	In a few cases	Low attention given	Marginal to same
8.	Maharashtra	-do-	-do-	-do-	-do-	-do-
9.	Meghalaya	-	-	-	-	-
10.	Orissa	To some extent	Partially attended to	In a few cases	Low attention given	Marginal to same
11.	Punjab	-do-	-do-	-do-	-do-	-do-
12.	Rajasthan	-do-	-do-	-do-	-do-	-do-
13.	Tamil Nadu	-do-	-do-	-do-	-do-	-do-
14.	Uttar Pradesh	-do-	-do-	-do-	-do-	-do-
15.	West Bengal	To a large extent	-do-	-do-	In some cases	High to marginal

* If respondents are more than 90 per cent in any category, that particular category is selected.
** (Partially / To some extent / To a large extent)

*** (In a few cases / In some cases / In many cases)

TABLE 4.15: **Infrastructural Position of Line Departments at the Gram Panchayat Level**

S.N.	Name of the state	Infrastructure for services / offices (Yes / No / Partial)										
		Primary edu.	Health centre	Drinking water	Road	AWC	Agriculture	Soil cons.	Vet.	Land (patwari)	Irrigation	Elect.
1.	Andhra Pradesh	Partial	Partial	Partial	Partial	Yes	No	No	No	No	No	No
2.	Assam	-do-	-do-	-do-	-do-	-do-	-do-	-do-	-do-	-do-	-do-	-do-
3.	Gujarat	-do-	-do-	-do-	Yes	-do-	-do-	-do-	Yes	-do-	-do-	-do-
4.	Haryana	-do-	-do-	-do-	-do-	-do-	Yes	-do-	-do-	-do-	-do-	-do-
5.	Karnataka	-do-	-do-	Yes	-do-	-do-	No	-do-	-do-	-do-	-do-	-do-
6.	Kerala	Yes	Yes	-do-	-do-	-do-	Yes	Yes	-do-	Yes	Yes	Yes
7.	Madhya Pradesh	Partial	Partial	Partial	Partial	-do-	No	No	No	No	No	No
8.	Maharashtra	-do-	-do-	-do-	-do-	-do-	-do-	-do-	-do-	-do-	-do-	-do-
9.	Meghalaya	-do-	-do-	-do-	-do-	-do-	-do-	-do-	-do-	-do-	-do-	-do-
10.	Orissa	-do-	-do-	-do-	-do-	-do-	-do-	-do-	-do-	-do-	-do-	-do-
11.	Punjab	-do-	-do-	Yes	Yes	-do-	Yes	Yes	-do-	Yes	-do-	Yes
12.	Rajasthan	-do-	-do-	Partial	Partial	-do-	No	No	-do-	-do-	-do-	No
13.	Tamil Nadu	-do-	-do-	-do-	-do-	-do-	-do-	-do-	-do-	-do-	-do-	-do-
14.	Uttar Pradesh	-do-	-do-	-do-	-do-	-do-	-do-	-do-	-do-	-do-	-do-	-do-
15.	West Bengal	-do-	Yes	Yes	Yes	-do-	-do-	-do-	-do-	-do-	Yes	Yes

Note : Partial means that part of the building exists, or drinking water is provided to some wards, or the quality of the water is not good, or roads are not provided to all the wards.

AWC : Anganwadi Centre, Vet.: Veterinary, Soil Cons.: Soil Conservation.

TABLE 4.16: **Manpower Position of Line Departments at the Gram Panchayat Level**

S.N.	Name of the state	Manpower for										
		Primary edu.	Health centre	Drinking water	Road	AWC	Agriculture	Soil cons.	Vet.	Land (tahsil)	Irrigation	Elect.
1.	Andhra Pradesh	Partial	Partial	Partial	Partial	Yes	No	No	No	No	No	No
2.	Assam	-do-	-do-	-do-	-do-	-do-	-do-	-do-	-do-	-do-	-do-	-do-
3.	Gujarat	-do-	-do-	-do-	-do-	-do-	-do-	-do-	-do-	-do-	-do-	-do-
4.	Haryana	-do-	-do-	-do-	-do-	-do-	Yes	-do-	-do-	-do-	-do-	-do-
5.	Karnataka	-do-	-do-	Yes	Yes	-do-	No	-do-	-do-	-do-	-do-	-do-
6.	Kerala	Yes	Yes	-do-	-do-	-do-	Yes	Yes	Yes	Yes	Yes	Yes
7.	Madhya Pradesh	Partial	Partial	Partial	Partial	-do-	No	No	No	No	No	No
8.	Maharashtra	-do-	-do-	-do-	-do-	-do-	-do-	-do-	-do-	-do-	-do-	-do-
9.	Meghalaya	-do-	-do-	-do-	-do-	-do-	-do-	-do-	-do-	-do-	-do-	-do-
10.	Orissa	-do-	-do-	-do-	-do-	-do-	-do-	-do-	-do-	-do-	-do-	-do-
11.	Punjab	-do-	-do-	Yes	Yes	-do-	Yes	Yes	Yes	Yes	-do-	Yes
12.	Rajasthan	-do-	-do-	Partial	Partial	-do-	No	No	No	-do-	-do-	No
13.	Tamil Nadu	-do-	-do-	-do-	-do-	-do-	-do-	-do-	-do-	-do-	-do-	-do-
14.	Uttar Pradesh	-do-	-do-	-do-	-do-	-do-	-do-	-do-	-do-	-do-	-do-	-do-
15.	West Bengal	-do-	-do-	Yes	Yes	-do-	-do-	-do-	Yes	-do-	Yes	Yes

Note : Partial means either there is less number of manpower than required, or one functionary is in-charge of more than one GP.

TABLE 4.17: **Funds Position, Planning Unit and Administrative Skills of PR Members at the GP Level**

S.N.	Name of the state	Funds (Yes / No)				Planning unit (Yes / No)				Administrative skills for planning and implementation *
		Centrally sponsored	Devolved funds from state plan	TFC grants	Own source	Manpower	Infrastructure	Equipments	Planning methodology	Good / Partial / Very less
1.	Andhra Pradesh	Yes	No	Yes	Yes	No	No	No	No	Partial to very less
2.	Assam	-do-	-do-	-do-	No	-do-	-do-	-do-	-do-	-
3.	Gujarat	-do-	-do-	-do-	Yes	-do-	-do-	-do-	-do-	Partial
4.	Haryana	-do-	-do-	-do-	-do-	-do-	-do-	-do-	-do-	Very less
5.	Karnataka	-do-	-do-	-do-	-do-	-do-	-do-	-do-	-do-	Partial
6.	Kerala	-do-	Yes	-do-	-do-	Yes	Yes	Yes	Yes	Good
7.	Madhya Pradesh	-do-	No	-do-	-do-	No	No	No	No	Partial to very less
8.	Maharashtra	-do-	-do-	-do-	-do-	-do-	-do-	-do-	-do-	-do-
9.	Meghalaya	-do-	-do-	Nil	Nil	-do-	-do-	-do-	-do-	-
10.	Orissa	-do-	-do-	Yes	Yes	-do-	-do-	-do-	-do-	Very less
11.	Punjab	-do-	-do-	-do-	-do-	-do-	-do-	-do-	-do-	-do-
12.	Rajasthan	-do-	-do-	-do-	-do-	-do-	-do-	-do-	-do-	-do-
13.	Tamil Nadu	-do-	-do-	-do-	-do-	-do-	-do-	-do-	-do-	-do-
14.	Uttar Pradesh	-do-	-do-	-do-	-do-	-do-	-do-	-do-	-do-	-do-
15.	West Bengal	-do-	-do-	-do-	-do-	-do-	-do-	-do-	-do-	Partial

* If respondents are more than 90 per cent in any category, that particular category is selected.

TABLE 4.18: **Capacity of Gram Panchayats**

S. N.	Name of the state	Capacity of Gram Panchayats (High / Medium / Low) *								Capacity to handle the development issues (L / M / H) *
		Educational level of PR members	Capabilities of PR members	Funds devolved	Infrastructure	Manpower	Logistics	Panchayat office	Panchayat secy.	
1.	Andhra Pradesh	Low	Low	Low	Low	Low	Low	Small office (1-2 rooms)	One for 3-5 GPs	Low
2.	Assam	-	-	Low	Low	Low	Low	-do-	-do-	-do-
3.	Gujarat	Low	Low	Low	Low	Low	Low	-do-	-do-	-do-
4.	Haryana	-do-	-do-	-do-	-do-	-do-	-do-	-do-	-do-	-do-
5.	Karnataka	-do-	-do-	-do-	-do-	Medium	-do-	Bigger office (2-3 rooms)	-do-	Medium
6.	Kerala	High	Medium	High	High	High	High	Full office building (5-6 rooms with library)	One for each GP	High
7.	Madhya Pradesh	Low	Low	Low	Low	Low	Low	Small office (1-2 rooms)	One for each GP	Low
8.	Maharashtra	-do-	-do-	-do-	-do-	-do-	-do-	-do-	One staff for 3-5 GPs	-do-
9.	Meghalaya	-	-	Low	Low	Low	Low	-do-	-do-	-do-
10.	Orissa	Low	Low	Low	Low	Low	Low	-do-	-do-	-do-
11.	Punjab	Medium	-do-	-do-	Medium	-do-	-do-	-do-	-do-	-do-
12.	Rajasthan	Low	-do-	-do-	Low	-do-	-do-	-do-	-do-	-do-
13.	Tamil Nadu	-do-	-do-	-do-	-do-	-do-	-do-	-do-	-do-	-do-
14.	Uttar Pradesh	-do-	-do-	-do-	-do-	-do-	-do-	-do-	-do-	-do-
15.	West Bengal	-do-	-do-	-do-	Medium	Medium	-do-	Bigger office (3-4 rooms)	One for each GP	Medium

* If respondents are more than 90 per cent in any category, that particular category is selected.

H : High M : Medium L : Low

infrastructural condition, adequate manpower and logistics support, besides higher capabilities of PR members.

As regards the handling of development issues, the people are of the opinion that these issues are not handled successfully by the panchayats. The reasons cited for such a state are: *first*, low capacities of panchayats to deliver; and, second, lack of abilities on the part of PR members to manage problems. But in both the above cases the findings are different in Kerala, which are well-presented in the concerned table.

- *Transparency in the Functioning of Gram Panchayat:* For the purpose of assessing the transparency four elements viz., identification of works, identification of work-sites, placement of work-order and display of accounts of works have been chosen. With regard to first two elements, except in Kerala, it is the chairperson of the gram panchayat in all the states who takes the decisions in most of the cases and the gram sabha does not take decision. With respect to third element the works are executed either by chairpersons of gram panchayats or by the departments, while in Kerala the beneficiaries committee implement most of the works.

  Similarly, the display of accounts (in spite of government order) of works carried out by the gram panchayat is not done in almost all the states with the exception of Kerala, and only in some cases it is done in the states of Gujarat, Karnataka, Madhya Pradesh, Maharashtra and West Bengal. (In this context, it also came out during the survey that in some cases the names of the beneficiaries are added even after the meeting of gram sabha and then forwarded to block.)

- *System for Addressing People's Grievances and Implementation of Programmes at the GP Level:* People's participation is the core of the panchayati raj system and addressing people's grievances is vital for the success of the system. It was attempted to ascertain the factors that affect the addressal of people's grievances. It revealed (see table 4.20) that the responsiveness of PR members is the most important of all the factors in all the states. This means that the PR members have vital role in addressing the people's grievances and the addressal mainly depends on their responsiveness. But in Kerala, as revealed by people, other factors such as people's knowledge and the role of gram sabha make equally important contribution in this context. It reflects that the people (in Kerala) have the opinion that the individual's knowledge is important in putting their grievances in the gram sabha, in which the PR members should attend to their grievances.

  As regards the implementation of programmes, the people in Kerala have stated that the factors that are crucial are 'beneficiaries' involvement', 'work by beneficiaries committee', 'manpower support' and 'logistics support'. In this context it is worth mentioning that in this state government has prescribed a very systematic procedure (for involving the beneficiaries, with adequate role of gram sabha and panchayat) for the implementation of programmes and it is followed by the panchayats meticulously. While in other states, as per the survey, one factor namely, 'manpower support' is of some significance, while the other factors do not have much importance. It could be that the people are not involved in the implementation of programmes, so they are not able to

TABLE 4.19: **Transparency in the Implementation of Works at the GP Level**

(In a few cases / In some cases / In most of the cases) *

S.N.	Name of the state	Identification of works			Identification of work-sites			Placement of work-order			Display of accounts of works
		In the gram sabha	By chair-person	By the GP body	In the gram sabha	By chair-person	By the GP body	To the beneficiaries committee	To the departments	By chair-person	Yes / No
1.	Andhra Pradesh	In some cases	In most of the cases	In a few cases	In a few cases	In most of the cases	In a few cases	No	In most of the cases	In some cases	No
2.	Assam	-do-	-do-	-do-	-do-	-do-	-do-	-do-	-do-	-do-	-do-
3.	Gujarat	-do-	-do-	-do-	-do-	-do-	-do-	-do-	-do-	-do-	In some cases
4.	Haryana	-do-	-do-	-do-	-do-	-do-	-do-	-do-	-do-	-do-	No
5.	Karnataka	-do-	In some cases	-do-	-do-	-do-	-do-	-do-	-do-	-do-	In some cases
6.	Kerala	In most of the cases	No	-do-	Yes	In a few cases	No	Yes	In a few cases	No	Yes
7.	Madhya Pradesh	In some cases	In most of the cases	-do-	In a few cases	In most of the cases	In a few cases	No	In most of the cases	In some cases	In some cases
8.	Maharashtra	-do-	-do-	-do-	-do-	-do-	-do-	-do-	-do-	-do-	-do-
9.	Meghalaya	-do-	-do-	-do-	-do-	-do-	-do-	-do-	-do-	-do-	No
10.	Orissa	-do-	-do-	-do-	-do-	-do-	-do-	-do-	-do-	-do-	-do-
11.	Punjab	-do-	-do-	-do-	-do-	-do-	-do-	-do-	-do-	-do-	-do-
12.	Rajasthan	-do-	-do-	-do-	-do-	-do-	-do-	-do-	-do-	-do-	-do-
13.	Tamil Nadu	-do-	-do-	-do-	-do-	-do-	-do-	-do-	-do-	-do-	-do-
14.	Uttar Pradesh	-do-	-do-	-do-	-do-	-do-	-do-	-do-	-do-	-do-	-do-
15.	West Bengal	-do-	-do-	In some cases	-do-	-do-	-do-	-do-	-do-	-do-	In some cases

* If respondents are more than 90% in any category, that particular category is selected.

TABLE 4.20: **Support System for Addressing People's Grievances and Implementation of Programmes at the GP Level**

S.N.	Name of the state	Factors for addressing people's grievances (H / M / L) *				Factors for implementation of programmes (H / M / L) *			
		People's knowledge	Responsiveness of PR members	Response of officers and staff	Role of gram sabha	Beneficiaries involvement	Work by beneficiaries committee	Manpower support	Logistics support
1.	Andhra Pradesh	Low	High	Low	Low	Low	Low	High	Medium
2.	Assam	-	-	-	-	-	-	-	-
3.	Gujarat	Medium	Medium	Medium	Medium	Medium	Low	High	Medium
4.	Haryana	-do-	-do-	-do-	-do-	Low	-do-	-do-	-do-
5.	Karnataka	-do-	-do-	-do-	-do-	-do-	-do-	-do-	-do-
6.	Kerala	High	High	Medium	High	High	High	High	-do-
7.	Madhya Pradesh	Low	-do-	Low	Low	Low	Low	-do-	Low
8.	Maharashtra	-do-	-do-	-do-	-do-	-do-	-do-	-do-	-do-
9.	Meghalaya	-	-	-	-	-	-	-	-
10.	Orissa	Low	High	Low	Low	Low	Low	High	Low
11.	Punjab	-do-	Medium	Medium	-do-	Medium	-do-	Medium	Medium
12.	Rajasthan	Medium	-do-	-do-	Medium	-do-	-do-	-do-	-do-
13.	Tamil Nadu	-do-	-do-	-do-	-do-	Low	-do-	-do-	-do-
14.	Uttar Pradesh	-do-	High	Medium	-do-	-do-	-do-	High	-do-
15.	West Bengal	-do-	-do-	-do-	-do-	-do-	-do-	-do-	-do-

* If respondents are more than 90 per cent in any category, that particular category is selected.

H : High

M : Medium

L : Low

visualise their role. And, as informed by the people during the survey, the implementation of works is normally the discretion of the chairperson of gram panchayat.

Miscellaneous Issues

- *Conflicts among PR Members and Officials:* The panchayat functioning is marked with various types of conflicting situations among PR members. These include (see table 4.21) inter-group conflicts, selection of project, placement of work-order and transfer of personnel. Among these the first and third are the dominant factors for conflicts among PR members. Conflicts arise due to differences among members of different groups and in some cases the rival group makes efforts to stop the execution of work. In most of the states, it was reported that it is often than not the panchayat functioning gets affected due to conflicts and that vitiates the working atmosphere considerably.

  Similarly, there are instances of conflicts between PR members and officers on various issues such as selection of project, placement of work-order and posting of field staff. And in the absence of proper demarcation of roles and responsibilities between them, the conflicts keep cropping up frequently. But in the state of Kerala, there are lesser conflicting situations due to better coordination and defining of the responsibilities of elected members and line departments.
- *Structure of PR system and structural problems:* The existing system of panchayati raj envisages three-tier arrangement at district, block and gram panchayat levels. Now, how this arrangement is working under the present system has been evaluated.

  The survey has shown (see table 4.22) that in all the states the problems of lower tiers are not attended to by the higher tiers. The reasons cited for this state of affairs are: *first*, lack of clarity about the roles and responsibilities among the members of higher tiers; *second*, the members of higher tiers have their own agenda which normally does not match with that of gram panchayats; *third*, inter-group conflicts; *fourth*, overlapping functions among three tiers; and, *finally*, lack of responsiveness among the members of higher tiers about the problems of gram panchayats. But in Kerala state, the problems of gram panchayats are attended to partially by the higher tiers, as certain measures have been initiated by the government for organic linkage of panchayats at all the three tiers.

  During the survey, majority of people opined that the chairperson of gram panchayat should be represented in all the three tiers, that the gram panchayats should be represented in all the three tiers, that there is no need for separate election for the constituencies of higher tiers and that the MLAs and MPs should not be represented in any of the three tiers. Such findings have come out due to the fact that the people want that the gram panchayats should get voice in the higher tiers.

  Due to these structural problems, the functioning of PR institutions is not smooth due to conflicts among three tiers. As ascertained, it is due to overlapping roles and functions among three tiers and also between PRIs on the one hand and departments on the other. All the tiers keep implementing similar works under various programmes without much co-ordination among them and come in conflict. While in the state of Kerala, the functioning

TABLE 4.21: **Conflicts among PR Members and Officials**

S.N.	Name of the state	Type of conflicts among PR members (H / M / L) *					Type of conflicts between PR members and officers (H / M / L)*			
		Inter-group conflicts	Over selection of projects	Over placement of work-order	Over development issues	Any other	Over selection of projects	Over placement of work-order	Over posting of field staff	Any other
1.	Andhra Pradesh	High	Medium	High	Low	-	Medium	High	High	-
2.	Assam	-	-	-	-	-	-	-	-	-
3.	Gujarat	High	Medium	High	Low	-	Medium	High	High	-
4.	Haryana	-do-	-do-	-do-	-do-	-	-do-	Medium	-do-	-
5.	Karnataka	-do-	-do-	-do-	-do-	-	-do-	-do-	-do-	-
6.	Kerala	-do-	Low	Low	Medium	-	Low	Low	Low	-
7.	Madhya Pradesh	-do-	-do-	High	-do-	-	Medium	High	High	-
8.	Maharashtra	-do-	-do-	-do-	-do-	-	-do-	-do-	-do-	-
9.	Meghalaya	-	-	-	-	-	-	-	-	-
10.	Orissa	Medium	Low	High	Low	-	Medium	High	High	-
11.	Punjab	-do-	-do-	-do-	-do-	-	-do-	-do-	-do-	-
12.	Rajasthan	-do-	-do-	-do-	-do-	-	-do-	Medium	-do-	-
13.	Tamil Nadu	High	-do-	-do	-do-	-	-do-	-do-	Medium	-
14.	Uttar Pradesh	-do-	-do-	-do-	-do-	-	High	High	High	-
15.	West Bengal	-do-	-do-	-do-	-do-	-	-do-	-do-	-do-	-

* If respondents are more than 90 per cent in any category, that particular category is selected.

H : High

M : Medium

L : Low

TABLE 4.22: **Structure of PR System**

S.N.	Name of the state	Issues					Structural problems inter-tier functioning smooth / workable/ conflicting situations*
		Whether presently the problems of lower tiers are attended to by the higher tiers (Y/N)	Whether the chairperson of GP should be the member in all the three tiers (Y/N)	Whether		Whether the MLAs and MPs should be re-presented in all the three tiers (%age of cases) (Y / N)	
				the GP should represent all the three tiers (Y/N)	there is a need for separate election for the constituen-cies of higher tiers (Y/N)		
1.	Andhra Pradesh	No	Yes	Yes	85 (No)	95 (No)	Conflicting situations
2.	Assam	-	-	-	-	-	-
3.	Gujarat	-do-	-do-	-do-	95 (No)	95 (No)	Conflicting situations
4.	Haryana	-do-	-do-	-do-	80 (-do-)	100 (-do-)	-do-
5.	Karnataka	-do-	-do-	-do-	80 (-do-)	80 (-do-)	-do-
6.	Kerala	Partially	-do-	-do-	90 (-do-)	95 (-do-)	Workable
7.	Madhya Pradesh	No	-do-	-do-	85 (-do-)	100 (-do-)	Conflicting situations
8.	Maharashtra	-do-	-do-	-do-	95 (-do-)	85 (-do-)	-do-
9.	Meghalaya	-	-	-	-	-	-
10.	Orissa	-do-	-do-	-do-	90 (No)	90 (No)	Conflicting situations
11.	Punjab	-do-	-do-	-do-	95 (-do-)	100 (-do-)	-do-
12.	Rajasthan	-do-	-do-	-do-	85 (-do-)	95 (-do-)	-do-
13.	Tamil Nadu	-do-	-do-	-do-	90 (-do-)	95 (-do-)	-do-
14.	Uttar Pradesh	-do-	-do-	-do-	95 (-do-)	100 (-do-)	-do-
15.	West Bengal	-do-	-do-	-do-	85 (-do-)	100 (-do-)	-do-

* If respondents are more than 90 per cent in any category, that particular category is selected.

is comparatively better as the roles and responsibilities have been clearly demarcated by the specific government order.

- *Perceptions and expectations of people about the panchayats:* The survey also tried to elicit the view of people on their perceptions about and expectations from the panchayats. In most of the staffs, they perceive the present environment at the panchayat level as conflicting or passive, with the exceptions of Kerala. While, in the state of UP, the environment is negative. As regards the capabilities of PR members and capacity of panchayats to deliver, their perception is on the lower side of the scale in all the states except in Kerala (see table 4.23).

  As per the survey, they seem to be having low expectations from the present status of panchayats. And regarding the future expected role from panchayats, they have expressed their desire for attending the issues like ensuring smooth functioning of schools for improved education and health centres for timely availability of medicines, presence of health staff; providing opportunities for employment, creating infrastructure for irrigation, roads, etc.; developing the marketing facilities for agriculture, handloom products, etc.; facilitating the availability of credit; providing essential commodities in time, facilitating in the availability of land and other certificates and so on.
- *Wide Variance between Actual Functioning and Expected Role from Panchayats:* If we carefully examine this issue, it is evident that there is a wide variance between what is being presently transacted in the gram sabha (or performed by the gram panchayat) and what the people expect from the panchayats. In this context the table 4.10 can be referred, which shows that the main focus of the gram sabha has been on issues like construction activities, selection of beneficiaries, complaints regarding PDS or absenteeism of school teacher or health worker and approval of accounts and budget, which do not encompass the development priorities that are needed in a village as evinced by people, as reflected by table 4.23.

Finances of Panchayats

- *Important Contributors in Total Taxes of Panchayats:* Contribution of three important taxes in the total taxes was studied at the gram panchayat level. These are personal tax (tax levied on personal income and property), income from panchayat property and user charges. It was found that the personal tax is high (see table 4.24) in the states of Kerala and Maharashtra. In these states contribution of property tax is significant and in addition to it, the profession tax has some share in tax revenue in Kerala. As regards the income from panchayat property, it is highly significant in the states of Punjab and Haryana and it has more than 80 per cent contribution in the total tax revenue. In these states the gram panchayat agricultural land (panchayat property[1]) is auctioned for raising crops, fetching

[1] The income from panchayat property is from gram panchayat agricultural land, which is auctioned for a certain period. Income is either through plantation or agriculture crop, in which normally the local people take part either from the same gram panchayat or nearby panchayats.

TABLE 4.23: **Perceptions and Expectations of People about the Panchayat Functioning**

S.N.	Name of the state	Perceptions of People			Expectations of People	
		Present environment at the panchayat level (Conducive / Conflicting / Passive/ Negative)	About the capabilities of PR members (Low / Medium / High) *	About the capacity of panchayats to deliver (Low / Medium / High) *	From the present status of panchayats (High /Medium / Low) *	Future expected role from panchayats
1.	Andhra Pradesh	Conflicting	Low	Low	Low	- To ensure smooth functioning of schools for improved education and health centres for timely availability of medicines, presence of health staff.
2.	Assam	-	-	-	-	
3.	Gujarat	Passive	Low	Low	Low	
4.	Haryana	Conflicting	-do-	-do-	-do-	
5.	Karnataka	Passive	-do-	-do-	Medium	- To provide opportunities for employment
6.	Kerala	Conducive	Medium	High	-do-	- To create infrastructure for irrigation, roads, etc.
7.	Madhya Pradesh	Passive	Low	Low	Low	
8.	Maharashtra	-do-	-do-	-do-	-do-	- To develop the marketing facilities for agriculture, handloom products, etc.
9.	Meghalaya	-	-	-	-	
10.	Orissa	Passive	Low	Low	Low	- To facilitate the availability of credit in time
11.	Punjab	-do-	-do-	-do-	-do-	
12.	Rajasthan	-do-	-do-	-do-	-do-	- To provide essential commodities in time
13.	Tamil Nadu	Conflicting	-do-	-do-	-do-	- To facilitate the availability of land and other certificates, and so on.
14.	Uttar Pradesh	Negative	-do-	-do-	-do-	
15.	West Bengal	Conflicting	-do-	-do-	Medium	

* If respondents are more than 90 per cent in any category, that particular category is selected.

TABLE 4.24: **Important Contributors in Total Taxes Collected by the Gram Panchayats (1997-98)**

(fig. in %age)

S.N.	Name of the state	Own tax (Personal tax*)	Own non-tax		Others ***	Percentage of households paying the taxes	Tax collection as percentage of demand
			Income from panchayat property **	Users charges			
1.	Andhra Pradesh	18	2	20	60	43	56
2.	Assam	Nil	Nil	Nil	Nil	Nil	Nil
3.	Gujarat	29	5	35	31	49	61
4.	Haryana	5	88	Nil	7	4	75
5.	Karnataka	12	7	29	52	46	66
6.	Kerala	39	4	32	25	79	72
7.	Madhya Pradesh	18	6	22	54	38	51
8.	Maharashtra	41	3	41	15	61	65
9.	Meghalaya	Nil	Nil	Nil	Nil	Nil	Nil
10.	Orissa	10	2	12	76	29	46
11.	Punjab	7	89	Nil	4	5	70
12.	Rajasthan	12	4	11	73	28	35
13.	Tamil Nadu	15	3	13	69	31	46
14.	Uttar Pradesh	7	4	Nil	89	6	45
15.	West Bengal	12	2	21	65	32	57

* Tax on Profession, Property, Vehicles and Animals.

** Panchayat property: It includes panchayat land, tanks, etc.

*** 'Others' will include income from royalty, fee, etc.

good revenue to gram panchayats. Higher income from panchayat property vis-a-vis other tax items reflects low contribution by individuals in Punjab and Haryana.

With regards to user charges, the states like Gujarat, Karnataka, Kerala and Maharashtra have better contribution. While the states like Haryana, Punjab and Uttar Pradesh have very insignificant contribution. Also, the performance of Orissa, Rajasthan and Tamil Nadu is poor. In sum, the contribution of user charges under non-tax revenue is not encouraging except in a few states. It only reflects that either the gram panchayats are not keen to impose user charges or the people are not willing to pay. And the income from other sources that mainly include royalty (from minor minerals in the mining areas) is quite significant in many states viz. Andhra Pradesh, Karnataka, Madhya Pradesh, Orissa, Rajasthan, Tamil Nadu, Uttar Pradesh and West Bengal.

If we examine the percentage of households paying taxes, it is less than 50 per cent in most of the states. Only in the state of Kerala and to some extent in Maharashtra, percentage is higher. As regards the percentage of collection of demand, it is more than 50 per cent in the states of Andhra Pradesh, Gujarat, Haryana, Karnataka, Kerala, Madhya Pradesh, Punjab and West Bengal, while in other states it is less than 50 per cent and the lowest is in the state of Rajasthan (and the collection in Meghalaya and Assam is nil).

The above observations lead us to conclude that in most of the states the contributions by individuals under personal tax is poor, also the contribution of user charges is low, and the main source of income remains panchayat property or royalty.

- *Composition of own Non-tax Income:* A specific attempt was made to know the composition of non-tax revenue. It revealed that there are three sources (see table 4.25) viz., income from panchayat property, user charges, and royalty from mining and license fee from small industries, which have major contribution in the non-tax revenue. The income from user charges is significantly good in the states of Gujarat, Karnataka, Kerala and Maharashtra. And the percentage of households paying user charges is high in the states of Kerala and Maharashtra, while in other states, less than 50 per cent households contribute and in the states like Assam, Haryana, Meghalaya, Punjab and Uttar Pradesh contribution is nil. As regards the income from panchayat property, it is high in the states of Haryana and Punjab. In the case of royalty from mining and license fee from small industries, it is significant in the states of Andhra Pradesh, Karnataka, Madhya Pradesh, Orissa, Rajasthan, Tamil Nadu, Uttar Pradesh and West Bengal (see Box 4.1).

  If we closely examine Box 4.1, in most of the states the main income for panchayats has come from royalty from mining and license fee from small industries, which in any case is not the contribution from local people as normally people from outside take permission for setting up industries or for mining purposes. The above findings also indicate that majority of the states does not attract much income from panchayat property and user charges. That means people in the gram panchayats are not in a position to contribute enough for the own income of panchayats.
- *Own Income, Devolved Funds and Grants:* The survey has revealed that the per capita

TABLE 4.25: **Composition of own Non-tax Income (1997-98)**

(fig. in %age)

S.N.	Name of the state	Own non-tax income				Percentage of households paying the users charges
		Users charges	Income from panchayat property*	Royalty from mining and license fee from small industries	Other sources	
1.	Andhra Pradesh	22	5	41	32	39
2.	Assam	Nil	Nil	Nil	Nil	Nil
3.	Gujarat	43	8	27	22	41
4.	Haryana	Nil	92	6	2	Nil
5.	Karnataka	34	9	37	20	42
6.	Kerala	42	11	21	26	76
7.	Madhya Pradesh	26	10	57	7	31
8.	Maharashtra	59	6	28	7	56
9.	Meghalaya	Nil	Nil	Nil	Nil	Nil
10.	Orissa	18	4	56	22	20
11.	Punjab	Nil	94	5	1	Nil
12.	Rajasthan	19	6	52	23	24
13.	Tamil Nadu	19	5	49	27	29
14.	Uttar Pradesh	Nil	6	78	16	Nil
15.	West Bengal	29	7	42	22	29

* Panchayat property: It includes panchayat land, tanks, etc.

BOX 4.1: Comparative Status of Various States regarding Tax Collection by Panchayats

S.No.	Type of tax	Item of taxes	States having more contribution
1.	Tax revenue	Personal tax	Kerala and Maharashtra
2.	Own non-tax income	- income from panchayat property	Punjab and Haryana
		- User charges	Gujarat, Karnataka, Kerala and Maharashtra
		- Royalty from mining and license fee from small industries	Andhra Pradesh, Karnataka, Madhya Pradesh, Orissa, Rajasthan, Tamil Nadu, Uttar Pradesh and West Bengal

own income is high (see table 4.26) in the states of Gujarat, Haryana, Karnataka, Kerala, Maharashtra, Rajasthan and Tamil Nadu. But a careful examination reveals that own income is higher in the gram panchayats, which are near to towns or industrial areas with the exception of Kerala. In the state of Kerala the gram panchayat in the rural area is having high income that is very encouraging. In this state, the gram panchayat income is as high as Rs.12.25 lakhs and the per capita income is Rs 57.50. While in other states, the same are comparatively much lower. If we look at the devolved funds at the gram panchayat level, it is only in the state of Kerala. Besides, the gram panchayat also has good amount under development grants and thus the total income with the gram panchayat is substantially high. The per capita availability of income with the gram panchayat is significantly high at Rs.403.58, which is much higher in comparison to other states. (Though average own income of gram panchayats in Punjab is low in the table 4.26, it only reflects about those where the field study was undertaken while the own income of other GPs is high, see table 4.27)

- *Own Income, Own Outlay and Devolved Funds in the Districts of Study Area:* The table 4.27 indicates that the devolved funds (untied) upon panchayats are only in Kerala, while in the states of Gujarat, Karnataka, Madhya Pradesh, Maharashtra and West Bengal, the funds are given to zilla parishad in the tied form, so the panchayats have no discretion. As regards the per capita income, it is very low in all the states except in Haryana, Kerala and Punjab, where it is Rs. 30.21, Rs. 39.59 and Rs. 30.23 respectively and the per capita own income as percentage of plan outlay stands at 7.07, 9.89 and 8.02 respectively.

In Kerala, significantly large devolved funds and own income of panchayats contribute a great deal in providing financial autonomy to panchayats.

4.3 Critical Observations

Based on the field studies and survey, as discussed in the preceding sections, the salient findings are summed up as follows:

TABLE 4.26: **Own Income, Devolved Funds and Grants at Gram Panchayat Level (1997-98)**

S.N	Name of the state	Av. total own income	Av. devolved funds	Av. grants (under CSP, TFC)	Av. total income	Own income as % age of total income	Average per family own income	Per capita						
								Own income				Devolved funds	Grants	Total income
								Of all GPs	Of GPs near towns and inds. **	Of GPs in other places	H/M/L			
1	Andhra Pradesh	4250	0.00	80,543	84,793	4.98	5.65	1.25	-	1.25	L	0.00	20.50	21.75
2	Assam	Nil	0.00	1,51,000	1,51,000	0.00	0.00	0.00	0.00	0.00	L	0.00	10.01	10.01
3	Gujarat (1)	12,19,545	0.00	2,15,000	14,34,545	85.00	59.52	12.12	12.12	-	H	0.00	2.11	14.23
4	Haryana *	1,25,300	0.00	1,50,000	2,75,300	45.51	153.22	30.95	30.95	-	H	0.00	9.50	40.45
5	Karnataka *(1)	3,11,000	0.00	95,000	4,06,000	78.529	310.40	67.50	67.50	-	H	0.00	16.25	83.75
6	Kerala	12,25,000	52,95,000	19,52,000	84,72,000	14.56	210.59	57.50	-	57.50	H	252.52	93.56	403.58
7	M.P.	12,538	0.00	1,35,565	1,48,103	8.46	30.25	6.50	-	6.50	L	0.00	58.50	65.00
8	Maharashtra *(1)	42,226	0.00	95,324	1,37,550	30.28	135.55	31.29	40.25	3.50	H	0.00	80.53	84.03
9	Meghalaya	Nil	0.00	54,000	54,000	0.00	0.00	0.00	0.00	0.00	L	0.00	64.53	64.53
10	Orissa	15,560	0.00	1,66,000	1,67,556	9.21	12.55	3.15	-	3.15	L	0.00	35.55	38.70
11	Punjab	17,785	0.00	65,870	83,655	21.19	38.28	7.95	-	7.95	M	0.00	34.64	42.59
12	Rajasthan * (1)	45,285	0.00	1,10,000	1,55,285	29.52	40.51	16.21	25.15	2.85	H	0.00	38.52	54.73
13	Tamil Nadu *	36,000	0.00	25,000	61,000	59.62	57.51	19.52	19.52	-	H	0.00	11.52	30.77
14	Uttar Pradesh	3,256	0.00	3,45,458	3,48,714	0.94	2.24	0.52	-	0.52	L	0.00	55.25	55.77
15	West Bengal	52,445	0.00	2,66,980	3,19,425	17.52	15.85	3.22	-	3.22	L	0.00	14.55	17.77

Source: Calculations based on data from concerned panchayat offices.

* In the GPs near to industries or towns, the own income of gram panchayats is high but in other GPs it is considerably low. And, this high income is not the representative picture of all the gram panchayats (see table 4.27).

(1) In these states, the income in other GPs of the district is comparatively far lower (also see table 4.27).

TABLE 4.27: **Own Income, Plan Outlay and Devolved Funds in the Districts of Study Area (1997-98)**

S. N.	Name of the state	Av. own income (of all tiers) (Rs. in lakhs)	Av. plan Outlay (Rs. in lakhs)	Av. devolved funds (untied) (Rs. in lakhs)	Per capita own-income of district (Rs.)	Per capita plan outlay in a district (Rs.)	Own-income as %age of total plan outlay	Per capita devolved funds (Rs.)
1	Andhra Pradesh	278.56	10,123,68	0.00	9.12	361.89	2.74	0.00
2	Assam	40.12	8,851.20	0.00	1.92	392.51	0.45	0.00
3	Gujarat	98.35	4,840.25	0.00 *	8.92	402.50	2.04	0.00
4	Haryana	121.52	1,710.31	0.00	30.21	410.21	7.07	0.00
5	Karnataka	225.65	6,124.59	0.00 *	15.56	408.56	3.81	0.00
6	Kerala	956.98	9,616.56	7,234.60	39.59	400.45	9.89	285.15
7	Madhya Pradesh	41.84	3,145.73	0.00 *	5.12	393.16	1.30	0.00
8	Maharashtra	425.15	12.367.87	0.00 *	14.15	412.52	3.43	0.00
9	Meghalaya	NA	-	-	-	-	-	-
10	Orissa	59.54	7,233.54	0.00	3.45	401.19	0.86	0.00
11	Punjab	615.35	7,524.56	0.00	30.23	376.97	8.02	0.0
12	Rajasthan	138.27	7,421.50	0.00	6.34	371.38	1.71	0.00
13	Tamil Nadu	224.56	17,200.56	0.00	4.12	380.89	1.08	0.00
14	Uttar Pradesh	58.22	7,243.91	0.00	3.29	393.68	0.84	0.00
15	West Bengal	96.36	8,795.52	0.00 *	3.94	387.57	1.02	00.00

Source: Calculations based on data from concerned block and panchayat offices.

*Though the funds are given to Zilla Parishads directly but these funds are basically earmarked for a particular department and also for a scheme.

Average per capita plan funds = Rs. 391.0, calculated from the above table.

NA : Not available.

- *Nomination of Candidates and Participation in Political Process:* The field observations reveal that the selection of the candidates for the panchayats is influenced by the existing political families or local elites and in many cases the candidates are relatives of the political people. It is invariably true in the case of woman members. Or, in other words, it is observed that common person (from the non-political family) has little chance of contesting and winning the elections. In a way, the present set-up at the panchayats level is facilitating the furtherance of the existing political base for a few political families or groups or village elites.
- *Election Campaign and Issues for Discussion:* The issues that are discussed during the election campaign have very narrow focus. The main issues for the discussion mainly pertain to construction of roads or village ponds or some such activities, while there is hardly any focus on the issues pertaining to improving the condition of primary education or health services or enhancing the crop yield or infrastructure. In several cases, even issues like settling political rivalry, dispute over personal or petty matters take precedent over socio-economic development problems. Thus, the issues concerning common person get overlooked.
- *Dummy Candidates:* There have been instances when some candidates have contested on behalf of someone else. It has been found mainly in the reserved category for SCs, STs and women. As, due to reservation, some people lose their chance to contest again so they propose the names of persons close to them for contesting election. In case they (reserved candidates) win they basically work on their proposers' behalf.
- *Election Process:* It is evident from field studies that the election process needs to be looked at seriously. The common man finds it difficult to participate or contest elections due to overwhelming or politically surcharged atmosphere. Instances of violence and other malpractices do not speak well about the process of elections. The political parties are keen to organise people during campaign and for casting vote on the day of poll, but not thereafter.
- *Election of Intermediate and Zilla Panchayats:* The Article 243C provides for direct election for members at all the three tiers. It stipulates for territorial constituencies at all the three tiers (while in the states having population less than twenty lakhs, the intermediate panchayats may be done away). The intermediate and district panchayats have electoral constituencies that are formed after combining the group of panchayats. Based on the field study, gram panchayat members and people have expressed that these higher tiers should be represented by the chairpersons of GPs. As such there should not be separate constituency for higher tiers, as they do not represent any particular GP or block. And, such constituencies (of higher tiers) are mere geographical boundaries (by combining part or full GPs or blocks, as the case may be).
- *Reservations for Women, SCs and STs:* If we examine the findings of the field study, it is quite evident though Acts have provided some political space to weaker sections, but there is no perceptible improvement in the functioning of panchayats as regards the handling of the problems of weaker sections. Presently, invariably in all the states with the exception

of Kerala, the gram panchayats activities are confined to, first, conducting gram sabha / panchayat meetings, second, selection of beneficiaries (which, in most cases, is the collection of names from each ward member or in some cases by other elected members viz., MLAs) and then followed by implementation of works that is mainly executed by the contractors (without the involvement of beneficiaries). And all these activities go on without looking into people's participation, planning needs, or accountability of elected members, leave alone the interest of weaker sections.

Besides, it appears that with the reservations, people under these categories (SC/ST and women) are restricting themselves to reserved seats. And due to low educational and economic level, landless people, SCs, tribals and women remain excluded from the panchayat functioning. Thus, reservations alone have only limited effects on inclusion, in the absence of programmes of education and empowerment for weaker sections.

- *Women as Chairpersons - Role of Husbands:* Under the new panchayat acts formulated by different states, 1/3rd of the seats are reserved for women. Even for chairpersons of gram panchayats, 1/3rd seats are reserved. It has provided good opportunity for the women to participate in the panchayat functioning. The literacy rate among women members is very low (many of them are illiterate or if literate they are just able to sign and only a few have crossed primary school) and there is a lack of awareness among them. These have led to a wide gap between the ability of the woman members (to function as chairpersons of GP) and the expected role. Not only this, as the seats have been reserved for the women, in many cases the wives of earlier elected representatives or influential people have contested election and become the chairpersons or ward members. These factors have made them dependent upon the family members, especially the husbands. For example, in Baulajholi GP in Orissa state, the woman GP *sarpanch* admitted during the village meeting (July 98) that she had to depend upon her husband for day-to-day work and mentioned, "The development activities and programmes are looked after by my husband", when she was asked how she managed the panchayat functioning. Similarly, in Andhra Pradesh the GP *sarpanch* (Tatpamla GP) had to depend upon her husband. In Tamil Nadu, the woman president of block panchayat (Wallajabad Block) had to be accompanied by her husband during block panchayat meetings and take advice from him for doing official work.

  There are several instances of inadequate performance but there are cases of competence among woman members also. For example, in the case of woman president of Pooyapalli GP in Kerala, she was able to officiate with full authority and to deliver efficiently. Rather, people were very particular for any aberration regarding the functioning of woman PR members. Similarly, in the case of Masoli GP in Uttar Pradesh, the woman *pradhan* was widely respected for her ability to run the panchayat functioning. Both these cases of success have one common factor — higher educational level and good knowledge about the panchayat functioning — which has helped these chairpersons in discharging their duties efficiently.

- *People's Participation in Gram Sabha:* The 73rd Constitution Amendment Act places high importance on the role of gram sabha and thereby seeks active involvement of people at the planning and implementation stages. The field studies clearly bring out that the people's participation is, by and large, overlooked by the panchayats. Only a handful of people, either village elites or those who are close to *sarpanch* speak in the gram sabha meetings. Or, otherwise, some opposition members raise voice, as if they have to settle some political score. As regards the gram sabha functioning, the agenda notes contain routine items like annual accounts, identification of beneficiaries or construction works. The issues discussed in the meeting have very limited focus. Further, the PR members seem to concentrate mainly on devolution of funds and functions while little thought is given to ensure full people's participation. There are certain categories of people, for example, women, marginalised groups (SCs / STs), labourers or debtors, who hesitate to speak in the village open meeting.

In a number of cases the quorum is not maintained in the first meeting due to low attendance and therefore another meeting is called where normally much lesser number attends and the necessary business is transacted (as no quorum is required in the second meeting). Here, if poor participation is analysed critically, it is mainly due to lack of information and knowledge with people, which is a result of poor education that deprives many from accessing basic information. Besides, the PR members do not make serious efforts for ensuring the attendance of people in the gram sabha (also see Box 4.2).

The performance of gram sabha is different in Kerala. The representative picture of attendance in the gram sabha is reflected categorically in the table 4.8 which shows that only Kerala is able to provide significantly high attendance of members in the gram sabha and other states are far behind. And high educational as well as awareness level among people have contributed a great deal in the state of Kerala.

During field study, people as well as panchayat members have expressed that they do not get the notice for the meeting. If sometimes they get, they just go to meeting for signing or putting the thumb impression. Sometimes the members of chairperson's groups put their signatures. More often the agenda items are read out to them, and without discussions, it is assumed that decisions are taken by doing so. It is observed that the chairpersons of gram panchayats try to avoid discussions in gram sabha or panchayat meetings due to a variety of behavioural reasons. Among others, there are factors like: the attitude that people should accept whatever they (chairpersons) propose; and ego, as how someone can question their authority. Cases are when they place their own agenda or ego over the genuine needs of village development. Generally, people try to avoid confrontation with or questioning of panchayat members, as it might lead to unending battle of ego or harassment.

If we take the case of Kerala, the environment building programme prepared people mentally (psychologically) and gave confidence to people and PR members that they can be a part of village development process. Besides, village level social structure is more egalitarian with fewer disparities on account of gender, caste or class. It has provided good foundation for grassroots democracy and contributed a great deal in people's participation meaningfully, from all sections especially weaker sections. It has provided a great strength to the process of decentralisation in general and strengthening of panchayats (local / people's institutions) in particular. While in other states, environment building has not been taken seriously and moreover there are wide disparities, especially on account of caste and gender that inhibit people to participate in local development.

As regards the propriety of the functioning of the gram sabha, there have been instances when the names of the beneficiaries are changed after the meeting. Also, in some cases the list of beneficiaries is prepared based on the list given by ward members or other public representatives, including MLAs. Due to non-transparent way of working, it would not be out of place to mention that the chairperson of GP and a few individuals have control over decision-making of gram panchayat.

BOX 4.2

Reasons for Poor People's Participation in Gram Sabha

- Inadequate information and knowledge with people.
- Lack of initiative by the PR members for organising gram sabha
- Negative attitude of opposition group as it is keener to pin the chairperson down, so chairpersons avoid holding GS and discussing issues.
- Indifference for people's participation and adequacy of culture of discussion and evolving consensus.
- Psychological barriers in people to raise issues.
- Disparities based on caste, class or gender.
- Insufficient procedures and rules to conduct gram sabha
- Structural problems —large members in the gram sabha, which leads to difficulty in managing the meeting.
- The gram sabha is able to do little for the majority of people, and they do not want to lose wages for the meeting.
- Lack of transparency in the preparation of proceedings.

- *Tendency to Centralise the Decision-Making:* It appears that there is a shift of decision-making from the state to lower panchayats through the process of decentralisation. However, there is no qualitative change with respect to people's participation in decision-making. Under the present state, there is an evolution of power centres at the district, block and the gram panchayat levels, where the decisions are taken by a few individuals. And, the people are not involved in the development process and they seem to remain marginalised.
- *PR Members' Role and their Approach for Local Development:* The PR members are mainly concerned with only convening the gram sabha or gram panchayat meetings, utilisation of funds, maintenance of accounts, etc., which are to be followed as per the

> If we take the case of Kerala, the environment building programme prepared people mentally (psychologically) and gave confidence to people and PR members that they can be a part of village development process. Besides, village level social structure is more egalitarian with fewer disparities on account of gender, caste or class. It has provided good foundation for grassroots democracy and contributed a great deal in people's participation meaningfully, from all sections especially weaker sections. It has provided a great strength to the process of decentralisation in general and strengthening of panchayats (local / people's institutions) in particular. While in other states, environment building has not been taken seriously and moreover there are wide disparities, especially on account of caste and gender that inhibit people to participate in local development.

statute or guidelines. But they are little concerned about the fundamental issues such as: how the people's participation should be encouraged; how the transparency in the functioning of panchayat should be brought; how the basic problems such as illiteracy, lack of health and sanitation that affect poor the most should be addressed; and how the resources of the panchayats can be augmented with the active participation of people. During the discussion in the panchayat, it has been abundantly clear that the PR members are more keen about, *first*, the funds and *second*, about the control over the transfer and postings of staff. For many of them powers and funds are an end itself. It is often observed that panchayat members are not inclined to involve people in discussions. Also, they do not have adequate perspective about people's participation, or resource planning, or transparency in functioning, let alone accountability.

Regarding their ability to deliver, it was observed that the elected representatives either lack confidence or are bogged down by group / party considerations or do not have sufficient capability to address the people's needs or are handicapped by low functional capacity (in terms of funds, infrastructure, manpower, etc.) of the panchayats.

- *Education, Training and Participation:* It is observed that the education (formal or informal) has far reaching impact on the capability of PR members and on the ability of the people to participate in the development process. The panchayat members with good educational background are able to appreciate and understand the functioning much better, while the members with illiteracy or low education find themselves in a disadvantageous position and are sometimes misled by panchayat secretaries or have to depend upon family members. The field studies indicate that:
    - Education and access to information have the most significant influence over the participation.
    - Participation rates among women rise considerably with higher education.
- *Lack of Responsiveness of PR Members:* As informed by people, lack of responsiveness among PR members has been noticed in a number of cases like functioning of PDS,

selection of beneficiaries, availability of drinking water, poor road conditions, etc. For example, during the field visit it was noticed, in the state of Uttar Pradesh, that the complaints of people (regarding PDS, drinking water, etc.) are not attended to by the *pradhans* of gram panchayats. Similar instances have been noticed in other states too. It has been quite evident during the field study that due to lack of addressal of problems, which can be sorted by chairpersons of GPs, they perceive little benefit from the panchayats.

- *Poor Manpower Support at Gram Panchayat Level:* Presently, in most of the states the available manpower at gram panchayat is only one functionary who is panchayat secretary (and in some states one functionary is in charge of more than one GP, see table 4.18). Under the new dispensation of decentralisation process, he is expected to perform the duties of various subjects entrusted to gram panchayat. These subjects vary from rural development to health, to agriculture, to irrigation and to marketing, which require certain technical knowledge and skills. It has been observed during the field visits that the present arrangement of staffing is not able to do the desired justice to the work. But in case of Kerala, the gram panchayat has better staff strengths and also the field staff of line departments report to gram panchayats for the works entrusted to them.
- *Poor Infrastructure at Gram Panchayat Level:* The infrastructural position at the gram panchayat level is very poor. The panchayats, except a few, do not have panchayat offices with meeting halls; school buildings do not have sufficient rooms; the health and veterinary centres are not available with all the panchayats; the offices of tube-wells and water supply departments are not constructed at the GP level; and infrastructure for marketing of agricultural products is not provided in all the panchayats. In the absence of these crucial infrastructural items, the gram panchayats find great difficulties in not only delivering the basic services to the people but also in conducting their office work. In the state of Kerala, infrastructural position is good and in some states like Haryana, Gujarat, Punjab, Karnataka and West Bengal some infrastructure is available partially.
- *Lack of Funds with Gram Panchayat:* The availability of funds with the GPs is small due to lack of devolution of funds upon panchayats and inadequate sources of their own income, and inability of panchayats to receive income. Besides, the funds that come under the programmes like SGSY, SFC and TFC are for certain pre-defined categories of works. Thus, small quantity of funds together with their earmarking for particular type of projects, leave very little option for the panchayats to take up activities of their choice. Although state PR Acts allow the imposition of certain taxes, including surcharge on land, fees for cattle market and slaughterhouses, tax for cleaning and lighting of streets, etc., yet the panchayats do not take concrete measures for the collection of taxes.

In most of the states, one point was raised about the funds received under JGSY. It was regarding the inability of panchayats to create good infrastructure due to mainly two reasons: *first*, the amount received by the gram panchayats normally varies from Rs.10,000 to Rs. 50,000, in which no major infrastructural project can be taken; and *second*, a large number of works are taken due to the demand of every ward member to take up some work in their wards in order to keep the people satisfied in their localities. People were not satisfied with this kind of funding and opined that this kind of approach of development is not helpful to panchayats in the long run.

- *Own Income of Gram Panchayats:* The own income of gram panchayats except for those that are near the town is poor. It is due to the fact that the panchayats are not willing to impose taxes and the people are also least concerned about the payment of taxes. It was also felt during the field visits that neither PR members nor people are keen to look into the issue of raising the panchayat income. PR members are scared of losing their popularity in case they impose some taxes and people are skeptical about the ability of panchayats to utilise the funds judiciously. Here the basic question is that the services should be made available to people effectively. Perhaps, if the people are convinced about the availability of services to them, they might start contributing and participating actively in the development process.

  In addition, it could be true that there is a lack of initiative on the part of the panchayats to levy taxes but hardly any attempt (by state government or PR institutions) is made to bring a suitable environment / culture to encourage people to pay taxes in order to meet the expenses for running the civil services like sanitation, street lighting, etc..

- *Development Planning and Implementation:* The concept of development planning at the panchayat level or at higher tiers seems to be completely missing. Action plan of gram panchayat or higher tiers is simply a compilation of proposals from various departments. No efforts are made to look into the preparation of database, assessment of local resources, sectoral analysis, backward and forward linkages, inter-sectoral analysis and so on.

  Also, the field observations reveal that the decision-making or the finalisation of plan and budget is the mutual understanding among the members of panchayats. For example, in case of preparation of plan (at each level), the funds are allocated based on the proposals submitted by the members, keeping in view their mutual understanding rather than looking from the point of view of rational or the feasibility of a project. As regards the role of people in planning at GP level, they hardly come for the gram sabha meeting and as far as the discussion is concerned, it mainly centres around the selection of beneficiaries for various schemes. And few other development issues pertaining to construction activities (which are guided by a few individuals) are also discussed. But other village development issues do not find much place in the discussion for the plan preparation of the village.

  In other words, as discussed above, the participatory planning at gram panchayat level is handicapped by a number of factors such as: lack of education and awareness among people, lack of capabilities in elected members and development functionaries at panchayat level to handle the task of planning, influence of individuals and lack of transparency in the decision-making process.

  As far as the implementation of programmes is concerned, it is done by the gram panchayat. But in practice, it is the chairperson and the secretary of panchayat (through contractors in some cases) who undertake the execution of work.

- *Existing Delivery System:* The delivery system in the villages in all the states, with the exception of Kerala, is poor as far as the availability of basic services for health, education, agriculture, veterinary, drinking water and credit is concerned. People have to struggle very hard for these basic services. The main reasons for such a state are poor infrastructure, inadequate manpower, lack of logistics support and insufficient administrative arrangement.

- *Transparency in the Gram Panchayat Functioning:* Some states (e.g. Rajasthan, Kerala) provide scope for availing the true copy of documents from the gram panchayats after giving nominal fees. But, in practice, people are hardly concerned for taking information and moreover if such information is to be provided by the panchayats, it would be an elaborate exercise. It is also evident that the chairpersons of the panchayats are reluctant to share the information with others. For instance, list of beneficiaries, amount spent for a particular work, etc. are not made available to people during gram sabha or panchayat meetings. Similarly, under the construction works, the bills are prepared without the knowledge of people and even without observing the desired quality of work and basically it (the completion of work) remains confined to the chairperson and the secretary of the gram panchayat.
- *Audit:* Presently, the panchayati raj department carries out the financial audit. The audit involves inspection of books of accounts, checking of vouchers, the procedure of purchases made, etc. This procedure of audit is very much resented by the chairpersons of panchayats as they find themselves in a difficult position to give account for each item and sometimes they are harassed by the auditors. Although the financial audit is important, yet some alternative should be worked out. As regards the social audit, it has not been established well and people are not able to make PR members accountable through the gram sabhas.
- *Accountability of PR Members and Functionaries:* It is more often than not found that the elected members are not accountable for their decision and various administrative actions. For example,
  - there are instances when the names of the beneficiaries are changed after the gram sabha meetings;
  - the works are executed by the contractors without the involvement of the beneficiaries;
  - the people are not provided with the financial details of the works;
  - the gram sabha meetings are not properly convened and the minutes of the meeting are not given to members or displayed; and
  - non-functioning of basic services like PDS, which are given to panchayats to manage.

Based on fields study, it is invariably true that under the present form of lack of accountability and the responsiveness of panchayats, people do not have much hope from the panchayats as their complaints are not heard and their grievances not attended to.

Similarly there are cases when the functionaries are unwilling to work with panchayats or people and they are not responsive to their problems, and people do not get services in time (see Box 4.3 for details). Under such circumstances functionaries are not held accountable. One can imagine, how panchayat level institutions would function and deliver goods to people.

- *Lack of Appreciation for Panchayats by the Functionaries:* The attitude towards panchayats and people's participation is not positive invariably among field officers and staff. Still, after about ten years of new system of panchayati raj, they find it difficult to cope with the new environment. One prominent reason that appears to be is the lack of sensitisation among them for the role of panchayats in development.

BOX 4.3

Accountability Issues: Observations from Field Studies

How accountability is not observed.

Political and Functional Accountability

- when members from upper caste do not like to participate in the meetings convened by chairperson of marginalised groups (SCs/STs)
- when the people from marginalised groups cannot attend the gram sabha if it is organised near or in the ward dominated by upper caste people
- when the people of marginalised groups have to sit at low pedestal in the gram sabha meeting
- when the women cannot sit with men in the meeting due to tradition, when men are sitting and discussing
- when the chairperson is of upper caste selects the beneficiaries from and take up works in locality dominated by his caste people. And the similar thing is repeated when the chairperson of other caste gets elected.
- if the notice is not displayed, especially for the second gram sabha and people do not come to know about it
- if the signatures of people are obtained even for not attending the gram sabha
- if the proceedings are drawn during the second gram sabha (it is called if the quorum is not maintained in the first meeting) meeting in which hardly a handful of people participates
- if the family members of woman chairperson do work on her behalf
- if the signatures of the panchayat members, who have not attended the meeting are taken for a resolution
- if the resolution is assumed to be passed or decisions are taken without discussion, and signatures of the panchayat members are taken
- if the members of panchayat do not participate in gram sabha or attend only a part of it
- if the names of the beneficiaries are changed after the gram sabha

....*Contd.*

BOX 4.3 *(Contd.)*

- if the chairperson does not respond to the complaints of people for matters over which panchayats have responsibilities to act
- when the works are implemented and the payments are made without the knowledge of people

Financial Accountability

- when tax is not collected by the panchayat
- when the details about the funds of the panchayats are not made public

Administrative Accountability

- when the functionaries are unwilling to work with panchayats
- when the panchayats complain of lack of responsiveness among functionaries, who do not listen to them
- when the panchayat members expect the departments to work as per their directions (which may not be appropriate always)
- when the functionaries are unwilling to work with people and they are not responsive to their problems, and people do not get services in time.

- *Lack of Capabilities in Field Functionaries:* The field functionaries lack requisite technical, administrative and behavioural skills for planning and implementation of programmes, especially in the area of participatory development. Presently, the functionaries are more keen to achieve physical target (as their performance is judged by it) without attending the real objectives of the programmes. It is observed that the functionaries at each level (district, block and GP) are not imparted adequate training.
- *Conflicts among PR Members, and between Panchayats and Departments:* Intra- and inter-panchayats conflicts were noticed very much in many gram panchayats. Intra-panchayat conflicts are mainly due to division of villages between pro- and anti-chairperson groups. In certain cases it is brought out that the members of anti-chairperson group would not allow the panchayat to implement the works. In certain cases, complaints are received by the district administration and sometimes the block or district officials have to intervene to sort out the problems. With regard to inter-panchayat conflicts, these are mainly due to, *first*, differences on approval of a particular project by higher tier, *second*, preparation of action plan by block and zilla panchayats overlooking the suggestions made by the lower tiers, and *third*, division among members on party lines. As regards the conflicts between panchayats and departments, the disputes are mainly due to transfer and posting of field staff, selection of work-site and placement of work order.
- *MPLADP and MLALADP Funds:* Regarding MPLADP and MLALADP funds, the PR members and officials have opined that these funds are not spent as per proper planning

and in many cases the funds are given for political considerations. That apart, these funds which are quite significant in terms of rupees (Rs. 4-5 cr. in a district) are not taken into consideration at the time of preparation of action plan of district or blocks, as these units are not sure of availability of funds. While in principle, the funds should be channelled in a definite manner either as per the action plan or master plan (may be for roads or schools or drinking water) so that the funds are optimally utilised and there is proper resource-matching and convergence of resources and services.

- *Membership of MLAs and MPs in Panchayats:* Many states have made provision for the representation of MLAs and MPs in the panchayats at intermediate and district levels (some exceptions like Kerala, Maharashtra). They have even been given the voting rights in the states of Andhra Pradesh, Assam and Bihar. As per democratic principles, the members should sit in the body for which they are elected, but in the case of panchayats, the members of state legislatures and parliament have been given membership to sit and also vote in panchayat bodies. The presence of MLAs and MPs is not only overwhelming for the panchayat members, who feel hesitate to speak in the panchayat meetings, but is also resented by panchayat members.
- *Small Size of Gram Panchayats:* In some states like Uttar Pradesh, Orissa, Madhya Pradesh, Punjab, etc., the average population of gram panchayat is about two thousand. Thus, there are about seven hundred and fifty GPs in a district and seventy five in a block. This small size of GPs has caused some practical problems for the gram panchayats to function effectively, as GPs are not able to provide services to people due to their low capacity.
- *Empowerment of the Present Elites and Political Groups, but Less of Common Man:* The present panchayat system that is influenced, to a great degree, by the extraneous factors such as use of physical or financial power rather by the merit of the case, is sending set of people, which has more inclinations in enhancing their political influence than attending to the development needs. This set is rooted in the culture of decision-making that is based on dominance by a few, or influenced by political or caste or economic consideration or personal interest or patronage. Such a system also promotes the tendency of rent seeking. The common man with an aspiration to look for development of village has very remote chance to be in race and these people get marginalised in the power game. Or in other words, panchayat system is leading to empowerment of the present elites and political groups, but less of common man.
- *About Scheduled Areas Act:* The contents of the Act reflect that the panchayats in the Scheduled Areas are expected to perform broadly two functions viz., development role and regulatory role. Besides, it is assumed that the panchayats would play the self-government role in future with the devolution of powers upon panchayats in these areas.

In this context, the studies have indicated that panchayats in the scheduled areas are marked with features like: *first*, insignificant participation of people in the gram sabha, *second*, lack of awareness in the people, inadequate capabilities among the panchayat members and poor capacities of the panchayats to handle the basic functions of development. In addition, the availability of basic services like primary education, health or drinking water is questionable and the panchayats are not able to attend to these very functions up to any satisfactory level. Moreover, the public awareness and action for such needs are not visible.

To conclude, when the panchayats are not equipped to handle the basic functions, which are very vital for people, we need to re-examine the issues of burdening the panchayats with too many regulatory functions. That apart, there is a danger that if the panchayats also look into regulatory job, the development may not be attended to in the desired way, due to not only their poor capacities to handle so many functions but also from the point of view of different perspective and approach attached to these two categories viz., 'development' and 'regulation'.

- *Merger of DRDA and Zilla Parishad (ZP):* Several states have either merged DRDA with zilla parishad, or planning to do so in order to provide effective control of ZP over DRDA. But the critical examination of the impact of such measure on the efficiency and effectiveness of the functioning of ZP reveals that it would not make much difference, whether we merge DRDA with ZP or not. What really matters is that the DRDA should be working under the overall direction of ZP and the PD, DRDA should be accountable to ZP. Abolishing one institution or changing its name is not going to serve much purpose, while the crucial point is how to strengthen the institutions and make them deliver effectively. Or in other words, we should be concerned about how the efficiency and effectiveness of DRDA (which has been in existence for long and people are familiar with the agency) for planning and implementation of programmes can be enhanced.

  Finally, such kind of measure of abolishing one institution or merging institutions are only going to give notional satisfaction. Rather, we should be concentrating our energy on: how to improve people's participation in planning; formulation of proper planning methodology; capacity building of PR members and field staff; devolution of funds, management of utilisation of funds including accounting; and transparency and audit system.

- *Factors Influencing the Panchayat Functioning at Grassroots Level:* From the findings of the field study the factors influencing the functioning of panchayats can be categorically identified as under:
  - Central decision-making tendency — people are not involved or their concerns are not cared.
  - Education level of people and of PR members — the low level of education has led to poor people's participation and ineffective panchayat functioning.
  - Caste factor — upper castes have dominance.
  - Rich *vs* poor — poor get marginalised.
  - Weaker sections do not get chance for participation.
  - Political groups' influence — party with a large number influences the decisions like the selection of beneficiaries or the construction-sites.
  - Political patronage — some works are done for a particular group or area to get some favour in future.

- *Lack of Focus on Development:* It appears at the panchayat level at all the three tiers, proving personal or group's superiority takes precedent over the development activities. The development issues that are attended to by the panchayats are very limited, but what is equally distressing is that these matters do not find place during various stages right from elections to planning to addressing people's grievances to implementation till the expiry of the term of the panchayat. The panchayat members remain more occupied in the routine matters or party politics.

Finally, in all the states, except in Kerala, in the absence of support from state government, the capacity of PR institutions is under serious question. They are handicapped by acute manpower, infrastructural and logistics shortcomings. Even the capabilities of the people manning these institutions are not of adequate standards and they seriously lack the necessary knowledge as well as skills. Due to their poor state they find it hard to function right from organising gram sabhas to attending people's grievances, to providing services to people, to implementing works and so on. In a way, the panchayats have been denied the role of self-government. The present status of panchayats is summarised in Box 4.4.

Some Creditable Efforts

Notwithstanding above, there have been cases of success stories where panchayats have done commendable work in a particular field due to initiatives by the elected members, but these are, normally, isolated cases and individual-specific. Some of the noteable cases are: the confident role played by the woman chairperson of Masoli GP in Uttar Pradesh; the strong initiatives initiated by the chairperson of Vellivallam GP in Tamil Nadu; the case of mobilising the resources for the construction of bridges by Chharikalan GP in Punjab; people's participation in Hariziana and Buddowal GPs in Punjab; and the construction of bridge by people's participation in Banachapada GP in West Bengal. (See state-specific case studies in section 4.1).

BOX 4.4

Present Status of Panchayats : Most Likelihood Scenario

- People perceive little benefit from gram panchayats
- There is considerable elite dominance in the village life
- Caste plays its role in the functioning of panchayats
- Landless people, tribals and women are excluded in the panchayat functioning
- Reservation alone, in the absence of proper environment building and educational base, has only limited effects on inclusion of weaker sections in the decision-making
- Women in rural society continue to depend on family members

Contd.

BOX 4.4 *(Contd.)*

- Though unintended, reservation appears to have led to restricting SCs/STs and women to mainly reserved seats
- Reservation do not appear to have an impact on improving the effectiveness of panchayats in terms of addressing the problems of weaker sections
- The presence of MLAs and MPs as members of panchayats overwhelms panchayat members
- People do not participate in the most visible accountability mechanism — the gram sabha
- At each tier, there seems to be no system of accountability at work
- Rules do not make departments accountable to elected representatives and there is a lack of sensitivity among functionaries for panchayats and people's participation
- Panchayats feel marginalised due to their poor capacities to deliver

But there are opportunities for future :

- Political will is the first prerequisite for decentralisation
- Factors with positive influence are critical for the smooth process of decentralisation, and the following are some of the prominent ones:
  - Education and access to information are the two most significant factors that influence participation;
  - Well-informed villagers and educated people are most likely to be active in the panchayat;
  - Participation rate among women rises considerably with improved education and higher access to information; and
  - From the institutional perspective, improving the capacity of the local institutions is necessary for making services available to people.
- Accountability is crucial for enhancing responsiveness towards people's grievances and building confidence of people in the local institutions.

Appendix 4.1

Note on District Councils in Meghalaya

Article 244(2) of the Constitution provides that the Sixth Schedule of the Constitution shall apply to the administration of tribal areas in the states of Assam, Meghalaya, Tripura and Mizoram. The Sixth Schedule is a self-contained code for the governance of the tribal areas. In pursuance of the Sixth Schedule, three Autonomous District Councils namely, the Khasi Hills Autonomous District Council (KHADC), the Jaintia Hills Autonomous District Council (JHADC) and the Garo Hills Autonomous District Council (GHADC) were set up in the state of Meghalaya, covering all the districts in the state. The District Councils are the Autonomous bodies consituted under the Sixth Schedule of the Constitution of India to safeguard the rights and interests of the tribal people within their jurisdiction.

Although they are autonomous bodies, the District Councils depend largely on government grants for implementation of various developmental schemes. For this purpose the government provides grants-in-aid every year both under Plan and Non-Plan Sectors to be implemented by themselves like construction of village roads, footpaths, small bridges, playgrounds, market places, ringwells, water tanks, councils' own office and improvement of rural markets etc.

Fund Released to the District Councils by the State Govt.

The position of fund released to the District Councils for the years 1997-98 to 1999-2000 is as indicated below:

(Rs. in lakhs)

Name of Council	Name of Scheme	Year	Amount sanctioned
KHADC	- Financing own Plan	1997-98	47.50
	- Special Grant (P)		100.00
	- Rural Communication		2.00
	- Financing own Plan		182.50
	- Construction of Buildings (P)		20.00
	- Rural Communication		3.60
	- Financing own Plan	1999-2000	182.50
	- Construction of Building (P)		20.00
	- Rural Communication (NP)		3.60

(Contd.)

(Contd. Appendix 4.1)

Name of Council		Name of Scheme	Year	Amount sanctioned
GHADC	-	Financing own Plan (P)	1997-98	40,00,000
	-	Special Grant		75,00,000
	-	Construction of building		No sanction released
	-	Repairs & Maintenance of certain roads (NP)		1,00,000
	-	Financing own Plan (P)	1998-99	160,00,000
	-	Construction of building		20,00,000
	-	Rural Communication (NP)		1,50,000
	-	Repairs & Maintenance of roads (NP)		1,00,000
	-	Rural Communication (NP)		1,00,000
	-	Financing own Plan (P)	1999-2000	160,00,000
	-	Construction of Building (P)		20,00,000
	-	Repairs & Maintenance of roads (NP)		1,80,000
	-	Rural Communication (NP)		1,60,000
JHADC	-	Financing own Plan	1997-98	32.50
	-	Special Grant (P)		75.00
	-	Construction of Building (P)		15.00
	-	Rural Communication (NP)		1.00
	-	Financing own Plan	1998-99	52.50
	-	Construction of Buildings (P)		15.00
	-	Rural Communication (NP)		2.40
	-	Financing own Plan (P)	1999-2000	52.50
	-	Construction of Buildings (P)		15.00
	-	Rural Communication (NP)		2.40

P : Plan and NP : Non-plan

Other Sources of Revenue of the District Councils

The other sources of revenue of the District Councils are as follows : The major sources of revenue for the Councils are forests (royalty), markets, fisheries, trades and profession etc.

The District Councils also get a share of the royalties collected by the state government on the mines, minerals, minor minerals, etc. This is shared in the ratio of 60:40 between the District Councils and the state government respectively.

The District Councils also get a major share of the tax on motor vehicles. After deducting the cost of collection, the Jaintia Hills District Council and the Garo Hills District Council get 100 per cent of the net proceeds, while the Khasi Hills District Council gets 60 per cent of the net proceeds.

Annual Expenditures of the District Councils

(i) Expenditure on Salaries: This Department have no records on the expenditure on establishment/salaries of the Autonomous District Councils. However, the same are being called for from the Autonomous District Councils.
(ii) Expenditure on Development Schemes: The Autonomous District Councils submitted the Utilisation Certificates for each grants-in-aid sanctioned to them for both plan and non-plan schemes and therefore the amount sanctioned appears to be fully utilised.

Role and Functions of the Autonomous District Councils

The District Councils have three wings—The Legislative, the Executive and the Judiciary.

Legislative

The elected and nominated members constitute the Legislative wing of the Council. It is headed by a Chairman and a Deputy Chairman, who are elected by the Council in session.

The business of the Council is transacted according to standard parliamentary practices.

Any of the languages spoken within the jurisdiction of the Council or any recognised language of the state may be used by the members in Councils, meetings/sittings.

The District Council Budget is discussed and voted in the Council. No funds can be spent from the District fund without the authority of the Council.

Executive

The executive functions of the Council are vested in the Executive Committee, headed by the Chief Executive Member. The Chief Executive Member (CEM) is elected by the District Council. Other members of the Executive Committee, generally called Executive Members, are appointed by the Governor on the advice of the Chief Executive Member.

At present, besides the Chief Executive Member, the Khasi Hills District Council has six Executive Members, the Garo Hills District Council has six Executive Members, the Jaintia Hills District Council has six Executive Members and one Deputy Chief Executive Member. The respective Councils can amend the Rules to increase the numbers of Executive Members or to add new category of members to the Executive Committee.

The Executive Committee is collectively responsible to the Council and may be removed on a vote of no-confidence by a majority of the members of the Council.

Judiciary

Para 4 and 5 of the Sixth Schedule empower the District Councils to constitute courts for the administration of justice in the Autonomous district. Under these powers, the District Councils have formulated their own Rules for the administration of justice.

Under these Administration of Justice Rules, three classes of courts were constituted by the District Councils:

- The Village Courts;
- The Subordinate District Council Courts and Additional District Council Courts; and
- The District Council Courts.

In Khasi and Jaintia Hills, the traditional Village Chiefs and Headmen elected according to custom are appointed as Chairman of the Village Courts. The Village Court shall consist of not less than two members and not more than six members.

In Garo Hills, the Village Court consists of the Lasker of the Village and two other members of the Village Council, elected by the Village Council by a majority of votes.

The Subordinate District Council Court is presided over by a Judicial Officer designated as a magistrate, appointed by the Executive Committee with the approval of the Governor. In Khasi and Jaintia Hills, the traditional Chiefs of Elakas, the Syiems, Lyngdohs, Doleis, etc. are designated as Additional Subordinate District Council Courts.

There is one District Council Court in every headquarters of the Autonomous District. The Court consists of one or more Judicial Officers, designated as Judge, appointed by the Executive Committee with the approval of Governor.

The Governor confers on the Courts, constituted by the District Councils, the powers for trial of suits or cases arising out of any law in force in the Autonomous District or for trial of offences, punishable with death, transportation for life of imprisonment for a term of not less than 5 years under the I.P.C or under any other law applicable to such District.

The High Court exercises its jurisdiction over the suits and cases decided by the District Council Courts.

Though the provisions of the I.P.C. and Cr.P.C. do not apply to the trial of cases, suits or offences in an Autonomous District, the spirit of these codes is followed in actual practices.

Powers

In terms of Para 3 of the Sixth Schedule, the District Councils have the powers to make laws with respect to following subjects:

- management (the allotment, occupation or use or the setting apart) of land other than any land which is a reserved forest;
- management of any forest not being a reserved forest;
- the use of any canal or water-course for the purpose of agriculture;
- the regulation of *Jhum* or other forms of shifting cultivation;

- the establishment of village or town committee or Councils and their powers;
- any other matter relating to village or town administration, including village or town police and public health and sanitation;
- the appointment of succession of Chiefs or Headmen;
- inheritance of property;
- marriage and divorce; and
- social customs.

Under Para 6 of the Sixth Schedule, the District Councils may establish, construct or manage primary schools, dispensaries, markets, cattle markets, ponds, ferries, roads, road transport and waterways in the District and may, with the previous approval of the Governor, make regulations for the regulation and control thereof.

Para 10 gives powers to the District Councils to make regulations for the control of money-lending and trading by non-tribals. The regulations prescribed that no one except the holder of a license issued on that behalf shall carry on wholesale and retail business in any commodity. However, no regulation have been formulated by any District Council to regulate or control money-lending in any of the Autonomous Districts.

Para 8 empowers the District Councils to assess and collect revenue from lands within the Autonomous District, in accordance with the principle for the time being followed by the state government in assessing lands for the purpose of land revenue.

Under Para 8, the District Councils also have the powers to levy and collect following taxes:

- taxes on professionals, trades, callings and employment;
- taxes on animals, vehicles, boats;
- taxes on entry of goods into markets for sale therein and tolls on passengers and goods carried in ferries; and
- taxes for maintenance of schools, dispensaries and roads.

All regulations made to provide for the levy and collections of taxes aforementioned will require the assent of the Governor.

Para 6 of the Sixth Schedule provides that the District Councils shall get a share of the royalties collected by the state government from licenses or leases for the purpose of prospecting or extraction of minerals from the areas within the autonomous areas. The proposition of share shall be as per mutual agreement. In the event of any dispute, the Governor shall determine the shares in his discretion.

An important provision, which was inserted in the Sixth Schedule in 1972 at the time of creation of a full fledged state of Meghalaya, is the paragraph 12-A. It provides that notwithstanding anything in the Constitution, if any provision of the law made by a District Council with respect to any subject or matter vested in the District Council, if repugnant to any provision of a law made by the Legislature of the state with respect to such subjects and matters, then the law of regulation made by the District Councils shall be void to the extent of repugnancy and the law made by the state Legislative shall prevail.

Of the subjects assigned to the District Councils, the state government have taken over the administration of primary education by an Act of the state Legislature. This was done on the basis of reports of three separate Commissions appointed under paragraph 14 of the Sixth Schedule to inquire and review the management and administration of primary education in the District Councils.

Finance

Para 7 of the Sixth Schedule provides for the constitution of a District Fund for each Autonomous District. The District Fund Rules have been framed by all the three District Councils, which provide the guidelines for custody, payment into and withdrawal of money from the District Fund.

Source : Panchayati Raj Directorate, Meghalaya, 2001.

Appendix 4.2

Administrative and Financial Devolution of Functions and Powers in UP

In June,1999, realising the importance of decentralisation, the State Government took various measures for administrative and financial devolution in order to strengthen the PRIs at three tiers. The salient features are given below:

I. A. At Gram Panchayat Level

Administrative Assistance to Gram Panchayat:

- The gram panchayats have been given the following twelve functions:

i. Education, ii. State Tubewells, iii. Hand pumps, iv. Youth welfare, v. Health and family welfare, vi. Women and children development, vii. Veterinary, viii. PDS, ix. Agriculture, x. Rural development, xi. Panchayati Raj, xii. Scholarships and Pensions.

- In order to operationalise the functioning at the GP level, one multi-purpose worker would be appointed as gram panchayat and development officer with the responsibility of the following activities:

i. State Tubewells, ii. Hand pumps, iii. Youth welfare, iv. PDS, v. Health and family welfare, vi. Agriculture, vii. Rural development, viii. Panchayati Raj

Note: Gram Panchayat and Development Officer may be from one of the above eight departments.

As per the order of the state government, the gram panchayat and development officer would be responsible for all the activities concerned with the above subjects and provide the necessary services to people. Additionally, he would also be the secretary of that gram panchayat.

In addition to the Gram Panchayat and Development Officer, the functionaries of four other departments will also be transferred to gram panchayat. These departments are Primary Education, Health and Family Welfare, Women and Child Development and Veterinary. The concerned functionaries will look after the functioning of their concerned subject.

- The state government would provide the infrastructure facilities for gram panchayat office and residential accommodation for gram panchayat and development officer.

Financial Assistance to Gram Panchayat:

- The gram panchayats would be given the financial assistance under the following categories:

Four per cent of State taxes	Rs. 328 crores
Rural Development Schemes	Rs. 583 crores
Tenth Finance Commission	Rs. 189 crores
Total	Rs.1100 crores

- Other sources of income of gram panchayat would be:
  - Irrigation cess
  - Surcharge on land revenue

Committees at Gram Panchayat:

- Planning and Development Committee;
- Education Committee;
- Implementation Committee;
- Health and Family Welfare Committee;
- Administrative Committee.

These committees would be responsible for the functioning of the subjects assigned to them.

Steps for improving education - Siksha Mitra Scheme

In case the existing teachers would retire or otherwise if there is any vacancy, the gram panchayat would engage the teacher and payment would be made by the state government It is also made mandatory that 50 per cent of the Siksha Mitra should be women.

- Education Guarantee Scheme

It is also proposed to start education centres in those areas where there is no school within one kilometre and for this purpose one Acharya would be appointed for each centre and the honorarium will be paid by the state government.

Transparency

As under decentralisation the gram panchayats have been given many functions and responsibilities, it becomes important to have transparency in the functioning of gram panchayats so that people would have confidence in them. Keeping this in mind, for improving transparency the gram panchayat members can take the copy of any document by paying nominal fees.

Audit

The income and expenditure by the gram panchayat would be audited and the gram panchayat would be required to produce them in the six-monthly gram sabha meeting.

I. B. At *Chetra* Panchayat (CP) Level:

The *chetra* panchayats have been entrusted with the following functions:

The rural development, primary health centres, veterinary, seed centres, marketing godowns, inter-gram panchayat works, *chetra* panchayat property.

Devolution of Funds : Chetra panchayat would be given 10 per cent of the devolved state income from taxes. It would be effective from 2000-2001.

Committees at Chetra Panchayat for Various Development Works:

Planning and Development Committee, Education Committee, Implementation Committee, Health and Family Welfare Committee and Administrative Committee

These committees will have 5-7 members and would be responsible for the functioning of the subjects assigned to them.

I. C. At Zilla Panchayat Level :

Restructuring of DRDA

- The President of the ZP would be the chairman of DRDA
- Governing body would also have the following members, besides the existing ones:
    - Presidents of 5 zilla panchayat level committees
    - By rotation 50 per cent *parmukhs* of *chetra* panchayat for one year.

Transfer of District Level Officers to ZP

The following officers will work under the ZP:

- Deputy Chief Medical Officer
- District Development Officer
- Primary Education Officer
- Executive Engineer Water Works
- Executive Engineer Tubewells
- District Youth Welfare Officer
- District Children Welfare Officer
- District Veterinary Officer

- District Agricultural Officer
- District Panchayati Raj Officer

Committees at the Zilla Panchayat Level:

Planning and Development Committee, Education Committee, Implementation Committee, Health and Family Welfare Committee and Administrative Committee.

These committees would have 5-7 members and would be responsible for the functioning of the subjects assigned to them.

District Planning Committee :

District Planning Committee (DPC) would have the following members:

(i) 4/5th members of the committee would be elected from the elected members of zilla panchayat and municipalities in the ratio of rural and urban population.

(ii) 1/5th members would be nominated by the state government.

(iii) It will also have the following members :

- One nominated minister who would be the President of the Committee.
- President of Zilla Panchayat who would be the Vice-President of the Committee.
- Nagar Pramukh of district municipality as Vice-President of Zilla Committee.
- District Collector as Ex-Officio Member.
- Any other member nominated by the Government.
- MPs and MLAs as invitees.

Source : Panchayati Raj Directorate, Uttar Pradesh, 1999.

5

ANALYSIS OF PROCESS OF DECENTRALISATION

The 73rd Constitution Amendment Act has heralded a new chapter in the process of decentralisation. The Act has provided a broad framework to states within which the panchayati raj (PR) institutions at three levels viz., district, block and gram panchayat, can become the units of development planning and implementation. The Act places the onus of its implementation on the states. It is up to a state how it attends to various provisions of the Act, creates the desired capacities of the local institutions to take up the development activities of their respective areas and provides opportunities to people in their village development. The states have initiated various measures in order to operationalise the Amendment Act. Some of them include the conduct of elections, reservations for the weaker sections, constitution of SEC, SFC and DPC, transfer of functions and powers and so on. The implementation of the Act varies in terms of content from state to state. However, there is definite trend towards decentralising the development system in the rural areas.

In chapters three and four, all the dimensions of decentralisation — political, functional, administrative and financial — have been covered. This chapter attempts to critically analyse the following issues in each of the dimensions:

- **Political Decentralisation**
  - Election to local bodies
  - Status of PR members
  - People's participation
  - Tenure of chairpersons of panchayats
  - Representation to weaker sections
  - Size of the gram panchayats
  - MLAs and MPs as members of panchayat bodies
  - Elections to the members to intermediate and district panchayats
  - Accountability of PR members

- **Functional Decentralisation**
    - Transfer of functions
    - Inter-tier demarcation of functions
    - Assigning subject-specific responsibilities

- **Administrative Decentralisation**
    - Institutional mechanism for planning
    - Mechanism for implementation, coordination and monitoring
    - Manpower support and capabilities of functionaries
    - Delivery system at the gram panchayat level
    - Transparency system
    - Institutional mechanism for resolving conflicts, settling disputes and arbitration

- **Financial Decentralisation**
    - Collection of taxes
    - Devolution of funds
    - SFC
    - Financial autonomy

The detailed description about the above dimensions is given below:

5.1 Analysis of Political Decentralisation

Election to Local Bodies: The elections to panchayats have been held in most of the states, while in Assam and Bihar the elections were held after the gap of 9 and 23 years respectively. In Andhra Pradesh and Madhya Pradesh, the elections were delayed due to petitions in the court. In Karnataka, these were delayed due to reorganisation of gram panchayats. In the state of Gujarat, the elections were not held simultaneously for all the three tiers, and the elections for gram panchayats were held in December, 2001, while the elections for intermediate and zilla panchayats were held in 2000. Similarly, in Punjab, the elections for intermediate and zilla panchayats were delayed due to petition in the courts.

The above are pointers to the fact that neither the elections are held in time nor held simultaneously for all the three tiers. It clearly indicates that the constitutional provisions of timely elections (Article 243 E) and the bar to court intervention (Article 243 O) have not been followed in the right spirit. And such a state will clearly undermine the continuity of the panchayats.

It has also come out during the field study that the election process is mainly sending representatives from the elite class or from political groups. Besides, the weaker sections, though their members get elected, find it hard to have their voice in the panchayats and get marginalised, and their participation remains mainly in the reserved seats and basically during election time. Similarly, the common person finds it hard to get the opportunity to contest election in a highly sensitive and surcharged political environment. The voices of common person who are concerned for village development do not get much attention during the election process. What is equally distressing is the means employed to win the elections, which among others include money, liquor and muscle power.

Status of PR Members: In all the states, in conformity with the 73rd Constitution Amendment Act, the state Acts have provided executive positions to PR members.

People's Participation: It is evident from the field studies that the functioning of gram sabha, a fulcrum of participatory development, is far from satisfactory, rather it is something that needs immediate attention. The poor attendance, lack of visible people's participation and the discussion on narrow agenda in the gram sabha present a poor account of functioning of panchayats at the grassroots level. The PR members are more concerned with the devolution of funds and functions, and control over officers and staff for the transfer and postings, rather than the involvement of people at every stage of development.

Moreover, as regards the discussion in the gram sabha, the proceedings are dominated by the discussion on the selection of beneficiaries or construction works. While other vital issues such as: how the education among poor can be improved; how the health and sanitation in the village can be improved; how the crop yield can be enhanced; how the income of landless people can be increased and so on, do not find much importance in the discussion during the gram sabha. And very little importance is given to look into the issues that are vital for the village development. But people cannot be blamed as adequate efforts have not been made to train the PR members or make people aware about the development needs in a holistic manners.

The functioning of gram sabha can be summed up as a forum where not many people attend or even like to attend the gram sabha meeting, even if those attend they find it hard to participate in the discussion, also the discussion is confined to a few issues and many vital issues of village development are overlooked.

Of particular importance is the issue of structure of gram sabha. It is a forum for eliciting the people's problems and needs, for having transparent way of informing people about the activities of gram panchayat and making PR representatives accountable to the people in the open forum. But, as indicated by field studies, it has its own limitations like: *first*, sheer large number of members makes it difficult (if the large number, say 200-300, of people attend the meetings) to organise meetings smoothly; *second*, difficulty in eliciting the views of people, especially of women and other weaker sections, due to dominance by vocal and influential people; and *third*, the planning which is a specialised exercise cannot be handled in gram sabha meeting alone. Quite often, the discussion leads to chaotic turn and goes beyond the control of the chairpersons of gram panchayats.

The above description is a clear reflection of less importance given to people's participation in the operational terms.

Tenure of Chairpersons of Panchayats: In certain states one feature has been noticed that the duration of chairpersons of panchayats has been fixed by state government for a certain period. For instance, in Karnataka, it is fixed for twenty months for chairpersons of taluk (intermediate) and zilla panchayats, and thirty months for chairpersons of gram panchayats. Similarly, in Maharashtra, for intermediate and zilla panchayats, earlier (in 1999-2000) the term was fixed for one year for intermediate and zilla panchayats, which has been raised to two and a half years. By any account, these are retrograde steps. Now, in this process, chairpersons hardly find sufficient time to perform and members are more occupied in identifying suitable substitutes (for future) than in working for development.

Representation to Weaker Sections: Article 243D makes provision for the reservation of women and SCs and STs and such reservation should be rotated. The states have construed that the rotation can be for every five years. Now, from the practical point of view, it has been noticed that the members from these categories take longer time to learn the official work due to their initial inhibitions and low educational level. Besides, one term is not sufficient for carrying out sufficient development activities if long term view is taken. It discourages members from taking innovative projects as they feel that they have no chance to become members again.

Size of the Gram Panchayats: The issue of size of gram panchayats was felt when it came to making panchayats capable of delivering services to people. Articles 243B and 243C deal with the formation of gram panchayats. It is on the concerned states to decide about the size of the gram panchayat. The states have formed the gram panchayats based on the population criterion. If we look into the average size of the population of one gram panchayat, it is normally in the vicinity of 3000 in most of the states, and only a few states like Assam, Kerala and West Bengal have population more than 10,000.

Now, if we examine critically, the small size of gram panchayats causes some practical problems for the gram panchayats to function effectively. *First*, the panchayats have not got the relevant staff for providing basic services for health, veterinary, drinking water, irrigation, etc. as the departments do not have sufficient number of field functionaries. It is estimated that if all panchayats were to be provided with the staff for these services, the number of field functionaries has to be increased by 4-5 times that would involve large expenditure on salary. *Second*, similarly, there is an acute shortage of infrastructure for the basic services to be provided to people, and if it were to be created at the GP level, it would require huge investment. *Third*, with so many panchayats, it becomes difficult to organise block level meetings (in which 50 to 100 members participate) and to monitor the financial performance of gram panchayats. Thus, from the points of view of financial, administrative and functional viability, it is vital that necessary support system should be provided to all the gram panchayats. And presently the size of gram panchayat is such which is making it difficult to make them viable units of development.

MLAs and MPs as Members of Panchayat Bodies: As per Article 243C, the states have made provision for the representation of MPs and MLAs in the panchayats at intermediate and district levels. In this regard, during field visits several objections have been raised by the panchayat members, as they feel overwhelmed and marginalised by the presence of MLAs and MPs in the panchayat meetings.

Election of Members of Intermediate and Zilla Panchayats: The field studies reveal that the elections of the intermediate and zilla panchayats have been a subject of discussion among members of gram panchayats. The Article 243C provides for direct election for members at all the three tiers. It stipulates for territorial constituencies for these tiers (while in the states having population less than twenty lakhs, the intermediate panchayats may be done away). Thus, the intermediate and district panchayats have electoral constituencies that are formed after combining the group of panchayats. Based on the field study, if we examine the present system of multi-level constituencies and the functioning of panchayats at all the three tiers, the following points emerge:

- *First*, the electoral constituencies of intermediate and zilla panchayats are simply geographical boundaries without any logical basis.
- *Second*, mere election of more members to higher tiers cannot be the criterion for more people's participation. While, by any logic the gram panchayats, which are the basic units of development, should get full representation in all the three tiers.
- *Third*, although the chairpersons of gram panchayats have been made the members of the intermediate panchayats and similarly the chairpersons of intermediate panchayats have been made the members of the district panchayat, still it is not effective due to the following reasons:
    - In states where the chairpersons of the lower panchayats are mere members without any voting right, then the concerned gram panchayats are not given true representation in the higher tiers for all practical purposes.
    - Even if the chairpersons of the lower panchayats have voting rights, they are not effective in the decision-making as the elected members of the higher panchayats have their own priority. Besides, the agenda for discussion is decided by the higher panchayat, which may not necessarily address the problems of lower tiers.
    - The number (which varies from 50 to 100 of members) in the higher tiers has become so large that it makes it difficult to conduct the panchayat meetings at intermediate and zilla panchayat levels meaningfully.
    - The views of the chairpersons of gram panchayats are not duly attended to by the higher tiers. While, in the gram sabha, which is the forum of accountability, it is the chairperson of the gram panchayat who has to answer to the questions of people. Thus, in a way the members who have to answer in the gram sabha do not have much say in the proceedings of higher tiers. In a way, it is irrational.
- *Fourth*, what is equally inconsistent is that the elected members of the higher tiers need not be from the same constituency in some states where they are contesting (and

may contest from anywhere in the panchayat area in some states e.g. in the state of Karnataka) but they should be in the electoral list of the intermediate or zilla panchayat as the case may be. In this process the members for the intermediate and zilla panchayats mainly contest more from the consideration of caste or religion or political influence, and the desired consideration of people's needs and aspirations or their participation takes backseat.

Accountability of PR Members: For observing financial accountability, Article 243J provides that the state may make provisions for the maintenance of accounts by panchayats and the auditing of such accounts. Accordingly, the audit section of the concerned panchayati raj department carries out the financial audit. The audit involves inspection of books of accounts, checking of vouchers, the procedure of purchases made, etc. This procedure of audit is very much resented by the chairpersons of panchayats as they find themselves in a difficult position to give account for each item, and sometimes they are harassed by the auditors.

In some states, the provisions for the social audit have been made but except in Kerala it has not taken proper shape. It is observed that so far there is no well-established system of making the chairpersons and the members of the gram panchayat accountable to people. Also, the decisions of members of higher tiers (intermediate and zilla panchayats) are not subjected to the scrutiny by the people in the gram sabha, while those decisions might affect the gram panchayats.

5.2 Analysis of Functional Decentralisation

The full transfer of functions under twenty-nine subjects has not taken place in almost all the states. Even, in the functional terms, the subjects under basic needs (like primary education, health, agriculture, veterinary, irrigation, etc.) have not been transferred. Also, inter-tier demarcation of functions has not been carried out resulting into overlapping of functions and conflicts in certain cases. Similarly, subject-specific responsibilities have not been assigned to each tier. In the absence of these vital aspects the panchayats are not in a position to take up the responsibilities under various subjects.

Regarding the issue of subjects under Eleventh Schedule, there are twenty-nine subjects that need to be transferred to panchayats. A careful examination indicates that this Schedule is asking for big responsibilities from the panchayats which range from education to health to natural resources management to handloom and handicraft to small scale industries to rural electrification. If we look at the capacity of panchayats, it is too large a responsibility to deliver and needs to be reviewed.

5.3 Analysis of Administrative Decentralisation

The issues studied under administrative decentralisation point towards how inadequate are measures that are initiated by the state governments to provide administrative authority to panchayats. Some of the critical observations have been summed up as follows:

Institutional Mechanism for Planning

Under this the issues of planning process, role of gram sabha, support system and district planning committee have been examined.

- The purpose of the participatory planning at the gram panchayat level is to bring out the critical issues of the importance to community with the involvement of people, so the prepared plan represents the felt-needs and aspirations of all the groups of the village and also the plan so prepared would be sustainable for the socio-economic development of the people. While, as revealed by the field studies, the concept of development planning at the panchayat level or at higher tiers seems to be completely missing. The studies have brought out the deficiencies in the present system of planning at local levels, the prominent among them include: *First*, there is no laid down process of planning for the action plan preparation at all the three tiers, and the planning exercise begins by inviting proposals from the departments without having any emphasis on analysis of data, inter-sectoral needs, etc. And the planning methodology for reaching the rational allocation of funds is not formulated. *Second*, the database that is the basic requirement for the planning is not developed for undertaking planning exercise. *Third*, the infrastructure in terms of adequate office building, record room for data-storage and facilities such as computers for data analysis and networking, is missing at the block and gram panchayat levels, and only partially some facilities are available at the district level, which are also not enough to carry out any meaningful planning exercise. And *finally*, the planning which is a specialised exercise involving good knowledge and skills is not supported by the adequate and trained manpower. Besides, participatory part of planning at gram panchayat is hampered by a number of factors such as: lack of awareness among people, poor people's participation, lack of capabilities in elected members and influence (over decision-making) of some individuals in the gram sabha meeting (see table 5.1).
- Integration of plans of three tiers which is very important in order to provide organic linkages to the plans of three tiers and also to assess the overall requirement of funds for the districts is not carried out. No efforts are made for the preparation of database; and the sectoral, backward and forward linkages, and inter-sectoral analyses are not attempted. The district plan is merely a compilation of proposals received from various departments, blocks and the gram panchayats.
- At the grassroots level, another dimension of lack of convergence of resources and services has been added due to the problems of multiple schemes, multiplicity of departments, and resource-gap and missing links within the programmes. The lack of convergence leads to inefficient utilisation of resources and lack of availability of

services to people. The development efforts continue without addressing this crucial issue of convergence that has strong bearing on the effectiveness and the efficiency of implementation of development programmes. It is a great challenge as to how the village development planning should be carried out in order to ensure not only the optimal allocation of resources but also the convergence of resources for their efficient end-use.

- *District Planning Committee:* For setting up of District Planning Committee (DPC), some steps have been taken by the states, but there are certain shortcomings in its formation. *First,* though the DPC has to look into the preparation of district plan based on the local needs, yet the chairperson of DPC is not an elected member from panchayats or municipalities in most of the states. *Second,* in spite of the fact that the planning requires specialised knowledge and skills, DPC does not have adequate experts as its members in order to provide technical inputs and make analyses for reaching rational decision-making. *Third,* DPC is formed but the supporting wing in the form of planning unit is not adequately placed. And, *finally,* no planning committee or unit exists at the block or GP level in order to carry out local level planning and also to provide vital inputs on local needs and resources to DPC.

Mechanism for Implementation, Coordination and Monitoring: For the implementation of programmes (see table 5.1) issues like beneficiaries' participation in the execution of work and procedure of supervision have not been addressed. The implementation of programmes is carried out by the gram panchayats through chairpersons or departments and in some cases the contractors also execute the works disregarding the involvement of beneficiaries. While the people's participation is very important, the beneficiaries' involvement at the execution and supervision stages remains negligible in all the states, with the exception of Kerala. Also, due to lack of administrative managements, coordination between PRIs and the line departments remains a problem in the planning and implementation of programmes. Similarly, the monitoring system, in order to assess the progress of works, is not rightly placed causing problems in knowing the physical and financial status of the projects/works.

Manpower Support and Capabilities of Functionaries

- To begin with, the placement of officers and staff of line departments with PRIs has not yet been done except in a few cases in some states (see table 4.6). In the absence of control of panchayats over the field staff of line departments, the panchayats find it difficult to implement and supervise various programmes. Besides, if we examine the available manpower at the block and gram panchayat levels, there is no addition to the strength of field staff since 1950s i.e. the time of community development programme, while there has been manifold increase in the officers and staff at the State and at the Central levels. In a way, at the cutting edge level, where the implementation of programmes takes place there is no improvement in the strength of manpower.

TABLE 5.1: **Problem Areas in Development Planning and Implementation at Panchayat Level**

S.No.	Areas	Item		Problems
1.	Functioning of Gram Sabha	(i) Participation	:	People hardly participate in gram sabha as they are disorganised and unaware
		(ii) Role of women	:	Women do not attend meetings. Only a few people dominate the proceedings
2.	Planning	(i) Data Collection	:	Proper data schedules not available and lack of facility in storage of data
		(ii) Data Analysis	:	Tools and techniques are not known at local level
		(iii) Problem identification	:	Only listing the problems without sequencing
		(iv) Prioritization	:	No objective criteria is applied
		(v) Project formulation	:	Not able to do in the absence of proper knowledge
		(vi) Plan preparation	:	No inter-sectoral and backward and forward linkages analyses are carried out
		(vii) Resource mobilisation	:	Not able to do through public contribution and other agencies
3.	Implementation	(i) Plan scheduling	:	Not prepared
		(ii) Beneficiaries committee	:	Not properly formed
		(iii) Training to executant of beneficiaries committee	:	Training is not given
		(iv) Manpower and logistics support	:	Work is started without looking into the details
4.	Monitoring	(i) Monitoring team	:	No earmarked team
		(ii) Monitoring formats	:	No users-friendly formatting is done
		(iii) Data analysis	:	Proper data analysis is not done.
5.	Evaluation	(i) Evaluation team	:	No earmarked team
		(ii) Evaluation of data analysis	:	Data analysis is not done to reach logical conclusion. No action for improvement in scheme-design is taken.
6.	MIS	(i) Identification of critical information (ii) Flow of Information	:	No data feeding, analysis and reporting system exists, to reach quick decision-making.

- *Administrative Control over Field Officers and Staff:* In some states (e.g. Madhya Pradesh, Maharashtra) the district-level officers have been designated as Addl. CEOs, zilla parishad, and they are required to report to ZP. Also, zilla parishad has been given powers of transfer and postings of district and lower level functionaries. Besides, the field level functionaries have been asked to report to the concerned tier where their office is situated. In this context, the two important observations have emerged. These are:

i. The district-level officers find it difficult to control their lower level functionaries due to multiplicity of control. As the works of field functionaries are now supervised and monitored by various institutions like GP, Block, ZP and their own departments. Under such state, sometimes, simultaneously all give instructions, which may not necessarily be in harmony with each other, to field staff and officers. Such situations, in many cases, have resulted into confusion in performing duty at the GP level.
ii. The panchayat functionaries report to the gram panchayat where they are posted while they are supposed to work for 3-5 GPs (as normally one field functionary of a particular department is in-charge of more than one GP). Thus, while working in all the panchayats of their jurisdictions, the functionaries are not accountable to those gram panchayats where they are not reporting.

- *Syndrome of achieve Somehow Target, and Touch and Go:* In the present setup of development the field officers and staff are not having proper direction for development. Their work basically pertains to, first, identifications of beneficiaries, then giving work-order, and finally, doing check-measurements. This is all very mechanical and there is a 'touch and go' tendency in them, and the focus of the work remains on achieving target somehow. Moreover, there is no concern among functionaries for issues like people's participation, quality of work, whether the beneficiaries are getting the intended benefits, etc. They practically have no knowledge of how the people are to be involved in the development process — village level planning, project formulation, management of implementation, monitoring and evaluation. Work goes on just on an *ad hoc* basis, without any planning with the sole objective of achieving the physical target. What is equally distressing is that the field officers are not trained to handle the task of village panchayat and the sole criterion of judging the performance is target achieved by the field officers and staff.

  In addition, much-needed subject-specific specialised knowledge in planning and management of programmes is very badly missing in the field functionaries. It is precisely one of the crucial factors, why the implementation of programmes suffers. As a result, programme objectives are not fully achieved.

Transparency: Though all the states have provided provisions for transparency, yet these have not been translated into action. For example, in case of gram sabha, in some states some of the decisions that are taken in the open meeting are not reflected in the proceedings, in some other cases the proceedings are not made available to people, the necessary physical and financial details are not displayed outside the panchayat office and so on.

Delivery System at the Gram Panchayat Level: At the gram panchayat level, the delivery system is poor as far as the availability of services for health, education, agriculture, veterinary, drinking water, irrigation, bank loan, PDS, etc. is concerned. People have to struggle very hard for these basic services. The reasons, as analysed from the study include: *first*, poor infrastructure at the GP level; *second*, inadequate manpower (e.g. the teachers or health workers or agricultural workers are not posted in the required number); *third*, lack of logistics support; *fourth*, lack of proper administrative system (delegation of responsibilities and transfer of power, etc.); and *finally*, poor people's participation. Here, it needs to be recognised that mere placement of funds will yield result is highly misplaced in the absence of proper delivery mechanism at the village level. And, more specifically, how presently the PR institutions are handicapped in ensuring the delivery of services to people is illustrated (Gupta, 2003) by the table 5.2. The following examples would further substantiate how the services are affected due to poor service mechanism:

Agriculture programme is handicapped by a number of constraints. *Firstly*, by non-availability of inputs viz., seeds, fertiliser, pesticide and credit at one point. *Secondly*, by necessity of availing technical guidance from multiple departments viz., agriculture, horticulture, soil conservation, irrigation and agro-industries. And, *thirdly*, by dependence on multiple programmes such as watershed development, seed multiplication programme, special area programme, special crop development programme and so on. With this kind of an approach, the beneficiaries have to run to a number of places for availing technical services and inputs. And, moreover, many of them do not get the desired benefits.

Health services are denied to people due to a number of reasons such as lack of health centre, non-placement of doctors or health workers and non-availability of medicines or equipments. In several cases it is found that some or the other item is missing and all the items are not placed at one place in order to provide a full package that would deliver health services to people with ease. It is often noticed that people prefer to go to a private doctor than to go to a public health centre.

Children are deprived of primary education due to scarcity of adequate buildings, want of teaching-aids and poor environment around the school. New buildings are added (moreover, in many cases the quality of construction is poor) without providing full facilities to schools in order to make them fully functional. For instance, due to paucity of funds and a desire to cover large number of villages, schools are provided with 2-3 rooms, and similarly because of shortage of teachers, normally 2-3 teachers are posted. Together with this, teaching-aids are not adequately provided, leave alone proper environment and sports facilities. Now, under such circumstances the schools are rendered ineffective and leave teachers discouraged, parents unenthusiastic and children disinterested. There is only quantitative addition but no qualitative improvement. Similarly, veterinary services are not made available to people due to poor infrastructural, equipments and medicinal support. And, due to want of logistics support, the field staff find it hard to organise field-camps.

TABLE 5.2: **Causal-Matrix Indicating the Availability of Services to People**

S.No.	Causes	Type of Services Affected
1.	If buildings are created, either these are not having sufficient space or lack electricity or water facilities, or officers and staff are not posted in desired number.	Health centres, Primary schools, Veterinary services
2.	Even if officers and staff are posted, they might be either not having sufficient training to carry out the desired job or lacking the requisite supporting infrastructure or equipments for enabling them to provide services to people.	Watershed development, Development planning, Primary education
3.	It is found in some cases that infrastructural or manpower support system is available but is located either at inconvenient locations or in a scattered manner, that deprives people from availing the services.	Banks, Agricultural inputs
4.	In certain other cases, programme requires the support of various departments and each of them may not extend the same due to either lack of funds or non-availability of support system, or lack of coordination.	Watershed development, Infrastructural development, IRDP (now SGSY)
5.	In some specific cases of education and extension, there is often lack of logistic support and extension-aids that restrict the reach of field functionaries to the intended target	IEC, Training
6.	Due to inefficient management of implementation, the services may not reach in time or in the desired sequence	Immunisation, Childcare and nutritional programme (ICDS)

Source : Gupta, 2004.

5.4 Analysis of Financial Decentralisation

Analysis of Panchayat Taxes

Tax-base and Per Capita Income: The per capita tax collection for all the three tiers together is significantly high in the states of Haryana, Kerala and Punjab and the figures are Rs. 32.92, Rs 34.16 and Rs. 25.64 respectively (see table 5.3). The same figure (which is less than Rs. 5.0), is very low in the states of Assam, Madhya Pradesh, Orissa, Uttar Pradesh and West Bengal. In other states, the collection is not that good but in Andhra Pradesh and Maharashtra, it is quite encouraging.

When we look at the tax collection at the gram panchayat level, the tax-base is higher in the states of Haryana, Kerala and Punjab. The per capita tax collection is about Rs. 32.88 for Haryana, Rs. 34.16 for Kerala and Rs. 21.95 for Punjab (see table 5.4). While in the states of Assam, Orissa, Madhya Pradesh, Rajasthan, Uttar Pradesh and West Bengal, the per capita collection is quite low and it varies from Rs. 0.28 to Rs. 4.11 (see table 5.4). If we look at the intermediate panchayat (IP) level, the average per capita tax collection Rs. 0.45, which is pittance (see table 5.5). As regards the collection of taxes at the district panchayat (DP) level, this figure is very low and is less than Rs. 3.0 in almost all the states (see table 5.6). In Kerala, IP and DP have not been assigned responsibilities for tax collection.

Thus, the tax-base for the collection of local taxes is low in most of the states and it is comparatively better in the states of Haryana, Kerala and Punjab. The low tax-base is reflection of low capacity of taxpayers to pay and also that of tax collection authority to collect taxes.

Contribution by Gram Panchayats in the Total Tax Collection: The contribution of tax collection by the gram panchayats in the total tax collection forms the majority with the exception of Uttar Pradesh and Rajasthan, especially the former. The all India average figure is about 84.00 per cent (see fig. 5.1). In Uttar Pradesh, the collection is very less due to lesser demand made by the gram panchayats for local taxes.

Percentage Annual Increase of Collection of Taxes: At the gram panchayat level the percentage annual increase of collection of taxes is quite high in the states of Andhra Pradesh (15.12), Kerala (27.25), Madhya Pradesh (16.38), Maharashtra (29.05), Punjab (19.16) and Tamil Nadu (18.24) (see table 5.4). When we look at the tax collection for all the tiers, the same states have higher percentage of annual increase (see table 5.3). These percentages are much lower in both the cases in the states of Assam (1.76), Rajasthan (-2.44), Orissa (2.24) and West Bengal (6.25). Overall, the percentage increase is low in majority of the states. In Maharashtra, it has picked up in the recent years due to enhanced rates of property and water taxes (based on field study). What is significant here is that not only the tax-base is low but also rate of increase is low in most of the cases (see tables 5.3 and 5.4). Besides, both (tax-base and percentage increase) are less in the same states such as Assam, Orissa, Rajasthan, Uttar Pradesh and West Bengal, which is a matter of serious concern.

If we look at the collection of taxes in Haryana and Punjab, it is mainly on account of panchayat own property i.e. agricultural land (which is leased out on rent) while the income from tax revenue is comparatively very low. It reflects low contribution by individuals in the form of taxes, which is not a healthy sign (based on field study).

Own Income as Percentage of Total Income: The total income earned by the panchayats at all the three tiers is miniscule (see table 5.7) in most of the states except in Assam, Haryana, Kerala and Punjab. The figure (22.32%) in respect of Assam is high, it is basically the reflection of low income from other sources or in other words the grants given to panchayats is less. Though this percentage is lower in case of Kerala vis-a-vis Haryana and Punjab but it is due to significantly high grants which is several times more than that of in other two states. The lower percentage in other states is a reflection of high dependence on government grants and their low internal resources.

TABLE 5.3: **Collection of Taxes by All Tiers in Different States**

S.N.	Name of the state	Tax collection (Rs. in lakhs)			Per capita (1997-98) (Rs.)	Average %age annual increase	Status (High/Medium/Low)
		1990-91	1994-95	1997-98			
1	Andhra Pradesh	6269.57	9294.67	13779.69	20.87	14.98	Medium
2	Assam	300.96	326.05	345.99	1.54	1.95	Very low
3	Gujarat	2745.07	3366.38	4036.11	9.77	5.90	Low
4	Haryana	2939.00	4272.00	5301.00	32.92	10.05	High
5	Karnataka	1733.05	2464.47	3013.72	6.69	9.12	Low
6	Kerala	3131.51	5561.33	9909.34	34.16	27.25	High
7	Madhya Pradesh	1194.17	2581.22	3203.83	4.85	21.50	Very low
8	Maharashtra	3420.51	6306.88	11217.00	14.19	28.35	Medium
9	Orissa	590.37	801.90	699.38	2.18	2.24	Very low
10	Punjab	2155.70	4533.16	5386.62	25.64	18.35	High
11	Rajasthan	2427.61	2554.04	3074.57	6.98	3.25	Low
12	Tamil Nadu	1571.59	2471.15	3403.77	6.07	14.15	Low
13	Uttar Pradesh	2275.35	3902.67	4665.17	3.35	13.05	Very low
14	West Bengal	1423.42	1457.67	1959.21	2.88	4.68	Very low
	All India	37036.41	47794.06	67707.85	9.02	10.12	Low

Source : Calculations based on data from EFC Report, 2000.

TABLE 5.4: **Collection of Taxes by Gram Panchayats in Different States**

S.N.	Name of the state	Tax collection (Rs. in lakhs)			Per capita (1997-98) (Rs.)	%age of total collection (1997-98)	Average %age annual increase
		1990-91	1994-95	1997-98			
1	Andhra Pradesh	5219.81	7694.67	11650.09	17.65	84.55	15.12
2	Assam	204.48	221.33	234.85	1.04	67.87	1.76
3	Gujarat	2036.48	2479.84	3158.25	7.64	78.25	6.89
4	Haryana	2939.00	4272.00	5295.00	32.88	99.88	9.98
5	Karnataka	1733.05	2464.47	3013.72	6.69	100.00	9.12
6	Kerala	3131.51	5561.33	9909.34	34.16	100.00	27.25
7	Madhya Pradesh	1171.70	2343.32	2718.24	4.11	84.86	16.38
8	Maharashtra	3169.73	5733.14	10550.38	13.35	94.05	29.05
9	Orissa	590.37	801.90	699.38	2.18	100.00	2.24
10	Punjab	1815.71	3951.96	4610.30	21.95	85.59	19.16
11	Rajasthan	1672.00	1305.00	1344.00	3.05	43.72	-2.44
12	Tamil Nadu	1031.82	1845.01	2575.30	4.59	75.66	18.24
13	Uttar Pradesh	332.20	484.26	382.13	0.28	8.19	1.89
14	West Bengal	859.07	853.81	1296.51	1.90	66.14	6.25
	All India	31562.79	39161.55	56880.50	7.58	84.00	10.05

Source : Calculations based on data from EFC Report, 2000.

TABLE 5.5: **Collection of Taxes by Intermediate Panchayats in Different States**

S.N.	Name of the state	Tax collection (Rs. in lakhs)			Per capita (1997-98) (Rs.)
		1990-91	1994-95	1997-98	
1	Andhra Pradesh	262.44	400.00	532.40	0.80
2	Assam	96.48	104.72	111.14	0.49
3	Gujarat	169.96	254.03	357.81	0.86
4	Haryana	0.00	0.00	0.00	0.00
5	Karnataka	0.00	0.00	0.00	0.00
6	Kerala	0.00	0.00	0.00	0.00
7	Madhya Pradesh	17.18	224.78	428.81	0.65
8	Maharashtra	73.87	134.13	188.43	0.23
9	Orissa	0.00	0.00	0.00	0.00
10	Punjab	255.10	461.10	550.17	2.61
11	Rajasthan	631.37	924.40	1230.37	2.72
12	Tamil Nadu	539.77	626.14	828.47	1.47
13	Uttar Pradesh	0.00	0.00	0.00	0.00
14	West Bengal	298.89	328.47	408.49	0.60
	All India	1713.69	2533.37	3405.72	0.45

Source : Calculations based on data from EFC Report, 2000.

TABLE 5.6: **Collection of Taxes by District Panchayats in Different States**

S.N.	Name of the state	Tax collection (Rs. in lakhs)			Per capita (1997-98) (Rs.)
		1990-91	1994-95	1997-98	
1	2	3	4	5	6
1	Andhra Pradesh	787.32	1200.00	1597.20	2.41
2	Assam	0.00	0.00	0.00	0.00
3	Gujarat	538.63	632.51	520.05	1.25
4	Haryana	0.00	0.00	6.00	0.04
5	Karnataka	0.00	0.00	0.00	0.00
6	Kerala	0.00	0.00	0.00	0.00
7	Madhya Pradesh	5.29	13.12	56.78	0.09
8	Maharashtra	176.90	439.60	478.20	0.61

(Contd.)

TABLE 5.6 *(Contd.)*

1	2	3	4	5	6
9	Orissa	0.00	0.00	0.00	0.00
10	Punjab	84.89	120.10	226.15	1.07
11	Rajasthan	124.24	324.64	500.20	1.24
12	Tamil Nadu	0.00	0.00	0.00	0.00
13	Uttar Pradesh	1943.15	3418.41	4283.04	3.08
14	West Bengal	265.46	275.39	254.21	0.37
	All India	3759.93	6099.13	7421.63	0.99

Source : Calculations based on data from EFC Report, 2000.

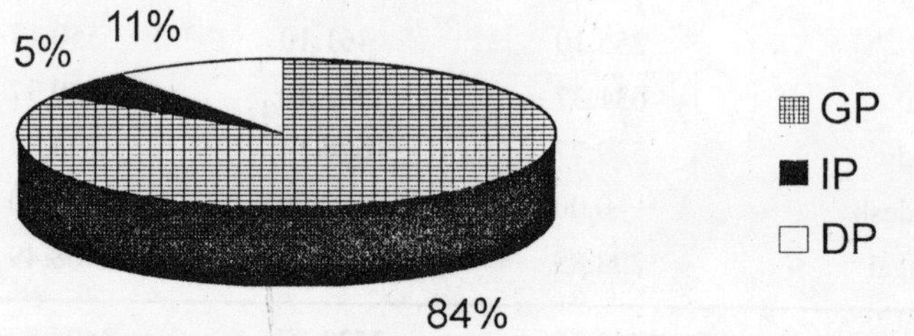

Fig. 5.1: Share of each Tier in the total Own Revenue of Panchayats (1997-98)
Source : Based on data given in EFC Report, 2000.

Contribution of own Tax vis-a-vis own Non-tax Income: It is important to know the composition of tax collection by the panchayats in order to know the tax income from 'personal income or property or business' on one hand, and the tax income from 'panchayat property and services (like health, drinking water, irrigation, panchayat land, etc.) provided by the panchayats', on the other. The former represents the capacity of people to pay for their own income or property, while the latter represents the capacity of the panchayats (local bodies) to charge for their property or for the services provided to people. The table 5.8 shows that the percentage contribution of own tax to total income is more than 50 in most of the states. The states like Assam, Karnataka, Kerala and Tamil Nadu have very high, more than 85 per cent, own tax contribution that reflects that the contribution from the individuals is higher. While in two states, Haryana and Punjab, this figure is exceptionally low, which reflects that the panchayats generate income from own property and people contribute less from their own income. Higher non-tax collection reflects that the panchayats have higher investment opportunities from their assets or more economic activities in their areas..

Efficiency of Collection of Tax: Efficiency of collection of tax in terms of : i. coverage of

TABLE 5.7: **Own Income vis-a-vis Total Income in Different States (1997-98)**

(Rs. in lakhs)

S.N.	Name of the state	Own income (Rs.)	Other income (Rs.)	Total income (Rs.)	Own Income %age of total income	Remarks	Overall rating of own income
1	Andhra Pradesh	13779.69	237378	251158.57	5.49	Good own income but low contribution in total income of panchayats	Good
2	Assam	345.99	1204.32	1550.31	22.32	Very low own income but higher percentage of total income due to low availability of funds with panchayats	Poor
3	Gujarat	4036.11	219217.60	223253.71	1.81	Low own income and low contribution in total income of panchayats	Poor
4	Haryana	5301.00	3221.00	8522.00	62.20	High own income and very high contribution in total income of panchayats (but low other income)	Very Good
5	Karnataka	3013.72	373792.82	376806.54	0.79	Low own income and low contribution in total income of panchayats	Poor
6	Kerala	9909.34	88367.25	98276.59	10.09	High income and good contribution in total income of panchayats (but higher income from other sources)	Very Good
7	Madhya Pradesh	3203.83	174697/64	177901.47	1.81	Very low own income and very low contribution in total income of panchayats	Very Poor
8	Maharashtra	11217.00	319530.01	330747.02	3.39	Good own income but low contribution in total income of panchayats	Good
9	Orissa	699.38	63302.87	64002.25	1.09	Very low own income and very low contribution in total income of panchayats	Very Poor
10	Punjab	5386.62	8154.42	13541.04	39.78	High own income and high contribution in total income of panchayats (but low other income)	Very Good
11	Rajasthan	3074.57	148946.18	152020.75	2.02	Low own income and very low contribution in total income of panchayats	Very Poor

(Contd.)

TABLE 5.7 *(Contd.)*

1	2	3	4	5	6	7	8
12	Tamil Nadu	3403.77	38812.64	42216.41	8.06	Low own income and low contribution in total income of panchayats	Poor
13	Uttar Pradesh	4665.17	83659.19	88324.36	5.28	Very low own income and low contribution in total income of panchayats	Very Poor
14	West Bengal	1959.21	46816.25	48775.46	4.02	Very low own income and low contribution in total income of panchayats	Very Poor
	All India	67707.85	1867846.53	1935554.38	3.49	Low own income and low contribution in total income of panchayats	Poor

Source: Calculations based on EFC Report, 2000.

TABLE 5.8: **Own Tax and Own Non-tax in Different States (1997-98)**

S.N.	Name of the State	Own Income (Rs.)	Own tax (Rs.)	Own non-tax (Rs.)	Own tax as %age of total income	Per capita own tax (Rs.)*	Per capita own non-tax (Rs.)**
1	2	3	4	5	6	7	8
1	Andhra Pradesh	13779.69	7990.07	5789.62	57.12	12.10	8.77
2	Assam	345.99	342.86	3.13	99.02	1.53	1.39
3	Gujarat	4036.11	3093.28	942.83	76.15	7.48	2.28
4	Haryana	5301.00	450.00	4851.00	8.21	2.79	30.13
5	Karnataka	3013.72	2592.43	421.29	86.23	5.76	0.93
6	Kerala	9909.34	8755.35	1153.99	88.36	30.19	3.97
7	Madhya Pradesh	3203.83	1167.10	2036.73	36.45	1.76	3.08
8	Maharashtra	11217.00	7459.15	3757.86	66.86	9.44	4.75
9	Orissa	699.38	462.34	237.04	66.25	1.44	0.74
10	Punjab	5386.62	69.85	5316.77	1.45	0.33	25.31
11	Rajasthan	3074.57	N.A	N.A	NA	N.A	NA
12	Tamil Nadu	3403.77	3293.80	109.97	96.22	5.88	0.19

(Contd.)

TABLE 5.8 *(Contd.)*

1	2	3	4	5	6	7	8
13	Uttar Pradesh	4665.17	865.36	3799.81	18.68	0.62	2.73
14	West Bengal	1959.21	784.61	1174.60	40.12	1.15	1.72
	All India	67707.85	37691.13	30016.72	55.12	5.02	4.00

Source: Calculations based on EFC Report, 2000.

* Higher own tax will reflect the higher own assets or higher own income of people.

** Higher own non-tax will reflect higher assets (of panchayats) or investment opportunities for the panchayats or more economic activities in panchayat area.

households (under all taxes including user charges) in the tax-net, ii. percentage collection of demand (see tables 4.24 and 4.25) and iii. the higher per capita collection (see tables 5.3 and 5.4) is much higher in Kerala. In Kerala, the panchayat of households paying taxes is 79% and the collection as percentage of demand is 72%. Though the tax collection is quite high in Haryana and Punjab, but it is mainly from the panchayat property (agricultural land) while the personal tax collection is far less.

In sum, based on the above analysis, the tax collection by panchayats is not satisfactory in all the states except in Kerala.

Correlation of Own Income with State Domestic Product and Infrastructure

There is a direct correlation of own income with state domestic product and the table 5.9 shows that its value is + 0.62. It shows that the income of people is going to be vital determinant for the panchayats to charge taxes and also to collect them. SDP covers the income in both rural and urban areas, however, such a correlation can be indicative of the direction of the two variables (per capita SDP and per capita own income of panchayats). Similarly, in most of the states, correlation is found with respect to infrastructural status and collection of taxes, and the table 5.9 shows that these two are in the same direction in most of the states. Also, it is indicated that the states (like Kerala, Punjab) with higher literacy rate are collecting higher taxes.

All these are pointers to the fact that the development policies, that are leading to higher individual income, infrastructural development and increased HRD, are going to result into higher tax collection.

Classification: Based on the own income of panchayats, as per table 5.3, the states can be classified as under:

High	:	Haryana, Kerala and Punjab
Medium	:	Andhra Pradesh, Maharashtra
Low	:	Karnataka, Rajasthan and West Bengal
Very low	:	Assam , Gujarat, Orissa, Madhya Pradesh and Uttar Pradesh

Critical Examination of Tax Collection

Based on field study, if we critically examine the collection of taxes, two factors are very crucial, *first*, the environment; and the *second*, income distribution. In spite of lower per capita income in Kerala, the tax collection is higher. It is due to above two factors. *First*, as the people are educated and aware, as well as the panchayats are well conscious about their responsibility of collection of taxes and taking up development works, the people pay tax. It indicates that the people show not only responsibility but also have faith in the abilities of panchayats to deliver services. Therefore, they make contribution as prescribed by the panchayats. Together

TABLE 5.9: **Own Income of Taxes by all Tiers in Different States vis-a-vis Per Capita State Domestic Product (1997-98)**

S.N.	Name of the state	Own income of all tiers (Rs in lakhs)	Per capita own income (Rs.)	Status of income (High/Medium/ Low)	Per capita state domestic product	Infrastructural status at gram panchayat level in the study area	Correlation direction between own income vis-a-vis infra-structural status at gram panchayat level
1	Andhra Pradesh	13779.69	20.87	Medium	10590	Poor	Not in the same direction
2	Assam	345.99	1.54	Very low	7335	Poor	Same direction (Positive)
3	Gujarat	4036.11	9.77	Low	16251	Poor	Same direction (Positive)
4	Haryana	5301.00	32.92	High	17626	Good	Same direction (Positive)
5	Karnataka	3013.72	6.69	Low	11693	Good	Not in the same direction
6	Kerala	9909.34	34.16	High	11936	Very Good	Same direction (Positive)
7	Madhya Pradesh	3203.83	4.85	Very low	8114	Poor	Same direction (Positive)
8	Maharashtra	11217.00	14.19	Medium	18365	Poor	Not in the same direction
9	Orissa	699.38	2.18	Very low	6767	Poor	Same direction (Positive)
10	Punjab	5386.62	25.64	High	19500	Good	Same direction (Positive)
11	Rajasthan	3074.57	6.98	Low	9356	Poor	Same direction (Positive)
12	Tamil Nadu	3403.77	6.07	Low	12989	Poor	Same direction (Positive)
13	Uttar Pradesh	4665.17	3.35	Very low	7263	Poor	Same direction (Positive)
14	West Bengal	1959.21	2.88	Very low	10636	Good	Not in the same direction

Source : Calculations based on EFC Report, 2000.

Note : 1. Correlation coefficient between own income of taxes by all tiers in different states vis-a-vis per capita state domestic product : 0.62.

2. Correlation direction between own income of taxes by all tiers in different states vis-a-vis infrastructural status at gram panchayat level: Same direction in most of the states.

with this, there is a good political environment in support of it. *Second*, the income of people in rural areas (in Kerala) is much higher unlike in other states where the income is confined to urban areas (even if the per capita income is lower in this state, there is a well distribution of income).

The own income in Haryana and Punjab is high. The main contribution is from the income from panchayat land. But we need to appreciate that these two states have considerably high entrepreneurship in agriculture. Moreover, there is a good scope for the success on account of higher income of people as the surplus can find good market. Besides, the panchayats have good established procedure for the collection of taxes. But if we look at the composition of collection of taxes in Haryana and Punjab, it is mainly on account of panchayat own property i.e. agricultural land (which is leased out), while the income from own tax is comparatively much lower. It reflects low contribution by individuals in the form of taxes, which is not a healthy sign.

For other states, the tax collection is not satisfactory. What is significant here is that in most of the states not only the tax-base is low but also increase in annual rate of collection is low. That apart, both (tax-base and percentage increase) are less in the same states such as Assam, Orissa, Rajasthan and West Bengal, which is a matter of serious concern. Also, the states of Assam, Orissa and Rajasthan have low per capita own income, low infrastructural base and low HRD level.

In sum, the above analysis shows that in three states of Haryana, Kerala and Punjab there is a good own income of panchayats which is much above that of in other states. It substantiates an important point that own income (or tax collection) is going to be higher in those panchayats where there is a good income of people, proper environment for tax collection and existence of appropriate tax collection mechanism.

Critical Issues of Financial Decentralisation

Degree of Fiscal Decentralisation

It can be measured in terms of:

- *Financial autonomy* — Measured by the ratio of local revenue from own sources to total local expenditure.
- *Revenue decentralisation* — Measured by the share of local revenue from own sources in total state government revenue.
- *Expenditure decentralisation* — Measured by the contribution of total local expenditure to state government expenditure.

Financial Autonomy

For all the tiers the financial autonomy is significantly low, due to low own income of panchayats. The all-India value of FAR is only 3.25 per cent for all tiers and 10.60 for GPs (see table 5.10 and fig. 5.2). Only two states : Haryana (36.50 per cent) and Punjab (33.89 per cent), and to some extent Kerala (13.78 per cent) have some reasonable value of FAR. In Gujarat, Karnataka, Madhya Pradesh, Maharashtra, Orissa and Rajasthan, FAR is lower than the national average. As a natural corollary to low financial autonomy, revenue dependency of panchayats on states and Centre is high. Higher FAR for GPs in comparison to that of all tiers, reflects that GPs are raising own income in excess of other tiers.

TABLE 5.10: **Important Ratios of Panchayat Finances in different States (1997-98)**

(in percentage)

S.N.	Name of the States	Financial Autonomy Ratio (FAR) (for all tiers)	Financial Autonomy Ratio (FAR) (for GPs)	Revenue Decentralisation Ratio (RDR) (for all tiers)	Expenditure Decentralisation Ratio (EDR) (for all tiers)
1	Andhra Pradesh	5.58	40.45	0.75	14.10
2	Gujarat	1.79	53.45	0.28	14.98
3	Haryana	36.50	38.78	0.67	1.88
4	Karnataka	0.82	12.37	0.24	29.32
5	Kerala	13.78	22.49	1.03	7.43
6	Madhya Pradesh	1.79	3.84	0.23	12.54
7	Maharashtra	2.45	19.63	0.39	16.56
8	Orissa	1.09	4.80	0.11	9.33
9	Punjab	33.89	37.23	0.59	1.67
10	Rajasthan	2.00	1.64	0.22	12.11
11	Tamil Nadu	6.94	10.84	0.20	2.81
12	Uttar Pradesh	5.14	0.51	0.19	3.42
13	West Bengal	3.55	4.11	0.13	4.08
	All India	3.25	10.60	0.28	9.16

Source: Calculations based on data given in EFC Report, 2000 and CMIE, 2002.

The funds (own income and devolved funds) over which the panchayats have rights to spend as per their own plans are very less in all the states except in Kerala, where per capita availability with the panchayats is Rs. 310.02 (57.50 + 252.52) (see table 4.26 of chapter four), the same varies from Rs 1.25 to Rs. 67.50 in all other states. Thus the low availability of funds that too coupled with tied form of grants makes it difficult for the panchayats to exercise their financial rights for the projects of local importance.

Similarly, at the all-India level the revenue decentralisation ratio (RDR) and expenditure decentralisation ratio (EDR) are 0.28% and 9.16 % respectively (see table 5.10), indicating low tax collection and expenditure by panchayats vis-a-vis state. What is significantly worrying is the decline in FAR since (see table 5.11) 1990-91, indicating erosion of autonomy of panchayats.

TABLE 5.11: **Financial Autonomy Ratio (FAR) at the all-India level for Panchayats of all Tiers**

(in percentage)

S.N.	Tier	FAR	Remarks
	1990-91	5.28	Decrease in financial autonomy
	1993-94	3.62	
	1997-98	3.25	

Source: Calculations based on data given in EFC Report, 2000 and CMIE, 2002.

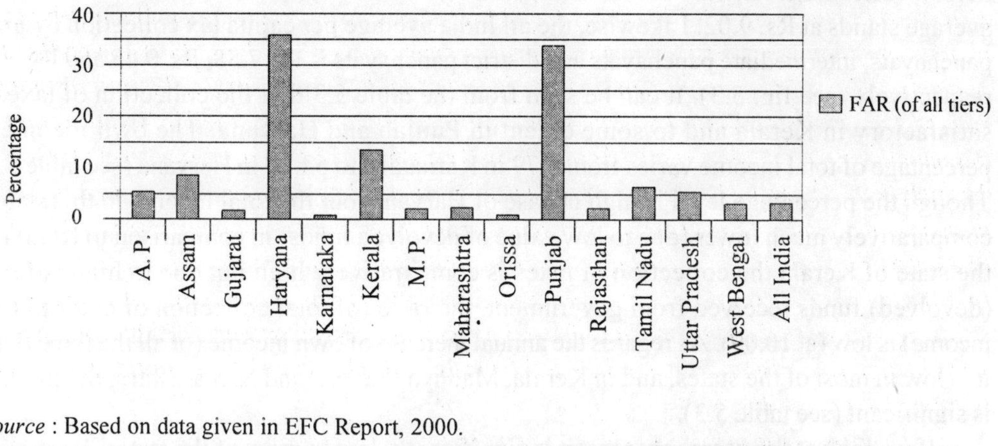

Source : Based on data given in EFC Report, 2000.

Fig. 5.2: **Financial Autonomy Ratio (of all Tiers) (1997-98)**

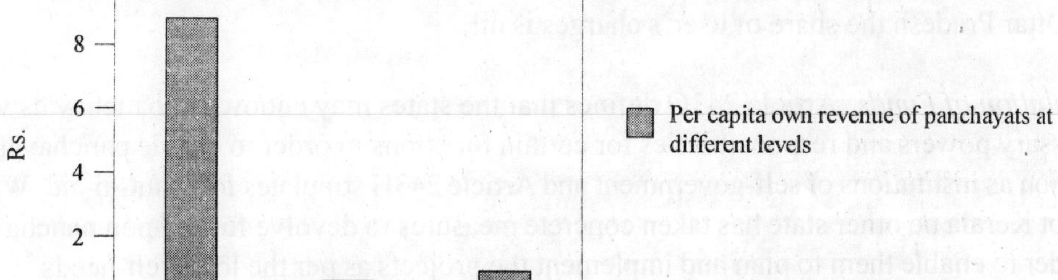

Source : Based on data given in EFC Report, 2000.

Fig. 5.3: **Per Capita Own Revenue of Panchayats at different Tiers (1997-98)**

Collection of Taxes: Under Article 243H the state may authorise the panchayats to impose and collect taxes. States have made provisions for the collection of taxes by the panchayats. However, the present status of panchayat finances is marked with low tax-base and poor institutional arrangements. If we examine carefully the poor state of collection of taxes, it will reveal that it is due to combination of various factors such as: *First*, lack of political will as there is a fear of losing popularity in the event of imposing taxes. *Second*, the existing income-base of the panchayats is very low, which leaves lesser scope for the panchayats to augment their income level significantly. *Third*, lack of confidence of people in the present set-up of PR institutions and delivery system, as people are skeptical about their abilities to provide services effectively to them. *Fourth*, the people are less concerned about the payment of taxes. Also, there is a lack of conducive environment in terms of educating and motivating the people for giving taxes in order to avail services. *Fifth*, the low income level of people to pay taxes. And, *finally*, high cost of collection of taxes at local levels.

If we examine the per capita total collection of taxes (tax and non-tax revenue) by all the tiers, it varies from Rs. 1.54 in Assam to Rs. 34.16 in Kerala (see table 5.3), while all India average stands at Rs. 9.02. Likewise, the all India average per capita tax collection by gram panchayats, intermediate panchayats and district panchayats is Rs. 7.58, Rs. 0.45 and Rs. 0.99 respectively (see fig. 5.3). It can be seen from the table 5.3 that the collection of taxes is satisfactory in Kerala and to some extent in Punjab and Haryana. The own income as percentage of total income varies from 0.79 in Karnataka to 62.20 in Haryana (see table 5.7). Though the percentage level is high in case of Haryana, but the total income in this state is comparatively much lower (due to low value of devolved funds) in comparison to Kerala. In the state of Kerala the collection of taxes is comparatively high but due to high value of (devolved) funds received from government, the ratio (of total collection of taxes to total income) is low (at 10.09). As regards the annual increase of own income (of all the three tiers), it is low in most of the states, and in Kerala, Madhya Pradesh and Maharashtra, the increase is significant (see table 5.3).

If we look at the users' charges, it is significantly low in most of the states. Its share in the total collection of taxes is reasonably good in the states of Gujarat, Karnataka, Kerala and Maharashtra (see table 4.24). While in certain states like Assam, Haryana, Meghalaya, Punjab and Uttar Pradesh the share of user's charges is nil.

Devolution of Funds: Article 243G defines that the states may endow the panchayats with necessary powers and responsibilities for certain functions in order to enable panchayats to function as institutions of self-government and Article 243H stipulates for grant-in-aid. While except Kerala no other state has taken concrete measures to devolve funds upon panchayats in order to enable them to plan and implement the projects as per the local felt-needs.

In Kerala, at the gram panchayat level in the study area, the per capita devolution of funds is Rs. 252.52 and as percentage of total income it is 63.85 (calculation based on table 4.26). The same figure in other states is nil.

SFC: As per Article 243I the states shall constitute state finance commission (SFC). The SFCs of almost all the states have submitted reports, still not much action has been taken to address the problem of panchayat finances. And no serious attempt has been made by the states to devolve funds upon panchayats to augment their own income. If we examine the salient recommendations (see appendix 1), these mainly pertain to the transfer of taxes, imposition of certain taxes, besides examining in general about panchayat finances. They have not looked into certain vital points such as requirement of development funds for panchayats, based on their needs how the resources to be raised by the panchayats or devolved by the state, minimum user charges, cross subsidy, tax collection mechanism and the measures for reducing horizontal and vertical imbalances. Although, in this regard, some recommendations have been made but they are not comprehensive.

Financial Autonomy of Gram Panchayats: As regards the financial autonomy, it is very badly restricted as the grants, mainly given to gram panchayats, are in the tied-form. The funds (own income and devolved funds) over which the panchayats have rights to spend as per their own plans are very less in all the states except in Kerala, where per capita availability with the panchayats is Rs. 310.02 (57.50 + 252.52) (see table 4.26 of chapter four), the same varies from Rs 1.25 to Rs. 67.50 in all the other states (while as per table in the state of Haryana the own income is very high, it is basically an exception, as explained in the footnote). Thus, the low availability, coupled with tied form of grants, makes it difficult for the panchayats to exercise their financial autonomy for the projects of local importance.

Self-government Role

Table 5.12 summarises the findings as presented above under the four dimensions of decentralisation. It also reflects that the panchayats have been denied the role of self-government, as per Article 243G. The panchayats have not been given autonomy under political, functional, administrative and financial spheres. They lack political autonomy due to government control over panchayats and untimely elections. As the functions have not been transferred to panchayats, the functional autonomy has suffered. Likewise, due to inadequate administrative arrangements for empowering panchayats with powers and support system (manpower, infrastructure, etc.), the administrative autonomy is affected. The insignificant devolution of funds upon panchayats has impacted on their financial autonomy. Besides, low tax-base of panchayats and low capacity of panchayats to raise taxes have further affected their own resources.

5.5 Implementation of Scheduled Areas Act

The contents of the Act reflect that the panchayats in the Scheduled Areas are expected to perform broadly development and regulatory roles. Besides, it is assumed that the panchayats would play the self-government role with the devolution of powers upon them.

TABLE 5.12: **Analysis of Panchayati Raj System**

S.N.	Dimensions	Items	Issues	Desired outcome (assumed)	Present status	Missing links
1.	Political	• Political status	Executive position to PR members	- PR members to be given executive status	- Executive position given	-
		• Election	Timely, free and fair elections	- Timely elections every five years will be held - Free and fair elections - Representation to wider sections - Village development needs will be covered in the election campaign	- Elections held. But delayed in Assam and Bihar for a long period and also in Andhra Pradesh, Gujarat Madhya Pradesh, Karnataka and Punjab - Elections marked with undesirable activities like use of more money and liquor, and also of violence in some cases - Influential people dominate the election process. Facilitating the political groups to expand their base. - Issues for discussion during elections are very limited and normally, the village development needs do not form the part of it	Election reforms lacking
		• People's participation	Attendance in the gram sabha	- People will attend the meetings in large number and participate in village development planning	- People do not attend meetings regularly and the attendance in the gram sabha is low.	- Lack of education and awareness - Disparities due to caste, class or gender affect participation

(Contd.)

TABLE 5.12 *(Contd.)*

S.N.	Dimensions	Items	Issues	Desired outcome (assumed)	Present status	Missing links
		• Functioning of gram sabha	People's needs and aspirations, and preparation of village plan	- The gram sabha will be able to address the people's problems and will prepare the village plan	- The gram sabha is not able to attend to people's problems adequately. It lacks transparency and is dominated by a few individuals.	- Lack of environment building. - Proper rules and procedure for functioning of gram sabha are lacking.
		• Accountability	Accountability of PR members to people	- PR members will deliver the desired results and will be accountable to people	- There is no well-defined accountability norm and the PR members are not accontable in any form for practical purposes	- Proper procedure and awareness among people for social audit are lacking
2.	Functional	• Transfer of functions	Transferring functions	- It will follow after the enactment of new panchayat Act	- Functions under most of the subjects are not transferred	- Lack of initiative by the departments at the state and centre levels
		• Assigning function-specific responsibilities	Giving responsibilities to panchayats for a particular function	- It was assumed that it will follow after the enactment of new panchayat Acts in the states	- Responsibilities are not clearly defined and there is confusion over the role of PRIs at the three tiers, and also between PRIs and departments	- Lack of appreciation for defining responsibilities
		• Inter-tier demarcation of functions	Demarcating subfunction under each subject for each tier	- It will follow after the enactment of new panchayat Act	- Demarcation not carried out in order to define clear responsibilities for each tier. There are overlapping areas of functioning among panchayats, resulting in confusion and conflicts	- Lack of appreciation for the need of demarcation of functions
3.	Administrative	• Planning - Planning unit	Planning system	- People and the PR members at the village	- Panchayats are unable to prepare plans due to	- Various components for planning not

(Contd.)

TABLE 5.12 *(Contd.)*

S.N. Dimensions	Items	Issues	Desired outcome (assumed)	Present status	Missing links
	- Planning methodology - Database - DPC		level will be able to prepare plans - DPC will be formed	poor people's participation, lack of knowledge and skills, and lack of support system - Functionaries are not provided training for local level planning - DPC not formed in all the states, and it has many deficiencies (see description in section 5.3) and is handicapped to take up the task of district planning	placed with the panchayats. - Moreover, there is a lack of appreciation for such needs (of planning)
	• Placement of officers and staff of line departments with PRIs	Administrative control over officers and staff	- Panchayats will have administrative powers	- Officers and staff are not placed with the panchayats and so they are not able to perform their duties	- State governments have not taken measures for deputation of officers and staff
	• Infrastructural and logistics support	Support system	- Panchayats will be able to deliver goods to people	- Support system is not provided to panchayats that is a big handicap for them	- No provision for strengthening the support system is made
	• Transparency	Transparency procedure	- Panchayats will provide scope for openness regarding the decision-making, and thus ensure transparency in the functioning	- Decision-making is marked with lack of openness and even the gram sabha's decisions are not transparent	- Lack of awareness among people to question about the decision-making and inadequate provisions for observing transparency

(Contd.)

TABLE 5.12 *(Contd.)*

S.N.	Dimensions	Items	Issues	Desired outcome (assumed)	Present status	Missing links
		• Institutional mechanism for planning, implementation, coordination and monitoring - Planning process and responsibilities - Implementation process and responsibilities - Coordination with different departments - Monitoring of progress of works	Institutional mechanism for the preparation of development plans and the implementation of works	- Panchayats will be able to perform their functions after they are constituted	- In the absence of proper procedure, the plans are not properly prepared and people's participation remains poor, and also not implemented by involving beneficiaries. It is the chairperson of the GP who undertakes the implementation of work - For want of training, functionaries lack requisite knowledge and skills for undertaking the task of village planning and implementation of programmes	- Proper measures not taken for defining responsibilities and the process for planning, implementation, coordination and monitoring - Beneficiaries' participation in the development process is not appreciated
4.	Financial	• Collection of taxes	Identification of items for taxes	- Panchayats will improve their internal resources through tax collection	- Own income of panchayats remains very low and there is a lack of initiatives by the panchayats for augmenting their income through collection of taxes and users charges - Tax collection mechanism poor	- Panchayats lack political will to impose taxes

(Contd.)

TABLE 5.12 *(Contd.)*

S.N.	Dimensions	Items	Issues	Desired outcome (assumed)	Present status	Missing links
		• Devolution of funds	Devolution of funds	- Panchayats will be able to deliver results for all development activities	- Panchayats have very little resources and the devolution of funds is insignificant	- State governments have not taken steps to devolve funds upon panchayats
		• Expenditure as per its own needs	Financial autonomy to panchayats	- Panchayats will be able to plan and spend as per their local need	- Panchayats virtually have no financial autonomy	- In the absence of devolution of funds, the panchayats' autonomy is affected

Note: The above observations are with respect to all the states except Kerala, the table 5.14 may be referred to for comparison of status in Kerala vis-a-vis other states.

Development Role

It pertains to approval and implementation of the plans, programmes and projects for socio-economic development, identification as well as selection of beneficiaries of poverty alleviation and other programmes, providing certification of utilisation of funds and control (clause 'm') over institutions and functionaries in all social sectors as also over local plans and resources for such plans including tribal sub-plans.

Regulatory Role (Consultative and Recommendatory Role)

It (as per clause 'm') pertains to enforcement prohibition of any intoxicant, ownership of minor forest produce, prevention of alienation of land; and to manage village markets and money lending. Similarly, regarding the acquisition of land, the Act has assigned consultative power to the gram sabha. For mining lease and grant of concession for the exploitation of minor minerals, the gram sabha has been given recommendatory role.

Self-government Role

The clause 'm' states that 'while endowing panchayats in the Scheduled Areas with such powers and authority as may be necessary to enable them to function as institutions of self-government.

Critical Observations

The same Body Exercising both Development and Regulatory Functions: Under the existing Act for Scheduled Areas, the panchayats will have to attend to both the roles viz., development and regulatory. In this context the following observations need to be taken into consideration:

The studies have indicated (field studies of Orissa, Madhya Pradesh and Maharashtra, see chapter four) that panchayats in the scheduled areas are marked with features like: *first*, insignificant participation of people in the gram sabha; *second*, lack of awareness in the people and poor capabilities among the panchayat members; and *third*, poor capacities of the panchayats and delivery system to handle the basic functions of development. Besides, the availability of basic services like primary education, health or drinking water is highly questionable, and due to lack of support from states the panchayats are not able to attend to these very functions up to any satisfactory level. Moreover, the public awareness and action for such needs is not visible.

To conclude, when the panchayats are not equipped to handle the basic functions, which are very vital for people, we need to reexamine the issues of burdening them with too many regulatory functions. Also, there is a danger that if the panchayats look into regulatory job, the development may not be attended in the desired way, not only due to their poor capacities to handle so many functions but also from the point of view of different perspective and approach attached to these two categories viz., 'development' and 'regulation'. Moreover, it is important to appreciate that we need to see the role of panchayats from the development perspective. With this kind of existing framework in which the gram panchayats will be handling both development and regulatory functions, the development is going to take backseat. No doubt, the regulatory functions are very essential, but these are to be handled by a separate body.

Envisaging the Self-governance Role in the Absence of Capacity Building: It is envisaged that the panchayats should function as units of self-governance. By assuming this role it enlarges their functional enormously. If we examine this aspect carefully, it will require handling of political, fiscal, and administrative subjects besides legislative roles (as per definition of self-government). Now this aspect should be looked in the light of two important points: *first*, what is the present capacity of local institutions, whether they are in a position to manage such responsibility; and *second*, what is the core responsibility of panchayats, which is undoubtedly the development. These two points should be borne in mind, while deciding the functional role of panchayats. And by assigning panchayats the role of self-governance, we will be asking them to look into too many functions, which may be difficult to handle in the absence of adequate capacity.

In sum, it appears that the present Act envisages too large a responsibility for the panchayats starting from village planning to implementation of plan to management of MFP and village markets to regulation of illicit liquor and money lending. With this kind of approach, there is no focused approach while. Rather development, which should be at the centre of the panchayat system in the tribal areas, has lost prominence. And it is likely that at the functional level, when the panchayats will start devoting their time and resources on regulation, the development of areas is further going to suffer. Moreover, experience shows that development and regulation require different approaches and cannot go hand in hand, so the efficiency of panchayats functioning, especially in respect of development, is bound to suffer. Besides, the following questions remain unanswered:

- *first*, what is not logical is as to why to give the dual responsibility (of regulation and development) to panchayats while both the functions require altogether different approach; and
- *second*, why the primacy of development has not been realised while the tribal areas with low HRD and infrastructural level require more focus on these issues.

No Power to Gram Sabha for Development Projects under Forest Land: As most of the tribal areas fall under forest areas (reserve or protected), so in the villages it becomes difficult to locate suitable land for development projects especially for check-dams or irrigation structures. It causes problems at the time of implementation of projects, and due to non-availability of suitable land, either projects get delayed or are not executed. But to handle this problem, which is very common in tribal areas, there is no power given to gram sabha in the Act.

5.6 Other Vital Issues

5.6.1 Observations from the People's Perspective

The major objective of the panchayati raj system has been to give opportunities to people to participate in the decision-making of the development process so that the grassroots problems can be reflected in the village development plans. Or, in other words, it was envisaged that the people would be given central position in the village development planning and implementation. But if we examine the observations made by the people during the field studies, the following points emerge:

Wide Disparities among People: There is a wide disparity among people on the basis of caste or income or property or affiliation to political party, which creates divisions among society. And in the absence of any proper corrective measure through sustained educational and economic programmes, the disparity continues to widen gap in some cases or to marginalise the disadvantageous people in many other. Environment for participation remains indifferent, passive and sometimes hostile. Such a state of village society is highly detrimental for the decentralisation process and needs urgent attention in order to involve people meaningfully in the village development. And without attending this vital issue the participatory development would remain a remote possibility.

Individuals are not Valued: Due to inherent tendency of central decision-making (existing political culture) and the tendency to project one's supremacy by PR members and elites, the individual's abilities are not given importance. The views of the individuals do not matter, and thus the possibility of participation as well as contribution by them is blocked.

'There is a wide disparity among people on the basis of caste or income or property or affiliation to political party, which creates divisions among society. And in the absence of any proper corrective measure through sustained educational and economic programmes, the disparity continues to widen gap in some cases or to marginalise the disadvantageous people in many other. Environment for participation remains indifferent; passive and sometimes hostile. Such a state of village society is highly detrimental for the decentralisation process and needs urgent attention in order to involve people meaningfully in the village development. And without attending this vital issue the participatory development would remain a remote possibility.'

Institutions are Inaccessible to People: In the absence of support system, local institutions do not attend to the basic needs of the people and fail to instil confidence in them.

Inadequacy of Proper Rules and Management: The present PR system does not give importance to rules and the procedures, as also it fails to recognise the need of management and professional approach for development and making basic services available to people. Thus, it puts the people on periphery as those who are manning the institutions can get away without following the norms and attending to the genuine needs of people.

Powers to Village Elites with little Accountability: Facilitating the political parties to get power, without accountability, in the absence of proper institutional mechanism.

Presently, with more focus on elections and certain other provisions on reservation, devolution of powers, etc., it appears that the PR system is assumed more as a political entity and of a source of power, rather than a means of providing services to people. In operational terms, there is a clear lack of vision as to how the people will get opportunities to participate, contribute and take advantage of development. Mere provisions on gram sabhas or elections or reservations or devolution of powers, though important, will not be enough for the people to participate, in the absence of conducive as well as enabling environment and without institutional development.

'Presently, with more focus on elections and certain other provisions on reservation, devolution of powers, etc., it appears that the PR system is assumed more as a political entity and of a source of power, rather than a means of providing services to people. In operational terms, there is a clear lack of vision as to how the people will get opportunities to participate, contribute and take advantage of development. Mere provisions on gram sabhas or elections or reservations or devolution of powers, though important, will not be enough for the people to participate, in the absence of conducive as well as enabling environment and without institutional development.'

5.6.2 Institutional Performance

Institutional role is vital in the development process, which will include planning of resources, implementation of programmes, monitoring and control, legal framework and making services available to people. A careful examination (see table 5.13) of factors responsible for institutional performance reveals how panchayats at the district, block and gram panchayat levels are incapacitated to perform. Some of the salient drawbacks are as follows:

To begin with, we take the case of *institutional processes*. It is marked with lack of procedures and norms for the conduct of gram sabha, transparency and accountability, planning and implementation of programmes. The work goes on without following systematic process, which results into confusion, loss of papers and documents, distrust and so on. As regards the HRD level of personnel of PR institutions, it seems to be the last priority, as if the planning and implementation of programmes can be handled without knowledge and skills. Here it is pertinent to mention that the functionaries are not properly equipped to handle the task of development due to lack of requisite technical, administrative and behavioural capabilities. They do not have skills for local level planning, management abilities to provide

TABLE 5.13: **Factors affecting Institutional Performance at the Panchayat Level**

S.N.	Component	Factors affecting Institutional Performance	Impact
1.	Institutional processes	- Inadequate procedure - Lack of transparency - No accountability of elected representatives	- Lack of direction for the functioning. Sometimes it causes confusion - Loss of papers and documents, which causes distrust - Decisions taken more by personal choice than by rational approach - The elected members are not accountable to people, so whatever members do there is a lack of control over that. There are instances of aberrations.
2.	HRD level of personnel	- Lack of technical, administrative and behavioural capabilities	- Personnel are not able to plan and implement programmes properly
3.	Financial system	- Poor financial base - Inadequate tax collection mechanism	- Lack of financial capacity and autonomy - Panchayats are unable to plan as per their local needs
4.	Planning	- Inadequate planning unit - No proper process and procedure of planning	- The planning of resources is on *ad hoc* basis, without following rational basis
5.	Management of implementation	- Lack of manpower and logistics planning - Poor infrastructural support - Inadequate management capabilities - Weak information system	- Management of implementation of works and the availability of services to people gets seriously affected
6.	Control and Monitoring	- Inadequate control and monitoring system	- Projects are not properly monitored - Financial position of the panchayat income and resources are not known in time.
7.	Legal system	- Weak mechanism to settle disputes and aberrations in decision-making	- There are inter- group conflicts, that disrupt the panchayat functioning and the implementation of works gets delayed - No check over aberrations or excess of power / control

services to people and the capabilities to work with and for the people. As for the financial system, it is handicapped by lack of resources, weak tax collection mechanism and inadequate procedure for finance and accounts. Regarding the issues of planning system, it is not placed in the desired manner of handling the task of participatory micro / district planning. Similarly, management of implementation suffers due to poor managerial abilities of functionaries and the lack of emphasis on involvement of beneficiaries in the implementation process. Likewise, monitoring and control of programme implementation suffer due to inadequate mechanism and the inabilities of functionaries. And, finally, the legal system is completely missing to address the disputes, which quite often arise.

It appears that, in the absence of vital fundamentals, the strengthening of local institutions is largely ignored or dealt with superficially. In practice, capacity-building of PR institutions remains a big cause of concern. The studies illustrate the infancy of the institutional development at the local levels.

In this backdrop, it is amply clear that the local institutions cannot be in a position to address the development needs and to meet the aspirations of people. It is simply assumed that panchayat Acts, though vital, would automatically lead to greater institutional capability. And simply conducting elections or extending powers will do very little, in the absence of adequate institutional support.

5.6.3 Salient Observations of Process of Decentralisation in the State of Kerala

Under people's campaign plan, the state government initiated several measures for decentralising the development process from district to gram panchayat level. The salient points are presented below:

Environment Building: In order to create conducive environment for the participation of people, instilling confidence in them and also for giving a sense of responsibility to PR members about the village development, the state took steps for building environment in villages. Under this programme, a number of activities such as distribution of literature on development issues, display of development activities through posters and charts, cultural programmes and orientation and training programmes were organised. The programme of environment building gave confidence to people and PR members that they can undertake the works of village development.

People's Participation: A special emphasis has been given to ensure people's participation in the gram sabha, in the decision-making process of development planning, as also in the implementation and supervision of programmes. For ensuring people's attendance in the gram sabha, activities like door-to-door contact programme, announcement in the villages and on radio, etc. have been taken up. Besides, development seminars at the gram panchayat level are organised. It has resulted in achieving four objectives: *first*, high attendance in the gram sabha; *second*, active participation in the discussion; *third*, collection of information on local problems and resources; and *fourth*, increased responsiveness of PR members for the problems of people and villages.

Institution Building: Government has initiated measures for institution building at all the three tiers. Infrastructural and logistics support has been added. The field officers and staff of line departments have been deputed to panchayats, which have been given working administrative powers. Also, these functionaries have been given training on local level planning, behavioural skills (to work with people and PR members), project formulation, implementation of works and so on. Transfer of functions, inter-tier demarcation of functions and devolution of funds upon panchayats have taken place. In a way, necessary functional, administrative and financial responsibilities and powers have been placed with the panchayats alongwith adequate support system that has provided good strength to the local institutions to perform their duties.

Devolution of Funds: The government has taken steps for devolving funds upon panchayats at all the three tiers. The funds are directly placed with the three tiers by the government. The devolution of funds was started in 1997-98 and 36 per cent of the state plan budget was earmarked for the municipalities and panchayats. Among panchayats, the gram panchayats were given bigger share in comparison to other two tiers. Under general sector, it was distributed to the gram panchayats, block panchayats and district panchayats in the ratio of 70:15:15. The devolution has improved the financial base of the panchayats significantly and resulted in providing financial autonomy to them in order to enable them to utilise funds as per local needs.

Planning: In order to make rational allocation of funds, a special drive has been undertaken for participatory planning. Under this, the elaborate guidelines and methodology for planning have been formulated. It includes a number of steps: *first*, defining planning process at the gram sabha and gram panchayat levels; *second*, formation of technical corps (groups) for giving technical inputs; *third*, database preparation and technical discussion about data analysis, backward and forward linkages analysis, inter-sectoral analysis, feasibility studies, project formulation and so on; *fourth*, project appraisal; *fifth*, finalisation of plan document at gram panchayat level; and *finally*, integration of gram panchayat plans with the block and district plans. Also, comprehensive training programmes for PR members and development functionaries were organised all over the state in order to equip them with the necessary knowledge and skills for planning.

Implementation of Programmes: Similarly, a detailed procedure for the implementation of works has been prescribed. It includes formation of beneficiaries committee, training of representatives of committee, supervision of quality of works by the beneficiaries, check-measurement procedure and monitoring of the progress of work.

System of Transparency and Accountability: In order to make people aware and to make panchayat functioning open, various steps have been taken for ensuring transparency in the functioning of panchayats. Some of them are display of accounts outside the gram panchayat office, disclosure of accounts in the gram sabha meeting, availability of proceedings of gram sabha and gram panchayat meetings, and involvement of beneficiaries in the implementation of works. With the increasing role of PR members and their responsibilities for the work, a system of social audit has been introduced in which people can ask questions to PR members about the decisions taken by them. Besides, financial audit has been introduced for checking accounts and the appropriateness of the financial procedures. These measures have helped not only in active participation by people but also in making PR members responsive to the people's needs and in observing the functional propriety, that has resulted in improving the effectiveness of PR institutions.

Overall, the measures initiated by the government in Kerala have led to good working environment, which has led to increase in demands from the people for their village development and has also provided opportunities to PR institutions to deliver goods. Finally, it has facilitated in improving the efficiency and effectiveness of local institutions in addressing the local development needs and aspirations of people.

In nutshell, in Kerala, unlike other states, the fundamentals are rightly placed and the comparative analysis is presented in the table 5.14. The state has given primacy to people's participation in a meaningful way and to developing capabilities of people at large and of PR members in particular. Genuine efforts have been made for institution building in terms of infrastructural, manpower, administrative and financial support. Initiatives have been taken for encouraging transparency in the functioning and for the accountability of elected representatives to people.

However, from the point of view sustainability of decentralisation process, the support from the state government is vital and should be on a sustained basis. Also, some aberrations that take place with regard to beneficiaries' selection, or engagement of proxy contractors for implementation of work, or inadequacy of social audit, need to be watched carefully and appropriate action needs to be taken for rectifying defects or improving procedures. And the overall spirit of decentralised governance that has been generated by people's plan campaign (PPC) should be sustained and further strengthened.

TABLE 5.14: **A Comparative Picture of Status of System of Decentralisation in Kerala and other States**

S.N.	Elements	Status in Kerala	Status in other states
1.	**Political Decentralisation**		
	Environment building	- Awareness building and training programmes at panchayat level	- No special efforts for environment building
	People's participation	- Improved attendance in gram-sabhas. Active participation by people due to better educational and awareness.	- Poor people's participation

(Contd.)

TABLE 5.14 *(Contd.)*

S.N.	Elements	Status in Kerala	Status in other states
	Role of PR members	- Active involvement by PR members due to their higher educational background, and improved knowledge and skills through training programmes	- Little interaction of PR members with people in development matters - Lack of initiative by the PR members for development activities
	Role of gram sabha	- High attendance. Active participation by the PR members and people	- Low attendance - Dominance by a few people
2.	**Functional Decentralisation**		
	Transfer of functions	- Transfer of functions for all the subjects has taken place - Also inter-tier demarcation of functions has taken place	- Transfer of functions has not been complete
3.	**Administrative Decentralisation**		
	Capacity building	- Well-organised training programme at all the three tiers. Close monitoring of programmes by the government	- Only a few programmes at concerned SIRDs but no comprehensive training programme
	Infrastructure	- Good infrastructure with gram panchayats	- Insufficient infrastructure
	Manpower support	- Good number of staff. Placement of staff and officers of other departments with gram / block / district panchayat	- Skeleton staff
	Planning		
	i. Planning unit	- Existing	- Partially existing
	ii. Database	- Prepared for each sector at GP, block and district	- Database not developed
	iii. Planning methodology		
	a. Procedure of planning	- Well-laid out procedure for planning at each tier	- No procedure developed
	b. Planning team at GP, block, and district	- Full-fledged planning team with experts.	- No earmarked team
	c. Technical team	- Formed at block and district	- No earmarked team
	d. Appraisal team	- Formed at block and district	- No earmarked team
	e. District planning committee	- DPC constituted	- Not constituted in some states
	f. Project formulation	- Proper procedure and techniques developed	- No attention is given
	g. Functions for each tier	- Clearly demarcated functions for each tier with regard to all	- Functions not clearly demarcated
	h. Integrated of GP plan with higher tiers	- Well-defined procedure	- No procedure prepared

Contd.

TABLE 5.14 *(Contd.)*

S.N.	Elements	Status in Kerala	Status in other states
4.	**Financial Decentralisation**		
	Devolution of funds	- About 40% of state plan devolved upon panchayats	- No devolution of funds
5.	**Overall Measures**		
	Role of Government	- People's plan campaign launched which resulted into higher people's participation	- No specific plan for strengthening participatory planning
		- Transfer of functions and devolution of financial powers upon panchayats	- No devolution of financial power

5.7 Indicators Analysis

5.7.1 Analysis of Prerequisites for Decentralisation

There are certain vital prerequisites (Manor, 1999), which need to be placed at the local levels, before any process of decentralisation should begin. These prerequisites are:

- Environment building: suitable behavioural and psychological factors;
- Sufficient powers to exercise substantial influence within the political system and over significant development activities;
- Sufficient financial resources to accomplish important tasks;
- Adequate administrative capacity to accomplish those tasks; and
- Reliable accountability mechanisms — to ensure both the accountability of elected politicians to citizens and the accountability of government officials to elected politicians.

Under each of the identified prerequisites, the analysis for assessing the status of prerequisites is carried out as per the specific initiatives taken by the states and the points have been given to each state (see tables 5.15 and 5.16).

- ***Under Political Decentralisation***

Political Devolution: The states have made suitable provisions in their panchayat Acts for timely election and giving executive position to the chairpersons of three-tiers.

Environment Building: Suitable Behavioural and Psychological Factors: Environment building is vital for providing a suitable environment for decentralisation so that the people can participate freely and actively. The state of Kerala has taken special measures under people's plan campaign in which awareness building activities like cultural shows, village meetings, door-to-door campaign, dissemination of information through visual and print media, etc. were organised. Also, under sensitisation programme, training programmes for PR members and other field officers and staff were organised at all the three tiers in a comprehensive manner. While in other states some efforts have been made partially for awareness building.

Reliable Accountability Mechanisms to ensure both the Accountability of Elected Politicians to Citizens and the Accountability of Government Officials to Elected Politicians

Though the states have made an attempt to ensure accountability, yet it has not been ensured fully in most of the states, except Kerala. As regards social audit, the government in Kerala has given orders and framed guidelines for it and the people have been made aware. In other states, some provisions have been made in the Act but necessary awareness among people has not been duly ensured. Regarding the accountability of officials to PR members, some steps, in terms of writing of ACRs of officers of line departments, have been taken in Kerala and the states under category B.

- **Under Functional Decentralisation**

Sufficient Powers to Exercise Substantial Influence within the Political System and over Significant Development Activities (transfer of functions): In order to provide the functional support to panchayats, the Kerala government has taken initiatives for transfer of functions to panchayats and also for demarcation of functions among three tiers. Whereas other states have taken some steps for transferring partially the functions to panchayats, but no concrete steps have been taken to demarcate the functions among three tiers.

- **Under Administrative Decentralisation**

Adequate Administrative Capacity to accomplish Tasks: In Kerala the steps have been taken by the government to transfer the services of field officers and staff of several (see chapter 3) departments at three tiers. The planning unit has been partially set up in terms of facility for database preparation, formulation of planning methodology and the planning process, and training to field officers and staff. Still, there is a need for creating infrastructure and providing equipments at all the three tiers. In other states, the transfer of field officers and staff to panchayat levels has not taken place, and also planning units have not been set up. In the states of Maharashtra and Karnataka, under the category B, only a few officers and staff have been placed partially with the zilla parishad.

Similarly, in the state of Kerala the measures have been taken to provide infrastructural and logistics support and to impart training to field officers and staff for various development programmes. As regards the transparency, it has been ensured by the Act and also measures have been taken to ensure its implementations by way of increasing public awareness. While other states are lacking in these areas, as indicated by table 5.15.

TABLE 5.15: **Analysis of Status of Prerequisites for Decentralisation — Procedure of Points**

Prerequisites	Indicators	Present status	Points	Category A	Category B	Category C
1	2	3	4	5	6	7
Political Decentralisation						
Political Devolution	- Timely election	i. Timely election ii. Untimely iii. Not at all	1 .5 0	Timely election provided by the Act	Timely election provided by the Act	Timely election provided by the Act
	- Political status to chairpersons of panchayats	i. Provided by the Act ii. Not provided	1 0	Provided by the Act	Provided by the Act	Provided by the Act
Environment building: suitable behavioural and psychological factors	- Orientation workshop in the villages	i. Very good ii. Good iii. Average	1 .5 0	Very good	Good	Average
	- Training for attitudinal changes among PR members & field officers and staff	i. Organised ii. Partially iii. Not organised	1 .5 0	Organised	Partially organised	Partially organised
	- Distribution of literature among villagers and conduct of gram sabha	i. Fully done ii. Partially done iii. Not done	1 .5 0	Fully done	Partially done	Partially done
	- Training to PR members for basic subjects	i. Fully provided ii. Partially provided iii. Not provided	1 .5 0	Fully provided	Partially provided (Only general purpose training)	Partially provided
Reliable accountability mechanisms to ensure both the accountability of elected politicians to citizens, and the accountability of government officials to elected politicians	- Accountability system with proper procedure (including social audit)	i. Full ii. Partial iii. Not done	1 .5 0	Partial (but significant steps)	Partial	Partial

(Contd.)

TABLE 5.15 *(Contd.)*

1	2	3	4	5	6	7
	- Accountability of government officials to elected representatives	i. Full ii. Partial iii. Not done	1 .5 0	Partial	Partial	Not done
Functional Decentralisation						
Sufficient powers to exercise substantial influence within the political system and over significant development activities (transfer of functions)	- Transfer of functions in each subject	i. Full ii. Partial iii. Not done	1 .5 0	Full	Partial	Partial
	- Subject-wise demarcation of functions at each tier	i. Full ii. Partial iii. Not done	1 .5 0	Full	Not done	Not done
Administrative Decentralisation						
Adequate administrative capacity to accomplish tasks	- Placement of field officers & staff with each tier	i. Full ii. Partial iii. Not done	1 .5 0	Partial	Not done (In Karnataka and Maharashtra, some staff deputed to ZP)	Not done
	- Planning unit at each tier	i. Set up fully ii. Partial set-up iii. No set-up	1 .5 0	Partial set-up	No set-up	No set-up
	- Training to field officers and staff for planning and implementation	i. Fully organised ii. Partially organised iii. Not organised	1 .5 0	Fully organised	Partially organised	Not organised
	- Infrastructural support for office, training centre, etc.	i. Fully provided ii. Partial iii. Little support	1 .5 0	Fully provided	Partial	Little support

(Contd.)

TABLE 5.15 *(Contd.)*

1	2	3	4	5	6	7
	- Logistics support	i. Fully provided ii. Partial iii. Little support	1 .5 0	Fully provided	Partial	Little support
	- Transparency system	i. Full ii. Partial iii. Not done	1 .5 0	Full	Partial	Partial
Financial Decentralisation Sufficient financial resources to accomplish important tasks	- Financial management and accounting system	i. Set-up ii. Partial set-up iii. No set-up	1 .5 0	Partial set-up	Partial set-up	Partial set-up
	- Devolution of funds	i. Full ii. Partial iii. Not done	1 .5 0	Full	Partial	Not done

Prerequisites

Category A — Kerala

Category B states — Gujarat, Karnataka, Maharashtra and West Bengal.

Category C states — Andhra Pradesh, Assam, Haryana, Madhya Pradesh, Punjab Orissa, Rajasthan, Tamil Nadu and Uttar Pradesh.

TABLE 5.16: **Summary of Points achieved by Different States for placing Prerequisites for Decentralisation**

S.N.	Category	Name of the state	Points for Prerequisite						Total points	Achievement as % of total points
			Political decentralisation			Functional decentra-lisation	Administrative decentra-lisation	Financial decentra-lisation		
			Political devolution	Environment building	Accountability	Transfer of functions	Capacity to function	Financial system and devolution of funds		
1	A	Kerala	2.0	4.0	1.0	2	5.0	1.5	15.5	86.11
2	B	Gujarat	2.0	2.0	1.0	.5	2.0	1.0	8.5	47.22
3		Karnataka	2.0	2.0	1.0	.5	2.5	1.0	9.0	50.00
4		Maharashtra	2.0	2.0	1.0	.5	2.5	1.0	9.0	50.00
5		West Bengal	2.0	2.0	1.0	.5	2.0	1.0	8.5	47.22
6	C	Andhra Pradesh	2.0	1.5	5	.5	.5	.5	5.5	30.55
7		Assam	NA	-	-	-	-	-	-	-
8		Haryana	2.0	1.5	5	.5	.5	.5	5.5	30.55
9		Madhya Pradesh	2.0	1.5	5	.5	.5	.5	5.5	30.55
10		Meghalaya	NA	-	-	-	-	-	-	-
11		Punjab	2.0	1.5	5	.5	.5	.5	5.5	30.55
12		Orissa	2.0	1.5	5	.5	.5	.5	5.5	30.55
13		Rajasthan	2.0	1.5	5	.5	.5	.5	5.5	30.55
14		Tamil Nadu	2.0	1.5	5	.5	.5	.5	5.5	30.55
15		Uttar Pradesh	2.0	1.5	5	.5	.5	.5	5.5	30.55

• Under Financial Decentralisation

Sufficient Financial Resources to accomplish Important Tasks: Kerala has taken concrete measure for devolving funds upon panchayats from the state plan. In the states of Gujarat, Karnataka and Maharashtra, funds are placed with the zilla parishad, but these are earmarked for certain schemes. But in other states there was no devolution of funds. With regard to setting up of system for financial management and accounting, it is not fully set up in all the states.

Based on the points secured, the states (about prerequisites) have been classified as under:

Category A :	Kerala
Category B :	Gujarat, Karnataka, Maharashtra and West Bengal
Category C :	Andhra Pradesh, Assam, Haryana, Madhya Pradesh, Punjab, Orissa, Rajasthan, Tamil Nadu and Uttar Pradesh

In sum, none of the states, except Kerala, have tried to place prerequisites for decentralisation, while operationalising their respective panchayat Acts. The efforts for creating conducive environment have not been made in order to prepare people especially from weaker sections to participate in local village development. There are various behavioural (due to gender and / or inter-caste, inter-class or inter-personal relationship) and psychological (mind-set, inertia) factors that have bearing on the way people interact and participate, but attempts are not made to bring attitudinal changes to create favourable factors for participation in the local development. Apart from these, the steps for transferring functions, and enhancing administrative capacity and financial resources together with accountability mechanism have not been taken as prerequisites to enable panchayats to function as institutions of self-government.

Finally, if we look at the summary of the points that are given to different states (see table 5.16), Kerala has got 15.5 points, which is 86.11 per cent of the total points, and the states under category B have got between 8.5 and 9.0 points, indicating 47.22 per cent to 50.00 per cent of the efforts required for placing prerequisites. And the points secured by the states under category C are 5.5, which is 30.55 per cent of the desired efforts for decentralisation. The analysis reflects that in Kerala more than eighty per cent (86.11) of the required efforts were made to place prerequisites in the desired shape at the local levels.

5.7.2 Analysis of Present Status of PR System

The findings in this section are analysed based on the field study and survey conducted, the salient point are listed below (see table 5.17):

• Under Political Decentralisation

Political Devolution

Timely Elections: Most of the states have conducted their panchayat elections in time but in

TABLE 5.17: **Measuring the Efficacy of Present Status of PR System - Procedure for points**

S. N.	Item	Issues	Indicator	Status	Points	Category A	Category B	Category C
1.	**Political Decentralisation**	Election	a. Timely election	i. Timely election ii. Untimely iii. Not at all	1 .5 0	Timely election	Timely election (but not in Gujarat, Karnataka and Punjab)	Timely election (But not in A.P. and M.P., and not held in Assam till 2000)
		Political devolution	b. Political position	i. Provided by the Act ii. Not provided	+1 - 1	Provided by the Act	Provided by the Act (term for the chairpersons deduced in Karnataka and Maharashtra)	Provided by the Act
	Environment in the panchayat	Socio-political environment	a. Socio- politico groups	i. Supportive ii. Neutral iii. Warring groups	+1 0 -1	Supportive	Normal	Normal (Warring groups in case of UP)
		People's participation	a. Attitude of people	i. Supportive ii. Normal (passive) iii. Negative	+1 0 -1	Supportive	Normal (passive)	Normal (Negative in case of UP)
		Participation of officials and staff	a. Attitude of officials and staff	i. Supportive ii. Normal iii. Negative	+1 0 -1	Supportive	Normal	Normal
	Accountability	Financial and social audit	a. Financial audit	i. Full system ii. Partial iii. No	1 .5 0	Full	Full	Full
			b. Social audit at GP level	i. Fully developed ii. Partial iii. No	1 .5 0	Partial	No (In Karnataka, *Jamabandi*)	No
2.	**Functional Decentralisation**	Functions at three tiers	a Transfer of functions (all subjects)	i. Full ii. Partial iii. No	1 .5 0	Full	Partial	Partial

(Contd.)

TABLE 5.17 *(Contd.)*

S. N.	Item	Issues	Indicator	Status	Points	Category A	Category B	Category C
			b. Transfer of functions upon panchayats for basic services	i. Full ii. Partial iii. No	1 .5 0	Full	Partial	Partial
3.	**Administrative Decentralisation**							
	Capacity of PR institutions	People's capacity	a. Literacy level	i. High ii. Medium iii. Low	1 .5 0	High	Medium	Low
			b. Awareness level	i. High ii. Medium iii. Low	1 .5 0	High	Medium	Low
		Capabilities of PR members	a. Education level of PR members	i. High level ii. Medium iii. Low	1 .5 0	High level	Medium	Low
			b. Ability to manage panchayat functioning	i. High ii. Medium iii. Low	1 .5 0	High	Medium	Medium
			c. Ability to do planning	i. High ii. Medium iii. Low	1 .5 0	Medium	Low	Low
			d. Ability to implement and monitor the programmes	i. High ii. Medium iii. Low	1 .5 0	Medium	Medium	Low
		System of local level planning (at all three tiers)	a. Planning Unit	i. Fully developed ii. Partial iii. Not existing	1 .5 0	Partial	Not existing	Not existing
			b. Database development facility	i. Fully developed ii. Partial iii. Not existing	1 .5 0	Fully developed	Not existing	Not existing

(Contd.)

TABLE 5.17 *(Contd.)*

S. N.	Item	Issues	Indicator	Status	Points	Category A	Category B	Category C
			c. Planning methodology	i. Formulated	1	Formulated	Not formulated	Not formulated
				ii. Partially done	.5			
				iii. Not formulated	0			
		Support system	a. Manpower	i. Full support	1	Partial	Weak	Weak
				ii. Partial	.5			
				iii. Weak	0			
			b. Infrastructural support	i. Full support	1	Full	Partial/Weak in case of Maharashtra	Weak
				ii. Partial	.5			
				iii. Weak	0			
			c. Logistics (equipments, vehicles, etc.)	i. Fully provided	1	Partial	Partial	Weak
				ii. Partial	.5			
				iii. Not provided	0			
		Administrative set-up (at all three tiers)	a. Administrative structure (control over deptt.)	i. PRIs have full control	1	Partial control	No control	No control
				ii. Partial control	.5			
				iii. No control	0			
			b. Writing of ACRs	i. Initiated by PR heads	1	Partial	Partial (not in Punjab and Haryana)	No
				ii. Partial	.5			
				iii. No	0			
		System of transparency and monitoring	a. System of transparency at GP level	i. Full system	1	Full	Partial	Partial
				ii. Partial	.5			
				iii. No	0			
			b. System of monitoring at GP level	i. Full system	1	Partial	No	No
				ii. Partial	.5			
				iii. No	0			
		Implementation of programmes	a. Implementation planning	i. Planning made	1	Planning made	Not done	Not done
				ii. Partial	.5			
				iii. Not done	0			
			b. Beneficiaries' participation	i. Good participation	1	Good participation	Not involved	Not involved
				ii. Partial	.5			
				iii. Not involved	0			

(Contd.)

TABLE 5.17 *(Contd.)*

S. N.	Item	Issues	Indicator	Status	Points	Category A	Category B	Category C
		Tax collection mechanism	Tax collection mechanism	i. Well established ii. Partially existing iii. Not at all	1 .5 0	Well established	Partially existing	Partially existing
4.	**Financial Decentralisation**	Financial devolution (at all three tiers)	a. Devolution of funds	i. Full ii. Partial iii. No	1 .5 0	Full	Partial (not in Punjab and Haryana)	No
		Taxation	a. Tax collection base at district level	i. High ii. Medium iii. Low	1 .5 0	High	Medium (High in Punjab and Haryana but low in Karnataka, Gujarat and West Bengal)	Low (medium in Andhra Pradesh)
			b. Financial management	i. Full system ii. Partial iii. No	1 .5 0	Full	Partial	Partial

Present status

Category A — Kerala

Category B states — Gujarat, Haryana, Karnataka, Maharashtra, Punjab and West Bengal

Category C states — Andhra Pradesh, Assam, Madhya Pradesh, Orissa, Rajasthan, Tamil Nadu, Uttar Pradesh.

Note : In Kerala in spite of some aberrations, the system of planning and implementation of programmes has been very well-placed in comparison to other states. Transparency, social audit and financial management are observed satisfactorily, though there may be a need of improvement.

the states of Andhra Pradesh, Karnataka and Madhya Pradesh, the elections were delayed, and in the states of Punjab and Gujarat they have been postponed. In case of Assam elections were held after the gap of nine years.

Political Position: All the states have provided the necessary political positions to elected representatives at all the three tiers.

Environment in the Panchayats: For assessing the environment in the panchayats the issues considered are: socio-political environment, people's participation and participation of officials and staff.

As per the information gathered about the indicators, it was revealed that in Kerala there are supportive socio-political groups that have helped in the decentralisation process. Also, the attitude of people and official and staff are found to be supportive. In this state, the government has taken initiatives for creating conducive environment through awareness building programmes and training for attitudinal changes that has resulted in favourable and supportive environment for participatory planning and development. The field observations revealed that in other states the environment in the panchayat is normal which does not inspire much confidence in the process of decentralisation. But the matter of particular concern is the presence of warring groups and negative attitude of several people (at the village level) in the state of Uttar Pradesh, which is having some dampening effect on the measures initiated by the state government (in 1999) for empowering the panchayats.

Accountability: The financial audit has been put in place in all the states, while in none of the states, except Kerala, the social audit has been given due importance in operational terms. Though the provisions have been made for the social audit, but in the gram sabha PR members are not very responsive for the questions raised by the people, whereas in Kerala the chairpersons of gram panchayats have to answer the questions in the gram sabha and take appropriate action if required. However, much more needs to be done to strengthen social audit in Kerala.

- ***Under Functional Decentralisation***

Except in Kerala, the functions have not been fully transferred to the panchayats. Even the subjects under basic services like primary education, health, drinking water, agriculture, etc. are transferred partially in other states.

- ***Under Administrative Decentralisation***

Capacity of PRIs

People's Capacity : To understand the capacity of people two parameters viz., literacy level and awareness level were identified. The observations and available information indicated that the literacy and awareness are high in the case of Kerala, while the same is medium in the states covered under category B and low under category C.

Capabilities of PR Members: For judging the capabilities of PR members the four indicators were chosen. These are: education level of PR members, ability to manage panchayat functioning, ability to do planning, and ability to implement as well as monitor the programmes. In all these indicators, Kerala's performance is much better.

System of Local Level Planning: Of particular importance was the need to assess the existing planning system at the gram panchayat level. We identified three fundamental factors: *First*, planning unit; *second*, database development facility; and *third*, planning methodology. Here also Kerala stands apart from other states and has taken concrete measures for improving the system of local level of planning.

Support System: It was of vital importance to study the support system available with the gram panchayats. For this we studied manpower, infrastructural and logistics support available at the gram panchayat level in order to enable it to implement development programmes (or deliver goods and services to people). The support system is far better placed with the gram panchayats in Kerala that has enabled them to have efficient delivery mechanism.

Administrative Set-up: Administrative set-up was studied to know the control of PRIs over the line departments. It brought out that in Kerala the PRIs have partial control over some departments viz., block, agriculture, animal husbandry, health, drinking water, ICDS and primary education. The other states do not have control over line departments for practical purposes. As regards writing of the ACRs, it is written by the chairpersons (of ZP and Block) only of CEO, ZP, BDO and officer of line departments in the case of Kerala, while in other states of category B, ACRs of only CEO, ZP is written by the chairperson of ZP.

System of Transparency: The states have made necessary provisions for maintaining transparency either through panchayat Act or government order, and these provisions make it mandatory for the panchayats to display their accounts outside their offices and at prominent places, to disclose the accounts in the gram sabha, and to provide the certified copies to people, if demanded. But in practice, it is Kerala which has been able to successfully implement the provisions of transparency. It is due to high awareness among people, the consciousness among PR members about the need of transparency in the functioning of panchayats and constant monitoring by the state government . While in other states people are not aware and PR members are not very keen about.

System of Monitoring: The system of monitoring at the GP level has been partially set up in Kerala, and the necessary physical and financial status of various programmes and schemes can be monitored smoothly. In other states, the status report is not available in time and also the status is not monitored properly.

Implementation: Implementation of programmes lacks proper planning and beneficiaries' participation, except in Kerala, though it may require improvement.

Similarly, *the tax collection mechanism* is not well-established in all the states, except in Kerala.

- ***Under Financial Decentralisation***

To examine the financial decentralisation, broadly three parameters viz., devolution of funds, tax collection base and financial management were identified.

Devolution of Funds: In Kerala, the funds have been devolved directly upon all the three tiers. As these funds are untied (in nature), panchayats have flexibility in having the schemes suited to the local needs. Though the states like Gujarat, Karnataka, Madhya Pradesh and Maharashtra are getting funds directly from the state plans but these funds are earmarked for a particular programme / scheme and the zilla parishads in these states have virtually no flexibility of having the schemes of their choice.

Tax Collection Base: As regards the tax collection base, it has significant base in Haryana, Kerala and Punjab, whereas in other states it is very low.

Financial Management: Except in Kerala, other states are not having adequate financial management in terms of trained personnel, fund planning, maintenance of books of accounts and management of tax collection.

Based on the analysis and the points assigned to states, the following classification (of present status) of states has been made (see table 5.18):

Category A : Kerala
Category B : Gujarat, Haryana, Karnataka, Maharashtra, Punjab and West Bengal
Category C : Andhra Pradesh, Assam, Madhya Pradesh, Orissa, Rajasthan, Tamil Nadu, Uttar Pradesh

Finally, the points given to different states have been summarised in the table 5.16. It shows that Kerala has got 26.5 points, which is 85.48 per cent of the total points, and the states under category B have got between 9.0 and 10.0 points with achievement level between 29.03 per cent and 34.25 per cent. But the points secured by the states under category C are very low and are between 3.5 and 6.0, signifying the achievement between 11.29 per cent and 19.35 per cent. This analysis presents a scenario which shows that all the states are lagging behind in decentralising the development system, but only in Kerala the process of decentralisation has

TABLE 5.18: **Summary of Points for Present Status of PR System in different States**

S.N.	Category	Name of the State	Points for present status						Total	%age maximum possible points
			Political decentralisation			Functional decentralisation	Administrative decentralisation	Financial decentralisation		
			Political devolution	Environment building	Accountability	Transfer of functions	Capacity of PRIs	Devolution of funds and taxation		
1	A	Kerala	2.0	1.5	2.0	3.0	15.0	3.0	26.5	85.48
2	B	Gujarat*	1.5	1.0	1.0	0	5.0	1.0	9.5	30.64
3		Haryana	2.0	1.0	1.0	0	4.5	1.5	10.0	32.25
4		Karnataka ***	1.0	1.0	1.0	0	5.0	1.0	9.0	29.03
5		Maharashtra **	1.5	1.0	1.0	0	4.5	1.5	9.5	30.64
6		Punjab *	1.5	1.0	1.0	0	4.5	1.5	9.5	30.64
7		West Bengal	2.0	1.0	1.0	0	5.0	1.0	10.0	32.25
8	C	Andhra Pradesh *	1.5	1.0	1.0	0	1.5	1.0	6.0	19.35
9		Assam ****	1.0	-	1.0	0	1.5	0	3.5	11.29
10		Madhya Pradesh *	1.5	1.0	1.0	0	1.5	.5	5.5	17.24
11		Meghalaya	NA	-	-	-	-	-	-	-
12		Orissa	2.0	1.0	1.0	0	1.5	.5	6.0	19.35
13		Rajasthan	2.0	1.0	1.0	0	1.5	.5	6.0	19.35
14		Tamil Nadu	2.0	1.0	1.0	0	1.5	.5	6.0	19.35
15		Uttar Pradesh	2.0	1.0	1.0	-2.0	1.5	.5	4.0	12.90

* Panchayat election delayed, and funds were not placed with ZPs till 1999.

** The term for the chairpersons reduced.

*** Panchayat elections delayed and the term for the chairpersons reduced.

**** Elections not held till 2000.

Note : The study of the above indicators is at the gram panchayat level, unless otherwise specifically mentioned.

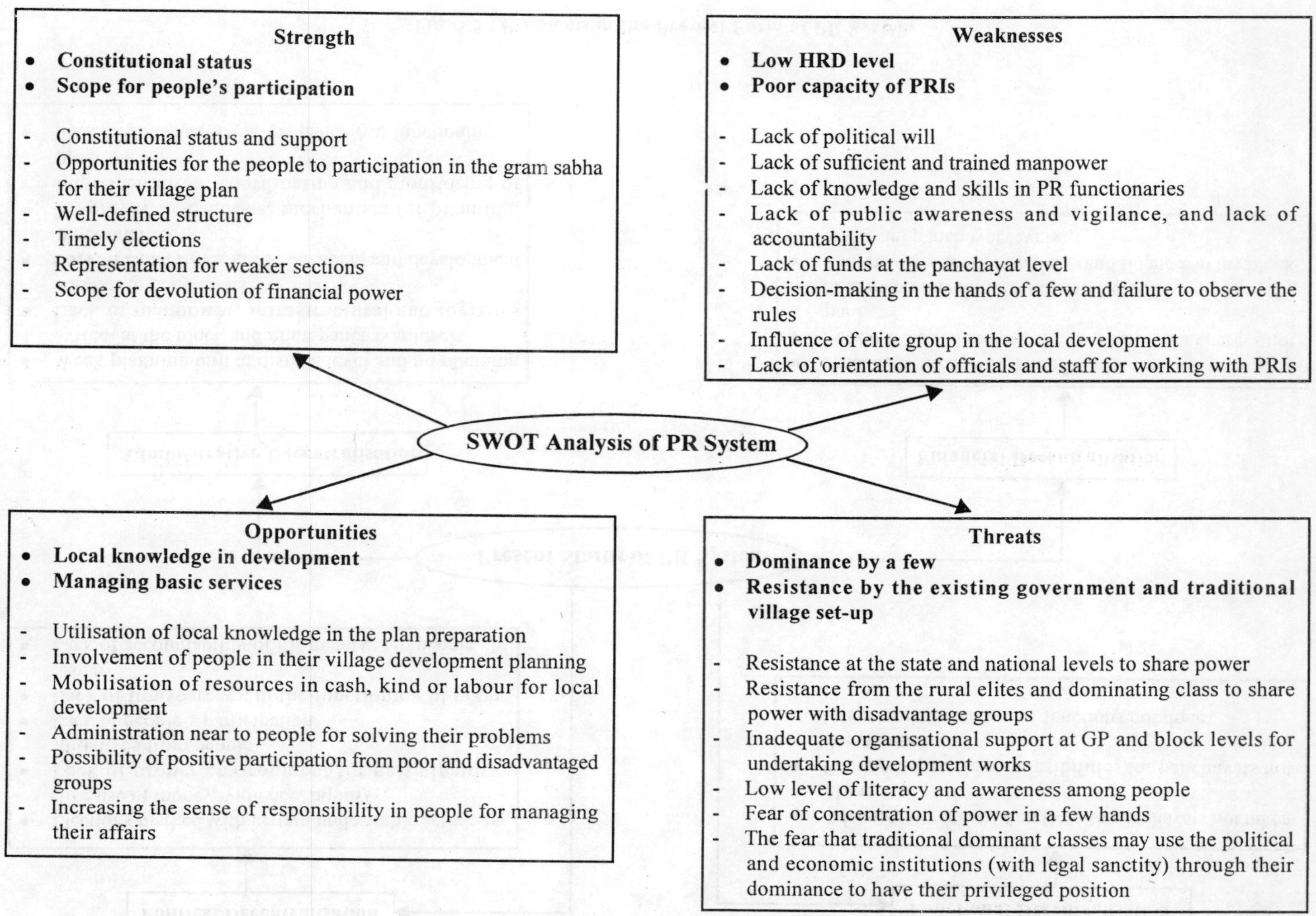

Fig. 5.4 : **SWOT Analysis**

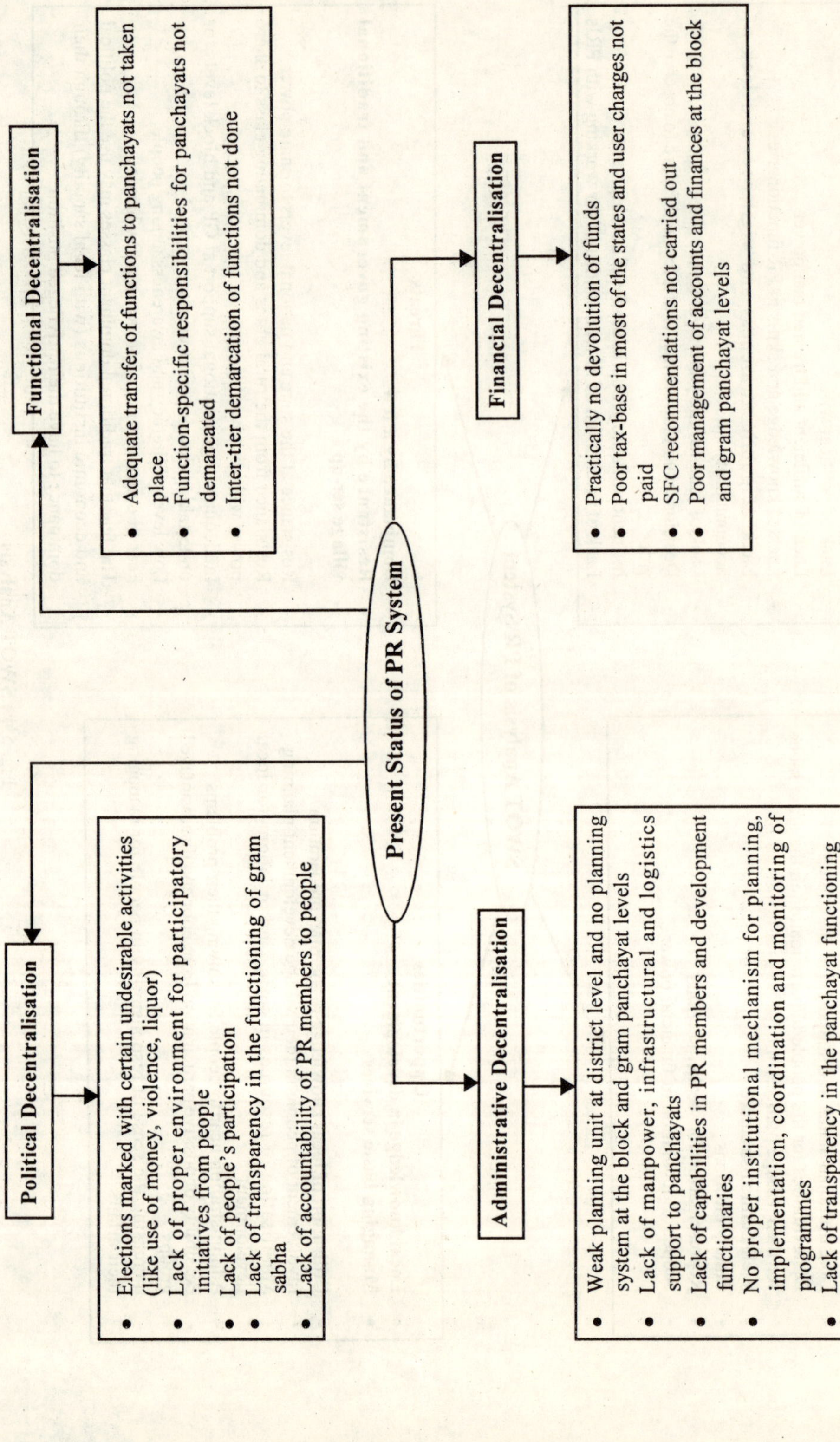

Fig. 5.5 : **Problems in the Present Form of PR System**

got some direction and also has got success in operational terms.

5.8 SWOT Analysis

In the backdrop of the findings as presented above, the SWOT analysis has been carried out, which is reflected by fig. 5.4. The salient points are indicated below:

Strength: The Act provides constitutional status to panchayats at all the three tiers, provisions for timely elections every five years, representation to weaker sections, the scope for transfer of functions and devolution of funds upon panchayats.

Weaknesses: The PR institutions are handicapped by lack of people's abilities to participate in the village development and poor capacities of local institutions to deliver.

Opportunities: The panchayati raj system opens a whole range of opportunities for the participation of people and local institutions in the village development.

Threats: There are a number of socio-economic and cultural factors such as disparities, dominance by village elites, resistance by existing political and government set-up, etc., that pose threat to the growth of local institutions and the process of decentralisation.

5.9 How the Present System is an Extension of the Previous System: Inadequacy of Governance

An attempt is made to draw a comparison between what existed before 1992 and what changes have occurred thereafter, as regards the implementation of the 73rd Amendment Act. A careful look at table 5.19 shows that even after the new Amendment Act, there has not been perceptible difference in achieving the objectives of decentralisation and in providing good governance at the grassroots level (see fig. 5.5). The specific points are summed up as follows:

- Firstly, we look *from the point of view of representation of people in the panchayat set-up.* It is amply evident that the traditional elites and political groups hold sway over others. Weaker sections do not get support and the voice in the panchayat functioning. Moreover, the reservation remains confined only to the reserved seats and that too mainly for the election purpose. During elections, the environment remains politically surcharged and overwhelming, and thus highly unconducive for the individuals. In the villages, it does not encourage common people to get associated in the election process and to participate in the panchayat functioning in a meaningful way.
- If we look *from the point of people's participation,* it is still elusive. The studies are replete with instances (of shortcomings) when the people are not able to participate

in the gram sabha. Besides, adequate efforts are not made by PR members to ensure their participation in the decision-making. Rather, the attempts are made to overlook their involvement. It is the chairperson of the gram panchayat or a few individuals who take the decisions. If we compare with the state of Kerala, it is evident in other states that the people's participation at the grassroots level is not forthcoming, and level of it is directly dependent on efforts made by the state government in this direction and the HRD level of people in the villages.

- When we look *from the point of planning*, no process or methodology has been formulated for the purpose of eliciting the information from people, database preparation, data analysis, and sectoral as well as backward-forward linkages analyses. In most of the cases, the selection of projects or the allocation of funds is done basically by the chairperson of the gram panchayat or by the members of his group. And no rational approach is followed while making panchayat plans.
- Also *from the point of implementation of programmes*, the beneficiaries involvement is almost absent. People are unaware about the cost of the project, the quantity of inputs used, number of people engaged and so on. The execution and supervision of works remain the concern of chairperson of panchayat, or any agency or contractor identified by the panchayat.
- As far as *the point of transparency* is concerned, the information about the projects, beneficiaries' selection, inputs used in the projects, proceedings of the gram sabha and panchayat meetings are not within the reach of people.
- As regards *the point of responsiveness*, it has not been forthcoming from the PR members as people have to struggle hard to make their grievances heard. Similarly, issues of landless farmers, poor and weaker sections are not attended to by the panchayats in their action plan, nor are efforts made for evolving consensus in order to meet the problems of these target groups.
- If we examine *from the point of raising of own income* by the panchayats, the income is low, people are reluctant to paying taxes and the panchayats do not have necessary political will to impose taxes. Or in other words, the panchayats have not been successful in mobilising resources.
- With regard to *the point of quality and efficiency of work*, there is not much perceptible improvement in the functioning of panchayats and the implementation of works.
- And *from the point of availability of services at the village level*, it is far from satisfactory, and people have to make rounds of visits to various offices for availing services.
- Finally, *from the point of accountability*, the chairpersons and the members of panchayats, in practice, are not accountable to people for their functional, administrative and financial decisions taken by them. Moreover, there is practically no sound mechanism or proper procedure for making them accountable for the actions taken by them.

Or in nutshell,

the fundamentals that are missing are:

- People's participation in discussion;
- Participatory planning;
- Responsiveness of PR members;
- Transparency in the panchayat functioning;
- Accountability of PR members;

inherent deficiencies are:

- Poor environment building;
- Poor HRD level in the village; and

other vital deficiencies are:

- Wide socio-economic disparities
- Lack of focus on electoral reforms;
- Dominance of a few;
- Lack of focus on institution building; and
- Weak delivery system.

Thus, in the backdrop of above and the inferences drew on the field studies, right from the planning to implementation to supervision to monitoring and to social audit, the people's participation is minimal. The chairpersons of panchayats or a few PR members and some influential individuals are the ones who take the decisions, and the people's involvement in the decision-making remains by and large absent. Not only this, there is a lack of transparency in the functioning of panchayats and the information are not made available to people. Even the decisions taken in the open gram sabha meeting are changed (especially the names of beneficiaries, which in some cases are pre-decided) while preparing the proceedings. Moreover, very little remedy is available to people for such a state of functioning of panchayats. PR members at all levels are more concerned with devolution of funds and control over officers and staff while important aspects like people's participation, transparency and accountability are completely overlooked.

In a way, the present system is not far different from the previous development system (prior to 1993), in which the decision-making was centralised and the funds were allocated more by the choice of a few than by rational planning (see table 5.19). The same mode of functioning has percolated from the then system to the present PR institutions. It is a pointer towards the unchecked drift of the philosophy of decentralisation towards concentration of decision-making in a few hands. It has been mainly the result of the lack of attention given to important aspects in the operational terms. Though the gram sabha has been constituted in every village yet not much has been done to educate people about their rights and role in the village development. Similarly, transparency and accountability system has not got the desired place, and even if the panchayats or PR members do not perform as desired, people have very little control to ensure their propriety in the functioning. Also, institution building and the strengthening of delivery system are not the area, which get attention. And thus, the functioning of panchayats continue without observing fundamentals. In this process the governance (especially in terms of accessing basic services) at the grassroots level remains a big casualty.

> 'Though the gram sabha has been constituted in every village yet not much has been done to educate people about their rights and role in the village development. Similarly, transparency and accountability system has not got the desired place, and even if the panchayats or PR members do not perform as desired, people have very little control to ensure their propriety in the functioning. Also, institution building and the strengthening of delivery system are not the area, which get attention. And thus, the functioning of panchayats continue without observing fundamentals.'

Thus, as reflected by the above discussion, in terms of fundamentals of decentralisation, the present form of development system, even after the initiation of process of decentralisation since 1993, is more or less an extension of previous system (the details are well-reflected by table 5.19). It (system) is not able to meet basic needs of people at the village level and that is leading to inadequacy of good governance. And, among others, the reassessment of various provisions enshrined in the amendment Act is very much needed.

5.10 Need for a Re-look at the Constitution Amendment Act

The analysis of various issues under different dimensions of decentralisation has brought out that the panchayats at all the three tiers are not in a position to perform as expected. The pace and the direction of decentralisation are not upto a satisfactory level. Neither people are empowered to participate meaningfully, nor are their needs addressed, nor panchayats have the capacity to deliver as per the local needs, and nor are there organic linkages among three tiers. Even the Central Act is not able to address these vital issues, and moreover most of the provisions like on taxation, devolution of funds and powers, etc., are indicative and not mandatory in nature. All these point towards for having a re-look at the 73rd Constitution Amendment Act, and for effecting necessary amendment in the backdrop of discussion presented in the preceding sections. The areas that require urgent attention are:

- Election of panchayat bodies;
- People's participation — role of gram sabha;
- Capacity of panchayats to function;
- Devolution of funds;
- Taxation;
- Constitution of various bodies such as DPC, SFC, etc.;
- Organic linkages among tiers;
- Transparency;
- Accountability; and
- Arbitration.

TABLE 5.19: **How is the present Status of System of Decentralisation vis-a-vis the Old System before 1992**

S.N.	From the point of view	Status prior to 1992 Act	Present status after 1992 Act	Remarks
1.	Representation of people in the election	- Hold of traditional elites over panchayats - Disparities due to caste, class and gender influenced panchayats	- Village elites and political groups have more representation - Weaker sections and common person in the villages have little chance of getting true representation, due to hold of influential people and political parties	There is no perceptible difference in the quality of representation
2.	People's participation	- Participation of people in the development activities insignificant - Central decision-making	- The gram sabhas are dominated by only a few individuals - Poor and weaker sections do not have voice in the gram sabha	Participation of people remains poor and the decision-making is confined to a few people
3.	Planning	- By way of compilation of proposals from various departments - People were not involved adequately	- Compilation of proposals from various departments and people are not involved. No systematic planning procedure followed	No difference, same as before
4.	Implementation of works	- Implementation by the line departments, people not involved	- Works implemented by the chairpersons of panchayats - People do not take part in the implementation	Practically, no difference, same as before
5.	Supervision	- By the departments, people not involved	- By the chairperson and secretary of panchayat	No difference, same as before
6.	Availability of services at the village level	- Poor availability of services - Time consuming	- Poor availability of services - Time consuming	No difference, same as before
7.	Quality and efficiency	- Poor quality - Assets not properly utilised	- Poor quality of work - Marginal improvement in the implementation of work	In some cases marginal improvement in quality

(Contd.)

TABLE 5.19 *(Contd.)*

S.N.	From the point of view		Status prior to 1992 Act		Present status after 1992 Act	Remarks
8.	Level of generation of own income of panchayats	-	Low own income	-	Low own income	No difference, same as before
9.	Responsiveness of functionaries at the decision-making level	-	Lack of responsiveness of departments	-	Lack of responsiveness of PR members	No difference, same as before
10.	Transparency	-	Lack of transparency in the functioning of departments	-	Lack of transparency in the panchayat functioning	No difference, same as before
11.	Accountability	-	Lack of accountability of departments to people	-	Lack of accountability of PR members to people	No difference, same as before

Summing up

The purpose of Amendment Act has been to strengthen the grassroots democracy and people's participation in order to make people partners in development, but it appears that our approach has been to look from the top. And, this is the reason why the focus has been on devolving more funds and powers from the top without having proper strategy for improving capabilities of people from within, which would empower them and augment their capacities to take part in village development. In a way, as per the findings, the present form of decentralisation is just an extension of powers from centre and states to district and lower level panchayats. It does not address the core issue of involving the people in the decision-making process and tapping their potential for the development activities.

Another fundamental drawback, that needs to be stressed pertains to political overtone given to panchayats. Under the present process of decentralisation, the elections, though important, have been assumed to be the final and almost the sole criterion of judging the performance of the panchayati raj set-up. It appears as if once the elections are held then panchayats will start functioning automatically, while this has not been the case and cannot be in the absence of fundamentals. In this context, it is also worth mentioning that the development role of the panchayats, in terms of looking into integrated nature of development and making services available to people, is not fully appreciated. What presently is basically assumed by the development is to allocate funds to different projects or select beneficiaries for various schemes, which is more of a exercise on political or patronage considerations than a system of planning and management of resources and services. If we go into deeper aspects of development, which entails issues of participatory planning, institutional development, delivery mechanism, management of services and so on. It appears that these basics are of little significance, while winning elections and control over resources become the prime importance for political groups and elected members. Or, we can say that the present panchayat set-up is evolved more from the political expediency than from the needs of village development and making basic services available to people.

Now, it has been almost a decade, when the process of decentralisation began, it is quite evident that there are still areas of concerns vital for the efficacy of local institutions. These include: *first*, the election process, though intended, is not able to provide representation to wider section of the society, as the traditional power centres in the panchayats first get hold over the nomination of the candidates and then the election process. *Second*, people's participation, which should be at the core of functioning of panchayats, is missing in the gram sabha. *Third*, panchayati raj (PR) members lack requisite capabilities for undertaking the task of development planning and implementation. *Fourth*, planning system does not have desired support at all the three tiers viz., district, block and gram panchayats. *Fifth*, delivery system at the gram panchayat level is weak and is not able to make the availability of basic services to people. *Sixth*, internal resources are too meagre to take up any viable project of local needs. *Seventh*, the size of gram panchayat is too small in most of the states that has raised the question of administrative and financial viability of local institutions. And, *lastly*, transparency and accountability system is not adequately placed. People do not have access to information, and decision-making is marked with lack of openness.

Finally, in the absence of proper education and awareness of people and due to the poor capacities of local institutions, the present panchayati raj system is promoting the elites and the patronage system with centralised way of decision-making. PR institutions fail to involve the people in the planning and implementation process, deliver services to people and are marked with non-transparent functioning without accountability of elected members. In a way, such a system of decentralisation is doing more favour to the interest of elites, who may be from political groups or influential people by virtue of muscle or money power, or caste or combination of all, than that of common people in the villages.

The offshoot of above discussion leads to the conclusion that the Constitution Amendment Act in its present form is not able to empower people and panchayats to take up the task of local development, and needs further amendment in order to address the basic objectives of people's participation in development; and enabling panchayats to deliver basic services to people and to meet their aspirations.

PART 2

Decentralisation and Governance : Needed Reforms

6

INTEGRATIVE APPROACH FOR DECENTRALISATION

The process of decentralisation got impetus with the enactment of Amendment Act in 1993. Since then a decade has passed, still it appears as if this process has not been fully grounded. The local institutions at district, block and gram panchayat levels are still struggling to come to terms with the reality and to take up task of village development. In this context fundamental issues concerning the decentralisation have been elaborately analysed in the part one of the book. And the analysis therein has categorically brought out the areas of concern especially in the context of governance. Against this backdrop, this chapter attempts to provide framework for institutional development of local institutions and suggest measures for bringing amendment in the Central Act in order to strengthen the process of decentralisation.

Institutional importance in a socio-politico development system may be judged from the status of that institution conferred within the legal framework. The legal status to any institution can be provided in a number of ways such as administrative power, statutory enactments or constitutional means. Among these, the constitutional status to any institution makes a difference in the hierarchy of institutions. Therefore, creating an institution within the constitutional law has provided high status to Panchayati Raj Institutions.

Presently, in spite of the constitutional status given to panchayats, the analysis presented in the chapter five has brought out categorically the deficiencies in the existing state of functioning of local institutions, and it is quite evident that there are still areas of concerns that are very crucial for the efficacy of the institutions. The areas of concern include poor people's participation, lack of requisite capabilities in PR members and development functionaries, weak planning system, inefficient delivery mechanism, insignificant devolution of funds, and lack of transparency as well as accountability. And due to such constraints, the panchayats are unable to deliver basic services to people and are unable to function as institutions of self-government..

But if we look at the process of decentralisation in Kerala, this state stands apart. In order to strengthen the PR institutions, it has placed specific components for environment building, transfer of functions, devolution of funds, training, planning, implementation, transparency and accountability in the right perspective.

No doubt, panchayati raj system has a lot to deliver to people, provided the fundamentals are rightly placed. We need to take problems as challenges and work on setting right the deficiencies and improving the functioning. There have been a number of instances where the panchayats have performed well but these are either isolated examples or are the exclusive initiatives of individuals as PR members or chairpersons {see the case studies of Kuthambakkam gram panchayat of Tamil Nadu (see appendix 6.1) and others}. What we need to do is to learn lessons from these successes and replicate them in other panchayats to institutionalise the process of success.

As indicated in the preceding chapter, there appears to be main focus of local institutions on devolution of funds and control over field staff. No doubt, these are important issues but the issues such as people's participation, giving opportunities to people, transparency and accountability should not be overlooked. For all these, we need to explore where does the problem lie, but certainly the people or the PR institutions cannot be faulted, and the moot question remains: whether the basics are addressed for operationalising the Act. And the underlying principle of integrative approach should be the basis of future action plan to give operational shape to the Central Act as well as state Acts. It will require the integration of people's participation and their actions; political, functional, administrative and financial support; institutional development; and finally, development policy.

Now, in the context of providing good governance at the village level, the need is to come to brass tacks and draw up a framework and the modalities for the implementation of the Act. The Act has provided framework for decentralisation. States have made attempts to give the Act an operational shape. But, still there are areas in the Act that need to be further strengthened in order to achieve the desired objectives of decentralisation and it should pass certain conditions for success. Now, what constitute the vital conditions are: political will, environment building and capabilities in elected members; transfer of functions and sufficient financial resources to accomplish important tasks; adequate capacity to accomplish those tasks; and reliable accountability mechanisms. In the context of these vital conditions, the fundamentals should be placed in their right perspective and also in an integrative manner before any viable and meaningful decentralisation process can begin. It will call for initiating the measures for institutional development and for establishing delivery mechanism, as also for bringing suitable amendments in the panchayat Acts.

6.1 Capacity Building of PR Institutions

Based on the existing state of the capacity of PR institutions, we need to be more realistic and pragmatic in our approach, and our focus should be to address the fundamental issues gripping the existing local institutional set-up and to give concrete shape to the process of institution building.

The task ahead is to deepen the process of institution building with a more focus towards sustainability, by allocating adequate resources for support system and upgrading the quality of the personnel who work from within. As a first step, we need to give thrust on human resources development through education and training for enabling them to work with the people, as also to plan and implement the programmes as per local felt-needs and resources. Also, efforts are required for running institutions by norms, rules, procedures and good practices. Such work is time-consuming, but in the latter stage of the development, institution building is going to hold the key for the success.

The institution building will include building infrastructure, placing manpower and logistics; improving capabilities of functionaries for technical, administrative and behavioural skills; and establishing good administrative arrangement for ensuring coordination, responsibility, accountability and good work culture (see fig. 6.1). It should be aimed at improving and strengthening:

- Personnel management
- Support system
- Management system
- Institutional processes
- Transparency
- Accountability
- Legal framework
- Value system

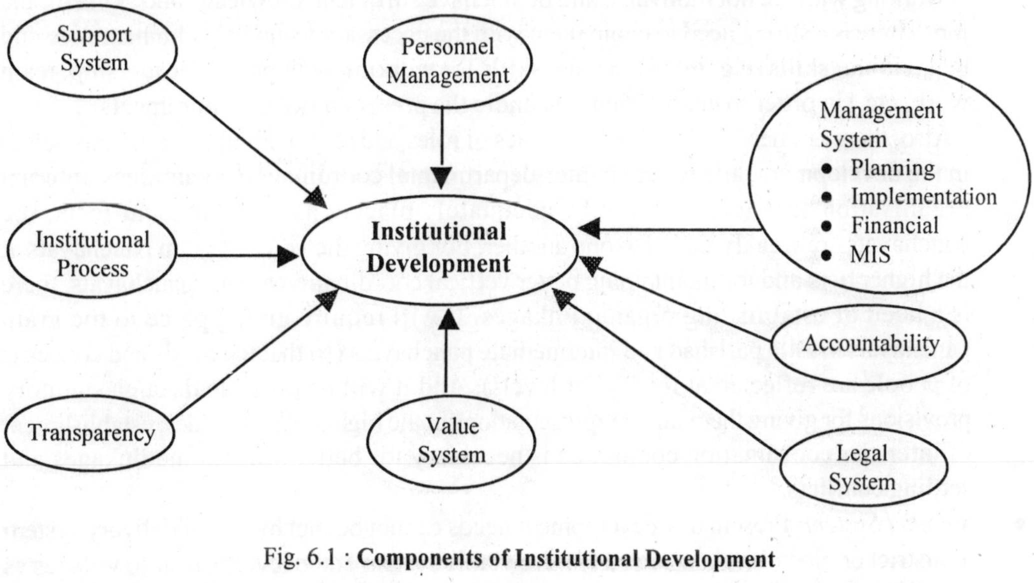

Fig. 6.1 : **Components of Institutional Development**

Important Ingredients for Institution Building

In the light of above discussion, what we need to borne in mind is that the institutions at the district level that carried out earlier mainly regulatory functions or implemented centrally sponsored programmes, which could be carried out through central command (or central decision-making), cannot straightaway handle the present day need of welfare-oriented functions wherein we need to work for and with the people. So, accordingly, the whole gamut of issues that go into institution building require restructuring. Under the new dispensation of development needs, the institutions assume high importance for the effective management of local services, and for instilling confidence in people and ensuring their participation and support in the development process. Under the present state, the institutions at the local levels have got constitutional status by virtue of Central Act. But the efforts cannot end here and to be taken further up and requisite measures need to be initiated. Now, what constitute the important ingredients for the institution building at the three tiers are indicated below:

- *Personnel Management:* Manpower planning, identification and placement of staff, job-specific training of field officers and staff, motivation and performance evaluation are some of the important measures that need to be initiated for utilising the potential of personnel to the best of their ability. Field studies indicate that the field functionaries lack necessary skills and expertise to perform their task, especially in the new set-up of participatory development. Besides, they lack work motivation. Under such a state no organisation can function successfully if people (departmental personnel) with whom it is working with are not motivated and do not have sufficient knowledge and skills for the job. There is a strong need to equip them with the necessary technical, administrative and behavioural skills (e.g. inter-personal skills for working with people, ieadership, team work, etc.) in order to enable them to handle the present day job requirements.

  Also, there is a need to look into the issues of roles and responsibilities of various actors in the development, and to set up inter-departmental coordination committees. Internal organisation structures need to be adequately placed, as in the present form, the panchayats are weakly linked to one another. For giving the voice of gram panchayats at the higher tiers and for maintaining better vertical coordination among panchayats, there is a need of establishing organic linkages. It will require giving place to the gram panchayats in zilla parishad and intermediate panchayats (so that the needs and concerns of people are reflected at the higher levels). And it will be possible through statutory provisions for giving them direct representations in the higher tiers. Besides, establishment of inter-tier coordination committee is necessary for better programme linkages and settling conflicts.
- *Support System:* Present day development needs cannot be met by far off delivery system at district or block level. We need to have viable system at the level as near to villages as possible. This will call for having support system not only for panchayats but also for delivery mechanism for various sectors such as primary education, health, drinking water, veterinary services, irrigation, electricity, agriculture marketing, land revenue and so on. This support system will be in the form of : *first*, infrastructure office building, schools, health centre, etc.; *second*, manpower, either permanently placed or deputed; and *third*,

logistics like office equipments, teaching-aids for schools, equipments for health centres, etc.

- *Management System:* In the context of development institutions, systems need to be placed for planning, implementation, finance and MIS.
- *Institutional Processes:* Rules and procedures are essential for bringing uniformity and clarity in the panchayat functioning.
- *Transparency:* Transparency is essential for making people aware about the manner of decision-making, so that they can judge the propriety of the decision-making before actual implementation takes place.
- *Accountability:* Accountability is a key element for instilling the confidence in people about the local institutions.
- *Legal Framework:* Legal framework is required for addressing disputable decisions, which may arise due to various financial and administrative decisions that are to be taken.
- *Value System:* Developing healthy organisational culture with a desired set of values is essential for efficient functioning of institutions.

Based on the above, in order to improve the capacity of the PR institutions, the following measures are required in each of the dimensions viz., political, functional, administrative and financial, and the requisite components are reflected in fig. 6.2.

6.1.1 Measures for Political Decentralisation

The political decentralisation is required for transferring decision-making, providing autonomy to democratically elected local institutions, and making them accountable to people. It requires initiating the following specific measures:

Creating Enabling Environment

Under political decentralisation, first and foremost, it is vital to create 'enabling environment' for panchayats to function. And the very success of local institutions depends largely on this. It would require initiating measures such as providing security and peace at the village level; secured status for local bodies; empowerment of people including, among others, protecting the interests of weaker sections and providing opportunities (social and economic); political will for providing autonomy to panchayats and their elected representatives; and improving capabilities of PR members and development functionaries to enable them to handle the development task of panchayats. And the specific measures needed are:

- *Providing Security and Peace:* It is a pre-requisite, and unless peace is maintained in the area and security is provided to people, the socio-political movement at the grassroots level cannot succeed. It would require steps for maintaining social harmony and law and order. It is important especially in violent prone areas.
- *Political Will:* To provide secured status and autonomy to panchayats through

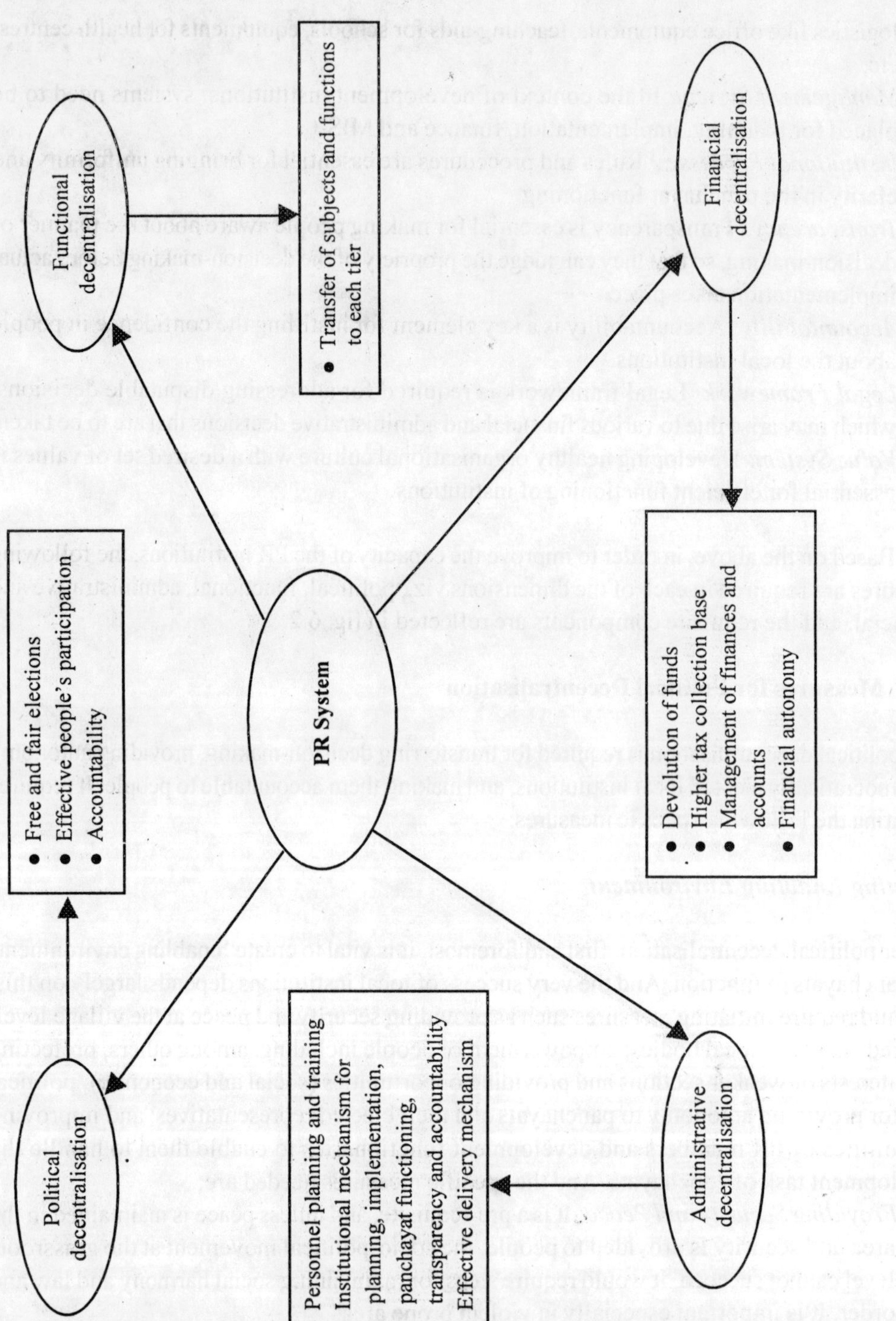

Fig. 6.2: Requisite Components of PR System

legislations. Though, secured status has been ensured through panchayat Acts, but steps are needed for providing functional and financial autonomy to panchayats.

- *Empowering people:* It would call for the following:

  - *Educating and sensitising people:* It would require organising educational programmes at village level through a variety of means such as seminars, audio-visual shows, cultural programmes and so on. These programmes should be well-funded on a long term basis and through them the people should be educated and sensitised about:

    On the attitudinal side:
    - cultural values - importance of participatory development, sensitivity for people' problems, especially, of the disadvantaged groups, respect for institutional norms, sense of belongingness for their village property, reducing biases based on caste, community and gender;
    - sound human values — human dignity, value for knowledge and work (people need to be educated that it is the education that will matter for their lives, and biases based on caste or gender are notional; that we need to judge a person from its conduct, knowledge and work not by its birth in a particular caste or community; and that we should respect human dignity);
    - contributing for the village development;
    - devoting time for community development and respect for the *shramdan* (voluntary work); and so on.

    On the knowledge area :
    - role of panchayats in village development;
    - constitutional rights;
    - need for local planning;
    - about sectoral programmes; and so on.

  - *Opinion Building:* There is a need to broaden the scope of discussion in the gram sabha and panchayat meetings. It will call for having sensitisation programme, which, among others, may include the following:

    If we go into the development needs of people they can be mainly classified as: *first*, HRD — availability of basics education, health, drinking water, etc.; and *second*, infrastructural development. Both of these will facilitate in providing opportunities to individuals for further development. There is a need to sensitise people about these fundamentals of development. For this, we need to first start the discussion (in the villages) on these issues, so that the people can understand about these needs. And then raise the level of discussion, so that people talk about them during the discussion in village meetings or gram sabha or during elections.

That is how the public action in the desired direction will emerge which will facilitate not only the emergence of vital issues for village development but also in giving scope to people to lead the public support for the pressing development needs. Finally, it will pave the way for the leadership that will be focused on 'development' and 'people's needs'.

- *Information sharing:* It is vital to impress that availability of information is very crucial. It will help people to understand and then take steps for improvement. For instance, if the people are provided with data on crop yield, then, there is a possibility that some of them may start working out on the need of improving crop yield. Or, in some other case, if people get access to data on water use efficiency and depletion of ground water, they may look for options for efficient use of water. Likewise, there may be a number of examples, where sharing of information is crucial to encourage people for solutions for their village development. It will require having the attitudinal change from the present state of 'keeping silent' to the culture of information sharing, suggesting options to people and then motivating people in finding solutions.
- *Protecting the interest of Weaker Sections:* The people of weaker sections (poor, lower caste people, women) need to be protected from the exploitive behaviour of village elites including upper caste and rich. Only when will this happen, the weaker sections will be able to participate successfully without fear. It would require two-pronged strategy of 'regulation' as well as 'positive interventions' such as education, awareness building for attitudinal changes (reducing biases based on caste and gender, inculcating sound values), and providing economic opportunities.

- *Improving Capabilities:* The knowledge and skills of PR members and development functionaries need to be strengthened in order to enable them to understand, appreciate and then perform their jobs.

Electoral Reforms

Under the given state of election process (as elaborately discussed in chapters four and five) at the panchayat level, electoral reforms are very much required in order to provide wider opportunities to individuals for participation in the elections at the grassroots level. Among the prominent measures that are required are: *first,* educating people about their rights and development needs of villages; *second,* elections on non-party basis; *third,* state funding of elections; and *fourth,* steps for checking malpractices in the election process. Also, steps are needed for timely and simultaneous elections for all the tiers at one time.

Functioning of Gram Sabha

Developing procedure for the conduct of gram sabha meeting becomes important in the context of large number of members attending the meetings (in some gram sabha, there may be as large number of people as 500 or even 1000). Besides, in order to have focused discussion, the resource groups for each sector should be constituted. Also, there is a need to develop the objective criteria (based on relative backwardness[1]) for the selection of beneficiaries in a transparent manner for various development schemes. And for those who are not able to come for the gram sabha there should be room for the people to get their grievances registered and then addressed. Finally, responsiveness of the gram panchayats to grievances is very important. Even if the people write or communicate through someone, it should be responded.

People's Participation

The studies, as elaborated in chapter four, are replete with instances of poor people's participation and central decision-making. In true sense, this is not what we should be expecting under the decentralisation where only a handful of people dominate the scene. The need is to appreciate the importance of making people aware and of educating them through well-organised educational programmes. This way only people's participation can be constructively encouraged and that is what we should be striving for. In a way, people's participation needs to be internalised by the PRIs. And it is where from every other thing should emanate.

Also, participation should not be judged only from the point of view of functioning of gram sabha. Rather it may be in one or the combination of the following ways:

- Expressing voice for the village problems and generating public opinion
- Informing the panchayats in time about the problems and participating in the village meetings including gram sabha
- Participating constructively in solving problems
- Making contributions in the development activities
- Writing to panchayats for the decision-making by the PR members

and so on.

Accountability

For ensuring the accountability of chairpersons and members of panchayats, the Central Act has provided for financial auditing. But it may require procedural simplification like inspection of accounts for projects or items above certain value, so that the panchayats are not questioned for every small detail, which may become counter productive. From the point of view of transparency, all the financial details must be displayed outside the panchayat offices and be

1. Relative backwardness can be considered based on the indicators of deprivations. For example under rural housing scheme, the indicators may be: i. No dependent, ii. No house, iii. No land, iv. Widow, v. No cattle. And for each of these one point can be assigned and whosoever gets higher score, he / she should be considered more backward among BPL families. (It is just an indicative example, like this the indicators can be selected for other schemes).

given to all the members. Besides, the auditing should be transparent i.e. the objections by the auditors should be given to all the ward members (at the preparatory stage), before the reply by the panchayat is prepared. And the final report should be placed before finance committee of the panchayat and the gram sabha. Under social audit, there is a need to have: *first*, proper procedure for raising questions; *second*, recording of proceedings; *third*, compliance by the members, if required; and *finally*, reporting to people about the action taken. Moreover, there is a need to have the mechanism for arbitration in case the action is not taken for rectification[2].

6.1.2 Measures for Functional Decentralisation

Functional decentralisation is essential for assigning specific tasks to panchayats. It requires the following measures:

Transfer of Functions

Presently, keeping in view the capacity of the panchayats, the subjects should be transferred in a phased manner with a focus on basic services. The first step should be to transfer basic subjects such as education, health, drinking water, woman and child development, agriculture and allied activities, PDS, etc. (see list I of box 6.1). Here, we need to appreciate that making basic services to people is of prime consideration. If these services are made available to people, it will be a very significant achievement. It should also be kept in view that mere transfer of subjects is not enough; what is basically required is to build the delivery mechanism, otherwise, panchayats will be expected to perform, but will not be able to do so. And gradually, the capacity of panchayats should be further enhanced, and, accordingly, as the capacity of panchayats improves, some more subjects as per the local needs should be transferred as illustrated in the lists II and III.

Inter-tier Demarcation of Functions

Now, with the 73rd Constitution Amendment Act, the 29 subjects are to be assigned to panchayats. The functions under these subjects should be undertaken by the panchayats as per the principle of subsidiarity. Keeping this in view, the transfer of functions should be made to each tier of panchayat (district, intermediate, gram panchayat). Now, there are functions that cover inter-gram panchayat area, so these functions should be handled by block panchayat. Similarly, the functions, which cover two or more than two blocks, should be handled by district panchayat. Besides, there are certain functions that can be suitably handled by district

2. There are cases like non-availability of essential commodities or non-payment of wages, which need to be attended to by the panchayats (for which the responsibilities are given to panchayats in some states like MP, Rajasthan, UP). But, in certain cases, actions are not taken by the panchayats (based on field study), in spite of complaints by the people. Such cases may be referred to tribunals.

panchayat, some can be managed by the blocks, and some others by the gram panchayats. For example, under agriculture, R&D can be best handled by district agriculture department, so it should be entrusted to the district panchayat; agriculture marketing can be handled by block as it can provide infrastructural support to the gram panchayats, so the block panchayats should be given the responsibility for this; and likewise, gram panchayat should be entrusted with the job of cropping pattern design as per local conditions. Keeping this in view, the table 6.1 outlines the sub-functions at each tier for each sector.

6.1.3 Measures for Administrative Decentralisation

The administrative measures are essential to provide operational shape to the functional role of local institutions. These mainly pertain to personnel management, planning, implementation, monitoring and transparency. The salient measures are suggested below:

Assigning Subject Specific Responsibilities to Panchayats

Under each of the subjects, each panchayat (district, intermediate, gram panchayat) should be given the specific role and responsibility. For example, under primary education, what the gram panchayat should be doing to ensure smooth functioning of schools. Whether it (GP) should inspect the schools or distribute the salary of teachers or do the maintenance of school, should be clearly defined. Likewise, under other subjects such responsibilities should be clearly defined. The broad roles and responsibilities of various institutions (PRIs, DRDA, line departments, people) in the development process are defined in table 6.2

Personnel Management

Placement of Services of Line Departments with PRIs and Manpower Planning: The services of line departments should be placed with the PR institutions. In this regard the transfer may take place as per the subjects (that are to be assigned to panchayats, in a phased manner) outlined in the list I, then followed by lists II and III (see box 6.1).

BOX 6.1

Phase-wise List of Subjects to be transferred to Panchayats

List I

Social

1. Education
   i. Education, including primary and secondary schools
2. Drinking water

..... *Contd.*

Contd. Box 6.1

ii. Drinking water

3. Health
   iii. Health and sanitation, including hospitals , primary health centres and dispensaries
4. Family welfare
   iv. Family welfare
5. Women and child development
   v. Women and child development
6. Social welfare
   vi. Social welfare, including welfare of the handicapped and mentally retarded
   vii. Welfare of the weaker sections, in particular of the SCs and STs

Economic

7. Poverty alleviation
   viii. Poverty alleviation programme
   ix. Maintenance of community assets
8. Public distribution system
   x. Public distribution system
9. Agriculture
   xi. Agriculture including agricultural extension
10. Natural resources management
   xii. Land improvement, implementation of land reforms, land consolidation and soil conservation
   xiii. Fuel and fodder

List II

1. Education
   i. Technical training and vocational education
   ii. Adult and non-formal education
   iii. Libraries
   iv. Cultural activities
2. Rural Connectivity
   v. Roads, culverts, bridges, ferries, waterways and other means of communication
3. Irrigation
   vi. Minor irrigation, water management and watershed development
4. Animal husbandry
   vii. Animal husbandry, dairying and poultry

..... *Contd.*

Contd. Box 6.1

5. Fisheries
   vii. Fisheries
6. Forest
   ix. Social forestry and farm forestry
   x. Minor forest produce
7. Housing
   xi. Rural Housing

List III

1. Energy
   i. Rural electrification, including distribution of electricity
   ii. Non-conventional energy sources
2. Industries
   iii. Small scale industries,
   iv. Khadi, village and cottage industries
3. Commercial Linkage
   v. Markets and fares

Note: The above list is indicative, the actual transfer of subjects to panchayats will vary from state to state and also from district to district. And while transferring the subjects two parameters are important, *first*, the present capacity of panchayats to handle the subjects, and *second*, the existing level of development.

In this context, it should be appreciated that the gram sabha is a forum for eliciting the people's problems and needs, for having transparent way of informing people about the activities of gram panchayat and making PR representatives accountable to the people in the open forum. But the basic groundwork has to be done by the field officers and staff for the planning and implementation of programmes as per the overall desire of the people. The studies (Mathur, 1986 and Gupta, 2001) have indicated that at the block and gram panchayat levels, there is acute imbalance between the available manpower and the needed work. The rural development works are implemented at the block and GP levels and there has been considerable increase in flow of funds, while there is a limited field staff at these levels and the number has increased marginally since 1960s (the time of community development programme), but on the other hand, the posts of the officers and staff have increased manifold at the Central and the state secretariats. In other words, where the presence of the officers and staff is most felt, it has not happened. Besides, the capabilities of the field staff do not match with the needed role in the present development scenario of complex issues related to 'participatory development', 'technology interventions', 'market dynamics', etc. Accordingly, the manpower planning and training needs identification are required.

TABLE 6.1: **Functions and Sub-functions for 29 Subjects (19 sectors) at three Tiers**

S.N.	Sector	Sub-functions at VP	Sub-functions at BP	Sub-functions at DP
1	2	3	4	5
1.	Agriculture i. Agriculture including agricultural extension	• Cropping Pattern at village level • Supply of inputs to households • Mobilisation of credit • Agricultural extension including technology transfer	• Cropping pattern at block level • Research and demonstration farms • Input management (procurement, storage & transport) • Seed multiplication farms • Marketing of agricultural products • Soil testing	• Cropping pattern at district level • District plan for inputs supply, marketing and agro-processing units • Inter-district marketing and exports • Perspective plan
2.	Natural resources management ii. Land improvement, implementation of land reforms, land consolidation, and soil conservation iii. Fuel and fodder	• Soil erosion control measures • Fuel-fodder management • Land development • Training at village level • Monitoring of implementation of land reforms measures	• Survey of soil erosion status • Training and research farms • Awareness programmes • Survey of surplus land under ceiling Act • Management of wasteland	• District profile of soil • District plan for fuel & fodder management
3.	Irrigation iv. Minor irrigation, water management and watershed development	• Water conservation strategy • Small check dam and WHS • Maintenance of irrigation channels • Water users' association	• Formulating MI project • Training programme for efficient water use • Inputs management	• Assessing the district potential for minor irrigation • District perspective plan for irrigation and water management
4.	Animal husbandry v. Animal husbandry, dairying and poultry	• Milch animals development • Development of poultry, piggery, duckery • Inputs supply to households	• Supply of good quality cattle	• Infrastructure development • Planning for dairying unit • Planning for breeder farms, hatcheries, etc.

(Contd.)

TABLE 6.1 *(Contd.)*

1	2	3	4	5
		• Marketing • Training of beneficiaries • Fodder development	• Research and demonstration farms • Market tie-up • Fodder management	• Marketing network for produce (like milk, eggs etc.)
5.	Fisheries vi. Fisheries	• Development of village ponds • Supply of inputs to beneficiaries • Awareness and training groups	• Fingerlings development farms • Feed management • Marketing of fish • Credit mobilisation • Training and research farms	• Infrastructure development planning • Processing of fish
6.	Forest vii. Social forestry and farm forestry viii. Minor forest produce	• Plantation programme • Joint forest management • Collection of MFP	• Awareness programmes for forestry • Marketing of MFP • Farm forestry management	• District forest plan • Processing of MFP • Exports of MFP to other districts and outside country
7.	Rural connectivity ix. Roads, culverts, bridges, ferries, waterways and other means of communication	• Village roads • Village road to GP • Drainage	• Village to block HQ road • Blacktopped road • Causeways and culverts & small bridges	• Inter-block roads. • Big bridges
8.	Housing x. Rural housing	• Houses for BPL families	• Group housing for non-BPL category • Credit mobilisation	• District housing plan • Credit mobilisation
9.	Commercial linkage xi. Markets and fares	• Survey of Agril. produce, and handloom and handicraft items	• Construction of market yards • Godowns & cold storage	• Inter-district marketing plan • Exports

(Contd.)

TABLE 6.1 *(Contd.)*

1	2	3	4	5
			• Arrangement for transport for commodities • Tie-up with household and cottage industries • Market intelligence • Credit mobilisation • Organising fares	• Infrastructure development • Tie-up with small scale food processing industries • Market intelligence
10.	Energy xii. Rural electrification, including distribution of electricity xiii. Non-conventional energy sources	• Application of bio-gas plants • Energy plantation	• Application of wind and solar energy • Training & Research • Energy plantation • Rural electrification plan • Supervision of distribution of electricity	• District plan for NC energy sources • Research and domonstration • District plan for electrification and distribution
11.	Industries xiv. Small scale industries, xv. Khadi, village and cottage industries	• Training • Household industries under self-help groups	• Cottage and small scale industries • ITIs • Linkages of local raw-material with industries	• Industrial development parks • Small and medium scale industries • Entrepreneurship development programme • Marketing facilities for products • Training and research
12.	Education xvi. Education including primary and secondary schools	• Primary education • GP library	• Middle school and high school	• Colleges • Technical education

(Contd.)

TABLE 6.1 *(Contd.)*

1	2	3	4	5
	xvii. Technical training and vocational education xviii. Adult and non-formal education xix. Libraries xx. Cultural activities	• Adult education • Cultural programmes	• Libraries • Cultural activities at block level	• District libraries • Cultural activities at district level • Linkages of technical education with industries
13.	Drinking water xxi. Drinking water	• Tube wells • Repair and maintenance of tube wells	• Pipe water supply • Tube wells • Repair & maintenance of water supply system	• District plan for drinking water
14.	Health xxii. Health and sanitation, including hospitals, primary health centres and dispensaries	• Health centres • Training to dais	• Management of PHCs & CHCs • Ambulance • Any serious disease prevention programme	• District hospitals • Training of medical officers and nurses • Supply of medicines to health centres, PHCs and CHCs
15.	Family welfare xxiii. Family welfare	• Family planning and awareness programme • Incentives for family planning	• Training programme for health workers • Medical camps	• District family planning plan • Supply of medicines & equipments to PHCs & CHCs
16.	Women and child development xxiv. Women and child development	• Asssessment of target group—women & children • Anganwadi centre • Training to adolescent girls	• Management of supply of medicines & foodstock • Infrastructure development • Training of field functionaries	• District plan for pre- & post-natal women and child care • District malnutrition control plan

(Contd.)

TABLE 6.1 *(Contd.)*

1	2	3	4	5
17.	Social welfare xxv. Social welfare, including welfare of the handicapped and mentally retarded xxvi. Welfare of the weaker sections and in particular, of the SCs and STs	• Availability of old age pension, maternity benefit schemes	• Survey of people under relevant group • Educational centres for handicapped	• District plan for social security • Creation of infrastructure (for creche, orphanage, schools for handicapped etc.) • Management of orphans
18.	Poverty alleviation xxvii. Poverty alleviation programme xxviii. Maintenance of community assets	• Implementation of beneficiary and village specific programmes • Maintenance of assets • Community participation • Training to beneficiaries	• Infrastructure development planning for the block • Watershed development • Survey of beneficiaries for anti-poverty schemes	• Strategy for poverty alleviation for the district • District plan for infrastructure development and income generation schemes • Credit plan
19.	Public distribution system xxix. Public distribution system	• Distribution of essential commodities at village level	• Construction of godowns and fair price shops • Management of transport • Supply of commodities to cut-off & inaccessible areas	• District PDS plan • Organising supply of commodities to block HQs

VP : Village Panchayat ; BP : Block Panchayat ; DP : District Panchayat.

TABLE 6.2: **Broad Roles and Responsibilities of Various Institutions in Development Process**

S. N.	Name of the institute	Broad nature of role and responsibility	Specific roles and responsibilities for				
			Planning	Implementation	Monitoring & supervision	Control	Evaluation
1	2	3	4	5	6	7	8
1.	PRIs	Mobilising & involving people in development process; coordination; monitoring & supervision	To coordinate with different line departments and to provide knowledge about local resources	To facilitate in arranging inputs in the formulation of beneficiaries committee	To supervise the quality of work	Check on time or cost over-run and check on financial transaction	To facilitate in the collection of information
2.	DRDA / DPU	Administrative and organisational support for planning, implementation, monitoring & evaluation at district level	To organize the line departments for planning exercise and conduct necessary pre-planning training programme	To provide necessary manpower and logistics support	To design monitoring system and compile necessary data and information and do different data analysis	• Development of formats for MIS for smooth flow of information	• To design evaluation system • The collection of information from the field and the necessary data analysis
3.	Line departments	Technical inputs for planning, implementation, monitoring & evaluation	• To provide technical inputs during programme design • Project formulation and appraisal	To provide technical guidance in the execution of work	• To inspect the quality as per standards • To provide feed-back at appropriate level	-do-	-do-
4.	Block and GP (office units)	Administrative and organisational support for planning, implementation, monitoring & evaluation at respective level	To organise staff and officers for planning	To provide necessary manpower and logistics	Supervise the quality of work. Necessary data collection and data analysis	-do-	Necessary data collection and data analysis

(Contd.)

TABLE 6.2 *(Contd.)*

1	2	3	4	5	6	7	8
5.	People (CBOs and NGOs)	In providing local knowledge in planning; in making contributions in the execution of works; supervision and monitoring	To provide local knowledge for planning	To help in organising inputs and provide contributions	To supervise the execution of work	Participation in social audit	To facilitate in the collection of information

Administrative Control: It is important to mention that the PR members at each tier should play the role of planning and monitoring, and the implementation task should be given to the concerned departments (but the beneficiaries' involvement during the implementation and supervision of works should be ensured through proper guidelines). The field staff and officers of the departments should work as per the plans and the overall direction given by GP or Block Panchayat or ZP (as the case may be). With regard to accountability, the concerned head of the department at each tier should report to the concerned chairperson. While the field staff and officers under each tier should report to concerned head of department at respective tier, in order to obviate the possibility of duality of control.

For exercising administrative control, the ACRs of head of the offices at zilla parishad, block and gram panchayats should be written by the chairpersons of respective panchayats. And the ACRs of line departments should be initiated by the CEO, ZP or BDO at their respective levels and then countersigned by the chairpersons of respective subject committees before sending it to the controlling authority of a particular department.

In order to avoid conflicting situations between PR members and line departments over placement of field officers and staff, and to maintain smooth functioning, it is important to have proper administrative framework at all the three tiers. The recruitment, transfer and postings of field officers and staff must be made, based on laid down procedure and guidelines and should be made by a board at the district level.

Also, to avoid having field staff including clerical staff from the local areas (where the local influence may work) and also to have uniformity in the selection pattern, there should not be separate staff with block and gram panchayats, field staff for these panchayats should be recruited at the district level and posted to panchayats from the district pool.

Organisational Structure: Keeping in view the above points, the organisational structures are suggested (see figs. 6.3 and 6.4) at the block and district levels (Gupta, 2001).

Roles and Responsibilities of Various Development Institutions: The integrated development planning involves not only the integration of plans of various sectors but also assimilation of efforts of various development functionaries, PR members and people. It, therefore, requires the defining of roles and responsibilities of all the concerned actors.

The roles and responsibilities of various development institutions are broadly outlined in the table 6.2. {for the subject-specific responsibilities for various actors in development, see Integrated Development Planning (Gupta, 2004)}. These have been suggested keeping in view that there should not be overlapping in the roles of functionaries in order to avoid conflicts and to have smooth functioning. Moreover, each functionary should be able to contribute maximum. Here, it should be kept in mind that the PRIs should play the role of planning, monitoring and supervision, while the departments should be given the responsibility of technical inputs and implementation.

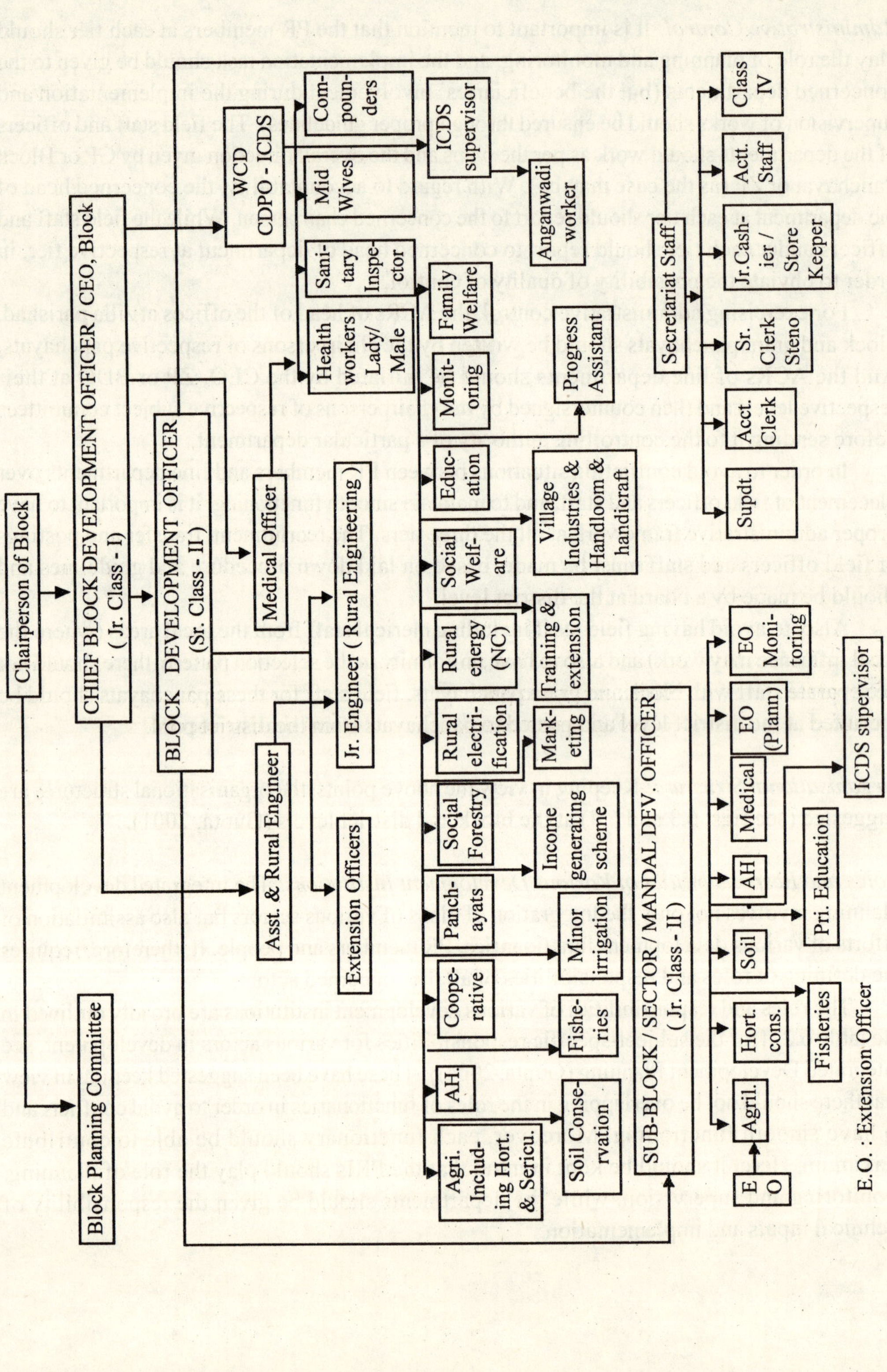

Fig. 6.3: Model Organisational Set-up at Block Level for Rural Development

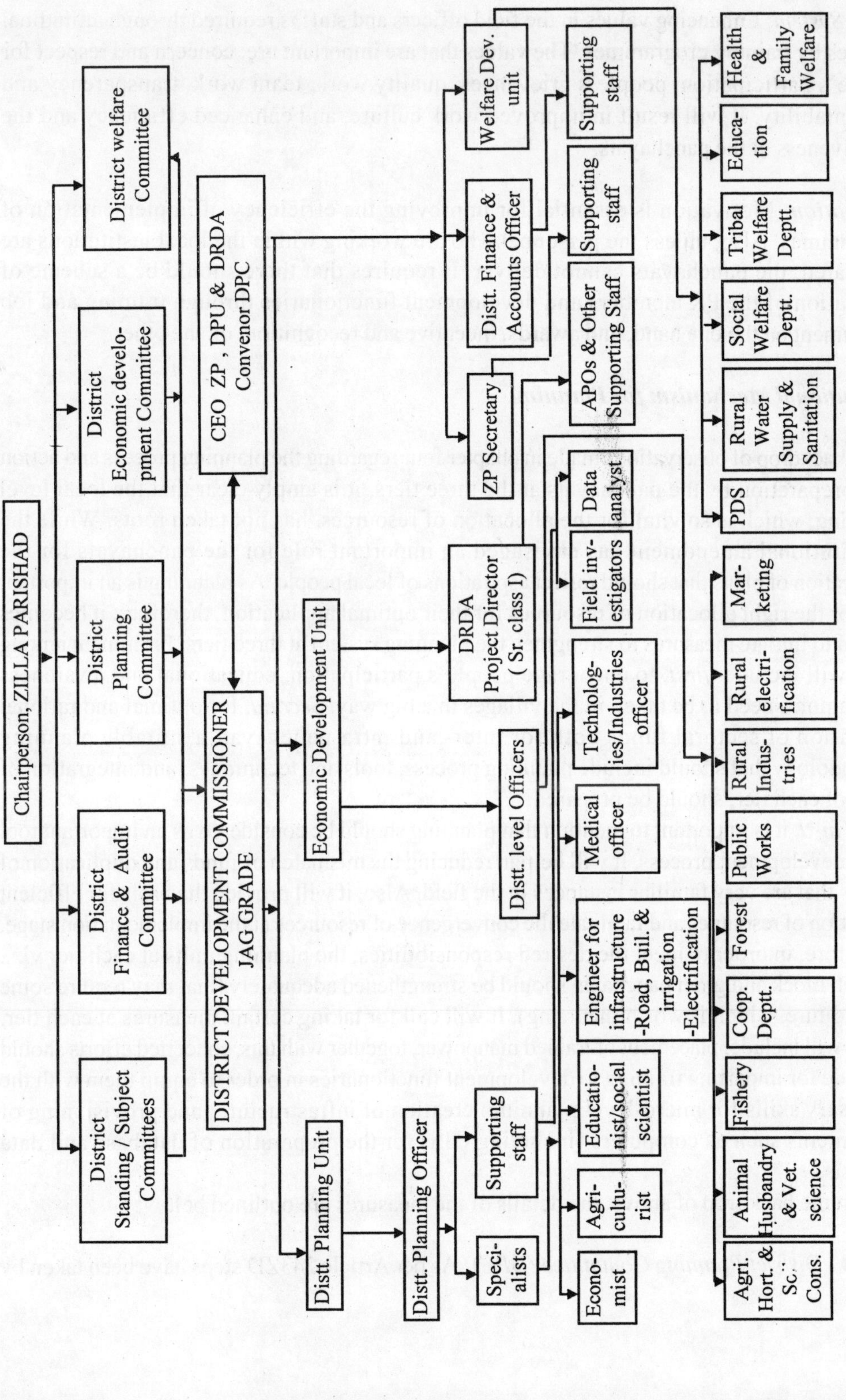

Fig. 6.4: Model Organisational Set-up at District Level — Zilla Parishad for Rural Development

Value System: Enhancing values in the field officers and staff is required through attitudinal changes by training programmes. The values that are important are: concern and respect for people's participation, people's grievances, quality work, team work, transparency and accountability. It will result in improved work culture, and enhanced efficiency and the effectiveness of the panchayats.

Motivation: Motivation is essential for improving the efficiency of implementation of programmes. Also, unless the personnel who are working within the local institutions are motivated, the panchayats cannot deliver. It requires that there should be a scheme of motivation of the PR members and development functionaries through training and job enrichment on the one hand, and awards, incentive and recognition, on the other.

Institutional Mechanism for Planning

In the backdrop of observations made in chapter four regarding the planning process and action plan preparation by the panchayats at the three tiers, it is amply clear that the local level planning, which is so vital for the allocation of resources, has not taken roots. While the constitutional amendment has envisaged an important role for the panchayats for the preparation of plans that should reflect aspirations of local people. As planning is an important tool for the right allocation of resources for their optimal application, therefore, it becomes crucial to initiate measures to strengthen the planning system at three tiers. Prominent among them will include: *first*, to encourage people's participation, educational and awareness programmes need to be taken in the villages in a big way. *Second*, for optimal and rational allocation of sectoral funds both for inter- and intra-panchayat, a suitable planning methodology that should include planning process, tools and techniques, and integration of plans of each tier, should be prepared.

Third, it is important to mention that planning should be considered as an important tool in the development process. It will help in reducing the mismatch of funds and duplication of efforts that are very familiar instances in the field. Also, it will provide the basis for efficient allocation of resources and facilitate the convergence of resources at the implementation stage. Therefore, in order to meet the desired responsibilities, the planning units at each tier viz., district, block and gram panchayat should be strengthened adequately (that may require some expenditure, which is worth incurring). It will call for taking certain measures at each tier. These will include: placement of trained manpower, together with this, concerted efforts should be made for imparting training to development functionaries in order to equip them with the necessary skills for micro-level planning; creation of infrastructure; and provisioning of equipments such as computers (including GIS) for the preparation of database and data analysis.

In the backdrop of above, the details of the measures are outlined below:

- *District Planning Committee (DPC):* As per Article 243ZD steps have been taken by some states for the formation of district planning committee (DPC), as discussed in the previous chapter, still there are certain lacunae in its formation. As planning can be a vital tool in the optimal allocation of resources and can facilitate the process of resource-matching which are very crucial in the development process, it, therefore, necessitates to initiate the following measures in order to strengthen the local level planning:

- DPC must have experts from various fields such as economics, HRD, technologies, agriculture, health, engineering (infrastructure) and management and their task should be to provide necessary technical inputs, to carry out the data analysis and assist in the preparation of action plan, and to monitor and provide feedback to the DPC and lower tiers (here, it should be appreciated that planning requires reasonably good amount of knowledge and skills that can be provided by experts). (see fig. 6.5 for framework of DPC).
- At each tier, planning unit should be created or the present level should be upgraded in order to provide effectiveness to the planning process. The planning unit should have: *first*, infrastructure and equipments; *second*, manpower with experts (who should be provided adequate training for local level planning); and *third*, facility for database preparation and data analysis.
- The chairperson of the DPC should be from among the elected members of ZP or municipality.
- DPC should be given the exclusive task of planning, as planning is an elaborate exercise that requires extensive as well as intensive efforts.
- Planning committees must also be formed at block and GP levels (to begin with, it may be done first at block and subsequently at GP).

- *Capabilities for Participatory Planning:* The capabilities of PR members and development functionaries need special attention in the context of their enhanced roles for local level planning. We may take clue from the findings of Charles V. Kidd (I980), who has noted, 'The interest in training arises from the realisation that lack of trained manpower poses obstacles to development as formidable as those pertaining to scarce resources, inadequate capital and insufficient technology '. Further, it is a matter of concern that the expenditure that is incurred on training is infinitesimal (Gupta, 2001) in comparison to total expenditure on development. In the context of participatory planning and development, it is crucial to have effective training system with adequate infrastructure and manpower support in order to equip the functionaries with appropriate knowledge and skills for planning of each sector of development.
- *Planning Methodology:* Development planning is a continuous process in which the initiatives are taken based on field situation, empirical analysis, programme design and management of implementation. People's participation has assumed important dimension in the planning in order to formulate the plan as per the felt-needs of people

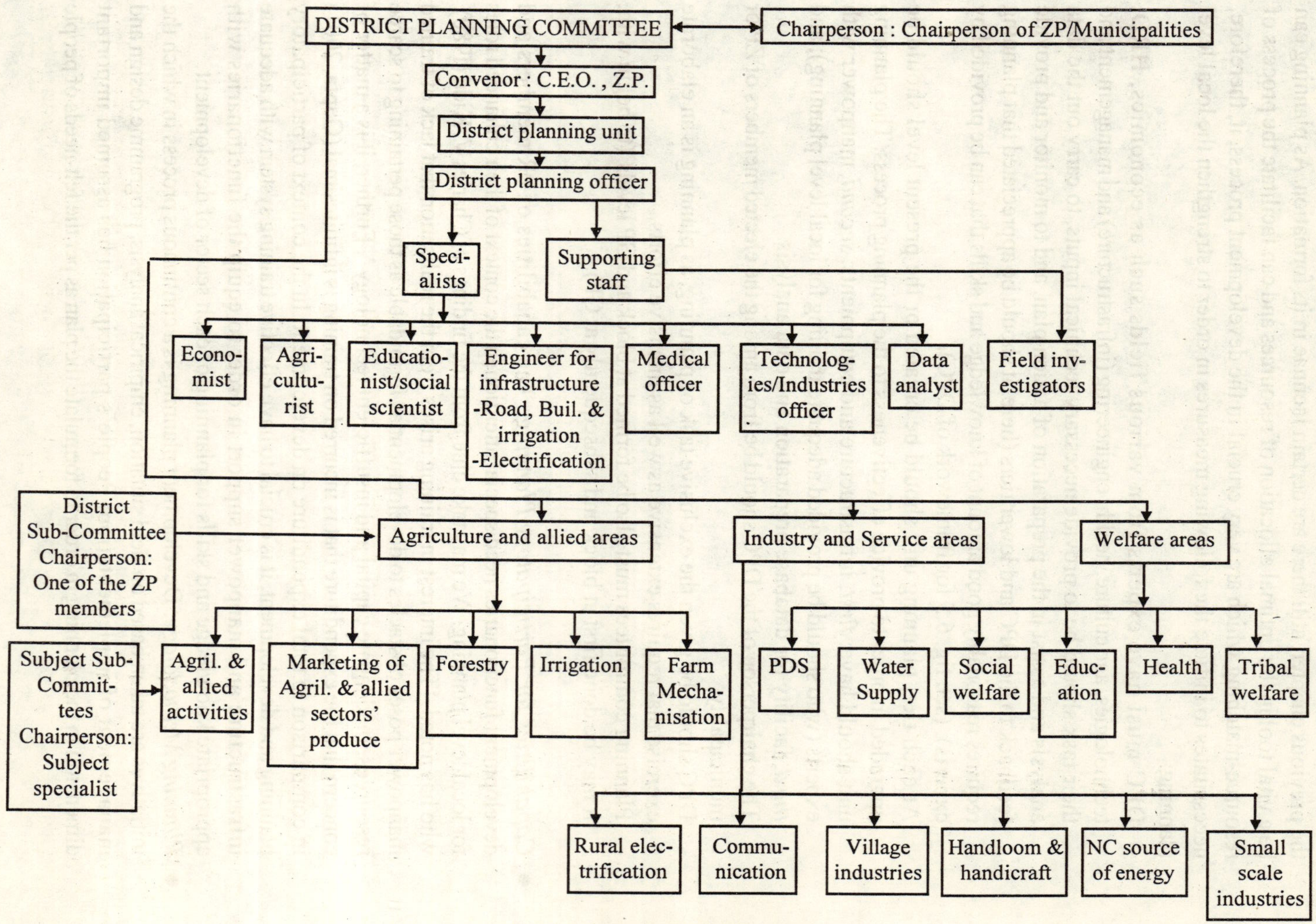

Fig. 6.5: **Suggested DPC Framework**

and also to tap the local knowledge during the process. The achievements and the outcomes of one plan become the inputs for the next plan. Thus, the planning is not a linear but it is a cyclical process. The planning cycle can be divided into different phases, i. situation analysis, ii. sectoral analysis, iii. programme design, iv. implementation, v. monitoring, vi. evaluation and vii. effecting modification. Specifically, the planning involves the following:

- The assessment of the existing resources, needs and problems
- Formulation of objectives and alternative status for development
- Designing suitable development progammes and / projects to fulfil the desired objectives of the plans.

Now, in order to facilitate the process of planning at the GP, block and district levels, planning methodology with tools and techniques should be developed in order to facilitate the preparation of comprehensive integrated plan, and the methodology should specifically include the following:

Situation Analysis: It involves the studies of facts and their synthesis into database about a particular area (which may be GP or block or district), necessary for an understanding of the situation existing at the ground. Database covers the entire gamut of social, cultural and economic sphere. (Needless to emphasise the need of database in decision-making which is very crucial for planning and implementation, it will require appropriate organisational support in terms of infrastructure, equipments and trained manpower, which is to be adequately supported by the government). This analysis also covers the identification of potential and problem areas, resource mapping and identification of constraints. To sum up, the situation analysis involves the study of the following:

- Data collection
- Data analysis
- Identification of potential, problems and needs
    - Resource matrix
    - Potential areas
    - Problem identification
    - Identification of target group
- Resource mapping
- Identification of constraints

Sectoral Analysis: The sectoral analysis is an essential element of the district plan formulation. In the context of 11th Schedule of 73rd Constitution Amendment Act, it is suggested to group the 29 subjects into 19 sectors (see appendix 6.2) in order to have sector-wise planning exercise. The planning for each sector would be carried out at the GP, block and district levels.

It, among others, would include areas of concern, prioritising the needs and identification of opportunities where thrusts in effort will achieve the most efficient results. Sector-wise analysis will include the following steps:

- Past performance
- Backward and forward linkages
- Problem areas
- Potential areas
- Priority areas
- Plan of action
    - Infrastructure
    - Family based schemes
    - HRD : Training, Research and Demonstration
- Perspective plan

Note 1: The planning may be first undertaken for subjects under primary sector (and for basic services) and thereafter as the capacity of the panchayats improve, the planning for other subjects may be added.

Note 2: As per the present state of support system for planning units, the planning may be undertaken at the district and block levels. And, simultaneously, the capacities of gram panchayats should be enhanced in order to enable them to undertake the task of village planning.

Preparatory Phase for Participatory Planning: In the context of strengthening the people's involvement in planning, it may require taking steps for rapport building. It requires developing good contacts with the people and building confidence through: village meetings, PRA exercise, participation in social functions by the field staff, informal discussion, workshop, etc.

Role of Gram Sabha: Under the 73rd Constitutional Amendment, the gram sabha has been given a prominent role in the village development planning. As per article 243 A, the gram sabha should be the focal point of the local level planning. As discussed in chapter four, the gram sabha has to be strengthened in order to enable it to perform efficiently. The successful functioning of gram sabha can be measured in terms of: *first*, improved knowledge and awareness among people; *second*, more attendance in gram sabha; and *third*, active participation of members, especially the poor and women. Therefore, the gram panchayat should take measures in order to ensure these three parameters for improving functioning of gram sabha.

The gram sabha should actively involve itself specifically for the following tasks:

- Providing local knowledge specific to its village
- Identification of resources and potential
- Identification of problems

- Needs identification and analysis
- Prioritisation of needs
- Suggesting solutions
- Resources mobilisation

Resource Groups : Development is a multi-dimensional process. It involves the role of various sectors viz., agriculture, animal husbandry, fisheries, education, health and so on. For the development of any area there is a need of integration of the activities of these sectors. It calls for making detailed analysis at panchayat level. And for this, we need a dedicated team for each sector that should devote itself fully for sectoral planning. But in order to assimilate the expertise from other relevant groups (in the village) and also keeping in view the present state of poor manpower available (with the planning units), especially at the gram panchayat level, it is crucial to widen the human resources base so as to improve the capacity of the planning system. It will require having resource groups at all the three tiers, in the following sectors and these resource groups should have representatives from PRIs, CBOs, experts from the local area and resource person from respective departments.

- Agriculture
- Natural resource management
- Irrigation
- Animal husbandry
- Fisheries
- Forest
- Rural connectivity
- Housing
- Commercial linkage
- Energy
- Industries
- Education
- Drinking water
- Health
- Family welfare
- Women and child development
- Social welfare
- Poverty alleviation
- Public distribution system

Functions of Resources Groups: The resource groups, so formed, should be associated with the preparation of action plan and be specifically responsible for the following tasks of their respective subjects:

- Problem identification
- Sectoral analysis
- Prioritisation of needs and problems
- Action plan preparation
- Implementation of plan
- Monitoring and evaluation

Note : As the gram sabha has large number of people (about 500 to 2000), so it is difficult to make indepth discussion in gram sabha about a particular subject. While, in a small group a detailed discussion and analysis can be attempted. So, these resource groups at the GP level can be usefully engaged for detailed analysis and planning for their respective sector. But, the analysis for potential, problems, and needs, and the allocation of resources should be done after the discussion in the gram sabha.

- *Planning Process:* Planning process includes broadly the roles of various functionaries and of committees, resource groups and subject committees; and the sequencing of relevant activities. The functionaries include PR members, line departments officers and staff, and people (including CBOs). The relevant activities are: awareness building, training programme, sectoral analysis and so on. The details of planning process are indicated by figures 6.6 and 6.7 (Gupta, 2004).
- *Integration of Plans of Three Tiers:* There is a need for integration of plans of all the three tiers in order to have proper resource matching and linkages of programmes. For this, while preparing the district and block plans, all the proposals of block and district panchayats should be sent to the concerned gram panchayats for discussion and recommendations of gram sabhas. This process is based on the principle that each proposal should be discussed, at first, by the concerned gram panchayat, followed by discussion at the block level, then, it should be discussed at district level based on the views expressed by the lower tiers. Together with this, the plan prepared by the gram panchayats should form an integral part of the block plan, and similarly, the plans of blocks should be integrated with district plan. This process will encourage the participatory planning from the below.
- *Support System:* The study of the planning system at district, block and GP levels, and the process of planning at local tiers, as discussed in chapters four and five, indicates evidently that each tier, the planning units are handicapped by lack of manpower, infrastructural and equipments support. Planning units lack the requisite expertise to undertake the micro-planning at gram panchayat level, there is a dearth of office infrastructure and equipments support. Under such circumstances, it becomes imperative to provide necessary support to planning units at all the three tiers, in order to make these units functionally viable so that they can perform the desired work of planning. The support includes infrastructure, equipments and manpower. The support system is outlined briefly below:

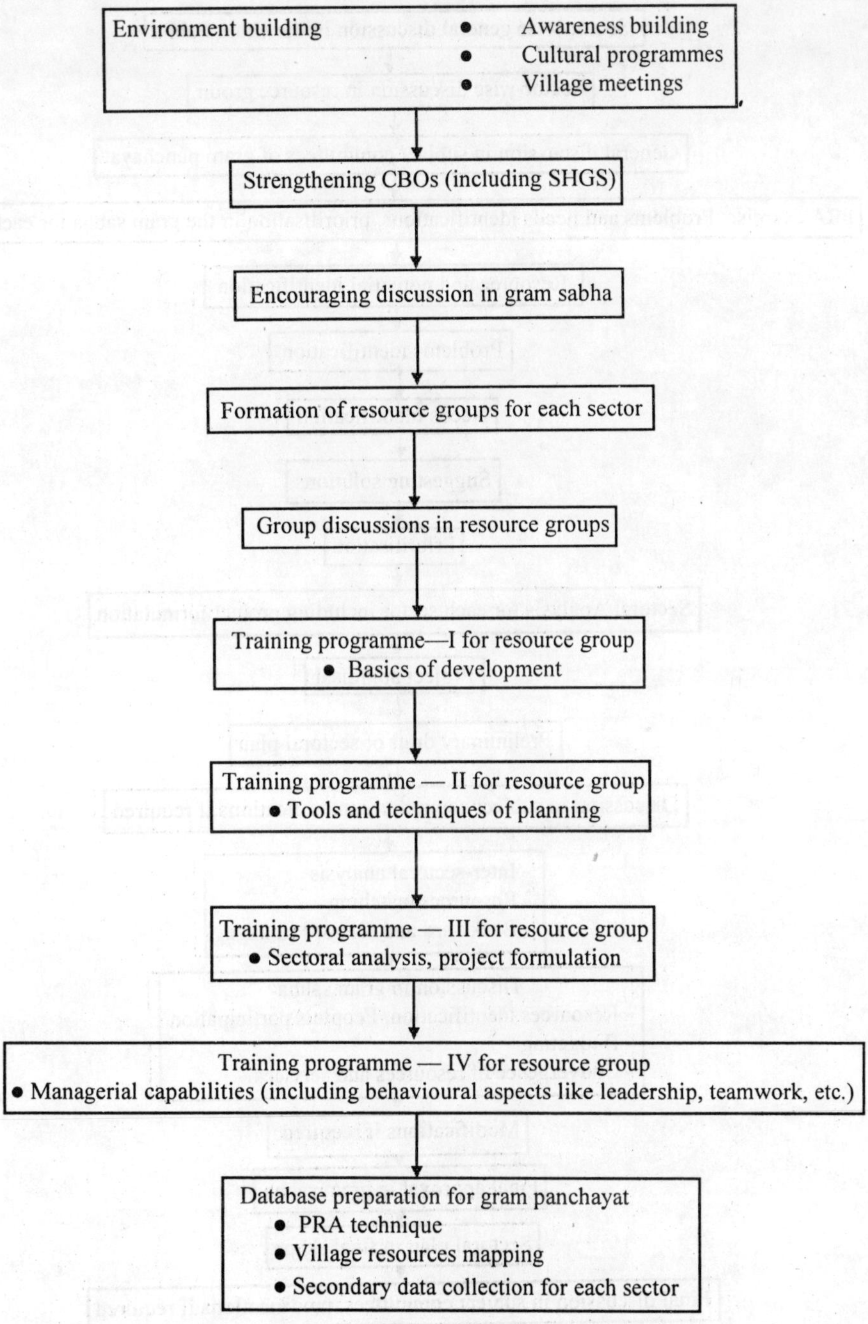

Fig. 6.6 : **Preparatory Phase for Planning at GP Level**

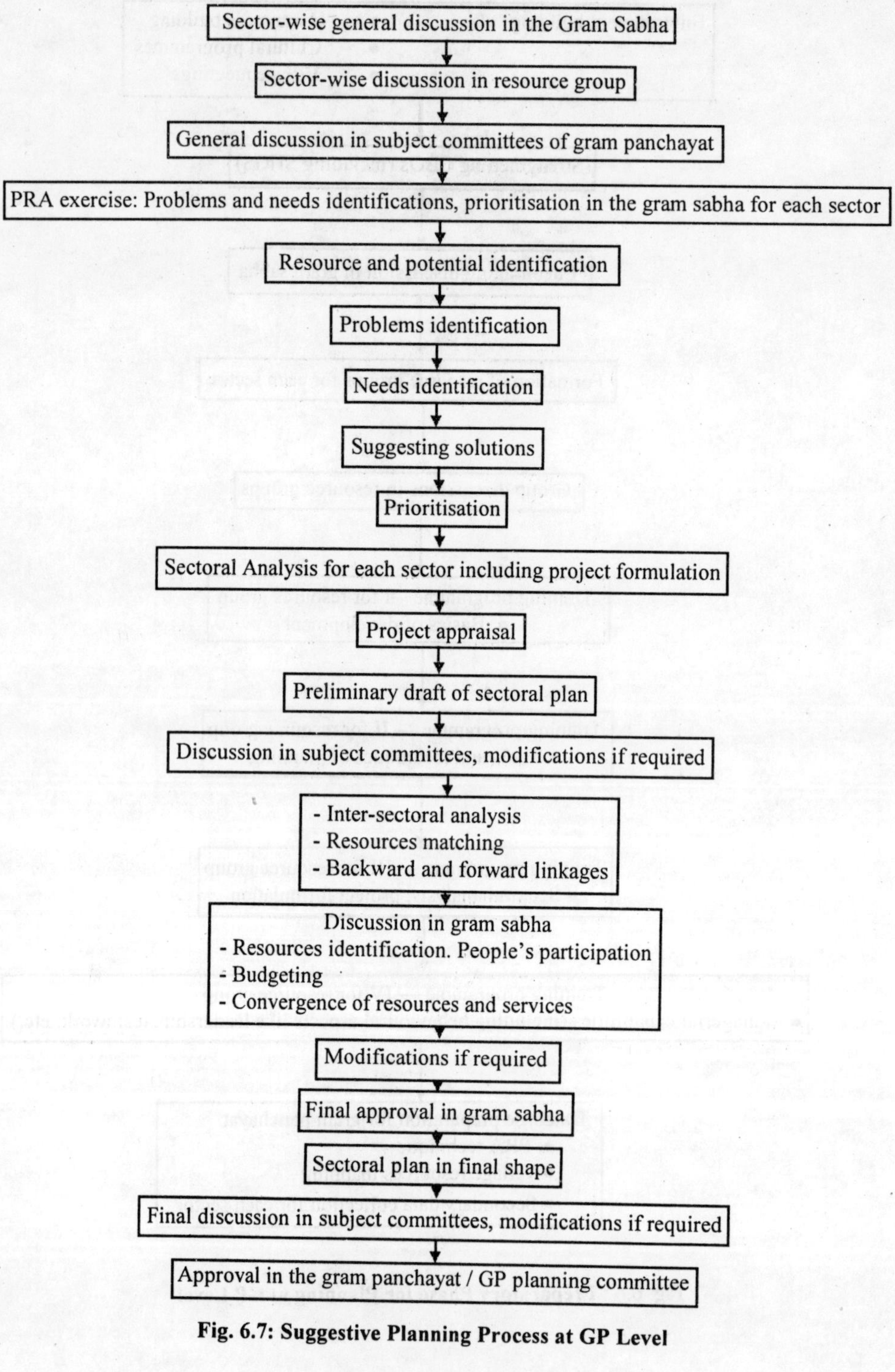

Fig. 6.7: Suggestive Planning Process at GP Level

- *Infrastructural and Equipments Support:* Infrastructure support is required at all the three tiers viz., gram panchayat, block and district. Infrastructure is necessary for conducting office work, for record room and for housing the equipments. The equipments and tools & aids include GIS, computers, appropriate software, etc. The necessity of application of GIS in planning has been realised in order to have development alternatives and to choose the best among them so as to optimise the output or make optimal allocation of funds. Besides, it will have help a great deal in handling of large database, quick monitoring and decision-making. It is suggested that GIS support can be provided to district planning unit, and this facility can be extended by district unit to blocks and GPs for their plan formulation. Based on the field level requirements, the details are presented in tables 6.3 to 6.6.

TABLE 6.3: **Additional Infrastructure and Equipments required for Planning at District**

(Rs. in lakhs)

Sl No	Name of the item		Name of the sub- item	Cost Rs.
1.	Infrastructure	i.	Planning unit (office infrastructure and computer chamber)	2.5
		ii.	Office infrastructure (additional)	10.0
			Sub Total	**12.5**
2.	Supporting equipments and aids	i.	Planning	
		a.	Computer	2.00
		b.	GIS package*	25.00
		c.	Design equipments (Engg. Works)	0.50
			Sub Total	27.50
			Total	**40.00**

*Web-based GIS Software, remote sensing software, etc.

TABLE 6.4: **Additional Infrastructure and Equipments required for Planning at Block**

(Rs. in lakhs)

Sl No	Name of the item		Name of the Sub- item	Cost Rs.
1.	Infrastructure	i.	Planning and M & E unit	1.5
		ii.	Office infrastructure	10.0
			Sub Total	**11.5**
2.	Supporting equipments and tools aids	i.	Planning	
		a.	Computer	1.00
		b.	GIS package (tied-up with DPU)	1.00
		c.	Design equipments for Eng. Work	0.50
			Sub Total	2.50
			Total	**14.00**

- *Manpower Support:* Presently, local institutions, especially the gram panchayats, do not have requisite manpower for carrying out various activities of planning. The activities include database preparation, training, planning exercise and so on. The required manpower for undertaking these activities is indicated in table 6.7. It has been suggested to provide experts both at district and block units in order to provide technical inputs for various items such as database preparation, project formulation, inter-sectoral analysis, project appraisal, spatial planning and application of various techniques like GIS and remote sensing.

TABLE 6.5: **Additional Infrastructure and Equipments required for Planning at Sector**

(Rs. in lakhs)

Sl No	Name of the item		Name of the sub- item	Cost Rs.
1.	Infrastructure	i.	Planning unit	0.75
		ii.	Office infrastructure	2.50
			Sub Total	**3.25**
2.	Supporting	i.	Planning	
	equipment	a.	Computer	1.00
	and tools aids	b.	GIS package (tied-up with DPU)	1.00
		c.	Design equipments for Engg. section	
			Sub Total	**2.00**
			Total	**5.25**

TABLE 6.6: **Additional Infrastructure and Equipments required for Planning at Gram Panchayat**

(Rs. in lakhs)

Sl No	Name of the item		Name of the sub- item	Cost Rs.
1.	Infrastructure	i.	Planning unit	0.75
		ii.	Office infrastructure	1.00
			Sub-Total	**1.75**
2.	Supporting	i.	Planning and Monitoring	-
	equipment	a.	Computer	0.75
	and tools aids			
			Sub-Total	**0.75**
			Total	**2.50**

Total Cost = 40.00 + 14.00 × 20 +5.25 × 60+2.50 × 240 = Rs. 1,235 lakhs

Percentage of total plan fund :{ 1235/250 (cr.) × 100 × 5 yrs. } × 100 = 0.98 %

Note : It is assumed that infrastructural and equipments support would be established in five years.

TABLE 6.7: **Recommended Officers and Field Staff and their Yearly Salary for Planning Units at District, Block, Sector, and GP**

(Rs. in lakhs)

S.No	Nature of Job	Name of post	Existing posts	Addl. posts	Total posts	Salary Existing (Rs.)	Total Salary for addl. Posts (Rs.)	Total Salary (Rs.)
1.	Planning (District)	i. District Planning Officer	1	-	1	1.80	-	1.80
		ii. Asst. Planning Officer	1	-	1	1.50	-	1.50
		iii. Investigators	4	2	6	4.00	2.00	6.00
		iv. Subject Experts	-	7	7	-	11.20	11.20
		v. Computer programmer	-	1	1	1.44	1.44	1.44
		vi. Computer operator	-	1	1	0.84	0.84	0.84
		Sub- total					**15.48**	**22.78**
2.	Planning (Block)	i. ABDO planning	-	1	1	-	1.2	1.2
		ii. Subject Experts	-	2	2	-	3.2	3.2
		iii. E.O. (Planning)	-	2	2	-	2.0	2.0
		iv. Computer operator	-				0.84	0.84
		Sub- total					**7.24**	**7.24**
3.	Planning (Sector)	i. EO (Planning)	-	2	2	-	2.0	2.0
		ii. Computer operator	-	1	1	-	0.84	0.84
		Sub-total					**2.84**	**2.84**
4.	Planning (GP)	i. EO (Planning)	-	1	1	-	1.0	1.0
		ii. Computer operator		1	1	-	0.84	0.84
		Sub-total					**1.84**	**1.84**

Addl. Salary = 15.48 + 7.24×20 + 2.84 × 60 + 1.84 × 240 =Rs. 772.28 lakhs
Percentage of total plan fund: {772.28/250 (cr) × 100} × 100 = 3.09 %

Total Salary = 22.78 + 7.24×20 + 2.84 × 60 + 1.84×240 = Rs. 779.58 lakhs
Percentage of total plan fund: {779.58 / 250 (cr) × 100} × 100 = 3.12 %

Note: Though as per above table, additional staff and officers are suggested, but these can be met from the existing departments, wherever there is a surplus and also from restructuring of existing departments and even from state directorates.

Finally, this support system is going to add considerable strength to planning units at the three tiers that would facilitate the local level participatory planning. It is worked out that the additional cost on account of infrastructure and equipments is 0.98 per cent of total development expenditure made in a district; and the recurring cost on establishment is 3.12 per cent (though as per table 6.7, additional staff and officers are suggested, but these can be met from the existing departments, wherever there is a surplus, and also from restructuring of existing departments, and even from state directorates. Thus there would be no need for fresh recruitment). It clearly shows that additional expenditure is a very small fraction of the total plan development expenditure made in a district, whereas these support systems are going to add to the quality of planning at all the three tiers to a very great extent, and would help PR members and other field functionaries not only in participatory planning but also in rational and optimal allocation of resources that is so vital for the process of development.

Note 1 : For the purpose of calculation the following data have been assumed (which are indicative):

District : 20 blocks ; rural population 25 lakhs; plan funds Rs. 250 cr. in rural areas. {Rs. 71,000 cr. allocation for rural areas by both states and Centre, MORD (2001a)}.

Block : 12 GPs ; population 1.25 lakhs.

Sector : 4 GPs ; population 40,000 (size of the sector may vary as per district specific need, and the number of GPs in a sector may be more in case the size of the population of GP is small). (60 sectors in a district)

GP : Population 10,000 (240 GPs in a district) (population may vary from district to district)

2. As regards the manpower support, in critical places new staff may be recruited, otherwise personnel should be drawn from the existing departments, even from state directorates.

Note 2 : In several states the average population of gram panchayat is about three thousand (even in many GPs the population is about 1200 or less) with the exception of Assam, Kerala and West Bengal where the population is more than 10,000 (in case of Kerala the average population is more than 25,000). In this context, it should be appreciated that for making a viable development unit, three components are very much necessary. These are, *first*, infrastructure, *second*, manpower, and *third*, equipments. Presently, the gram panchayats do not have any of these support systems. Now, under such circumstances in which the size of the gram panchayat is very small, the states may find it very difficult to provide manpower and infrastructural support to each GP to make it a viable unit. Besides, block is too far a unit (from the GP) to provide services to people, and gram panchayats are too small units to be viable enough to provide services to people. Therefore, for the purpose of providing support to GP in order to make it a viable unit, either minimum size of GP having population 20-25000 should be fixed, or one sector may be formed for cluster of GPs. At sector level, the necessary support should be given, which would provide support to the concerned GPs (for bigger GPs having population above 25,000 there is no need for creating sector, and the necessary support system should be provided right at the GP level).

Note 3 : In case the size of GP is big (population above 25,000), the support system should be provided right at the GP level. For small GPs, full support system should be given to sector, but bare minimum support system should be given to GP also.

Note 4 : The items for infrastructural, equipments and manpower support are indicative, but as per the district-specific needs the actual requirements are to be worked out. But the proportionate requirements in a district as per the population are going to remain more or less the same.

Also, in the context of participatory planning, we can take the lessons from the success of people's plan campaign of Kerala. Here, for strengthening participatory planning, the steps have been taken to educate and train people, PR members and development functionaries about planning; for formulating planning methodology and the process of planning; and for providing necessary manpower and infrastructural support to planning units at all the three tiers. It clearly shows that the necessary requisites for local level planning have duly been recognised and also attended to in order to make participatory planning a success. For rational allocation of funds and their efficient matching with the local resources, participatory planning assumes high importance. It calls for placing the necessary requisites in right perspective as discussed above, before people's involvement can be sought and the resource planning can begin at local levels.

Institutional Mechanism for Implementation of Programmes

Implementation of programmes is an important component for realising the intended objectives. For efficient implementation, there is a need to look into implementation planning, inputs management and beneficiaries participation. In the context of involvement of beneficiaries in the implementation of programmes, the following points need to be attended to:

- Implementation mechanism;
- Formation of beneficiaries committee;
- Training of representatives of the committee;
- Inputs management; and
- Monitoring and supervision and so on.

The details of the implementation process with the roles and responsibilities of PRIs, departments, people and CBOs, are pictorially reflected in fig. 6.8.

Institutional Mechanism for Panchayat Functioning

For smooth panchayat functioning, conduct of panchayat meetings, monitoring and coordination, among others, assume high significance at the panchayat levels. The salient steps that require to be taken are indicated below:

- *For Functioning of Panchayat Meetings*: Firstly, for the purpose of streamlining the functioning of panchayats, there is a need for having a set of rules and procedure for the meetings (including gram sabha), that should include the following:

  ▸ *Rules and procedure for:*
  - Agenda preparation;
  - Convening of meetings;

Role of line department	Activities	Role of PRIs	Role of people and CBOs
	After identification of work		
Line department to prepare technical estimate	Preparation of work estimates	-	-
Field staff to participate during formation of committee	Formation of beneficiaries committee	To form beneficiaries committee	To facilitate in the formation of committee
-	Identification of secretary of committee	By beneficiaries committee	-
To provide training for necessary execution of work	Training to representative of beneficiaries committee about basics of work including maintenance of muster - rolls and accounts	To supervise training programme	To participate
To provide inputs	Organising inputs for works	Supervise supply of inputs	Helping the committee in arranging inputs
To provide necessary technical skills	Execution	To supervise the work	To help representative of the committee in the execution
To supervise technical parameters	Supervision	To supervise the quality of work	To supervise the progress
To measure necessary indicators	Monitoring	Review the Progress of the work	To provide feedback
To participate in the discussion	Social Audit	To reply to the questions of people in the gram sabha	To participate in the discussion
Audit section to do inspection	Financial Auditing	Facilitate in the audit work	-
To collect information about various parameters	Evaluation	Facilitate in the collection of information	Facilitate in the collection of information

Fig. 6.8: **Requisite Implementation Process**

- Conduct of business of meeting;
- Procedure of voting;
- Noting of proceedings;
- Circulation of proceedings;
- Inviting objections; and
- Reply of objections.

- *For MIS*

  - *Database and Information System:* At each tier database for all development activities needs to be developed, and shall be made available to people, PR members and departments in user-friendly format for smooth flow of information.
  - *Monitoring*: At the panchayat level there are a number of crucial functions such as addressing people's grievances, transparency, accountability, etc., that require constant monitoring, and the following monitoring committees are essential:
    - Grievance handling
    - Implementation of works
    - Transparency and accountability (social audit)
  - *Control System*: Definite indicators are to be developed and information should be provided at the appropriate level for necessary control.

- *For Coordination*: At various stages of development like planning, implementation, monitoring, supervision and control, there is a need to have coordination among panchayat members and departments. It will require having the following committees:
  - Inter-tier coordination committee
  - Inter-department coordination committee
- *For Transparency*: Transparency in the panchayat functioning is very essential, so a proper modality for transparency should be worked out, which may include the following:

  - Procedure for
    - Decision-making in the gram sabha and panchayat meetings;
    - Noting of decisions and publicising the decisions taken;
    - Display of information about accounts, projects, beneficiaries list, etc.; and
    - Providing information to people on demand.
- *For Accountability*: For the purpose of having accountability of elected members to people, we need to address both financial as well as social audit.

  - *Financial audit committee at the panchayat level with defined powers and functions:* The role of this committee should have twin objectives: *first*, keeping watch over finance and accounting system; and *second*, advising panchayats for improvements.

Specifically, the committee should look into audit objections (by the auditors) and examine the financial matters on a selective basis, and guide the panchayats on three main aspects: *first*, bringing transparency in the transactions; *second*, simplification of procedure for timely availability of wages to the beneficiaries (engaged in the works); and *third*, observance of financial norms for accounting.

- Social Audit, we need to address the procedure for :
  - Mode of asking questions;
  - Reply of objections;
  - Noting of proceedings;
  - Circulation of proceedings;
  - Availability of proceedings for people; and
  - Compliance for the corrective measures.

Simultaneously, through appropriate accountability mechanism, the efforts should be made for ensuring the accountability of departments to panchayats for their performance

Miscellaneous Issues

Merger of DRDA with ZP: Various state governments have taken measures for merging the DRDA with zilla parishad (ZP) in order to provide effective control of ZP over DRDA. During the field study, it has come out that there is no qualitative difference in the functioning of ZP as far as the implementation of anti-poverty programmes is concerned, as was evident during the discussions with some ZP members, CEOs and district-level officers.

But if we critically examine the impact on the efficiency and effectiveness of the functioning, it is not going to make much difference, whether we merge DRDA with ZP or not (even if DRDA is not merged, the ZP would continue to provide direction to DRDA, as it would be accountable to ZP). What really matters is that the DRDA should be working under the overall direction of ZP and the PD, DRDA (or CEO who is Chairman of DRDA in some states) should be accountable to ZP. Abolishing one institution or changing its name is not going to serve much purpose, while the crucial point is how to strengthen the institutions and make them deliver effectively. Or in other words, we should be concerned about how the efficiency and effectiveness of DRDA for planning and implementation of programmes can be enhanced.

Finally, such kinds of measure of abolishing one institution or merging institutions are only going to give notional satisfaction. All the more we should be concentrating our energy on: how to improve people's participation in planning; formulation of proper planning methodology; capacity building of PR members and field staff; devolution of funds, management of utilisation of funds including accounting; and creation of transparency and audit system.

Training

The field studies have categorically reflected the low level of capabilities among PR members and development functionaries, still there seems to be serious lack of training in bridging the gap between the desired role and the existing state of capabilities. While in the ever changing economic and technological scenario, training can play an important role in improving the capabilities of individuals and organisations. The purpose of training involves the process of learning new skills, acquiring knowledge and attitudinal changes. In the context of decentralised planning, the PR functionaries should acquire knowledge and skills pertaining to the local level planning process: tools and techniques required for micro-planning, participatory techniques, resources mobilisation; implementation of programmes; monitoring and evaluation.

If we look at the state of Kerala, it has done considerably well in training the PR members and development functionaries. It has created conducive environment for smooth functioning of the panchayats. Or in other words, it is evident from the field studies that HRD including training, the fulcrum on which the Kerala's decentralisation has depended, is in poor state in other states.

In the context of building capabilities, the following observation (Montgomery, 1980) deserves mention:

'In the past the panchayati raj institutions could not function in the manner envisaged, and one of the important reasons has been the lack of local level expertise to cope with the growing complexities of development'.

While realising the importance of reasonable educational background that enables a person to reach threshold level which facilitates him in acquiring further knowledge and skills, there is also a strong need for continuous training programmes not only to make people and PR members aware about the development programmes, but also to enable the PR members to do necessary development planning and then to manage the implementation of programmes successfully.

It is pertinent to point out that the capability level of PR functionaries is very crucial and determining factor in the success of functioning of local bodies. Even if we delegate the powers to local bodies and provide necessary funds along with institutional arrangements, but for village development planning, to allocate the resources optimally and to ensure efficient implementation of programmes at the field, it will require individual skills and organisational capabilities, only then would the desired objectives of participatory development be achieved. Not only this, the fast changing socio-economic scenario, changing market conditions, emerging new technologies and increasing people's demands also make it necessary that the functionaries of local bodies should enhance their capabilities to meet new realities and changing conditions at the field.

- *Magnitude of Problem for Training for Panchayats*

▶ *Large number of Field Functionaries and PR Members:* Under rural development, besides panchayat members, a large number of development functionaries at district, block and gram panchayat levels are engaged in the implementation of various development programmes. It is estimated that the number of development functionaries is 29,97,550 and that of PR members is 28,37,050 — together about six million (see tables 6.8 and 6.9).

TABLE 6.8: **Total number of Field Functionaries and PR members**

S.No.	Levels	Number of functionaries * in each tier (Average)		Total Number (All India)	
		Development / Departmental Functionaries *	PR members	Development / Departmental functionaries	PR members (No. of chairpersons)
1	District	50	30	27,550	17,050 (550)
2	Block	45	20	2,70,000	1,20,000 (6000)
3	Gram Panchayat	12	12	27,00,000	27,00,000 (2,25,000)
	Total			29,97,550	28,37,050

* It includes all the departments, DRDA / zilla parishad and Banks.

TABLE 6.9: **Total Number of Field Officers and Staff at District and All India Level**

S.N.	Level	At the District level *			At the all India level *		
		Field Officers	Field staff	Total	Field Officers	Field staff	Total
1	District	50	-	50	27,500	-	
2	Block	250	200	450	1,50,000	1,20,000	
3	Gram Panchayat	-	4,800	4,800	-	27,00,000	
	Total	300	5,000	5,300	1,77,500	28,20,000	29,97,500

* *Note* : The figures are average and will vary from state to state.

▶ *Problem of Physical-reach:* Normally at the state level, the availability of physical infrastructure for training is confined mainly to state institute of rural development (SIRD) and extension training centre (ETC) levels. At the district and below, the training infrastructure is very much lacking which restricts the reach of training programmes at the block and gram panchayat levels. Thus, a large number of field functionaries and PR members are deprived of getting proper training.

- *Training not given in the form of a Package*

This aspect will be clear from the following two examples:

- It is often found that the officers or field staff at a particular level are not covered fully for a specific training programme. For example, for the training of BDOs in a state, only a few of them are covered for a particular programme and so all of them are not given training on a uniform basis. This approach leaves many officers at the same level without getting training and thus do not get the desired inputs which is essential for implementation of programmes.

  Or it could also be that some officers would be given training on planning, some others on programme design and the remaining on monitoring and evaluation, but the training in the form of a package is not imparted to the officers so that they can get full view of the development scenario.
- Similarly, the participants do not get training in a comprehensive way, or in other words only a part of development programme is covered while the rest is not given adequate attention. For example, for the training of PR members, the training is mainly given on basics of constitutional provisions for panchayati raj whereas the issues like planning methodology, programme implementation, monitoring and evaluation, that are also very crucial, are normally not imparted to PR members.

  Thus, in a way, the training programmes are organised without covering all the members of a particular clientele group and without giving the training inputs to trainees in the form of a package.

- *Other Shortcomings in the present Training Programmes*

The following points specifically highlight the shortcomings in the present form of training programmes:

- No scientific assessment is made to identify the training needs of the elected members and field functionaries.
- Generally, it is found that the field functionaries learn on the job and no specific-in-service training is imparted for various programmes or development issues that are important for improving their conceptual understanding.
- There is a lack of infrastructural support and training-aids with the training institutes.
- More often, the training is imparted based on the pre-defined training modules, irrespective of the knowledge base of clientele group.
- Very little efforts are made to assess the impact of the training and the need for future requirement.

▸ *Observations about the Functioning of Field Officers and Staff*

- *Problem of Lack of Sensitisation:* Normally, field officers and staff are not aware about the aims and objectives of the programmes. It is found that the officers and staff are not properly sensitised about the need of the programmes. It is reflected in their lack of commitment for the work in rural areas.
- *Problem of Lack of Appreciation for Quality Work:* Field observations indicate that the attitude of field officers and staff is to achieve targets somehow. What really happens is that they are given targets by the state departments to district, and then in turn by the DRDA or zilla parishad to lower tiers. More often than not, officers start implementing the programmes without caring much for the people's participation, inter-sectoral or backward and forward linkages planning, specific guidelines for providing assistance to target group and so on. More specifically, in the case of SGSY (anti-poverty programmes), it is found that the field staff do not prepare the projects specific to the needs of a block, and the applications are sponsored to Banks without looking into backward and forward linkages. Similarly, in other programmes like JGSY or EAS work-orders are issued and they are implemented by contractors or departments without involving beneficiaries for whom the programmes are intended to. And the funds are spent for achieving the targets without looking into the quality of work.
- *Problem of Lack of Appreciation of PRIs and People's Participation:* It is found that the attitude towards PR institutions and people's participation are not encouraging among field officers and staff. Besides, in several cases, people do not get the desired services in spite of a number of visits to offices, and little is done for considering this aspect at the implementation stage. It only reflects about the lack of sensitivity for the problems of people.

These findings reflect that the field officers and staff lack the necessary behavioural skills.

● *Required Actions*

▸ *Objectives*

- To improve the reach and the quality of training in order to provide training to rural development functionaries and PR members at district, block and gram panchayat levels, so as to enable them to implement the programmes effectively.
- To cover all the development issues in the form of a package (which may be in a phased manner over a certain period).

▸ *Required Capabilities:* The development is a multi-dimensional subject and requires integrated approach wherein the activities of various sectors have to be integrated rather than having sectoral or activity-based approach. Therefore, the panchayat members, especially the chairpersons of panchayats at all the three tiers, should be given training-cum-orientation for the integrated development of a village. Also of importance is to train them about the development programmes in totality so that their vision for the holistic village development gets broadened.

Now, with the introduction of 73rd Constitutional Amendment, the field officers and staff have to deal with a variety of new problems that cannot be handled effectively by the traditional ways of doing development-oriented work. It requires that the training should include not only the technical and managerial skills, but also the skills in human relations that have usually been neglected. Skills, for example, in communicating with local people and local participatory organisations (PRIs, CBOs, etc.). It will call for training programmes, which should focus on attitudinal changes in the field functionaries in order to enable them to accept the role of PR functionaries and role of people in development, and to work with people.

For performing various activities for rural development at the gram panchayat level, the PR members and development functionaries require different capabilities (Gupta, 2001). These include technical, managerial / administrative and human / behavioural capabilities. Technical capabilities involve the understanding and learning of methods of planning, basic technical knowledge of different subjects and also exposure to various Acts pertaining to gram panchayat, land revenue, etc and so on.

Managerial / administrative capabilities include mobilisation of resources, coordination, monitoring and supervision. Human capabilities are concerned with ability to deal with other people like officials, staff members and the people in the villages. These include abilities to lead others, motivate, generate team spirit and resolve conflicts. Some of the capabilities can be summed up as follows:

Technical Capabilities

- Panchayati Raj System—philosophy, 73rd Constitution Amendment, powers and functions of PR bodies;
- Technical knowledge about 29 functions under the 11th Schedule to the Constitution;
- Planning Methodology—resource inventory, identification of problems and potential areas, indicators analysis, prioritisation of problems and needs, and action plan preparation;
- Budgeting of GP plan;
- Exposure to different Acts like GP Act, Land revenue act, and other miscellaneous-Acts related to 'income certificate', 'death certificate', etc.;
  and so on.

Managerial /Administrative Capabilities

- Resources Mobilisation-Mobilisation of resources through different departments, agencies and banks, convergence of resources and services;
- Implementation of programmes;
- Monitoring and supervision of programmes;

- Other official works—conducting plan and review meetings, maintenance of records and accounts, office inspection and coordination;
  and so on.

Human / Behavioural Capabilities

- Commitment for work;
- Role and responsibilities of PR functionaries;
- Leadership quality;
- Motivation and team-work;
- Interaction between officials and elected representatives;
- Responsiveness for people's problems and interaction with people for conducting village meetings and understanding their problems;
  and so on.

▸ *Attitudinal Changes :* There is a need to bring the attitudinal change in the field officers and staff. It will involve bringing shift from the present approach of 'achieve somehow target' and 'touch and go' to appreciate the importance of participatory planning and management of implementation, need of project formulation, necessity of monitoring and MIS. They need to be trained that development is just not giving work-orders, doing check-measurements, or identifying beneficiaries. It also involves the issues of making people understand about the programmes, involving them in the decision-making, improving their capabilities to develop entrepreneurship, planning the resources for their optimal application, management of services and monitoring for exercising controls.

In sum, there is a need for a personnel policy that should specifically address the issues of attitudinal changes and skill development through training and motivation, so that they can perform their job efficiently. Therefore, the focus of training needs to be on:

- Attitudinal changes for:
  - commitment for rural development,
  - appreciating and accepting the role and position of PR members,
  - sensitivity for the people's grievances,
  - working with people, and
  - quality and efficiency of work.
- To provide appropriate technical advice to panchayats and people
- To work for planning, implementation, supervision and monitoring of works as per the action plan of the panchayats.

• *Types of Training Required*

Based on the nature of rural development programmes and the necessity of understanding of certain fundamental issues, the training needs have been classified broadly in four categories:

Category 1: Development Issues

It concerns general issues pertaining to development and includes the following:
- Development concepts;
- Development policies and strategies;
- Planning (sectoral planning, participatory planning);
- Implementation of programmes (methodology, management techniques, behavioural aspects); and
- Monitoring and evaluation.

Category 2: Specialised Programmes

There are a few development issues as indicated below that require special input in order to enable the concerned development functionaries to handle those issues:
- Gender issues;
- Community participation— PRA technique;
- Equity issues;
- Behavioural issues in development;
- Technique of local level planning; and
- Specific management techniques like, i. Management by objective (MBO), ii. Problem- tree analysis, iii. PERT & CPM, iv. TQM, etc.

Category 3: Anti-poverty Programmes

Ministry of Rural Development is having a number of anti-poverty programmes which have their own mandate and require specific training component for a particular programme in order to make functionaries to appreciate philosophy behind these programmes; specific guidelines; and planning, implementation and monitoring aspects of the programmes. The important programmes are listed below:
- JGSY
- SGSY
- EAS
- DPAP
- Rural Housing
- Drinking Water and Sanitation, etc.

Category 4: Sectoral Programme

- For each socio-economic sector.

Finally, against the backdrop of above points, it is essential to design the training programmes for: i. Field officers (at State, District, Block, Gram Panchayat levels); ii. Field staff (Block, Gram Panchayat); and iii. PR members.

Also, the factors that need to be taken into account are : duration of training; frequency of training; and institute for training.

- *Approach for improving Physical Reach and Quality of Training*

Now, in order to train such a large number of functionaries, which are about 30 lakhs in case of departmental functionaries, and about 28.50 lakhs in case of PR members (at the all India level), we need to have sound strategy. For a successful training programme, which can reach all the gram panchayats in all the districts, and also to all the concerned functionaries and PR members, it is vital to consider the decentralised form of training system. Under this, we need to have comprehensive strategy as outlined below:

- *Strengthening the Existing Institutions:* Firstly, the existing training institutes viz., National Institute of Rural Development (NIRD) at the national level and State Institute of Rural Development (SIRD) at the state level should work as nodal institutions. And these need to be strengthened in terms of infrastructure, qualified as well as trained manpower and teaching-aids.
- *Networking:* Besides, these institutes at their respective levels should identify other institutes (private as well as government) which can provide training on a sustained basis to the development functionaries, and make liaison with them so that they can provide support in terms of: *first*, inputs and the resource persons for the programmes to be organised by NIRD or SIRD, as the case may be; and second, conducting training programmes in which these (other) institutes may be having specialised courses (see fig. 6.9).
- To focus on training of trainers (TOTs) so as to upgrade the capabilities of existing faculty of NIRD, SIRD and ETC so that these institutes can provide training to field officers and staff at the district level and so on, as indicated below:
  - At the apex level, NIRD along with IRMA, IIM, XLRI, BIRD, etc. can provide training to training instructors of SIRDs as TOTs who, in turn, can provide training to district level officers.
  - At the state level, SIRD can provide training to ZP/DRDA officials and training instructors of ETCs who, in turn, can provide training to block level officers.
  - At the district level, ZP/DRDA and ETCs can provide training to officials of blocks, line departments and NGOs as TOTs, who, in turn, can provide training to officers and field staff of blocks and gram panchayats, and PR members.
- *Strengthening Decentralised Training through SATCOM :* Through SATCOM, the block and district officials can be linked to state training institute for enhancing the reach of training.

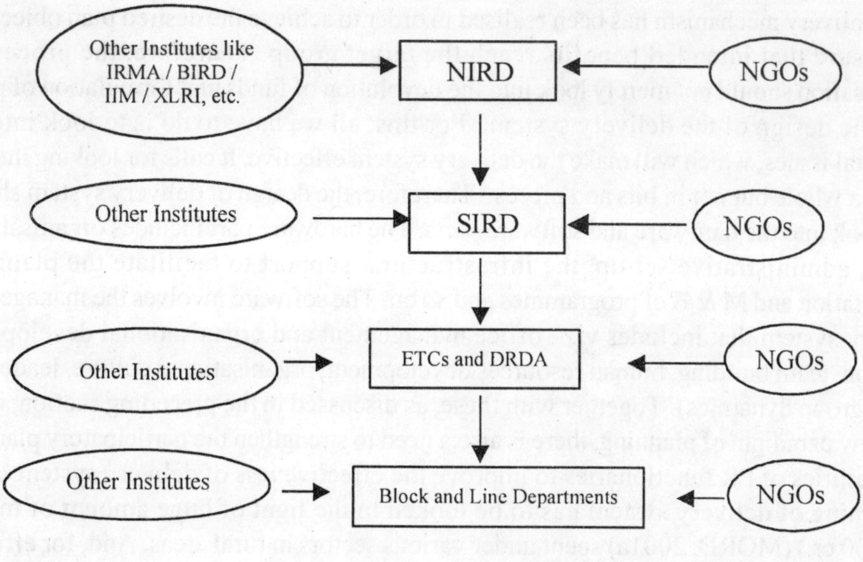

Fig. 6.9: **Training Network**

Note : 1. It may not be possible to provide training to all at a time but based on the available resources, the priorities are to be fixed and then training needs have to be identified for each level and each category of functionary.

Note : 2. In order to cover a large number of members of panchayats, at first orientation workshops may be organised. Structured training may follow it.

Note : 3. Through SATCOM, the training programme can be organised by the SIRDs which can reach to blocks and districts in a cost-effective manner.

Note : 4. Internal capabilities of ZP/DRDAs, line departments and blocks need to be enhanced in order to enable them to organise in-house training for field functionaries and thus increasing the reach of training.

Finally, although there is no clear evidence of linking the educational background with his or her ability to perform, but barring exceptions, it is observed that education and training are very much required for a number of requirements such as understanding the programme design, assessment of local needs, planning of resources, funds management, monitoring of programmes, carrying out official work, and so on. Also, under the decentralised system, the PR members and development functionaries have to assume a new role for development of villages, and this changed role needs to be attended to carefully. The changes envisaged involve changes of attitude and approach working through a new and by no means a complex system. It is this area where a great deal of effort has to be made through training.

Improving Delivery System Design

The discussion in chapter five has brought out emphatically that the delivery system in the present form is completely incapacitated due to a variety of factors, and the necessity of efficient delivery mechanism has been realised in order to achieve the desired plan objectives and to ensure that intended benefits reach the target group. Therefore, the process of decentralisation should not merely look into the devolution of funds and formulation of plans but also the design of the delivery system. For this, all we have to do is to look into the fundamental issues, which will make the delivery system effective. It calls for looking into the system as a whole but not in bits and pieces. Therefore, the design of delivery system should broadly look into the hardware and software parts. The hardware part includes organisational structure, administrative set-up, the infrastructural support to facilitate the planning, implementation and M & E of programmes and so on. The software involves the management of delivery system that includes viz., office management and organisational development (motivation, team building, human resources development, organisational culture, leadership and inter-group dynamics). Together with these, as discussed in the preceding section, in the light of new paradigm of planning, there is also a need to strengthen the participatory planning and capabilities of PR functionaries to improve the effectiveness of delivery system. Also, strengthening of delivery system has to be looked in the light of huge amount of money (Rs. 71,000 cr.) (MORD, 2001a) spent under various sectors in rural areas. And, for efficient implementation, the efficacy of delivery system in rural areas needs to be improved substantially.

In this direction the Ninth Plan approach paper (1997) has also mentioned that 'an area of priority is to improve project implementation and delivery mechanism and to ensure that intended benefits actually reach the people'. And, finally, it adds 'no new programme or project should be launched without paying sufficient attention to these aspects'. Therefore, the design of effective delivery system will require the integration of the following elements (Gupta, 2001):

- ***Hardware***

▸ *Well-structured Planning Unit:* In the context of participatory planning, the planning unit at the district and sub-district levels needs strengthening, which will require infrastructural support, the placement of appropriate number of experts and the creation of proper database at district, block and GP levèls

▸ *Strengthening Support System:* Effective implementation of programmes will call for sound organisation to carry out the task as envisaged in the plan. It necessitates the strengthening of support system which includes the following:

- *Manpower Support:* With the increase of allocation of funds the necessary manpower planning should be made to absorb the increase in work. It should look into the quantum of money to be handled, number of works to be supervised, the distance factor (i.e., the distance of work sites from the headquarters) and complexity involved in the works, together with the capabilities of the functionaries. But in order to economise, it may be prudent to keep some core technical staff, and additional staff can be engaged on a temporary basis as and when need arises or the big works may be contracted out.

Infrastructure: For physical reaching at the ground, the development agencies need to have adequate infrastructure such as godowns, farms, nurseries, marketyards, even office buildings (see table 6.10) at GP level, etc. in order to facilitate in carrying out required activities such as to make timely availability of inputs to beneficiaries and at the work site for construction, plantation, etc.; and also to provide facility for storage and marketing of various products. Together with these special emphasis has to be given for creation of infrastructure for education, health, safe drinking water, etc. (see table 6.11). Only when the infrastructure is placed as per the need, will it make possible to carry out the implementation of programmes and to provide necessary services to people at the field level. Besides, the infrastructure for training should be developed in order to provide training to officers, staff and beneficiaries. It should necessarily be created at district, block and gram panchayat levels in order to impart training effectively to the desired clientele.

Logistics Support: Need of logistics including vehicular support and equipments should be pre-determined and should be matched with the requirement of work (see tables 6.10 and 6.11). Logistics support should be adequately provided or provision should be made to hire them in time. The special care should be taken in remote and inaccessible areas where the public transport and availability of private owners of equipments are scarce.

- *Efficient MIS:* In the ever increasing functions and responsibilities of delivery system, the MIS is an important management tool which can be very useful for planning, controlling and decision-making. For making effective MIS, necessary support system, in terms of computer facility, computer networking with other offices at different locations; and trained manpower to collect, store, process the data and provide information in the user-friendly reporting formats to supervisors and officials for necessary action at their end, should be provided.
- *Strong M & E System:* The need for M & E system emerges from the two important points: *first*, programme implementation follows a process approach (in which, while implementing monitoring and concurrent evaluation are done and necessary changes are made from time to time) rather than blueprint; and *second*, there are several objectives, usually inter-related, are pursued at the same time which require close watch. Besides, M & E enables modifications to be made in the mid-course, thus resulting in considerable savings in the long-run. Monitoring systems will also help senior officials at the centre to remain fully informed on all matters connected with projects on the ground, thus, further obviating the need for a highly centralised system of administration (as planning and implementation of programmes can be done at local level). The evaluation of the programmes will help in determining their relevance, effectiveness and the impact, in order to take corrective measures for future planning, project design and implementation. Therefore, in order to improve the efficiency of implementation, properly designed system

TABLE 6.10: **Support System for PR Institutions—A Select List**

S.N.	Purpose	Item	Manpower	Infrastructure	Logistics	Remarks
1.	Office	GP office	Office Staff	Office building	Office eqipments	-
		Block office	-do-	-do-	-do-	-
		District office	-do-	-do-	-do-	-
2.	Planning unit	GP planning unit	Field Staff	Building	Computer, GIS package, etc.	-
		Block planning unit	Expert and field staff	-do-	-do-	-
		District planning unit	Expert and field staff	-do-	-do-	-
3.	Implementation	At GP level	Field staff	Building	Equipments for Construction, plantation, etc.	As per the specific need at the field level
		At Block level	Field officers and staff	-do-	-do-	-do-
		At District level	-do-	-do-	-do-	-do-
4.	Monitoring	At GP level	Investigators	-	-	-
		At Block level	Investigators and analysts	Building	Computer, etc.	-
		At District level	-do-	-do-	-do-	-

Note : The above list is only indicative.

TABLE 6.11: **Necessary Components of the Delivery Mechanism for Certain Services—A Sample**

S. No.	Type of service	Necessary components of the delivery mechanism	Remarks *
1.	Primary education	i. School Building ii. Teachers iii. Teaching aids iv. Sports and play-ground v. Drinking water	Awareness building programmes for encouraging people to send children to schools
2.	Health	i. Health centre ii. Doctors iii. Specialists iv. Equipments for testing v. Vehicular support for mobile team vi. Medicines vii. Ambulance	Health camps and mobile units can be set up
3.	Drinking water	i. Water treatment plant ii. Chemicals iii. Instruments iv. Vehicular support for mobile team v. Trained staff	Mobile repair units can be set up
4.	Agriculture inputs	i. Agriculture centres ii. Demonstration farms iii. Distribution centres for inputs iv. Credit v. Technology input vi. Marketing centre vii. Trained field staff	Agriculture camps and mobile units for inputs supply can be set up
5.	Veterinary services -Dairy	i. Veterinary centre ii. Cattle-feed centre iii. Medicines iv. Bulk coolers v. Mobile van vi. Chilling plant	Veterinary camps and mobile units can be set up
	-Poultry	i. Veterinary centre ii. Centre for supply of chicks iii. Cattle-feed centre iv. Mobile van v. Marketing centre	Veterinary camps and mobile units can be set up
6.	Irrigation	i. Field staff ii. Training centre	Village meetings and demonstration of irrigation systems including sprinkler and drip system
7.	Land settlement	i. Court building ii. Record rooms iii. Field staff iv. Vehicular support	Mobile courts for settling cases

* This column tries to present the alternatives for augmenting the reach of the delivery mechanism.

Source : Gupta, 2004.

of monitoring and evaluation must be installed; and it will call for strengthening infrastructure, placement of trained manpower and facility for data analysis.

- *Organisational Development*

Organisational development is a long term effort to improve an organisation's effectiveness through an effective management of organisation culture with a view to bring changes in the beliefs, attitudes, values and structure of organisation so that it can better adapt in the fast changing environment. Under OD, a systematic set of interventions viz., training, job enrichment, conflict management, reengineering, value clarification, prescribing procedure manuals and team building, are introduced in the organisation.

- *Changes in the Value System:* There is a need of bringing changes in the values in the field functionaries. For example, bringing shift from centralised decision-making to the role of people and panchayats in development, from achieving somehow target to quality and efficient work, from working away from people to having sensitivity for the problems of people in rural areas and so on.

  Similarly, the value changes are necessary in the panchayat functioning like from control and command to involving people in the decision-making, from closed system to having the need of transparency and accountability and so on.
- *Team Building:* The need for convergence of resources and services is very much felt at the grassroots level. That calls for effective coordination and harmony among field functionaries and panchayats, in order to pool the resources of different departments and generate synergy for effective implementation of programmes. So, teamwork at the planning and implementing stage is very crucial for the success of development efforts. It requires team-building efforts at all the three tiers.
- *Personnel Management :* Improving the efficiency of work calls for enhancing the effectiveness of officers and staff. For this a well-defined personnel management policy should be worked out for field officers and staff. It should include induction training at all levels, in-service training, criteria for placement of officers and staff, norms for transfer, awards as well as incentives and career planning.
- *Leadership Development :* Good leadership is necessary for creating enthusiasm and motivating people for achieving higher efficiency, thus enhancing the effectiveness of the organisation. Under the present circumstances in which the work environment has become very challenging due to rising aspirations of people and complexity of problems, the leadership development for the head of development agency / department and chairpersons of panchayats assumes significance in order to enable them to take best out of development functionaries, especially at the implementing stage and to deliver effectively.

  In the above context, the support system that is required for the panchayats at the three levels is reflected in table 6.10, and the required components that are to be provided to some of the important services are indicated in table 6.11. Though, it is indicative, the needed support should be placed as per local specific needs.

Finally, in the context of making basic services available to people, it is crucial to have efficient delivery system so that the panchayats can effectively meet basic needs of villagers. The expenditure on creation of delivery mechanisms should be viewed as investment, and more so in the context of large money spent in rural areas every year (about Rs. 35 lakhs per year on an average in one GP). Without such investment, the funds for the rural development are not going to be utilised purposefully and will result into underutilisation of funds and existing infrastructure. It may also lead to misutilisation or poor quality of output. Finally, only when the appropriate mechanism (for delivery) is rightly placed, will it be possible for panchayats to attend services like primary education, veterinary services, agriculture, drinking water and so on.

6.1.4 Measures for Financial Decentralisation

The financial decentralisation is important for augmenting the financial strength of panchayats. It includes important issues like devolution of funds, role of SFC, tax collection and financial management. The salient measures that are necessary are indicated below:

Minimum Devolution

The devolution should begin in a phased manner, for the subjects under list I (see box 6.1) then followed by that of under the lists II and III. Also, in the initial stage, the devolution may take place, say for ten per cent of the plan funds for certain functions (of local importance) under a particular subject. And after assessing the performance and the constraints, further devolution should be initiated.

Redefining the Role of SFC

As discussed in the previous chapter, it is observed that the role of SFC is very limited. It is mainly confining itself to suggesting the transfer of taxes (from state to panchayats) for a variety of items such as entertainment tax, cess on land revenue, stamp duty, motor-vehicle tax and so on, besides looking in general about panchayat finances. Now, in order to improve the financial system of the panchayats, rather than just looking into the issue of tax collection and transfer of grants, there is a need to address all the issues like capacity of the panchayats to manage the functioning and to deliver, requirement of funds, tax-base and problems in tax collection, environment in the panchayat for paying taxes, devolution of funds, transfer of grants, and financial management in an integrated way. It requires that SFC should have wider role of assessing the physical and financial capacity of panchayats, and also it should be given some statutory recommendatory powers with regard to devolution of funds, tax collection, especially user charges, cross subsidy and allocation of funds among panchayats.

In a way, the scope of role and responsibility of SFC requires to be widened and the following steps are necessary for this purpose:

- *Role of Assessment of Panchayats' Finances and their Capacity*

▸ Firstly, the SFC should provide the basis as well as assess the development funds (infrastructural and recurring cost) requirement for rural development, for various categories as indicated below:

i. Office Infrastructure
ii. Basic Sectors
  - Education
  - Health
  - Drinking water
  - Agriculture
  - Veterinary
  - Fisheries
  - Irrigation
  - Rural roads
iii. Industries
iv. Other Sectors

This requirement of funds will help in taking two vital decisions; *first*, the extent of devolution of funds to be made by state government upon panchayats; and *second*, the level of funds that can be generated through internal tax collection by the panchayats.

▸ *Assessing the Tax-base and Tax Collection Mechanism:* To assess per capita tax collection of taxes by panchayats and the efficacy of the present tax-collection mechanism.

▸ *Capacity of Panchayats to deliver:* Based on the manpower and infrastructural support, capabilities of PR members and development functionaries at various levels, especially at the gram panchayat level, and the past experience of panchayats' functioning, the realistic assessment of the capacities of panchayats to handle funds and the implementation of programmes should be made.

- *Recommendatory and Management Role*
  - SFC needs to be given more teeth with mandatory provisions for suggesting not only devolution package but also users' charges and norms for cross subsidy for various services.
  - Transfer of tax collection by the state to panchayats. It should be done by giving certain percentage of total collection of taxes by the state to the panchayats, rather than transferring for particular item (for example, under entertainment tax, cess on

land revenue, stamp duty, etc.) in order to avoid cumbersome procedure of accounting, and this way the purpose will be served as what is important is to transfer grants to panchayats.

- Identifying possibilities of raising taxes by the panchayats. Improving the tax collection mechanism and the possible alternatives for improving the efficiency (percentage of collection) and effectiveness (covering more items under tax basket) of tax collection.
- System of financial management at panchayat level including manpower requirement for funds management.
- It should also give recommendations on reducing horizontal and vertical imbalances.

- *Constitution of SFC*

Finally, as regards the constitution of SFC, it must have experts from economics and fiscal management. As the issues like statutory recommendatory powers with regard to devolution of funds, tax collection, especially user charges, cross subsidy and allocation of funds among panchayats are involved that have political significance, so the members should be selected by an expert body through a process of political consultations with various political parties.

Financial Management

It will include finance and accounting system of the panchayats. It becomes important, as in future the gram panchayats will be required to handle large funds to the tune of, say, ten lakhs that will require the support of trained manpower and prescribing proper financial procedures and norms. More specifically, the management will involve maintenance of accounts registers, accounting procedure, tax collection by panchayats, cash flow and accountability of functionaries for financial transactions.

Other Issues

- *Vertical and Horizontal Imbalances:* Usually, two types of imbalances occur. The imbalances at different levels of government (inter-governmental) are known as vertical fiscal imbalances, while those at different units of the same level of government (inter-jurisdictional) are known as horizontal fiscal imbalances. If the distribution of revenue sources and expenditure responsibilities between the centre and the states is such that the centre raises more than it spends while the states spend more than they raise it is called vertical imbalance. Horizontal imbalances occur when the ability to raise revenues or the unit cost of providing public services vary widely among different jurisdictions. This can cause significant differences in the standard of public services provided unless those with lower ability to raise revenue or higher unit cost of public services levy taxes at higher rates. These imbalances are going to pose serious problems (as it may cause imbalances in development) if there are large inter-tier and intra-tier differences in the income.

The table 6.12 shows that there is a wide difference of availability of funds among three tiers of panchayats. For example, in case of Andhra Pradesh, per capita income of the district panchayat is Rs. 256.57, block is Rs. 115.56 and gram panchayat is Rs. 21.75 (see table 6.12). Similarly, there is a wide gap in the availability of income between the gram panchayats in the same block. For instance, in Andhra Pradesh, Pipalpahad GP has per capita income of Rs. 33.52, which is about twice that of Chirkonda GP. Such

TABLE 6.12: **Income of Select Gram Panchayats of Select States in the Study Area**

(1997-98)

S.N.	Name of the state	GP income (Rs.) (under the same block) *		Total available income at three tiers (average)		
		GP1	GP2	District (Rs. in lakhs)***	Block (Rs. in lakhs)***	GP (Rs.)***
1.	Andhra Pradesh	(Pipalpahad)	(Chirkonda)	70,345	110.50	84,793
		1,20,000	40,000	(256.57)	(115.56)	(21.75)
		(33.52)	(17.85)			
2.	Haryana	(Umri) **	(Jirbari) **	1284.29	125.50	1,03,70,189
		2,06,93,221	2,94,557	(267.72)	(128.65)	(603.00)
		(1997.86)	(259.56)			
3.	Kerala	(Pooyapalli)	-	2,354	78.82	84,72,000
		84,72,000	-	(91.23)	(50.56)	(403.58)
		(403.58)				
4.	Punjab	Mahana	Lasrala	51,348	125.54	83,655
		89,200	55,000	(254.45)	(120.45)	(42.59)
		(121.45)	(18.54)			
5.	Uttar Pradesh	Seikhpur Zafar	Magasil	5,067.59	129.56	3,48,714
		1,10,000	2,25,000	(265.69)	(121.40)	(55.77)
		(61.24)	(45.24)			

Figures in bracket represent per capita income.
* The names of panchayats are indicated in table 4.1.
** as per 1999-2000 data.
*** *Source*: Field Survey.

differences are also noticed in other states like Haryana, Punjab and Uttar Pradesh, to name a few. Such differences may result into imbalance causing uneven development and neglect of certain areas in the district.

For rational allocation of funds among tiers and equitable distribution of income across the blocks and gram panchayats, there is a need for making rational basis for funds allocation and distribution of income (collected from own sources). It will require assessing the funds requirement that are to be handled by each tier viz., district, block and gram panchayats. Simultaneously, the basis for redistribution of panchayat income (of some panchayats, which have higher income above a certain level, to other panchayats) should be made. And such a task can be suitably handled by SFC.

- *Institutional Mechanism:* The institutional arrangements need strengthening in terms of infrastructural and manpower support, sound accounting procedure and transparency in the maintenance of accounts. Also, in order to reduce the cost of collection of taxes, it may be collected at one point especially where we have small gram panchayats and the cost of collection is high.. And keeping in view the principle that greater the distance, more likelihood of higher collection, so, the tax collection authority may be away from the taxpayers. Thus, it may be prudent to have tax collection authority at the block level (middle tier) for all the three tiers, or / and the assistance of the existing revenue department may also be sought. In the event of such an arrangement for tax collection, if block panchayat collects the taxes on behalf of gram panchayats (GPs), GPs should have the right of fixing taxes for their respective panchayats, and the procedure of tax-sharing among three tiers should be well-laid out.
- *Cross Subsidy:* Keeping in view the disparities in income among people, the user charges for various services availed by the people can be different for different categories of people. After calculating the average charges, the rich may be charged above the average value, while the poor can be charged below the value. These charges can be fixed by the expert body like SFC in order to cover at least the recurring and maintenance expenses. And later on, as the income level increases, the replacement cost may also be covered by user charges.
- *Loan by Local Institutions:* Before the panchayats can enter into the loan-based development activities, it will be prudent that the panchayats should first set their own houses in order. It will require improving tax-base, improving the capacity of delivery mechanism to implement programmes effectively and provide services to people efficiently, and establishing proper accountability system.
- *Fiscal Management:* There is a need of keeping balance between the income and the expenditure by the panchayats. The recurring liabilities by the panchayats should be kept in control, in case new staff or equipments are to be added to the panchayat's support system. Besides, while making plans for raising taxes and panchayat development, existing and the likely liabilities of panchayats should be mandatorily taken into consideration.
- *Tax Collection and Development Policies:* The income of the panchayats cannot be achieved by mere stressing on bringing more items under tax-basket for augmenting the tax collection by the panchayats. As shown by the table 6.13 that even if the tax collection is increased by 100 per cent, it will still remain just a small fraction of the total plan funds available at the district level (for all the panchayats at the three tiers). For example, the average tax collection at the all India level, when increased by 100 per cent, remains just

at 4.62 per cent of the total plan funds, while the same is 1.72 per cent for Orissa and 1.68 per cent for Uttar Pradesh. Thus, as analysed in the previous chapter, besides the poor capacity of panchayats to collect taxes, the low ability of people to pay taxes is also a major limiting factor for raising the resources for the panchayats. The examples of Kerala, Haryana and Punjab have shown that the own income in these states is much higher in comparison to many other states like Andhra Pradesh, Gujarat, Orissa, Uttar Pradesh and West Bengal. As analysed, the own income level in Kerala is much higher due to higher per capita income of people and better HRD level, that have enabled people to contribute more in the form of taxes. While in the states of Haryana and Punjab, the panchayat income is mainly from agricultural land of the panchayat, and it is possible only due to the fact that there is a good inputs and infrastructural support that has enabled the lease holder (who takes land from panchayat on rent) to cultivate crops successfully and raise good income.

So, in the light of the above context, it will call for initiating proper development policies, which should enhance the income level of people. It may require investment in infrastructure, education, health, technological interventions and so on. It should be borne in mind that it is the enhanced income of people, through sound investment policies, that will lead to increased tax-paying capacity, not the other way round.

- *Tax Collection and Delivery System:* Improvement in the delivery system is crucial so as to provide the services to people efficiently. It will instil confidence in the people so that in case they pay user charges, it will result into availability of services to them.
- *Tax Collection and Accountability:* For the financial decisions taken by PR members, their accountability to people and the local institutions is vital, so that people will have confidence that funds will be properly accounted for and utilised judiciously.
- *User Charges and Tax Collection:* The collection of user charges is very important for the running of services to be provided to people. Otherwise, in the long run it may just not be feasible to have the mechanism for providing services such as drinking water, primary education, health, irrigation, veterinary services and so on. Moreover, also from the points of view of sense of involvement and optimal use of resources, it becomes important to have certain user charges. With a special reference to water, both for irrigation and drinking purpose, due to scarcity, it is crucial for conservation of water, and also to enhance water use efficiency in case of irrigation. Now, as discussed in the previous chapter, except in the states of Gujarat, Karnataka, Kerala and Maharashtra, the contribution of user charges in the total panchayat income is very less in other states. And in many states, the per capita payment in a year is less than Rs. 5.0 (see table 6.14), while in certain states like Assam, Haryana, Meghalaya, Punjab and Uttar Pradesh, it is nil. Therefore, keeping in view the low payment of user charges in many states and also the necessity of running the utilities, there is a need to evolve political consensus and educating people for paying minimum user charges.
- *Devolution Index :* Regarding devolution index for the grants-in-aid to local bodies, in order to bring higher efficiency of resource management, besides giving weightage to

TABLE 6.13: **Percentage increase in Collection of Taxes of Panchayats: Alternative Scenario**

S.N.	%age increase	Per capita tax of all the tiers (fig in Rs.)			Per capita tax as %age of total plan funds **		
		Present level *	if 10 % increase in tax collection	if 100 % increase in tax collection	Present level	if 10 % increase in tax collection	if 100 % increase in tax collection
1.	Andhra Pradesh	20.87	22.96	41.74	2.74	3.01	5.48
2.	Kerala	34.16	37.57	68.32	9.89	10.88	19.78
3.	Orissa	2.18	2.39	4.36	0.86	0.95	1.72
4.	Punjab	25.64	28.20	51.28	8.02	8.22	16.04
5.	Rajasthan	6.98	7.68	13.96	1.71	1.88	3.42
6.	Uttar Pradesh	3.35	3.69	6.70	0.84	0.92	1.68
7.	All India level	9.02	9.92	18.04	2.31	2.54	4.62

* Average figures as per the EFC report (see table 5.3).

** Average plan funds taken for the districts of the study area (from table 4.27).

population criteria and regional imbalance, the index must include: *first*, capacity building of panchayats; *second*, institutional reforms (improved work culture, transparency and accountability, etc.); *third*, incentive for tax collection; and, *fourth*, expenditure efficiency. It would be necessary to work out impact indicators like human development index and infrastructure index for every district.

Possibility of Increasing the Tax-base of the Panchayats

Though there is a low tax collection by the panchayats, but the field studies have indicated that there is a possibility of increasing the tax collection by the panchayats. It will require for having an objective assessment of possibility of collection of taxes. As calculated, through a detailed exercise, box 6.2 indicates that there is a possibility of raising own tax by the panchayats to the tune of Rs. 98.72 per family in a year. For this a conservative estimate of the income of three categories of households has been made, and taxable value has been arrived at by assuming certain percentage (10 per cent for poor and non-poor, and 15 per cent for semi-rich

BOX 6.2

Rationale for the Possibility of Increasing the Own Income of Gram Panchayats

The following calculations reflect how there is a possibility of raising the taxes:

Income (per family):

- Income of poor: Rs 8,000 *
- Income of non-poor (APL) but not rich: Rs. 16,000 *
- Income of semi rich to rich: Rs. 20,000 *

Disposable income(per family)(DI):

- Disposable income for poor: (assuming 65% expenditure on essential items including food) **
  DI = 35% of Rs. 8,000 = Rs. 2,800
- Disposable income for non-poor: (assuming 65% expenditure on essential items including food) **
  DI = 35% of Rs. 16,000 = Rs. 5,600
- Disposable income for rich: (assuming 60% expenditure on essential items including food) **
  DI = 40% of Rs. 20,000 = Rs. 8,000

...... *Contd.*

TABLE 6.14: **User Charges and Own Income in the Gram Panchayats and Districts of the Study Area**

S.N.	Name of the State	User charges				
		for gram panchayats			at district level	
		User charges as %age of own income of GP	User charges as %age of total income of GP*	Per capita at the GP level * (Rs.)	User charges as %age of total funds at the district level *	Own income as percentage of total plan funds *
1	Andhra Pradesh	20	0.99	0.25	0.59	2.74
2	Assam	0	0.00	0.00	0.00	0.45
3	Gujarat	35	29.75 **	4.24	0.71	2.04
4	Haryana	0	0.00	0.00	0.00	7.07
5	Karnataka	29	22.77 **	19.75	1.10	3.81
6	Kerala	32	4.65	18.40	3.16	9.89
7	Madhya Pradesh	22	1.86	1.43	0.29	1.30
8	Maharashtra	41	12.41 **	12.82	1.36	3.43
9	Meghalaya	0	0.00	0.00	0.00	0.00
10	Orissa	12	1.10	0.38	0.10	0.86
11	Punjab	0	0.00	0.00	0.00	8.02
12	Rajasthan	11	3.24	1.78	0.19	1.71
13	Tamil Nadu	13	7.75	2.54	0.14	1.08
14	Uttar Pradesh	0	0.00	0.00	0.00	0.84
15	West Bengal	21	3.68	0.68	0.21	1.02

* Based on the calculations (see tables 4.24, 4.26 and 4.27).
** High percentage is due to low total income of GP (in comparison to Kerala).

.... *Contd.*

Likely tax collection (per year)

(per family)

- For poor : 10% of Rs. 2,800 (disposable income) = Rs. 280
- For non-poor : 10% of Rs. 5,600 (disposable income) = Rs. 560
- For semi-rich to rich : 15% of Rs. 8,000 (disposable income) = Rs. 1,200

Total possible tax collection (per family) = (Rs. 280) × 0.42 +
(Rs. 560) × 0.5+
(Rs. 1,200) × 0.08 = Rs. 493.60

i. Possible per capita tax collection = Rs. 98.72

ii. Possible per capita tax collection as %age of per capita plan funds at the district level = 25.24%

iii. Present per capita income (at the all India level) = Rs. 9.02 (see table 5.3)

iv. Present per capita income as %age of per capita plan funds at the district level *** = 2.31%

Finally, (per family)

Tax payment by poor = 3.50% of their total income
Tax payment by non-poor but not rich = 3.50 % of their total income
Tax payment by semi-rich to rich = 6.00% of their total income

Assumptions:

The above is possible if the following conditions are met:

- Political will and consensus
- Conducive atmosphere for paying taxes
- Efficient tax collection mechanism
- Effective delivery mechanism
- Proper accountability system

Note 1: The average income for poor, non-poor and semi-rich to rich for the all the states has been assumed.

Note 2: Assuming 42% poor as per household survey, 50% non-poor but not rich and 8% semi-rich to rich (non-poor category has been taken between poor and semi-rich to rich, as in the rural areas majority of the people who are not poor do not have sufficient income. So as a conservative estimate, this is assumed).

Note 3: The average income per family assumed for each category is on the conservative side.

Note 4: As the average income per family and the number of poor in each state are taken on the conservative side so the disposable income is likely to be much higher and so also the tax collection.

Note 5: The actual calculations can be done as per GP or district specific data, but the present calculations provide a broad indicator for the possible income that can be generated by the local institutions.

..... *Contd.*

* -	Per capita income ceiling, which is Rs. 266.27 × 12 (months) × 5 (family of five) =15976.20 or say 16,000 (Ministry of Rural Development, 1996-97).
-	For income of poor: Assuming average 50% of the per capita income ceiling for poverty line (all India average), assuming a normal distribution.
-	For non-poor (but not rich), income level is assumed at the cut-off poverty line (and Rs. 16,000 has been taken as round-off figure).
-	For semi-rich to rich, a conservative level of income (Rs. 20,000) is taken.
-	Population below poverty line is 41.23%, as per ninth plan data (Ministry of Rural Development, 1996-97), but for the sake of calculation assuming 42% population below poverty line.
-	Assuming 50% non-poor but not rich and 8% semi-rich to rich.
**	As per NSS data (Rural Development Statistics, NIRD, 1998).
***	Taking the per capita plan (Rs. 391) outlay from the table 4.27 (for 1997-98).

to rich) of disposable income as tax. It shows that the tax payment by poor will be 3.5 per cent of their total income, the same by non-poor but not rich and by semi-rich to rich 6.0 per cent of their total income, and in terms of average value, the monthly payment of taxes will come to about Rs. 23.3, Rs. 46.6 and Rs. 100 for these respective categories. Certainly, these are very reasonable figures and the households would be able to contribute. If we look into its percentage of total plan funds in the district then it will stand at 25.24 per cent or in other words an additional quarter of the total available funds can be added by the tax collection.

But from the point of view of planning of the tax, as analysed from field studies, the following assumptions are to be taken into account:

- Political will and consensus;
- Conducive atmosphere for paying taxes;
- Efficient tax collection mechanism and financial management system;
- Effective delivery mechanism for providing basic services; and
- Proper accountability system.

Similarly, a detailed exercise (based on the field study) in this context has been carried out in table 6.15, which shows how there is a possibility of having minimum to maximum level of collection by fixing rational charges as per the category of households. To be more precise, the principle of cross subsidy has been applied. In case of minimum level, the per capita collection can be Rs. 21.72 (which is more than twice of the figure at 1997-98 level, at the all India level), and the percentage of total contribution of taxes in a district to total plan funds would be 5.55 per cent, and the same figures for the maximum level are Rs. 97.21 and 24.87 per cent.

Note: There are minor variations in the calculations as indicated by Box 6.2 and table 6.15, but figures (for possible per capita tax collection) are almost same. For the purpose of calculations in the box average values have been taken, while in the table there is an attempt to give figures for various tax items.

Can we Raise the Panchayat Taxes Indefinitely

Now from the perspective of raising the income of panchayats, can we rely on raising taxes alone? The answer is to be seen in the context of the following explanation:

It is important to keep in mind that present level of availability of funds at the district level is much lower than the requirements for the development in the villages. There is always demand in the villages for the school building, health centres, drinking water, roads and so on. (In some cases, the point is also raised about the availability of large unspent funds with the panchayats. Here it will be pertinent to point out that in certain cases, as pointed out normally, the funds are not utilised fully, but it is more due to the poor capacity of the delivery system to utilise funds than any other factor. And lack of utilisation of funds does not mean that there is a decline in people's needs, or in other words utilisation of funds may be low but people's demands may be much higher due to ever-increasing needs for village development.)

Now the question is how to meet the rising demand of funds for development activities. One possible way is tax collection. But the present level of tax collection by various states indicated that it is a small fraction of the available plan funds (see table 4.27). And at the all India level the ratio of tax collection to present availability of funds at the district level stands at mere 2.31 per cent, which is much lower in the cases of Orissa (0.86 per cent), Uttar Pradesh (0.84 per cent) and West Bengal (1.02 per cent). Even, assuming 100 per cent increase in the tax collection, it is possible to increase the tax ratio to 4.62 per cent (see table 6.15), which is still small. Thus, expecting that enhancing the tax collection is the solution for augmenting the panchayat income is highly misplaced. But certainly raising the collection of taxes by the panchayats is one of the options, and before we plan to do so, as discussed above, there is a need to appreciate the fundamentals.

For enhancing the tax, based on field studies and above discussions, the people are going to be guided by mainly four factors: *first*, present level of savings that will depend on the present income level of people; *second*, capacity of the panchayats to function effectively; *third*, sound delivery mechanism; and *fourth*, the accountability of panchayats to them. Or, in nutshell, people will pay taxes only when they have adequate income and also have faith in the ability of the panchayats to deliver.

Finally, in the light of above discussions, we need to have sound planning and management of the entire system of tax collection and to move ahead keeping in view the fundamentals in mind. As a first step, conducive climate should be created through educational and awareness programmes in order to make people understand the need of paying taxes / users' charges for the recurring cost of the availed-services. *Second*, evolving political consensus for appreciating the need of payment of taxes. *Third*, bringing more items under the tax baskets. *Fourth*, initiating proper development policies, which should enhance the income level of people. The development policies, that are crucial for giving boost to human resources development and augmenting the income of people, need to be initiated. *Fifth*, the delivery mechanism at the local levels needs to be strengthened in order to make desired services available to people so that they can have confidence in the abilities of the local institutions.

TABLE 6.15: **Estimated Possible Collection of Taxes at the District Levels (Annually)**

S.N.		Type of Taxes	Physical asset	Tax collection (Minimum possible) (Scenario I)						Tax collection (Maximum possible) (Scenario II)						% age of total funds at the district (taking the average from table 4.27) & per capita values	
				Per family payment (Minimum possible) (Rs.)				Per GP (Rs.)	For the district (Rs. in lakhs.)	Per family payment (Maximum possible) (Rs.)				Per GP (Rs.)	For the district (Rs. in lakhs.)		
				Poor (42%)	Non-poor (APL) (50%)	Semi-rich to rich (%)	Total (Av.)			Poor 42%)	Non-poor (APL) (50%)	Semi-rich to rich (8%)	Total (Av.)			Scen-ario I	Scen-ario II
1	2	3	4	5	6	7	8	9	10	11	12	13	14	15	16	17	18
	Tax Revenue	House property		5	10	50	111.0	11100	44.4	25	50	250	55.5	55,500	222.0	-	-
		Vehicle - I *	200 *** (100,50,50)	5	10	20	2.0	2000	8.0	10	20	50	4.5	4,500	18.0	-	-
		Vehicle - II **	50 *** (0,0,50)	-	-	20	1.0	1000	4.0	-	-	100	5.0	5,000	20.00	-	-
		Animals	1000 *** (500,200,300)	5	10	15	9.0	9000	36.0	25	50	100	52.5	52,500	210.00	-	-
		Profession	-	10	20	50	18.2	18200	72.8	25	100	250	80.5	80,500	322.0	-	-
		Land (cess) (in ha.)	1000 *** (500,200,300)	5	10	25	12.0	12000	48.0	25	50	100	52.5	52,500	210.0	-	-
		Sub-total	-	30	60	180	53.3	53,300	213.2	110	270	850	250.5	2,50,500	1002.0	2.72	12.81

(Contd.)

TABLE 6.15 *(Contd.)*

1	2	3	4	5	6	7	8	9	10	11	12	13	14	15	16	17	18
	Non Tax Revenue	User charges - I (Drinking water)	-	10	15	25	13.7	13700	54.8	50	75	150	70.5	70,500	282.0	-	-
		User charges - II (Irrigation water)	100 ha.	(10% irrigated land) (Charges: Rs. 50 per ha.)			5.0	5000	20.0	100 ha.	(10% irrigated land) (Charges: Rs. 250 per ha.)		25.0	25,000	100.0	-	-
		User charges - III (Roads)	-	5	10	15	8.3	8300	33.2	25	50	120	45.1	45,100	180.4	-	-
		User charges - IV (Street lights)	-	5	10	15	8.3	8300	33.2	25	50	120	45.1	45,100	180.4	-	-
		Miscellaneous: Panchayat property/ license fee/ royalty on mining		-	-	-	-	20000	80.0	-	-	-	-	50,000	200.00	-	-
Sub-total				20	35	55	35.3	55,300	221.2	100	175	390	185.7	2,35,700	942.8	2.83	12.06
Total				50 +	95 +	235+	88.6	1,08,600	434.4	210 +	445 +	1240+	436.2	4,86,200	1944.8	5.55	24.87
Per capita payment by individual households in a GP																17.72	87.21
Per capita collection by gram panchayats from all sources																21.72	97.21

* Cycles ; ** Scooters / Tractors

*** The figure represents the total physical asset possessed (rough estimate) by people in a GP. And the figures in the bracket represent the values for a particular category i.e. poor or non-poor or semi-rich to rich (e.g. in the case of ' vehicle - I', 100 is for poor, 50 is for non-poor, and 50 is for semi-rich to rich); + It is the maximum value that will be paid by an individual in a given scenario (except for irrigation charges) and the actual payment will depend upon the assets held by him.

GP population: 5,000 (assuming 5 in a family). District population (rural areas): 20 lakhs (assuming 400 GPs).

Note 1: 42% poverty level (Ministry of Rural Development, 1996-97); and assuming 50% for non-poor but not rich; and 8% semi-rich to rich.

Note 2: Figures are based on the discussion held with the people in the villages. The figures are representative indicators and may vary from place to place, but in the most likelihood cases, these are going to be more or less the same.

Note 3: Per capita collection is more than per capita payment by the individual household as the former includes the fee/royalty, which may not necessarily be paid by all the individual households.

Sixth, strengthening the tax collection mechanism. And, *seventh*, placing the accountability system in the right place.

6.2 Frequently Raised Issues

During the course of study of panchayati raj institutions, there were interactions with a large group of people, including PR members, field officers and staff, people in the villages, senior officials, representatives of voluntary agencies and so on. They expressed a variety of viewpoints, which have been organised as follows:

- ***Expected Outcome from PR Institutions but Need for Caution***

- *Establishing Gram Sabha will bring People's Participation:* The gram sabha is a body to discuss the issues pertaining to village development. Now it is up to the people how they get themselves involved in the discussions, which will depend upon their ability to understand various development issues and their confidence to put forth their problems to and get their grievances registered or redressed from the gram sabha. Besides, from the common man's perspective, it is crucial how he gets the legitimate share in the development process while facing the adverse conditions, sometimes hostile conditions, which could arise due to conflicting interests, especially that of rich and dominant class.

  The moot point is that the gram sabha has provided a forum for discussion, it cannot be taken as the ultimate thing to ensure the people's participation. What really will matter is the HRD level of people and socio-economic and political environment in the village.

- *People's Participation can bring all the Changes:* People's participation in the development has been stressed basically for eliciting the local knowledge about the problems, needs and aspirations for the planning as well as implementation of programmes, as also to ensure that the people become the partners in the development not just the receivers of some benefits from government, and to enhance the accountability of development agencies.

  It should be well appreciated that development is a function of various parameters. These parameters include development policies, strategies, programme design, institutional development and management of implementation, besides people's participation. Therefore, for achieving the objectives of development, we need to focus on each parameter as each one of them has vital role to play in the success of development initiatives.

  The moot point is that the people's participation is one of the parameters of vital importance which is going to add to the efficiency and effectiveness of the implementation of the programme, while all other parameters need to be adequately attended to.

- *PRIs can do all the Development Activities:* It is envisaged that the PRIs can attend to all the development activities under 29 subjects. These subjects have a wide range of activities starting from primary education to higher education to water supply to industries and so on. To handle such wide ranging subjects, the capacity of panchayats should be assessed before taking final decision. It is an indisputable fact that the development needs to be decentralised but at the same time the role of other organisations like NGOs, CBOs, industrial organisations, etc. and the initiatives by the individuals should be recognised and promoted in order to generate synergy in the system. Also, the panchayat leadership needs to be supplemented by technical know-how.

The moot point is that the development requires teamwork and all the actors as discussed above have important role to play. The PRIs should focus on providing basic services such as primary education, family welfare, health, drinking water and local natural resources management, to people and at the same time play the facilitating role for development activities in other sectors. And if the panchayats assume their major role in all the subjects, they might have to stretch beyond their capacity to deliver. The panchayats should focus on core subjects that impinge on the life of people at the local levels and should play the role of facilitator as regards the functions under other subjects. Besides, PRIs should become a good link between the people and other professional organisations in the field of social works, business, industries, research, etc.

- *PR Members can implement all the Programmes:* In ideal situation it is said that the PR members can implement all the development programmes. It needs to be appreciated that development requires professional skills and knowledge for planning, implementation of programmes. Also, technical inputs from various departments such as agriculture, animal husbandry, fishery and so on are vital for the development initiatives.

  The moot point is that the PR members should provide a conduit between the needs and aspirations of people on one hand and the administrative, technical and management of planning and implementation of programmes on the other. What is crucial is to appreciate the roles of various functionaries / agencies (people / CBOs / NGOs, line departments) and assign them the desired responsibilities with defined accountability and that PR members should coordinate with effectively.

- *Earlier Government Departments have failed, PRIs can succeed in achieving the desired Development of the Local Area:* May be in certain areas, development efforts have not been in the desired direction, but certainly the departments cannot be fully blamed for it, as there are a number of factors such as lack of capabilities in field personnel, poor people's involvement, weak delivery mechanism, inadequate institutional framework for administrative support (like control, coordination) that have led to the present state of development.

  The moot point is that we need to evaluate the development process and identify the factors that have been hindering blocks. And the PRIs should make endeavours to take people's participation in development and fill the critical gaps that have been missing so far.

- *PR System will bring Efficiency, Transparency and Accountability:* It is expected that the decentralisation will bring efficiency in the implementation of programmes and also transparency in the functioning of local institutions / departments. But it will depend upon the capacity of panchayats to handle the development works. Besides, due to local-effect in which the local representatives will be more in contact with the people, they will be more accountable to people for their actions. For this to happen, people should be vigilant and should question the decisions of PR members in case there is a genuine need and also participate actively during discussions in the panchayats.

The moot point is whether the people in the gram panchayats are aware about their role in the functioning of panchayats. Also of importance is how the PR members take initiatives in this direction. Simultaneously, efforts are needed for having the system of guidance, evaluation and control.

- *Panchayats will be able to raise Funds to meet their Needs:* It is expected that the panchayats, once set up, will be able to raise funds. But we need to take notice of ground realities, which reflect that the per capita own income of panchayats is Rs. 9.02; rate of increase of tax revenue is 10.12 per cent (see tables 5.3); and what is more striking is the percentage share of own income in the total income, which stands at 3.49 per cent (see table 5.7). From the practical point of view, panchayats would be able to raise their income marginally in a year and thus can meet only a small part of their needs. And, among other factors, the main reasons for small panchayat income are low income level of people (see section 5.4, analysis of panchayat finances) and lack of political will.

  The moot point is how do we first raise the income of people, who in turn should be in a position to make savings for paying taxes, besides political will is necessary for encouraging people to pay taxes.

- ***Concerns for PR Institutions but Need for Positive Approach***

- *Departments will oppose the Strengthening of PR Institutions:* It is feared that line departments, which may lose their control over funds or flexibility in their functioning, will not like the strengthening of PR institutions. It may not be altogether a correct assessment and there are precedents in various states where the strengthening of PR institutions, barring a few voices or initial resistance or reluctance, has got down very well till the last tier starting from state to gram panchayat. The states, where such a system has got good grounding are Maharashtra, Karnataka, Gujarat and West Bengal. Recently, Kerala has shown how well-organised programme for strengthening PR institutions can be successful. Also, Uttar Pradesh and Madhya Pradesh have taken measures in this direction. And in all the states the line departments are working with the panchayats as per the directions from the state governments.

  The moot point is how the message of decentralisation is carried forward from the state to the gram panchayat that is something very important. And with a strong political will and a well-laid out strategy by the state government the departments will join the process of decentralisation and participate actively.

- *There will be more Problems in the Planning and Implementation of Programmes due to Low Capacity of PRIs:* Initially, when the process of decentralisation is taken to lower tiers, there may be some problems as the institutions have not got adequate opportunities in the past to take up such an assignment. But with the passage of time through a process of learning, the local institutions will be able to come upto the desired level of functioning. It may require the support from the government in terms of manpower, financial and administrative measures in order to enhance the capacities of PR institutions.

The moot point is how the PR institutions have been equipped with the necessary capabilities for planning and administrative skills, and how the necessary support system including manpower, infrastructure and logistics is provided to these institutions.

- *PR Members cannot do much due to lack of Capabilities:* The PR members come from diverse background and are not homogeneous group in terms of educational background, past experience, leadership qualities and so on. Moreover, a significant percentage of members is having low educational background, so it may make it difficult for them to perform as desired. But they can certainly do a good job as has been found in Kerala, if they are provided with adequate training, and the local institutions are strengthened administratively, with infrastructure and logistics support, and financially.

The moot point is that the measures need to be taken for enhancing the capabilities of PR members through a well-organised programme of training.

- *PR System will bring more Conflicts:* The conflicts are likely to come to the surface either among PR members or between line departments and PR members. It is important that for avoiding such a situation to happen, we need to organize a good number of orientation training programmes for bringing attitudinal changes and for inculcating good values so that each functionary (of line departments) and PR member can appreciate one's role and contribute as a team member in the process of development.

The moot point is how the measures are taken to develop healthy traditions and good work culture so that the PR members can transact the business of panchayat meetings purposefully and work effectively. Besides, it will also ensure a good work climate for joint functioning of line departments and PR members.

- *PR System will lead to more Groupism in the Villages / Dominance by a particular Party or Group of People:* This fear may be true if proper environment building at the grassroots level does not take place and the people do not get opportunity to participate in the discussion, which may lead to dominance by a few individuals. Here, what is crucial is to make people aware about their roles and responsibilities in the village development. Also, there is a need to develop healthy conventions (good practices) for the working of panchayats so that the conflicts are resolved through fair discussions.

The moot point is that if PR system or the process of decentralisation has to succeed, the people must be educated and made aware about basics of development only then the common person will get the desired voice in the panchayat and will also deter the elites or dominant people in the panchayats to dominate the functioning.

- ***Limitations of PR System***

- *Limitations of Gram Sabha:* As emerged from the field study, the gram sabha has got limitations due to mainly three factors. *First*, sheer size of the gram sabha having two to five hundred members (this figure may be one to two thousand members in some cases). This big size poses various operational problems in terms of participation by members, recording of proceedings (as several voices express opinion for a particular issue), uncontrolled way of raising issues and lack of focussed discussion on some critical issues or on accountability aspects of a particular PR member. *Second*, dominance by a few vocal people; and *third*, the technical nature of numerous problems under various subjects, which may not be within the capacity of gram sabha to handle.

- *Limitations of PR Members:* The PR members have limitations in terms of their capabilities to work. Besides, under the present socio-politico-economic scenario, different factors such as caste, class, affiliations to a particular party, etc. play their role, which may have negative bearing on their abilities to perform.
- *Limitations of PR Institutions:* The panchayats have limitations in terms of delivering services and to meet development works in all the subjects due to lack of manpower, infrastructure and resources.

- ***Opportunities for PR System***

- *Opportunities for the People:* The panchayat system opens an opportunity for any individual to exercise its political rights and also participate in the development process of his village. Through panchayats, local needs of the people can be identified and then addressed in time.
- *Opportunities for PR Members:* It provides a good opportunity to elected representatives for both political purpose and participation in local development.
- *Opportunities for PR Institutions:* The local institutions can successfully address the needs of local people with regard to basic services and the local development works, which otherwise are difficult to be attended to.

6.3 Need for Further Amendments

In the backdrop of field study and the analysis presented in chapter five, the following amendments are suggested :

6.3.1 Amendment in 73rd Constitution Amendment Act

The analysis as presented in chapter five brings out categorically the need of making amendments in the Constitutional Act. Accordingly keeping in view the fundamental concerns that the people should be able to meaningfully participate in the socio-politico and economic process of development at the village level, that the panchayats should become the units of development, and that the panchayats should emerge as institutions of self-government, the further amendments (see table 6.16) are suggested for the Central Act. Such amendments are suggested for Central Act in order to provide uniformity across the states, and thereafter suitable amendments are required in the state panchayat Acts. However, the states, if they so desire, may initiate measures beforehand for amendment in their panchayat Acts.

- *Environment Building and Functioning of Gram Sabha:* In the context of lack of conducive environment for people to participate and the inability of the gram sabha to address the issues of local development, it is evident that the gram sabha finds it hard to do justice to people. So, it demands that the necessary correctives should be brought in Article 243 A, which may include the following:
  - Programme for environment building (for empowering people) with financial support; and
  - Defining the modalities of the functioning of gram sabha within a definite time-frame.
- *Size of Gram Panchayats:* Article 243B deals with the formation of panchayats. It is on the concerned states to decide about the size of the gram panchayat. The states have formed the gram panchayats based on the population criterion. If we look into the average size of the population of one gram panchayat, it is normally in the vicinity of 2000 in most of the states (only a few states like Assam, Kerala and West Bengal have population more than 10,000). But, if we examine the case of Kerala the state is in a position to provide services to people due to necessary manpower, infrastructure and logistics support that has been provided by various departments at the gram panchayat level. And to some extent the same is true with regard to West Bengal

  Now, if we examine critically, the small size of GPs has caused some practical problems for the panchayats to function effectively. *First*, the panchayats have not got the relevant staff for providing basic services for health, veterinary, drinking water, irrigation, etc., as the departments do not have sufficient number of field functionaries. It is estimated that if all panchayats were to be provided with the staff for these services, the number of field functionaries has to be increased by 4-5 times, that would involve large expenditure on salary. *Second*, there is an acute shortage of infrastructure for the basic services to be provided to people, and if it were to be created at the GP level, it would require huge investment. *Third*, with so many number of panchayats, it becomes difficult to organise block level meetings (in which 50-75 members participate) and to monitor the financial performance of GPs. Thus, from the point of view of financial, administrative and managerial viability, it is vital that necessary support system should be provided to all the gram panchayats. It will require amendment for having minimum size of a gram panchayat with a population of around 15,000 or for about 100 sq. km. area (in case of scarcely populated areas) so that GPs can become viable development units, and the gram sabha should be organised at the village level. (If it is difficult to have minimum size of GP, a sector / mandal may be created for 4-5 GPs, but below block, with necessary support system).
- *Elections to three Tiers:* With a view to give true representation to needs and problems of people and their collective voice through gram sabha, there is a need of organic linkages

TABLE 6.16: **Further Amendments required in the Central Acts**

S.N.	Issues	Section	Present status	Amendments needed for: Making panchayats viable development units with a focus on — people's participation and institution building — for Good Governance
1	2	3	4	5
A. In the 73rd Constitution Amendment Act				
1.	Environment building	A new section to be inserted	No emphasis on having environment, which will foster people's participation in a meaningful manner	For creating conducive environment for free and meaningful participation by people in the social, political and economic activities
2.	Functioning of gram sabha	243A	Lack of proper direction for the conduct of gram sabha meeting	Modalities for the functioning of gram sabha to be defined by states within a timeframe
3.	Size of the GP	243B	The states have to decide about the size of gram panchayats	Minimum size for the gram panchayats should be fixed in order to make them viable development units
4.	Elections to three tiers	243C	Separate territorial constituencies for the elections of intermediate and district panchayats	- Separate territorial constituencies for the elections of intermediate and district panchayats to be done away with - The chairpersons of the gram panchayats should represent the intermediate panchayat, and the chairpersons of intermediate panchayats should be the members of the district panchayat
			- Elections not held in time and simultaneously for all the three tiers - Elections based on party basis, leading to divisions in the villages on party lines	Provisions for timely elections (not to be postponed for any reason), and simultaneous elections for all the three tiers and on non-party basis. SEC should be given more powers.

(Contd.)

TABLE 6.16 *(Contd.)*

1	2	3	4	5
5.	Membership of MLAs and MPs	243C	Memberships to MLAs and MPs in the panchayat bodies	Membership of the panchayat bodies should be only for the elected members of the panchayats
6.	Reservations for weaker sections	243D	- Reservations for five years - Lack of meaningful participation by weaker sections in the panchayat functioning	- The rotation for the reserved seats for the weaker sections should be after two terms - There should be educational and training programmes (with adequate financial support) focussed for the weaker sections
7.	Duration of period of chairpersons of panchayats	243E	In some cases the duration of the chairpersons of the panchayats reduced	- There should be fixed tenure of five years for the chairpersons, and their removal should be by the concerned panchayat as per laid-down procedure - There should be minimum period for chair-persons before that, they cannot be removed.
8.	Transfer of functions	243G and 11th Schedule	Transfer of subjects has not taken place in most of the states	There should be a fixed timeframe within which the transfer of subjects should take place, and it should be in a phased manner as per the capacity of the panchayats to handle functions. While transferring the functions, the focus should be on the subjects pertaining to basic needs (see box 6.1).
9.	Devolution of funds	243G	Except in the state of Kerala, the devolution of funds has not taken place	Provision for minimum devolution from the state budget within a timeframe
10.	Transfer of departments and deputation of officers and staff	-	The field officers and staff of line departments are not deputed to panchayats in most of the states	Within a definite time period, the field officers and staff should be deputed to panchayats as per the functions transferred to panchayats
11.	Imposition of taxes	243H	Low tax collection	Certain tax items especially user charges must be brought under tax-basket within a definite time period and a separate list of items for tax collection by panchayats should be added in Schedule VII

(Contd.)

TABLE 6.16 *(Contd.)*

1	2	3	4	5
12.	Constitution of SFC	243I	It lacks necessary statutory powers	SFC should be given some statutory powers to suggest taxes, especially the user charges, cross subsidy, and devolution of funds
13.	Transparency	A new section to be inserted	There is a lack of transparency in the panchayat functioning	Provision of transparency in the panchayat functioning must be added
14.	- Accountability (Social Audit)	243J	Social audit and accountability of elected members not ensured	Provision of social audit and accountability should be added
	- People's watch committees	A new section to be inserted	There are certain cases of inappropriate functioning of various activities (elections, panchayat functioning, transparency, etc.) related to panchayat, but little is done to improve functioning	People's watch committees should be set up at the district and block levels
	- Constitution of tribunal	A new section to be inserted	There are certain cases of inappropriate administrative and financial decisions, and inter- and intra-tier panchayat conflicts but there is nobody to address them	Tribunal should be constituted at the district level
15.	Constitution of DPC	243ZD	DPC lacks necessary capabilities to prepare district plans	- Constitution of DPC needs to be enlarged to include experts, and it needs to be provided necessary support (infrastructural, equipments) to undertake district planning - Planning committees should be formed at blocks and GPs to encourage bottom-up planning
16	Support System Planning unit	A new section to be inserted	There is a lack of support at the district level and no planning units at the block and gram panchayat levels for undertaking micro-planning	Planning units with necessary support system should be set up at all the three tiers

(Contd.)

TABLE 6.16 *(Contd.)*

1	2	3	4	5
	Delivery system	A new section to be inserted	Low capacity of delivery mechanism (education, health, drinking water, animal husbandry, etc.) at the panchayat level to make basic services available to people	Delivery system needs strengthening with necessary support
17.	Regulatory functions like check on money lending and prohibition of illicit liquor	A new section to be inserted	Presently the gram panchayats are not assigned these functions	A separate body of elected representatives (other than panchayat members) should be set up at the district and block levels for regulatory functions
B. Scheduled Areas Act (Act 40 of 1996)				
1.	Regulatory functions of prohibition of any intoxicant, ownership of minor forest produce, prevention of alienation of land, and to manage village markets and check on money lending	Clause 'm'	Presently the gram panchayats are entrusted with both the regulatory and development functions	A separate body (viz., Tribal Advisory and Regulatory Board) of elected representatives should be set up at the district and block levels for regulatory functions
2.	Use of forest land for crucial development activities	A new section to be inserted	Presently no powers to gram sabha	A new section to be added for providing powers to gram sabha for utilising forest land for development purpose (like construction of school building, health centre, checkdams, etc.)

Note: Also, in the view of the above suggested amendments, there is a need to bring appropriate changes, wherever necessary, in the Articles of the Central Act from 'state may' to 'state shall' in order to bring mandatory nature in the Act for strengthening the panchayats.

among three tiers. For this purpose, the lower panchayats should have direct representation in the higher tiers. It requires having chairpersons of gram panchayats as the members of intermediate panchayat and one of them should be elected as chairperson of intermediate panchayat. Similarly, all the chairpersons of intermediate panchayats should be the members of zilla panchayat and they, in turn, should elect the chairperson of zilla panchayat. This system (after bringing amendment in Article 243C) would not only help in reducing the multiplicity of constituencies, especially those of intermediate and zilla panchayats (as these are artificial boundaries created by merging the GPs and do not serve much purpose), but also in achieving two major objectives as envisaged in the Constitutional Amendment Act. These are:

First, the GP members will be fully represented in all the three panchayats. Thus, it will give direct voice to every panchayat in the decision-making process at all the three tiers.

Second, as the members in intermediate and zilla panchayats will be from the GPs, which are the basic units of development, it will provide opportunities to GP chairpersons to put forth local problems effectively. That will provide right projection of people's needs in the development meetings of intermediate and zilla panchayats, and the plans so prepared will reflect the local needs and aspirations. Thus, it will encourage the people's participation in a more meaningful way. That apart, another fundamental point is that the chairperson of a gram panchayat is accountable to people at the gram sabha level. He has to answer to people for their problems. He has to put the problems and needs of the people at the higher tier, to suggest the projects and to get them approved, and then answer back in the gram sabha about the action taken by him. While, under the present system the chairpersons of intermediate and zilla panchayats are not accountable to people in the gram sabha. So, the gram panchayats through their chairpersons should get full representation in all the three tiers. *Finally*, keeping in view the spirit of democratic decentralisation, the membership in each tier should solely be based on the fundamental basis that 'gram panchayats should get full representation in all the three tiers' so that the gram panchayats are able to project their needs and problems at the higher tiers and also to ensure that they are attended to. In fact, what is really required is the aware and vigilant members from the gram panchayats who will like to project their problems in right perspective and see that the projects are implemented effectively. And, certainly not the large number.

Also keeping in view the delay in conduct of elections, that elections of all tiers are not held at one time (thus causing the problem of organic linkages, as some tiers do not have elected members, while other has), and that elections are dividing villagers on political lines, amendment is needed for timely elections, simultaneous elections for all the tiers, and elections on non-party basis (keeping the primacy of development role of panchayats).

- *MLAs and MPs as Members of Panchayat Bodies:* Article 243C specifies that the states may provide representation to MPs and MLAs in the panchayat bodies. The states have made provision for their representation in the panchayats at intermediate and district levels. In this regard, some objections have been raised due to the following points:

First, the PR members are elected as per the panchayat Act, and thus are accountable to people for their decision-making and implementation of programmes. So only they should be the members in the panchayats.

Second, the elected PR members find it difficult to cope with MLAs and MPs during panchayat meetings, as there persists differences in opinion about the development needs between PR members on one hand and MLAs and MPs on the other. Also, the PR members are overwhelmed by their presence.

Besides, from the logical point of view the elected members should sit in the body for which they are elected, so in the panchayats only the PR members should have membership. So it calls for making amendment in the Act for the membership of the panchayats, and only the elected members of the panchayats should be the panchayat members at three tiers.

- *Reservation of Weaker Sections:* Article 243D makes provision for the reservation of women SCs and STs and such reservation should be rotated. The states have construed that the rotation can be for every five years. Now, from the practical point of view, it has been noticed that the members from these categories take longer time to learn the official work due to their initial inhibitions and low educational level. Moreover, one term is not sufficient for carrying out sufficient development activities if long term view is taken. Also, it discourages members from taking innovative projects which require long term planning as they feel that they have no chance to become members / chairpersons again. In a way, there is no incentive for re-election. So, the rotation of these reserved seats should be done for every ten years in order to provide sufficient opportunities and incentives to the members to perform their duties effectively.
- *Duration of Tenure of Chairpersons of Panchayats:* It is in the context of fixing of the duration of tenure of chairpersons of panchayats in the state of Karnataka, (where it is fixed for twenty months for chairpersons of taluks and zilla panchayats and thirty months for chairpersons of gram panchayats) and in Maharashtra (where the term was fixed for one year for intermediate and zilla panchayats, it has been raised to two and a half years). Now, in this process, chairpersons do find get sufficient opportunities to work, and such a move is self-defeating. It, therefore, requires that the tenure of the chairpersons of panchayats should be fixed for five years and only the members of the panchayats should have the right to remove the chairpersons as per laid-down procedure. Also, to provide stability, these should be minimum period, before that the chairpersons cannot be removed.
- *Transfer of Functions, Devolution of Funds, and Levying Local Taxes:* Article 243G defines that the states may endow the panchayats with necessary powers and responsibilities for certain functions in order to enable them to function as institutions of self-governance. While, except Kerala no other state has taken concrete measures to transfer necessary functions to panchayats, to devolve funds upon them and levying of

local taxes. In this context the following steps are essential:

The transfer of functions should be done within a definite time period, and the focus should be on basic subjects which should be transferred first. The priority of subjects has been made in box 6.1. Simultaneously, with the transfer of functions, the field officers and staff of the concerned line departments should be deputed to panchayats.

As regards the devolution of funds, it is necessary to devolve minimum percentage of state budget within a definite time-frame. As far as the levying of local taxes is concerned, the panchayats should be entrusted with the mandatory responsibility of collection of user charges (for drinking water, electricity, irrigation, roads, health, etc.). Initially these may be low but gradually should be increased. Also, the principle of cross subsidy should be applied so that the poor are not subject to too much of burden. Together with this, a separate list of items of tax collection should be added to Schedule VII.

- *Constitution of SFC:* SFC requires revitalisation. It needs to be given more teeth with certain mandatory provisions for suggesting not only devolution package but also users' charges and norms for cross subsidy for various services. As regards the constitution of SFC, it must have experts from economics and fiscal management.
- *Transparency:* Mandatory provision of observing transparency needs to be incorporated. Also, a proper information system needs to be developed so that the people can access the information easily.
- *Accountability*
  - *Social Audit:* Article 243J provides that the state may make provisions for the maintenance of accounts by panchayats and the auditing of such accounts. Accordingly, the states have made necessary provisions. But, this financial audit should be seen as more an exercise in bringing corrections in the procedures and maintenance of finance and accounts of panchayats than merely finding objections and faults. For maintaining accountability of elected members to people, a system of 'social audit' (with proper procedure, and noting of minutes of discussion, its circulation to all ward members and also its display outside the panchayat office, and provisions for taking remedial measures by PR members) and compulsory display (fortnightly/monthly) of expenditure on each item should be introduced.
  - *People's Watch Committee:* Keeping in view the distortions in the present form of panchayat functioning, which is also marked with malfunctioning in electoral process (as reported during the field visits and survey in various states), poor functioning of gram sabha, and lack of transparency and accountability, there is a necessity of constituting people's watch committee from among senior citizens (non-political) at the district and block levels. Its role should be that of an ombudsman and should play advisory role. From people's perspective, it should examine the procedural shortcomings and bottlenecks in the implementation of panchayat Act. Among others, it should recommend about electoral reforms, quality of people's participation, planning and implementation process, transparency in the functioning, and accountability of elected members.

- *Constitution of Tribunal:* There are certain legal problems (which may crop up due to irresponsible decisions, partial decisions and unlawful decisions) that keep hampering the functioning of panchayats. So the necessity of constitution of tribunal arises for examining and adjudicating cases pertaining to malfunctioning—administrative as well as financial, and to resolve inter-panchayat and intra-panchayat conflicts.

▸ *Constitution of DPC:* Article 243ZD stipulates for setting up of district planning committee (DPC). Accordingly, some steps have been taken by the states for the formation of DPC, still there are certain lacunae in its constitution as outlined in chapter five. The following measures are suggested for providing functionality to district planning:

- DPC must have experts from various fields such as economics, HRD, technologies, agriculture, health, engineering (infrastructure) and management whose task should be to provide necessary technical inputs, to undertake feasibility studies, to carry out the data analysis and assist in the preparation of district plan, and to monitor and provide feedback to the DPC and lower tiers (here, it should also be appreciated that planning requires good amount of knowledge and skills that can be provided by experts).
- The chairperson of the DPC should be from the elected members of ZP or municipality.
- DPC should be given the exclusive task of planning, as planning is an elaborate exercise that requires extensive as well as intensive efforts.
- Planning committees must also be formed at block and GP levels (to begin with, it may be done first at block and subsequently at GP).

▸ *Support System*

- *Planning Unit:* In the backdrop of description about local level planning in the chapter five, it is amply clear that the local level planning, which is so vital for the allocation of resources, has not taken roots. Therefore, to strengthen the planning system at three tiers, it becomes crucial to initiate measures like, *first*, to encourage people's participation, educational and awareness programmes need to be taken up in the villages in a big way. *Second*, for optimal and rational allocation of sectoral funds both for inter- and intra-panchayat, a suitable planning methodology that should include planning process, tools and techniques, and integration of plans of each tier should be prepared. *Third*, the planning units at each tier viz., district, block and gram panchayat should be strengthened adequately that may require some expenditure, which is worth incurring, unless such support system is provided the planning process at the local level will not succeed. The items that are required for planning unit are placement of trained manpower, creation of infrastructure; and provisioning of equipments (see tables from 6.3 to 6.6, and 6.16).
- *Delivery system:* The delivery system in the villages is poor as far as the availability of services for health, education, agriculture, veterinary, drinking water, irrigation,

availability of bank loan, etc. is concerned. People have to struggle very hard for these basic services. And among others, the reasons are poor infrastructure, inadequate manpower, lack of logistics support, and poor people's participation. The basic aim of decentralisation is to provide basic services to people as close to their village as possible. This will be possible provided we create support system in terms of manpower, logistics and infrastructure (especially for basic services like health, agriculture, veterinary, irrigation, etc.) at the gram panchayat level (see tables 6.11 and 6.17).

The above support system, which is vital for improving the capacity of panchayats, should be provided within definite time period in order to enable the panchayats to deliver at the village level.

- *Regulatory Functions:* There are certain issues like moneylending and illicit use of liquor (as these two are widely prevalent) that directly impinge on the life of the villagers considerably. It requires that a separate body of elected representatives should be set up at the district and block levels for regulatory functions like check on money-lending and prohibition of illicit liquor. Also, other crimes having wider social ramifications for the society can be brought under this regulatory body.

Note: Wherever necessary, there is a need to bring changes in the Articles of the Central Act from 'state may' to 'state shall' in order to bring mandatory nature in the Act for strengthening the panchayats

6.3.2 Scheduled Areas Act

As elaborately discussed in section 5.5, the Scheduled Areas Act provides large responsibilities of regulation and development in the hands of panchayats, which, under the given state of panchayat functioning, is quite disproportionate to their capacity to handle. So, in order to avoid the situation of giving the panchayats too many functions and the dual role (of development and regulation), the following specific points are suggested:

- *Focus Needs to be on making Basic Services Available to People:* What is crucial for a villager is to have access to basic services like primary education, health and sanitation, safe drinking water, proper roads and timely availability of essential commodities. It will provide scope for human resources development (HRD), which is so badly lacking in the tribal areas. Therefore, the provisions in the Act should be amended to give focus to basic services.
- For Regulation, a separate body of representatives of tribal areas requires to be constituted. In order to address the important issues of acquisition of land, alienation of land, minor forest produce, village markets, money lending, consumption of any intoxicant, license or mining lease for minor minerals, Tribal Advisory and Regulatory Board should be constituted at the district and block levels for the regulatory function.
- *Use of Forest Land for crucial Development Activities:* A new section needs to be added for providing powers to gram sabha for utilising forest land (within a certain permissible

limit for each activity) for development purpose like construction of school building and health centre, checkdams, etc. The regulation of which should be done at the district level. It would facilitate in desired identification of land, which is suited for development activities of a village (which is not possible presently, and several development projects in tribal areas get delayed or are not executed).

Note: Also, the necessary amendments suggested in 6.3.1 should be incorporated for the Scheduled areas.

Finally, the further Amendments that need to be brought in should provide definite direction to the states for bringing changes in their state Acts. Also, in order to operationalise the Act, certain degree of mandatory nature has to be provided especially with regard to empowerment of people, transfer of functions and devolution of funds, transparency, accountability, planning unit and delivery system. And only when are these addressed by the Act in concrete terms, the process of decentralisation can get the desired shape. Notwithstanding the need of bringing the amendments, even if some provisions are not provided in the Act, it is vital to take appropriate steps for strengthening the panchayats keeping in view the spirit of the Constitution Amendment Act.

6.3.3 Requirement of Funds for the Support System

In the light of above discussion, in order to operationalise the 73rd Constitution Amendment Act, the capacity of the panchayats needs to be strengthened. And it will call for having appropriate support system. To put it in a simple way, for having active participation of people, it requires conducive environment in panchayats; for efficient functioning of panchayats, it requires trained manpower with requisite capabilities; for preparing plans as per local felt-needs, it necessitates that planning unit should be placed; and for meeting the basic needs of people, the delivery mechanism needs to be strengthened. And without this support system the panchayats will not be able to function, which has been the case in all the states, except in Kerala where the support system has been provided.

The support system that is required is reflected in table 6.17, which shows that over a period of five years, the funds requirement would be Rs. 55.95 cr., which is quite a reasonable sum (against the average plan funds of Rs. 1250.00 cr. in rural areas over a period of five years) for making panchayats to get functional strength, and the requirement would be 4.47 per cent (see table 6.18) of total plan funds in a district. And this will provide the necessary support to panchayats that is very badly needed presently by the panchayats to function. Even after five years, we should continue to invest in this support system, as the capacity of panchayats may require further strengthening, and the role of the panchayat is most likely to increase.

It is critical that the allocations for support system for environment building, training, planning unit and delivery system should necessarily be made and these allocations must be considered as investments. The underlying need of this support emanates from the urgency of involving people meaningfully in the functioning of panchayats, improving the capabilities of

TABLE 6.17: **Suggested Requirement of Funds for Support System for Panchayats in a District**

(Rs. in lakhs)

S.N.	Support system	Sub-items	Funds requirement for each tier, for the five years *** (Rs.)				Total funds requirement in a district (Rs.) ****	Funds requirement as %age of total plan funds
			GP	Sector	Block	District		
1.	Environment Building	- Educational and awareness building programmes	1.00	-	-	-	240.00	0.20
2.	Training	- Infrastructure	1.00	2.00	10.00	50.00	625.00	0.50
		- Imparting training to PR members and development functionaries						
3.	Planning Unit	- Infrastructure *	2.50	5.25	14.00	40.00	1235.00	0.98
		- Equipments (like computers for database preparation, GIS package) (see tables 6.3 to 6.6)						
4.	Delivery System	- Infrastructure Primary edun.	2.00	-	-	-	500.00	0.40
		- Logistics (Equipments) Others **	-	20	50	100	2,300.00	1.84
		- Panchayat offices (see also table 6.10) - Office building, office equipments	1.5	2.00	7.5	50.00	695.00	0.55
						Total	5595.00	

(Contd.)

TABLE 6.17 *(Contd.)*

* See tables from 6.3 to 6.6 for support system for planning units.
** For primary health, ICDS, Agriculture, etc.
*** It is assumed that it may take five years for providing the support system.
**** Assuming that this support system would be established over a period of five years (The funds requirement has been calculated based on field experience, and is a rough approximation, except for the planning units for which tables 6.3 to 6.6 have been used).

Note 1 : For the purpose of calculation the following data have been assumed :

District: 20 blocks ; rural population 25 lakhs; plan funds Rs. 250 cr. {Rs. 71,000 cr. for all the districts in rural areas, (MORD, 2001a)}
Block : 12 GPs ; population 1.25 lakhs.
Sector : 4 GPs ; population 40,000 (size of the sector may vary as per district specific need, and the number of GPs in a sector may be more in case the size of the population of GP is small). (60 sectors in a district)
GP : Population 10,000. (240 GPs in a district) (population may vary from district to district)

Note 2: As regards the manpower support, in critical places new staff may be recruited, otherwise personnel should be drawn from the existing departments (even from state directorates).

TABLE 6. 18: **Suggested Allocations (for Support System for Panchayats) as Percentage of Total Plan Funds**

S.N.	Support system	Sub-items	Suggested allocations for support system, as percentage of total plan funds	
			In the first five years ***	After five years ****
1	Environment Building	- Educational and awareness building programmes	0.20	0.20
2.	Training	- Infrastructure	0.50	0.50
		- Imparting training to PR members and development functionaries Recurring Cost *	0.50	1.00
3.	Planning unit	- Infrastructure	0.98	0.50
		- Equipment (like computers for database preparation, GIS package)		
4.	Delivery ** System	- Infrastructure, logistics (Euipments)	2.24	1.00
		Panchayat office (see also table 6.10)	0.55	0.10
		- Office building, office euipments		
		Total	4.47	3.30

Note 1. The above requirements (for support system) are indicative based on rough estimate (as analysed during the field visits). But actual requirements have to be assessed based on the specific needs.

2. As regards the manpower support, in critical places new staff may be recruited, otherwise personnel should be drawn from the existing departments (even from state directorates).

* Taking the approximation of .5% of plan funds as recurring cost in the first five years as it will take time in building infrastructure, then 1% for the next five years.

** For primary education, agriculture, health, etc.

*** Taking figures based on the calculations in table 6.17.

**** For the next five years, based on the rough approximation.

Note : For recurring cost of delivery system, it is assumed to be met by State Govt. The above table includes cost which is only additional to the existing cost, but necessary for providing support to panchayats.

those who have to work from within and enhancing the capacity of local panchayats to deliver. Besides, this support system is vital for the very success of process of decentralisation in general and for making panchayats as the 'unit of development' in particular. And only when is the support system placed, would the panchayats be able to function and deliver as expected from them.

> 'It is critical that the allocations for support system for environment building, training, planning unit and delivery system should necessarily be made and these allocations must be considered as investments. The underlying need of this support emanates from the urgency of involving people meaningfully in the functioning of panchayats, improving the capabilities of those who have to work from within and enhancing the capacity of local panchayats to deliver. Besides, this support system is vital for the very success of process of decentralisation in general and for making panchayats as the 'unit of development' in particular. And only when is the support system placed, would the panchayats be able to function and deliver as expected from them.'

Finally, in the light of above discussions, the implementation of the process of decentralisation should be in a phased manner, keeping in view the capacity of the panchayats. Accordingly, the phase-wise interventions are indicated in table 6.19. And the specific interventions, that are required to operationalise the Act, have been reflected in table 6.20.

Summing Up

The process of decentralisation got new impetus with the enactment of 73rd Constitution Amendment Act. The states have taken some measures to strengthen the panchayats in order to enable them to take up the task of local development. Though the Central Act envisages that the people will be able to represent themselves in the gram sabha and the panchayats will be able to meet local development needs, while the present state of functioning of panchayats speaks that the process of decentralisation is gripped by the unequal opportunities available to different segments in the villages, central decision-making, control of local elites, weak local institutions and poor accountability system.

In this very context, this chapter has suggested measures that are vital for operationalising the Act. It has stressed that the success of decentralisation process will be determined by two fundamentals: *first*, whether the people have opportunities to participate meaningfully in the development process; and *second*, whether the panchayats have adequate capacity to address the needs of people and deliver basic services, and that is where from the initiatives for decentralisation should begin. And, alongside every other initiative for decentralisation, an enabling environment should be fostered so that public participation can be strengthened and local institutions may find sufficient room to function. Measures required for strengthening panchayats must address all the dimensions viz., political, functional, administrative and financial, in an integrated manner. And the necessary amendments in the Central as well as state Acts should be effected to underpin the local institutions, so that they can come to a stage of delivering services to people as per their needs and meet the standards of good governance.

TABLE 6. 19: **A Suggestive Model for Phase-wise Interventions for Systematic Development of PR System**

Phases	Core focus	Capacity building		Administrative arrangements	Organisational support	Infrastructure development	Transfer of functions and devolution of financial power
		Environment building	Knowledge & skills improvement				
1	2	3	4	5	6	7	8
Phase I	Preparatory phase	• Rapport building programme • Awareness building about participatory planning • Attitudinal changes in development functionaries	-	-	-	Construction of panchayat office building	-
Phase II	Capacity building-I		• Improvement in capabilities for planning & implementation of programmes	• To develop methodology of planning at GP, block & district • To provide necessary administrative guidelines for placement of field staff of other line deptt. with PRIs	• Placement of field staff and officers of DRDA, blocks and GPs with respective PRIs	Creation of additional office building for line deptt. office	• To transfer functions and devolve funds for subjects of list I (Box 6.1)

(Contd.)

TABLE 6.19 *(Contd.)*

1	2	3	4	5	6	7	8
Phase III	Capacity building-II ● Strengthening planning exercise	• The capacity building programme should continue in all the phases in order to sensitise the people about participatory planning and their involvement in the gram sabha besides equipping the development functionaries with necessary knowledge and skills for planning and implementation of the programmes)		• To define administrative and financial limits for functioning at GP, block & district for each subject • To define the roles, and responsibilities of PR members, line departments and CBOs	•Placement of officers and staff of line departments of primary and social sectors with respective PRIs	-	-
	● Strengthening delivery system	-		• To provide necessary M & E system and MIS for smooth monitoring and control & for incorporating desired changes • To develop the accountability system (social audit)		• Creation of infrastructure at the GP level for education, health, drinking water, marketing, training, etc. • To provide equipments (computer etc.) & logistics support	
	● Improving accountability, M & E system and MIS	-					
Phase IV	Capacity building-III	-		• Commensurate increase in administrative support (procedures, rules, etc.)	• Deputation of officers and staff of line department of other sectors with respective PRIs	• Improving need-based infrastructure	• To transfer functions and devolve fund for other subjects of list II (Box 6.1)
Phase V	Capacity building-IV	-		-do-	-do-	• Improving need-based infrastructure	• To transfer functions and devolve fund for other subjects of list III (Box 6.1)

TABLE 6. 20: **Required Interventions for Operationalising the 73rd Constitution Amendment Act**

S.N.	Dimensions	Items	Critical issues	Required interventions
1	2	3	4	5
1.	**Political**	• Election	- Discussion during the election campaign - Dominance by village elites and a few groups - Candidature of dummy candidates - Use of money, increased consumption of liquor	• Electoral reforms for - Educating people about their rights and village development needs - Elections on non-party basis - State funding of elections - Measures to check use of physical power and consumption of liquor • Constitution of citizens committee (to work as ombudsman) to oversee the conduct of elections • Educational and awareness building programmes to educate people about need, rules and procedure of elections • Timely elections and elections for all the tiers at one time
		• Functioning of gram sabha - People's participation	- Low attendance in the gram sabha - Lack of people's participation - Narrow focus of agenda item - Poor participation of women - Dominance by a few - Lack of transparency in the preparation of proceedings - Difficulty in the preparation of village plan	• Educational and awareness programmes • Sensitisation programme for the role of gram sabha in the development • Developing rules and procedure for the conduct of the gram sabha meeting and recording of proceedings • Developing the objective criteria for the selection of beneficiaries for the development schemes • Improving value system for participation and decision-making • Information sharing • Large number of members in GS — formation of resource groups

(Contd.)

TABLE 6.20 *(Contd.)*

1	2	3	4	5
		• Accountability	- Accountability of PR members and chairpersons of panchayats to people is lacking	• Proper procedure with adequate guidelines for social audit needs to be developed • Introducing the system of arbitration for settling disputes, ensuring compliance of rules, and observing financial and administrative propriety
2.	**Functional**	• Transfer of functions	- Transfer of functions as per the 11th schedule not done	• Defining the functional role of panchayats • Transfer of functions to panchayats, in a phased manner, starting with subjects under list I, then followed by lists II and III (Box 6.1)
		• Inter-tier demarcation of functions	- Demarcation of sub-functions under each subject for each tier is not carried out	• Demarcation of sub-functions under each subject for each tier to be undertaken in order to clearly define the roles and responsibilities for each tier
3.	**Administrative**	• Assigning functions specific responsibilities to panchayats	- Responsibilities to panchayats for a particular function have not been defined	• Defining function-specific responsibilities in order to give specific role and responsibility
		• Placement of officers and staff of line department with PRIs	- Manpower planning - Placement of officers and staff to PRIs not done in almost all the departments	• For improving the manpower support to PRIs, the officers and staff of line departments should be placed with the PRIs with

(Contd.)

TABLE 6.20 *(Contd.)*

1	2	3	4	5
		• Recruitment, transfer and posting of field officers and staff • Roles and responsibilities	- No administrative control over officers and staff - Adequate procedure for transfer and postings are lacking - Roles and responsibilities of concerned PRIs and departments are not defined	properly laid down rules of administrative control • Board should be set up at the district level for recruitment, transfer and posting of field officers and staff • Under each subject, the roles and responsibilities of concerned PRIs, line departments and of people should be defined in order to avoid overlap and conflicts • Motivation for PR members and development functionaries through awards, incentive and recognition. • Enhancing value system for improving work culture
		Institutional mechanism for planning, implementation, panchayat functioning, transparency and accountability • Planning - Planning unit - Planning methodology - Database - DPC	- Planning system at all the three tiers is in poor shape. At the district level, planning unit is not equipped to take up planning exercis. At the lower levels planning units do not exist. Database is not being prepared. There is no planning methodology. DPC not constituted in all the states, and wherever constituted, it is not effective	• DPC should have experts from various fields • Planning methodology should be formulated with steps for reaching the logical conclusion • Database preparation at the panchayat levels should be undertaken • Planning units with infrastructure, manpower and logistics support should be created at all the three tiers

(Contd.)

TABLE 6.20 *(Contd.)*

1	2	3	4	5
		• Implementation - Role of beneficiaries - Supervision - Logistics support	- Beneficiaries are not involved in the execution and supervision of works - Works are implemented by the chairpersons of GPs themselves in some cases, or by departments or contractors in other cases	• Proper procedure for involvement of beneficiaries in the execution and supervision of works should be prescribed • Necessary logistics support to be provided
		• MIS - Information system - Monitoring system - Control system	- Mechanism to collect data and information and their processing is not in place - Monitoring system is not placed to assess the progress of the works - Control system inadequately placed	• MIS to be set up
		• Coordination - Coordination committee	- Lack of coordination among PRIs and departments	• Coordination committees required for inter-panchayats and inter-departmental functioning
		• Infrastructural and logistics support	- No support system provided to panchayats	• Necessary infrastructural and logistics support should be extended to PRIs in order to improve their capacity to perform
		• Transparency	- No proper procedure for maintaining transparency	• Sound system of transparency with simple a procedure should be laid down with adequate accountability of the concerned functionary
		• Delivery mechanism	- Poor capacity of delivery mechanism	• Sound delivery mechanism especially for basic services like education, health, drinking water, agriculture, animal husbandry, etc. • Simplification of procedure • Information sharing and facilitation centres at the gram panchayat level

(Contd.)

TABLE 6.20 *(Contd.)*

1	2	3	4	5
		• Training	- Lack of capabilities among PR members and dvelopment functionaries	• A comprehensive programme of training required
4.	**Financial**	• Devolution of funds	- Devolution of funds has not taken place	• Certain minimum devolution of funds should take place
		• Collection of taxes	- The collection of taxes is poor - There is hostile or indifferent environment for paying taxes	• The sources of tax collection should be increased and tax collection mechanism needs strengthening • People should be sensitised about the need for paying the taxes and user charges to panchayats in order to maintain the panchayat assets and running of various services • The PR members should show courage and leadership in imposing taxes and at the same time they should instil confidence in people that the panchayats will provide better services to people in return of tax paid by the people
		• Management of finance and accounts	Inadequate procedures	• Adequate procedure for maintenance of panchayat finances and accounts
		• Financial autonomy	Lack of financial autonomy to panchayats to utilise resources as per local needs	• Financial autonomy of panchayats to be augmented by improving ther resource-base

Note: The above issues are applicable to all the states in varying degree, except Kerala.

APPENDIX 6.1

A. Case Study of Kuthambakkam Gram Panchayat in Tiruvallur District of Tamil Nadu

The study of functioning of Kuthambakkam Gram Panchayat was made to present a success story of the panchayat at the lowest tier. A brief description is given below:

- In 1997, the newly elected president of the gram panchayat had difficult task at his hand for socio-economic development of his gram panchayat. He first began his work by mobilising people through door-to-door visits and awareness building meetings. He laid special emphasis on the formation of self-help groups (SHGs). He met with some success. Then he organised training and workshops for panchayat members for making them aware about panchayat Act, development programmes and so on. It was followed by orientation workshops for the people, who were motivated to attend the gram sabha meetings, and to participate and to make suggestions during planning process, and to make contributions in the implementation of programmes. During the village meetings, people were oriented for the importance of *shramdan* (voluntary labour contribution) and were encouraged to do so in their village work. Such a strategy helped the panchayat in creating a good environment for people's participation and for development activities.
- The main activities of this gram panchayat have been in the area of primary education and health, drinking water, training, and providing value addition to agricultural produce and thereby creating additional employment opportunities. The GP has taken measures for setting up of units for animal feeds, groundnut oil, eco-friendly bags and handicraft items. The GP has also added considerable infrastructure like roads, school, community centre, etc., which has helped people in various socio-economic activities. The panchayat is also making efforts in the field of agriculture, floriculture, poultry and so on.
- In achieving the success in the development of panchayat, the planning has played an important role. In this direction, the village database has been created (by using computer), and village plan has been prepared by the panchayat with a focus on meeting the basic needs in the area of education, health, agriculture, employment, infrastructure, etc. Also, management and monitoring of implementation have been adequately taken care of. In doing so, the president has played very important role in providing requisite knowledge and skills in every stage (planning, project design, implementation, monitoring) of development.
- At the implementation level, the training of beneficiaries under each programme has been ensured, and the people have been involved in making contributions for development activities and in the monitoring and supervision of programmes.

If we examine the factors behind the success of the functioning in the Kuthambakkam Gram Panchayat, these can be counted as higher capabilities (which has been strengthened by the good educational background) of panchayat president, social mobilisation, positive people's participation, training of elected members, infrastructural and logistics support to panchayat office, and the right planning and implementation mechanism.

Finally, in the overall analysis, it is the commitment and leadership of the panchayat president that has provided an effective and positive leadership to the people. Also his capabilities in planning and implementation of programmes added momentum to the development process.

B. Successful Cases in People's Participation and Local Development by GP Chairpersons

S. No.	Name and address	Achievements
1.	Shri Rajendra Kumar Sarpanch, Village Chamund Hisar District Haryana	- Village infrastructure development like schools, health centres, etc. - Took initiative to resolve disputes in the village - Organised women to solve water problem in the village
2.	Smt. Kamala Mahato Pradhan Bandoan Village Purulia District West Bengal	- Drinking water - Organised the women in a number of remunerative activities related to poultry, dairy, livestock, etc. - Solved many household problems
3.	Smt. Fatima Bi Sarpanch Kalva Village Kurnool District Andhra Pradesh	- Village infrastructure development like metalled roads, construction of school building etc. - Organised thrift societies and self-help groups - Handled social problems like child marriage

Source : Planning Commission, 2001

APPENDIX 6.2

Development Sectors

1. Agriculture
   i. Agriculture including agricultural extension
2. Natural resources management
   ii. Land improvement, implementation of land reforms, land consolidation and soil conservation
   iii. Fuel and fodder
3. Irrigation
   iv. Minor irrigation, water management and watershed development
4. Animal husbandry
   v. Animal husbandry, dairying and poultry
5. Fisheries
   vi. Fisheries
6. Forest
   vii. Social forestry and farm forestry
   viii. Minor forest produce
7. Rural connectivity
   ix. Roads, culverts, bridges, ferries, waterways and other means of communication
8. Housing
   x. Rural housing
9. Commercial linkage
   xi. Markets and fares
10. Energy
   xii. Rural electrification, including distribution of electricity
   xiii. Non-conventional energy sources
11. Industries
   xiv. Small scale industries,
   xv. Khadi, village and cottage industries
12. Education
   xvi. Education including primary and secondary schools
   xvii. Technical training and vocational education
   xviii. Adult and non-formal education
   xix. Libraries
   xx. Cultural activities
13. Drinking water
   xxi. Drinking water
14. Health
   xxii. Health and sanitation, including hospitals, primary health centres and dispensaries

15. Family welfare
    xxiii. Family welfare
16. Women and child development
    xxiv. Women and child development
17. Social welfare
    xxv. Social welfare, including welfare of the handicapped and mentally retarded
    xxvi. Welfare of the weaker sections, and in particular of the SCs and STs.
18. Poverty alleviation
    xxvii. Poverty alleviation programme
    xxviii. Maintenance of community assets
19. Public distribution system
    xxix. Public distribution system

7

CONCLUSIONS : SETTING REFORM AGENDA

The principal objective of the study of decentralisation in India was to assess the processes leading to establishment of local institutions in the backdrop of Central as well as state Acts. The study covered wide ranging issues and examined them under four dimensions viz., political, functional, administrative and financial (specific issues are reflected in box 7.1). Specifically, the focus was on the following vital aspects discerning their inter-relationships and to examine what is the impact of one on the other and in turn on the whole panchayat system:

- *first*, social, political, economic and cultural factors influencing the process of decentralisation,
- *second*, the role of state in strengthening the local institutions, and
- *third*, the role of institutions in involving people in the participative process and enhancing the delivery of services.

7.1 Salient Findings of the Study

The field studies and survey provided a first hand account of the decentralisation and the functioning of PR institutions at all the three tiers. The salient findings that have emerged, as elaborately discussed in the chapters four and five, are summarised below:

Assessment of Factors Influencing the Process of Decentralisation

The field study is a pointer to the fact that there are a number of factors viz., social, political, economic and cultural values that are influencing the process of decentralisation. A brief description is as follows:

As analysed, the factors like caste (discrimination), position of village elites, manner of decision-making (tendency to dominate, central decision-making), isolation of weaker sections in the panchayat functioning influence the functional environment in the villages. Also, for elites, the prestige for winning elections and having control over village panchayat are other

BOX 7.1

Issues Analysed in the Study of Process of Decentralisation

- **Political Decentralisation**
  - The degree to which the political status has been given to the PR members
  - The degree to which the elections to the local bodies have been conducted successfully
  - The degree to which participation is ensured in the village development planning and implementation
  - The degree to which the accountability system has been placed
  - The degree to which the responsiveness for the local needs has improved

- **Functional Decentralisation**
  - The degree to which transfer of functions has taken place
  - The degree to which inter-tier demarcation of functions has taken place

- **Administrative Decentralisation**
  - The degree to which institutional mechanism for planning, implementation, coordination and monitoring has been placed
  - The degree to which the transparency in the functioning of panchayats has been ensured
  - The degree to which the roles and responsibilities have been assigned to various functionaries in the process of development
  - The degree to which the mechanism for resolving conflicts, settling disputes and arbitration has been set up

- **Financial Decentralisation**
  - The degree to which devolution of funds upon panchayats has taken place
  - The degree to which the powers have been given for the collection of taxes and also the environment has been created for raising taxes
  - The degree to which the powers have been given for utilising funds as per the local needs

And finally

- The degree to which the people have access to and opportunities for the socio-politico-economic participation in the villages
- The degree to which the decentralisation has helped in improving the effectiveness of local institutions in meeting development needs and in providing basic services to people
- The degree to which the development policies have role in the process of decentralisation

factors that influence the panchayat polls. In such cases the tendency to spend more money or to use physical (muscle) power increases. And, often, the elites end up using local public services for the promotion of their personal and / or political interests.

The village environment remains politically sensitive and overwhelmingly against the possibility of participation in the political process by the individuals. The affiliation by people to a particular political party is another issue that divides the village on political lines.

Besides, the panchayat functioning at all the three tiers is marked with individual approach, domination by a few, ego conflicts, lack of collective approach, lack of responsiveness to weaker sections, poor capabilities for planning and implementation of programmes, lack of appreciation for technical opinion or expertise and low priority given to quality of work. The lack of possibility of raising of legitimate grievances and settling of political or personal scores are common sights in the gram sabha meetings.

Assessment of Role of State in Strengthening the Local Institutions

The 73rd Constitution Amendment Act has provided framework for decentralisation. As panchayat being the state subject, the onus of implementation of the Act has been entrusted to states. The states have made attempts to give the Central Act an operational shape. The prominent measures, in varying degrees, initiated by the states include representation to weaker sections, conduct of elections, transfer of subjects to panchayats, constitution of SFC, DPC and SEC, devolution of powers and funds, and collection of taxes by the panchayats.

A careful analysis reveals that much of the concern for decentralisation centres around the issues pertaining to the powers. Perhaps, the mindset of the concerned opinion makers, whether they be in politics or in academics or in non-government organisations or in government or in among general intelligentsia, is governed by the negative and regulatory thought of taking powers from one form of system — which is centralised form of development agencies — and transferring it to another form of system — which is panchayats. It appears as if it is perceived that the present form of development is something to do with only exercising powers and deciding on the allocations of funds and control over departments. While development is a much bigger task that will entail participation of people in development, providing basic services, addressing people's grievances, responsiveness to the people's needs, attending to the problems of weaker sections and so on. All these will require more of effective local institutions and good knowledge and skills in the personnel managing local affairs than just devolving powers. To be more precise, the issues like: how to take the people's aspirations and needs in the plan formulation, how to elicit the information from people about local resources, how to reach to rational decisions, how to allocate the funds judiciously, how to address the grievances of weaker sections without prejudice, how the services are provided to people in time and with ease, how to resolve conflicts, how to take people's contribution in the development, are very vital, and the success of development depends on how these are attended to. These are the areas that have not been addressed in the operational terms by the states.

In this very context, Dreze and Sen (1995) have also observed that the measures in question include mandatory elections at regular intervals, reservation of seats in village panchayats for women and members of scheduled castes or tribes and devolution of some government responsibilities to local authorities. These legislative reforms certainly provide opportunity for correcting the current failures of local governance in rural India. Nevertheless, it would be naive to expect too much from them unless the other causes of this problem are also addressed. For instance, the reservation is one of the components for giving voice to weaker sections that basically addresses the negative aspect, which is control and power, but we have to look at the problem in a much bigger context of development and to appreciate the need of initiating positive measures, which include improving capabilities of weaker sections and giving them socio-economic opportunities through suitable development policy measures.

If we examine the case of Kerala's success in decentralisation, and by contrasts the failure of other states, it combines in its own way three major elements: i. high educational and awareness level, ii. high capacity of local institutions, and iii. efficient delivery mechanism. And in this regard, Kerala made specific comprehensive interventions, which other states have not.

Assessment of Institutional Performance

The local institutions have vital role in order to operationalise the panchayat Acts. The findings presented in chapter five point towards serious weaknesses about the capacity of the panchayats to perform. In practice, capacity-building of PR institutions remains a big cause of concern. The studies illustrate the infancy of the institutional development at the local levels. Among the prominent weaknesses are: lack of procedures and norms for the conduct of gram sabha, transparency and accountability, and planning and implementation of programmes; poor HRD level of personnel, inadequate planning and financial system; weak control and monitoring system; and inadequacy of legal system. Now, it is evident that in the absence of these vital fundamentals, the local institutions would find it hard to deliver and meet the development needs of the people.

About Scheduled Areas Act

The provisions provided in the Scheduled Areas Act empower the gram sabhas with both development and regulatory roles. Besides, it is assumed that, in future, the panchayats would function as self-government with the devolution of powers upon panchayats in the Scheduled Areas.

Now, with this Act broadly two questions emerge. *First*, how far the panchayats (through gram sabhas) would be able to handle both development and regulatory functions. If we examine carefully both require specialised way of handling and differ in terms of content and approach, while the former requires 'participation of people' and the latter requires 'control', which do not go hand in hand. So whether the same (panchayat) body will be able to address both the roles requires deeper assessment. *Second*, whether the panchayats would be able to perform duties as the units of 'self-government', though necessary, under the present state of poor socio-economic conditions and weak delivery system in tribal areas.

What Decentralisation has not achieved — The Question of Governance

From the study of the provisions of the panchayat Acts and based on the findings that have emerged from the field studies, it is quite evident that the focus of decentralisation has been more on: *first*, conduct of elections; and *second*, control over power, funds, departments and personnel than on enhancing people's participation and improving institutional capacities. The thinking has been that the panchayats will look after all the development interests of villages, once they are constituted. But it has not been the case. And in this process the vital fundamentals viz., *first*, participatory approach in development; *second*, availability of basic services to people; *third*, gender equality and equity in development; and *fourth*, institutional capacity to deliver, have not been addressed by the states and such vital issues do not form the part of main debate on decentralisation (presently the debate is mainly on power, funds, and control). And, such a state has raised the question about the governance at the village level.

In the backdrop of above discussion, it is evident that we are still struggling in the process of decentralisation, even after the new thrust given to it under the Constitution Amendment Act, 1993. Though states have initiated some measures, as revealed by the field studies, but except Kerala, none of the states have been in a position to provide credible decentralised system for ensuring good governance at the local level. The prominent reasons, as revealed from field studies, for such a state are: *first*, the limited representation to people in the election process, due to hold of traditional power centres and wide disparities; *second*, poor people's participation in development activities; *third*, weak planning system; *fourth*, lack of requisite capabilities in panchayati raj (PR) members for undertaking the task of development planning and implementation; *fifth*, weak delivery system to make basic services available to people; *sixth*, meagre financial resources of panchayats; and *lastly*, inadequate transparency and accountability system. And such a state is leading to vicious cycle of poor people's participation, lack of transparency, inadequate accountability and decline in performance (see fig. 7.1).

7.2 Vital Issues

This section identifies certain important issues that directly impinge on the process of decentralisation. These are briefly summed up below:

Disparities

The panchayats have to operate in a very complex setting at the village level. This setting is marked with various disparities on account of social, economic and cultural patterns. These disparities among people have impact on inter-personal relationships and the way panchayats

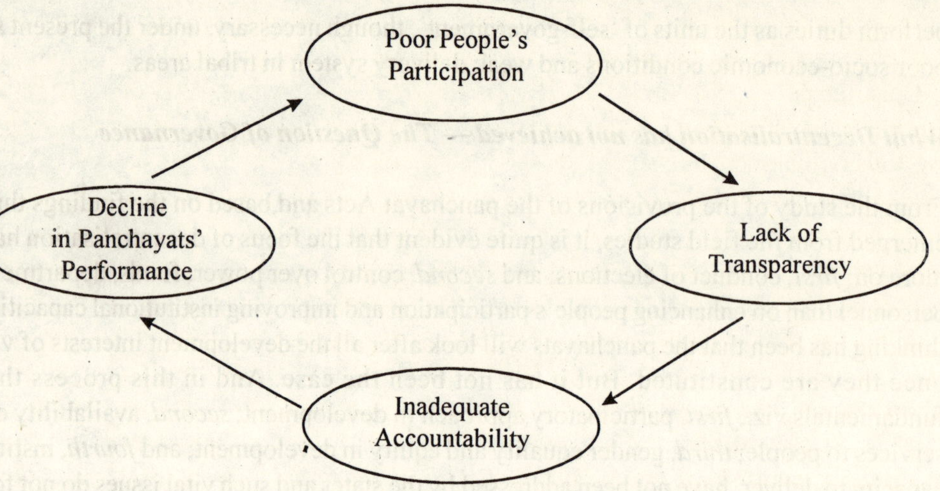

Fig. 7.1: Vicious Cycle of Poor People's Participation

take decisions, implement the programmes and deliver the services to people. Based on the field studies, some of the disparities that are commonly noticed at the grassroots level are illustrated below:

- *On Account of Caste:* Caste factor is quite prominent at the village level. The decisions at the panchayat level are influenced by the alignments of people on the caste lines. For example, where the tube-well will be sunk, where the road will be laid, and who will be the beneficiaries for the anti-poverty programmes are some of the instances in which the decision-making takes place keeping in view the caste factor.
- *On Account of Class:* There is a division between the rich and the poor. The rich have access to information, resources, technologies, while the poor do not have. The rich have more confidence and voice in the gram sabha, while the poor lack the same. And similarly, the rich can reap the benefits from the development activities more than what the poor can..
- *On Account of Biases:* There are cases of biases, while handling the institutional functioning or development activities. It is quite often noticed that there are cases of biases against the poor or small farmers. These biases could also be from the administration. For instance, when a prominent person in a village complains, it is given more weightage and attended to promptly, while that of the poor does not get the same treatment. Similarly, the problems of small farmers do not get prominence, while the rich and big farmers get the ears of administration.
- *On Account of Cultural Values:* There are certain cultural factors like central decision-making or dominance over others by elites that bring cultural divide between those who are in position and those who are at the receiving end. The propensity to take decisions by a few (panchayat president or elites) in the gram sabha or panchayat meeting is the result of such a value system.

- *On Account of Deprivation:* There are certain economic factors that bring the divisions between the rich and the poor, or the haves and the have-nots. And in the traditional set-up, the poor and have-nots are deprived of their freedom to express or participate in the development process. For example, the dependence of the poor on money lenders or that of small farmers on traders deprives them from expressing freely their views in the gram sabha or in other fora.
- *On Account of Gender:* Due to a number of inequalities (on account of education, profession, ownership, etc.), the women suffer in their socio-economic life and that affects their ability to participate in the village development, while there are a number of issues like fuel-fodder management, drinking water, health and family planning, where women have a vital role to play. So in a way, lack of participation of women has bearing on the abilities of the panchayats to handle these critical issues.
- *On Account of Lack of Capabilities:* Lack of education is a big hindrance for people to access information and participate in the village development. Also, such disparity deprives many from availing opportunities. The poor, among whom the illiteracy is more, are always in a disadvantageous position, and will benefit less from decentralisation unless the programme of improving their capabilities is initiated.
- *On Account of Political Affiliation:* There are instances that the elections on the party lines have divided many villages on political affiliations. Moreover, what is important to mention is that, more often than not, the decisions in the gram sabhas or panchayat meetings are taken on political considerations. For example, the selection of beneficiaries in the gram sabha is influenced by the affiliations of beneficiaries to a particular political party.
- *On Account of Community:* Quite often the communities are divided over profession, religion, regional affiliation and land ownership. They make groups for defending their own interests.
- *On Account of Structural / Policy Issues:* There are certain policy interventions, though necessary, may benefit only a section of community. For example, in Punjab and Haryana after the success of green revolution through technological interventions, big farmers have benefited a great deal, while the small and marginal farmers and the landless labourers, especially scheduled castes, have not benefited so much. Similarly, the existing policies, which have lack of focus on HRD — basic education, skills development, health and family welfare continue to assist more to the rich than to the poor.

PR and other Important Issues

- *PR and Local Knowledge:* The panchayat system provides good opportunity, if duly channelised, for tapping local knowledge in the process of development, which will improve the efficiency of the local institutions to implement the programmes. It calls for having a suitable database of local knowledge that can provide inputs for planning.
- *PR and Voluntary Contribution:* There is a need to encourage the voluntary contributions

by the people in the implementation of programmes. It could be by way of either contribution in kind or money, or *shramdan*. It will facilitate in augmenting the resources of panchayats.

- *PR and Regulatory System:* Under the Scheduled Areas Act, the panchayats have been entrusted with the dual role of development and regulation (of liquor, mining lease, minor forest produce, etc.). It needs to be assessed whether the present set-up should continue or the separate body for regulatory work should be set up. There is also a need of similar set-up (with separate regulatory body) for regulation in non-scheduled areas.
- *PR and Information System:* For the success of process of decentralisation in general, and for the involvement of people and the preparation of village plans in particular, the access to information is vital. The information that is vital includes database for each sector, financial allocations and expenditure, physical achievements, etc. And without information system at the three levels, the panchayats would find it hard to function.
- *Subjects under 11th Schedule:* The Act envisages to assign 29 subjects to panchayats. Though all the subjects are essential, but, keeping in view the existing state of capacity of panchayats, we need to focus on basic subjects such as primary education, health and sanitation, drinking water, agriculture and allied activities and natural resources management, and then as the capacity of the panchayats gets built up in future, the other subjects should be assigned to panchayats.
- *PR and Globalisation:* The emergence of globalisation, including WTO in all sectors of economy, is going to impinge on the economic life of people at the village level. Its impact has started showing signs of distress in many parts of the country. The panchayats would be required to keep themselves abreast with the latest developments, especially about the trade of agriculture-related commodities, and take either direct appropriate measures or raise public awareness thereby drawing attention of government.
- *PR and Cultural Insensitivities:* The insensitivities[1] of people regarding certain cultural values may affect the functioning and the decision-making ability of the panchayats. There would be a need for sensitising people about certain values like people's participation in development, problems of weaker sections, necessity of efficiency and quality of work and so on.
- *PR and Disparities:* The socio-economic and cultural disparities affect the people's participation and decision-making of panchayats. It is crucial that the analysis of these disparities should be made in order to know the precise reasons, and then the efforts are required to be made for reducing the disparities through suitable policy interventions.
- *PR and Governance:* The success of panchayati raj system will be judged by the quality of governance. It is expected that for good governance, the basic needs of people should

[1] 'Cultural insensitivity' pertains to the state when the people become insensitive to certain values such as concern for weaker sections or for quality work or for people's grievances. For example, instances like lack of appreciation for the development needs of landless people in the gram sabha, or refusal by the panchayat to attend to the pressing problem, say, of drinking water in remote hamlet, or implementation of works by functionaries for achieving the target without fulfilling quality standards.

be attended to, people's participation in the discussion should be encouraged, decision-making should be transparent and there should be accountability of elected members. All these are required to be addressed by the panchayats.

- *Leaning towards Control and Power, but lack of Positive Focus:* The focus of the PR system under the new Act is towards giving directions through statutory provisions, while the support system for people's participation, institution building and improving delivery mechanism continues to be wanting. Measures are required for making interventions in order to improve the capacity of panchayats to deliver as per local needs.

7.3 Fundamental Issues Influencing Decentralisation

How HRD is Crucial for the Decentralisation and for People's Participation in Particular

Human resources development (HRD) refers to acquiring human capabilities that will include knowledge, skills and potential through educational and health programmes. The high level of HRD is one of the crucial indicators of social and economic development. In the context of decentralisation, particularly about people's participation, how specifically the higher level of HRD can be useful is indicated below:

- Improved human capabilities through a well-defined educational and awareness programmes can lead to improved freedom (due to higher confidence level) to speak in the meetings that can facilitate meaningful participation in the development process.
- From the point of view of political significance (Dreze and Sen, 1998), the interpersonal connections, strengthened by education and health programmes, can be of high utility. For example, a village may benefit generally from the development attention it gets through the efforts of active groups within the community. Likewise, the greater education and awareness will help in acquiring more information that will give fillip to collective demands which, in turn, will help in the improvement of the availability of basic services and lead to better utilisation of local resources. In a way, it will strengthen the public action. For example, check on absenteeism of teachers in the schools, availability of medicines or the application of immunisation, timely distribution of essential commodities can be better monitored by vigilant community and reported at appropriate level for corrective action. (And without this collective voice, presently, mainly due to lack of education, people, especially from weaker sections, have little power to question the wrong decisions or anomalies in the functioning.)
- Similarly, HRD will help in reducing traditional inequalities of caste, class and gender, thereby reducing the gender-inequalities and gap between the rich and the poor. And that will enhance upward mobility of weaker sections socially, politically and economically. More specifically, it will also help in empowering people to resist the wrong decisions and improve their abilities, especially of disadvantaged groups (weaker sections), to organise politically for collective action and against oppression.

- Also, higher educational level may help in enhancing their participation in the economic activities. As the use of economic opportunity by one can, in many circumstances, open up for the opportunities for others, through backward and forward linkages in supply and demand (Dreze & Sen, 1998).
- Finally, improved knowledge and freedom to speak, through the confidence and opportunity of questioning (encouraged by collective desire) of decision-making, will lead to increased transparency and enhanced accountability of local institutions to people. For example, people can ask about the amount spent on a project, wages paid to people, quality of works and so on (which, otherwise, in the present state of panchayat functioning go unquestioned due to lack of initiatives by people). Also, they can question the elected representatives in the gram sabha meetings about the decisions taken by them.

In sum, the improved HRD level has considerable significance in terms of availing opportunities, shaping the political agenda, empowerment of people, and participation in the process of institution building. And, it will lead to virtuous cycle of higher people's participation, improved transparency, accountability and performance (see fig. 7.2).

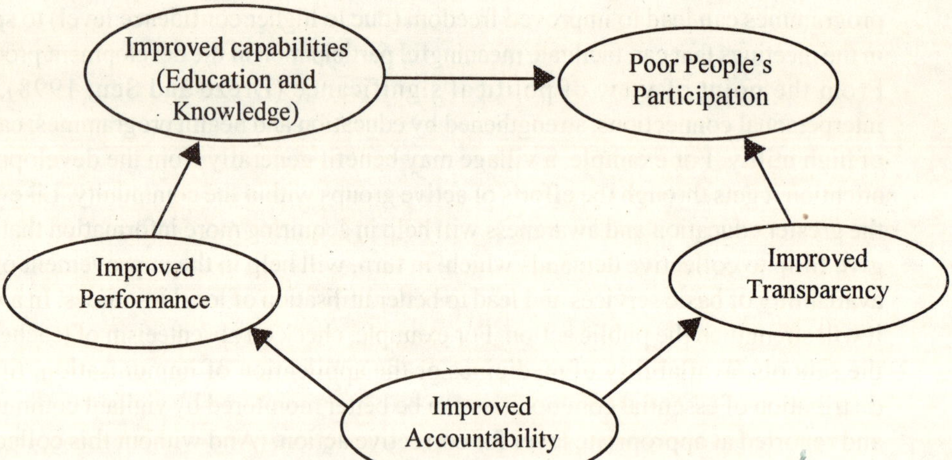

Fig. 7.2: **Virtuous Cycle of Higher People's Participation**

How Institution Building is Vital in the Process of Decentralisation

Institutions are central to sustainable development. The institutions set the process of evolution of policies, formulation of strategies, planning, mobilising resources, management of implementation of programmes and delivery of services.

The impact of programmes aimed at providing services and infrastructure depends upon the efficacy of institutions responsible for planning and implementing the projects / schemes. The institutional machinery provides the means through which the problems are identified, priorities are articulated, resources are identified, projects are formulated and implemented, and inter-sectoral linkages are accomplished. It serves as the most critical intervening factor through which human and economic resources are channelled for, among other things, promoting rural development.

To be more specific, at local level, there are a number of public services that have to be made available to people in order to promote equity and ensure minimal social security. For instance, primary school is one such basic service available for people. Similarly, there are a whole range of other services such as anganwadi centres, primary health centres, drinking water, public distribution system, agricultural inputs, veterinary services, land rights and so on, that are essential at local level. The effective and efficient management of these services is essential which can be ensured by having institutions that can deliver. To explain further the necessity of institutions, we take the case of distribution of essential commodities at the village level. Under this the delay in distribution of commodities, excessive time in queue which could be half a day and sometimes full day for those coming from distant villages (resulting in loss of wages thus offsetting the gains made from the low price of commodities), poor quality of commodities, irregularity in supply of commodities, pilferage by the salesman, etc. go on unattended for all practical purposes. It is a case in point as to where the people should report for their grievances and go for the redressal of their legitimate problems. Here, what needs to be emphasised is that the villagers in remote places find it hard to communicate or report to the higher offices about any form of irregularities, which need to be addressed at the panchayat level only, so that the timely and appropriate action is initiated.

Likewise, in case of IRDP (now SGSY), the study (Research Study, 1998) has shown that the beneficiaries have to move to different offices about 4-5 times incurring an expenditure of about Rs.450 (excluding the loss of wages during their visits to offices) before they get the loan. Likewise, for availing bank loan, the small farmer is first required to get the application forms and get it filled with the assistance of others, followed by a round of visits to different offices viz., revenue inspector office, tehsil, co-operatives, banks and agriculture department for the collection of various certificates and NOCs. So, a farmer in need for credit urgently normally prefers to go to the local money-lender rather than wait indefinitely the sanction by the bank. This example is a pointer towards the fact that how lack of institutional support at the panchayat level is depriving the needy villagers their due share in the process of development.

Similarly, there are innumerable examples which indicate that the services to people, whether these be in primary education or health or veterinary services or drinking water, do not reach the target group due to weak institutions at the local levels, and the functionaries responsible for providing these services are not accountable to any institution at the gram panchayat / village level where it matters the most.

Besides, there are a number of statutory functions that are to be regulated by the local institutions. Money-lending, for example, is one such issue, which is widespread, that goes unabated in its repressive form and it robs people off the hard-earned money. Likewise, the list also includes other regulatory / community functions such as control of illicit liquor consumption, management of minor forest produce, local markets, water bodies and so on. All this will demand that there should be institutional framework for the regulation of these functions. To illustrate it more specifically, we can take the case of money-lending. How the money-lenders are charging higher interest, how the people are forced to part with their belongings or money as interest, can be best noticed and checked at the local levels. Under the present system of centralised or far away control system, supervision and check have proved to be quite ineffective, as there remains fear and hesitation among people to report at the higher level and so the incidents continue without being reported. Also, there is indifference in the functionaries at the higher level to attend to the problems of people in far away villages. As the things stand there is no viable mechanism to ensure the check on money-lending at the village level. It would be desirable, for regulatory functions, if the requisite institutional support (e.g. regulatory body at the block and gram panchayat levels) is provided to monitor and regulate the implementation of regulatory functions such as control over money-lending, consumption of liquor, etc.

Thus, in the backdrop of above discussion, the necessity of local institutions is strongly felt, which can be responsive to the needs of people at the village level and will be accountable to people for delivering results.

Cultural Factors hindering the Evolution of Institutions

The cultural factors have an important role in the functioning of local institutions and have strong bearing on their capacities to manage local development affairs (see Box 7.2). The cultural factors have been grouped into two categories: *first*, socio-economic and political factors; and second, the HRD factor. These are examined below:

First, socio-economic and political factors. If we examine critically, over a period of centuries and in the context of centralised command of the government since independence, one of the major weaknesses of panchayats (local institutions) has been of the tradition of control over people by rural elites (who may be handful in number). The historical roots of such a state of functioning is due to socio-economic and political factors. Among social factors, caste and status have played their role; economic factors in villages typically comprise of *jamindari* and money-lending system; and political factors mainly include, among others, system of centralised governance during colonial period.

Under the social scenario the functioning of local institutions greatly suffers due to lop-sided social-equilibrium. The low involvement of women or *dalits* in the development process is the reflection of this problem. As has been observed in most of the states, the gram sabhas have very less participation from these sections. There are instances where the local panchayats are in the hands of upper-caste men (directly in the capacity of chairpersons or indirectly through dummy candidates), who are not accountable to the community and often utilise local public services for their own benefits and sometimes as instruments of patronage (see tour

BOX 7.2

Vital Cultural Factors affecting the Panchayat Functioning

The functioning of panchayats is influenced by a large number of stakeholders such as elected members, social and political groups, village elites, development functionaries and people in the villages. Their priorities, aspirations and concerns vary from each other. And the cultural factors have influence on their attitudes, approach and commitment, which have bearing on socio-political system at village level:

- *Political will:* Political will is vital for giving direction to the course of public action. It would determine the psychological factors at the grassroots level. Political will is essential in determining the vital issues such as: how much should be decentralisation; what should be the way of achieving it; and stability and continuity of local institutions. Experiences have shown that the political will has guided the course of decentralisation in many states (e.g. in Kerala, Karnataka, MP or West Bengal). The political will is determined by the value system of a political party in power.
- *Political Culture:* Values such as tendency to dominate panchayat functioning by political elites, chairperson-centric approach, lack of appreciation for people's participation, affect the functioning of gram panchayats. Such values determine: how the decisions are taken by political parties, how parties value people's participation, how political groups or individuals value 'village development' vis-a-vis 'personal gains or ego'.
- *Administrative Culture:* The centralised way of decision-making and the inability to work with people, lack of appreciation for transparency and accountability, etc. affect the functioning of panchayats and delivery of services to people.
- *Cultural factors at the grassroots level:* Socio-political situation is considerably affected by cultural values[2], and inhibitions, due to mind-sets[3] for and inertia[4]. Such factors greatly influence the participation by women and marginalised groups in the development activities.
- *Inter-group Dynamics:* It is due to conflicts between representatives at higher levels and lower levels; inter-tier panchayat conflicts; inter-panchayats and departments conflicts; and group rivalries at grassroots level. To elaborate further, the representatives at higher levels (state and national levels) may not always be inclined to support the panchayats, which sends wrong signals at the grassroots level. Differences and distrust among three tiers of panchayats and between panchayats and

... *Contd.*

2 Lack of culture for discussion, tendency of dominating in the decision-making, discrimination based on caste, women should be in *purdah* (gender bias), inability to work with people, elites (upper caste people, landlords) have right to control panchayats.

3 Women are weak and cannot perform, cannot work with officials, women and members from marginalised groups (SCs / STs, etc.) cannot manage panchayats

4 Women, marginalised groups (SCs / STs), labourers or debtors hesitate to speak in the village open meeting.

.... *Contd.*

departments disturbs the harmonious functioning. Group rivalries (mainly on political account) within village, create enormous distrust among people and vitiate the atmosphere, and discourage people to participate in the gram sabha and local development.

reports of states in chapter four). In many cases, these elites have their own agenda of development (see crowding-out effect)[5], which may not favour the interest of the weaker sections and the empowerment of disadvantaged groups.

Under the economic perspective, the village rich men, including traders and money-lenders have major role in the utilisation of village property like forest land, village pond, community land and so on, or in the creation of new facilities and services for people. For example, the issues like where the school building is to be created, who should be the beneficiary for the rural development schemes, what should be the priority of development, how the village income should be utilised, are influenced by the interests of rich, and may not necessarily by the gram panchayats or gram sabhas. They may control the decisions directly or indirectly through the clutches of economic dominance by tilting public opinion in their favour. To be more specific, people depending on the money-lenders are hardly going to speak against their wishes, or poor farmers dependent on traders hesitate to articulate their problems collectively.

From the political point of view, the centralised form of decision-making has been consistently followed by the government since independence, which has been inherited from the colonial period. This is why, the institutions at the lower levels, especially at the gram panchayat level, have remained neglected. Though at the block level some steps have been made yet they have not been sufficient to address the problems in totality. Besides, at the district or sub-division level, reasonably good efforts have been made over a period of time to evolve institutions, but as these levels are too far from the villages so their effectiveness for dealing with a large number of people and their problems goes down drastically. Moreover, earlier institutional set-up dealing more with law and order and revenue related matters finds, itself anachronistic for handling the development programmes at the village levels which require approach of working with people rather than giving command. And, studies show that the present administrative set-up is unable to meet the new development paradigm of people's participation.

---

[5] Crowding out effect: With a focus on a few issues like construction of roads or repair of ponds, repair and maintenance, etc. that are normally raised, discussed and followed during the preparation and implementation of the GP action plan. The real issues like people's participation, improving the quality of education, availability of essential commodities get low priority, which affect poor and disadvantaged groups the most. Thus, too much of focus on construction activities that are mainly the concerns of elites (including upper caste influential people, contractors, money-lenders to further their interests) crowds out the other important development issues like primary education, health, agriculture, etc.

The political decisions in terms of community activities, selection of representative for a ward or village, identification of village needs and problems, to a very large extent, are still controlled by the centralised way of decision-making of the political parties. Also of significance is the role of political groups. There are instances, when these groups in a village do not leave any opportunity of taking upper hand in the decision-making through its sheer physical power, and thus putting people into submission. There are innumerable examples (as indicated by field studies in chapter four), which amply show that in many cases, the decisions in the gram sabhas are taken by the chairpersons of gram panchayats, while the views of people are ignored. Even the issues like where (location) a particular project will be taken up, who will execute the work, say, construction of road, who will be engaged for the labour works are decided by political groups and in many cases by the chairpersons of the panchayats. Moreover, validity of these decisions is not questioned and, if it is done that too in a few cases, no satisfactory action can be expected and no accountability of elected representatives is ensured.

Second, the HRD factor. The success of participatory way of functioning in the local institutions is greatly affected by low level of HRD. Basic education can help people to understand the functioning of the system, to deal with the government functionaries, to put forth their grievances, to be aware of their rights, to make their claims, to appreciate local problems, and to acquire knowledge and skills for enabling them to contribute in the local development process. Particularly in the context of decentralised planning, which is highly dependent on the ability of people at the local level, it will get support by the availability of expertise at the local level, if educated and well-informed people are present. For example, during gram sabha, educated people can better articulate local problems, participate in the plan discussion and contribute during implementation and monitoring of programmes. Above all, the good education will provide confidence to them to learn more and to raise questions in the meetings.

This hypothesis has been well-tested in Kerala and found to be exceptionally successful. The wide participation of people through training, coupled with their higher education level, has contributed a great deal in the decentralised participatory planning. The higher educational level has raised the level of institutional effectiveness, and has helped the local institutions distinctly in three ways: *first*, by improved participation in gram sabha. *Second*, by further acquiring knowledge and learning new skills for planning and implementation, and thus by contributing significantly in the planning, implementation, monitoring and supervision either through discussion and advice, or by making manual or monetary contribution. And *finally*, by improving the transparency of panchayat functioning and accountability of elected members to people. While, in other states, the common sight of silence of majority of people in the gram sabha and the inabilities of people to question the decisions of elected representatives are inhibiting the evolution of local institutions, which is a cause of serious concern.

In addition, there are instances of conflicts due to inter-personal behaviour arising out of personal-ego and political rivalries. Decisions in the gram sabha or panchayat meetings are also taken on such considerations. Personal prejudices or political leanings take precedence over rational or objective criteria. And the panchayats get divided over conflicting issues.

Finally, the aforementioned cultural factors, seriously undermine the functioning of local institutions and pose big challenge for the creation of democratically run public institutions at the local levels, and cannot be overlooked in the process of decentralisation.

Social Capital

Social capital refers to certain aspects of the social structure that affect relations among people. These include, in particular, the existence and traditions of co-operation, social networks, associations, and trust between people, as well as social and economic homogeneity of the population. In addition to human capital, the existing level of social capital in the society influences infrastructure delivery (Putman, 1993).

The civil society organisations that are based on collective action have a comparative advantage in the provision of common pool good-type infrastructure services (Ostrom 1990). Social capital affects primarily the effectiveness of delivery mechanisms that rely on collective action, particularly at the village level. The present socio-economic and political set-up, which is marked with disparities, does not add to social capital. Lack of social networks, lack of trust among various groups (including political), and disparities between rich and poor and among various castes affect cohesion in the society that undermines the participatory process of development.

How Development Policies affect the People and in turn the Process of Decentralisation

Policies are essential for setting the goals or objectives that are required to be achieved, while the strategies and programmes are drawn to translate policies into expected outcomes. The local institutions, through a process of decentralisation, are required to translate the programmes into outputs. Thus, in a way, the efficacy of local institutions to deliver will depend considerably on the existing policies and programmes. Under the given state of policy environment, how the decision-making at the panchayat level takes place is illustrated below:

Firstly, under the rural development programmes the main focus is more on wage employment. Under this, for instance, the present policy is so directed that panchayats have to take up the works pertaining to small works and that too mainly *kutcha* (digging of ponds, formation of road repair / maintenance) type, with a focus on achieving the target for wage employment. A careful examination reveals that in a year (in 1996-97) on an average in a village the employment generation programmes (JRY and EAS) were able to provide employment to less than 31 per cent of the BPL families under JRY and only 41 per cent under EAS, and that too only for 7.5 days in case of JRY and 11.4 days through EAS (i.e. employment for less than half a month) (Gupta, 2001). Moreover, the earned-wages are consumed as 'one-time consumption' and do not enable people to utilise wages for any productive gains in the absence of adequate infrastructural base and entrepreneurship (capabilities), and thus don't add future economic value for them (who continue to be engaged as labourers without any significant improvement in their future earning capacity). Moreover, at the macro-level, the wage employment is providing just 0.92 per cent of the total employment (Gupta, 2001), which is only miniscule, while funds of the order of Rs. four thousand cr. are spent every year.

Thus, it is clear from above that wage employment is not a sustainable solution for the employment problem. Moreover, there are instances which show that the same works on road formation or digging of ponds are repeated every four-five years (as *kutcha* works require treatment every year) for achieving the target of wages, while for such *kutcha* (or maintenance) type of works there is a need of people's contribution. Spending money on a repetitive basis is virtually a drain on precious resources, whereas the investment in the creation of productive assets like irrigation, plantation, agroforestry, in soil and water conservation; marketing infrastructure; and in human resources development can provide higher dividends in the short as well as long run. But such investment gets low priority. The productive assets cannot only help people to raise their income in future, for example, through agro-forestry or irrigation or wasteland development, but also in providing additional employment to farmers by double-crop in irrigated area, to landless people on wasteland, besides facilitating an efficient utilisation of natural resources. Similarly, the higher HRD will raise the capabilities of people to take advantage of existing economic opportunities and also to facilitate them to further explore for the new opportunities. These measures will promote sustainable development, while such an approach gets overlooked.

Secondly, thinly spread of funds: In the case of JGSY (earlier JRY programme), the funds given to gram panchayats are normally small (as the funds at Central level are divided among 2.25 lakhs GPs in the country), which vary from Rs. 10,000 to Rs. 50,000, and due to this the panchayats are not able to take up projects (e.g. water harvesting structure, small bridge for fair weather road, etc.) that require large funds but are of importance for villages. Besides, tendency by panchayat members to have works in each ward leads to further division of funds (which are small) given to GPs.

Thus, against the backdrop of above, it needs to be emphasised that present policy, under which the small funds are made available to panchayats, does not encourage investment in productive assets due to a variety of reasons such as focus on wage employment, strict guidelines and lack of appreciation for infrastructural and productive assets. Under the programme of JRY (now JGSY) about Rs 35,000 crores (till March, 2002) have been spent since 1989, and out of which about 60 per cent (in some gram panchayats it may be as high as 75 per cent) i.e. Rs. 21,000 crores are on activities like repair, maintenance, *kutcha* work (including repetitive works), etc., which in a way is very highly unproductive investment of such a big magnitude. Similarly, the programmes of other departments are thinly spread in too many areas and items, which lead to creation of some physical assets (like roads, schools), or demonstrations or field trials (e.g. under agriculture and allied activities), or providing some services (like medicines, essential commodities, etc.) at so many places, with very little technical and economic viability. Thus funds are sub-optimally allocated resulting into underutilisation, and also wastage due to non-utilisation of assets (e.g. tube wells with non-potable water or health centres without equipments, water and electricity, are found non-functional in many villages for want of funds. These existing assets remain unutilised while the fresh funds are spent for creating assets in other places) in a large number of cases.

Thirdly, there is an issue of comprehensive approach of development[6]. More often, the development programmes are designed to meet a particular problem[7], and with a set of guidelines which are required to be adhered to. Also, for all practical purposes, there is little linkages among various programmes. It leads to compartmentalised approach of each programme. Coupled with this, at the planning stage (at the village level) there is a very myopic view of development — with a thrust on construction works[8 & 9]. If we look carefully the action plan of any gram panchayat (also of block and district panchayats), it reveals that the majority of works pertains to construction activities, and the following observations can be discerned:

- if school building is constructed, how the quality of education should improve is not attended to;
- if drainage is constructed, how it should be maintained is not taken into account;
- if the same road is constructed repeatedly every four-five years, why the efforts for making the *pucca* road are not made;
- if the well is constructed which has water that is not potable, why the further steps are not taken to improve the quality of water;
- if health centre is constructed, why it does not have medicines or basic equipments for testing, and so on.

Comprehensive Approach : How comprehensive approach in development is missing is explained by some cases as under:

[6] Comprehensive approach is required for attending to all the items in a particular sector. For example, for health sector, all the items viz., infrastructure, placement and training of health workers, availability of medicines, health centres with beds, equipments, etc. need to be placed in the form of a package in order to address the health sector comprehensively.

As regards the integrated development, the inter-sectoral linkages are needed wherein the efforts and activities of all the sectors viz., education, health, drinking water, agriculture, irrigation, marketing, etc. are to be integrated for holistic development of a village.

With regard to the implementation at the village level, the comprehensive approach will also include planning, programme design, project formulation and management of implementation.

[7] There are several programmes launched by a number of departments. These programmes have specific guidelines and address only their sectoral objectives or that of a particular activity, without having inter-sectoral linkages. Such an approach leads to compartmentalisation of programmes and does not serve much purpose as regards the integrated development.

[8] The development has been assumed to be synonymous with the 'construction work', which in fact is only a part of the whole development work. Even in the watershed development projects, the major portion (say, 80%) of the project cost is spent on construction activities like embankments, water harvesting structure (WHS), etc., while other items like cropping pattern, agroforestry, soil and water management by farmers, fodder and cattle management, etc. do not find adequate attention at the planning and implementation level. Often, the decisions for such projects are taken by a few, which may include contractors or elites, who may want to pursue their own interests.

First, let us take the case of primary education, which is very important in the context of decentralisation. Presently, the panchayats are keen to take up the works of construction of school buildings. Here, it should be emphasised that just mere creation of a school building is not enough. How is the quality of teaching? How would the dropout in the schools be checked? How is the environment of teaching? Such are the questions that are concerned with the positive aspect of development are not attended to by the panchayats. The focus of attention remains on the regulatory aspect that is the absenteeism of teacher, which is vital but not the end for the management of primary education. In order to initiate the positive action for bringing certain corrections in primary education, we need to look at policy aspect and programme design. It may call for redefining the policies, which can facilitate the channelisation of funds in attending to the fundamental requirements (like teaching-aids, teachers training, good learning environment, etc.) for improving school education, and for improving the capabilities of panchayats for designing programmes as per local needs. It may also require for bringing attitudinal changes (through educational and training programmes) in the functionaries of departments and elected members for understanding the development concepts and for managing comprehensively the affairs of panchayats. And only then will the panchayats be able to provide good primary education to people.

Similar instances can be found in other areas as well. For example, the health centres are run without basic equipments; veterinary centres normally do not have adequate facilities for artificial insemination or medicines. And it is not to suggest that the construction works are not desired, but what is important is to look for important issues of comprehensive development in a particular sector for ensuring optimal use of resources.

Second, there are certain other areas where critical inputs remain missing, which affect the economic viability[9]. For instance, marketing of agricultural produce suffers due to poor infrastructural support, likewise under scarce water areas (for irrigation) there is a possibility of adopting water conservation techniques for efficient water management or of applying technologically advanced equipments for raising water use efficiency (WUE), but these are not available to people. Similarly, we may take the case of loan assistance given under Swarnjayanti Gram Swarjaya Yojana (SGSY). It is found that in this programme the support for training, technology and marketing is not available at the village level but the loan is given to a number of beneficiaries, which normally results into underutilisation of assets. And such examples are in plenty, the funds are utilised for some or the other activities without attending to these very inputs.

---

[9] It is often noticed that the mindset among elected members, field officers and staff is to choose works of construction activities. It is precisely for various reasons such as *first*, cultural factors like i. preference among the panchayat members and field functionaries for construction activities, as they feel that these are easy to identify, and also these will give visible impact, ii. in some other cases, decision-making is controlled by elites who have interest in construction works (see note 8), and iii. the target-oriented approach which encourages construction works, as targets can be easily achieved by giving works to contractors. *Second*, policy and programme design factor - which focuses mainly on employment generation. And, *third*, knowledge factor - due to low level of knowledge the functionaries are not able to visualise that investment in other areas can be productively utilised (see note 10).

Third, if we examine from the management point of view, another point of importance has been that the construction activities give more visibility[10], whereas improving the performance of school in terms of quality of teaching, though may be crucial, is less visible, at least in the short term, but may require more efforts in the form of hard work and persuasion over a long time, but is not appreciated as one of the important components of development. Likewise, there may be some no-cost inputs like motivating parents to send children to school, persuasive management skills and the need to work with people for timely immunisation of children, that do not form the part of the discussion for the plan preparation at the panchayat level. Similarly, an efficient management of public distribution system (PDS) may help save time for the people (which may be in some cases half a day thus resulting into loss of wages, which offsets the gains made through lower prices of essential commodities) for the people to purchase commodities. Similar examples can be sighted for non-availability of agricultural inputs and the medicines, at a point and in right time. But these do not find priority with the panchayats and departments. These are the basic services that matter a lot to poor but are given less attention, while the rich are able to manage the services due to their higher resources.

Fourth, there is a problem of lack of convergence of resources and services. For example, various programmes under agriculture, rural employment, irrigation, agro-industries run in isolation of each other resulting into resource-mismatch, underutilisation of created assets and finally leading to wasteful expenditure in a large number of cases. It is due to proliferation of various departments with so many programmes and schemes (without inter-linkages) dedicated to particular target groups, and also partially due to thinly spread of funds. It leads to a problem of integration of programmes at planning and implementation stages. The dimension of this problem assumes high significance from the fact that it is estimated (MORD, 2001a) that the funds allocated to states and districts under twenty-nine subjects are Rs. 31,575 cr. and Rs. 40,818 cr. under centrally sponsored programmes and the schemes of state plan outlay respectively. Their total comes to Rs. 72,393, which is a very substantial sum (see appendices 2 and 3). Similarly, under MPLADP and MLALADP, funds worth Rs. 2,500 cr. are earmarked in a year. While panchayats have little control over their allocations for the purpose of resource-matching at the village level. All these programmes are planned and run practically independent of one another without inter-sectoral linkages, and integrative nature of development needs are not taken into account. As such, funds are allocated without addressing the issue of 'optimal utilisation of resources'. And, unless policy changes are made in the process of planning and implementation of programmes, such huge funds are not going to make much improvement in the socio-economic life of villages, which has been a case presently.

Finally with this kind of development approach, neither are people able to improve their quality of life nor are they able to improve their income any significantly. And low level of

[10] The investment under irrigation (minor or medium or lift or well), agriculture and allied activities, agro-forestry, plantations or soil conservation measures are more productive and useful (but require more efforts in terms of planning and implementation) for people in the long run than programmes with mere emphasis on wage-oriented works like digging of ponds or *kutcha* roads formation, which are presently norms for the development activities at the panchayat level.

purchasing power is very much noticeable among people and is a major cause of depression in the village economy.

> 'The dimension of this problem assumes high significance from the fact that it is estimated (MORD, 2001a) that the funds allocated to states and districts under twenty-nine subjects are Rs. 31,575 cr. and Rs 40,818 cr. under centrally sponsored programmes and the schemes of state plan outlay respectively. And this total comes to Rs. 72,393, which is a very substantial sum (see appendices 2 and 3). Similarly, under MPLADP and MLALADP, funds worth Rs. 2,500 cr. are earmarked in a year. While panchayats have little control for their allocations for the purpose of resource-matching at the village level. All these programmes are planned and run practically independent of one another without inter-sectoral linkages, and integrative nature of development needs are not taken into account. As such, funds are allocated without addressing the issue of 'optimal utilisation of resources'. And, unless policy changes are made in the process of planning and implementation of programmes, such huge funds are not going to make much improvement in the socio-economic life of villages, which has been a case presently.'

All the above indicate how policies are going to affect the decision-making of panchayats and the implementation of programmes. It is quite evident that the policies are skewed and favour less the poor and disadvantageous groups. Also, there is incongruity between policies and development needs at the local levels. And the process of decentralisation can be of little aid to panchayats for meeting the local needs, unless some policy-specific corrections are introduced.

Policy and Programme Design—Need of Macro-Micro Convergence

There are three issues in this context. *First* pertains to existing policies and programmes. Since 1993, after Constitution Amendment Act, the process of decentralisation has been underway. And the states have taken measures to legislate panchayat Acts. Under the new dispensation the panchayats have been established at all the three tiers in almost all the states in the country and the elections have been conducted. Certain measures have been taken by the states to transfer functions and devolve funds upon panchayats. The panchayats are expected to deliver goods to people, but the abilities of panchayats to do so depend, to a very large extent, on the existing development policies and programmes of the Centre and states. For instance, the issues like whether the programme will give priority to infrastructure development or wage employment, whether the human resources development will be attended to on a priority basis, whether the diversification of agriculture will be undertaken and the marketing support to farmers will be provided, what would be measures for natural resources management and so on are determined by the Centre and states. So, in a way, among other factors, the efficacy of panchayats to deliver will be determined by — how the Centre and states address the issue of development policies and programmes.

Second is looking from the point of view of the need of policy direction keeping in view the dimension of national as well as state priorities. And for meeting such priority areas, certain programmes may be necessary at the national as well as state level in order to provide policy direction and funds. For instance, oilseeds and pulses development becomes important in order to meet the domestic (national) requirements; similarly immunisation and family planning, social welfare, providing essential commodities in the remote and backward areas are other crucial areas, where the intervention of state is important.

Third is about the considerations that are required to be taken while designing the policies and programmes. The devolution of funds is one aspect, and setting 'right' policies and formulating programmes to have integrated development are equally important. It would require that at the national and state levels, policies need to be framed, which would provide broad direction within which the panchayats should formulate the programmes to achieve objectives. Policies should be such which reflect the pressing needs of the people at the grassroots level and the programme design should be left to panchayats. In case the programmes are to be formulated at the national or state level, it should provide broad guidelines so that there is enough scope for the panchayats to design schemes / projects as per the local conditions, and there should not be any problem at the planning and implementation level. Also, national or state level programmes should take into consideration the existing other programmes, possibility of tie-up with other programmes and the available delivery mechanism, so that there is backward and forward linkages, as also convergence of resources and services.

Besides, for enabling the panchayats to undertake the task of planning, programme design for integrated development, the capabilities of panchayat members and development functionaries need to be built up through capacity building programmes. Such capabilities are required in all the sectors. For instance, under the policy of free and compulsory primary education, the panchayats would be required to formulate the programmes to ensure that the children get quality education at the village level. Similarly, under the policy of self-employment, panchayats should be able to draw programmes and design the schemes suited to local conditions.

Concluding Remarks

The above analysis (of HRD, institution building and policies) brings to the fore how the decisions of the panchayats at the grassroots level are influenced by various factors. Quite a few decisions are affected by cultural factors such as interest of a particular group, disregarding the interest of weaker sections; for example, the priority given to construction activities in the gram panchayat plan (by contractors as they are normally elites in the village settings, who wield considerable influence over the decision-making) over issues of education, health, drinking water, etc., which matter more for the poor in their day to day life. Some are institutional-centric, such as quality and timely availability of basic services to people, for example, the smooth functioning of village schools or the timely availability of essential commodities, which will determine the quality of services and require institutional support, are not attended to during the plan formulation stage by the panchayats and departments. And others are policy specifics; for instance, emphasis on wage employment, lack of emphasis on integrated development in the centrally sponsored programmes (compartmentalised approach), thinly spread of funds; such policies result into more focus of gram panchayats on narrow development activities and lack of convergence of resources.

Why the Process of Decentralisation has not been Successful: Fundamental Issues : In the light of discussions in the aforementioned sections, it is evident that the process of decentralisation has not been successful in achieving the desired objective of meeting the aspirations of people. The specific issues are summed up below:

HRD Specific

First, the representative democracy has been narrow at the village level — with a restricted scope for the people to participate in the election process and with a very limited concern for development (the basic issues like education, health, agriculture, etc. are overlooked).
Second, the participation of people in the process of development has been elusive.

Institutional Specific

Third, weak institutional systems.
Fourth, the transparency in the panchayat functioning is not observed.
Fifth, the poor capacities of panchayats to deliver.
Sixth, accountability of elected members to people has not made its presence.

Policy Specific

Finally, narrow and compartmentalised approach of development — with a focus on limited or narrow issue of development without addressing the problem in totality; and with the approach of specific programmes by departments and rule-based strict guidelines without inter-sectoral linkages. The policies lack comprehensive and integrated development approach and restrict the autonomy of panchayats to plan as per their local needs, and in the present state of decentralisation the local bodies are able to do little.

7.4 Panchayati Raj and Governance

▸ *Why Governance*

The question of governance has been of prime importance as without good governance — in the absence of rule of law, administrative consistency, performance matching efficient delivery mechanism, and responsive, transparent and accountable institutions — no amount of funding or statutes will be able to provide the desired direction for the village development. Based on the findings from the field study (see chapter four), the issue of governance needs to be looked at from the following perspective:

- The frequency and the degree of inappropriateness of functioning are so much that there appears to be blurring of line between what is appropriate and what is not. People seem to have accepted wrong doings as a part of life and stopped talking of such, let alone demanding actions against them. In certain cases these become so glaring that the question of governance becomes very critical.
- In the context of wide disparities — which could be social or economic or political — that have the effect of depriving the large section of society.
- In the context of decentralisation, governance becomes more crucial as it will put decision-makers (at the grassroots level) on test to handle successfully development issues, which are presently entrenched with prejudices and marked with a variety of conflicting interests.

Promoting governance is not just the ability of the institutions to deliver but also to strengthen the village society. The healthy and vibrant society can contribute a great deal for the economic development.

How to Judge Good Governance

Enhancing governance should be the ultimate goal of decentralisation that will instil confidence in people about the panchayati raj system. In the context of present state of functioning of panchayats, the good governance will be determined by:

- When the people have access to information and their grievances are attended to by the local institutions;
- When people have access to basic services in their gram panchayat area;
- When the people have opportunities for social, political and economic activities in the village; and
- When the local institutions can meet unforeseen situations and instil confidence in people.

Challenges for Governance

The observations from the field visits have shown that the panchayats at the grassroots level are faced with insurmountable task of addressing the problem of governance. The experiences bring to the fore the need of addressing the challenges faced by the panchayats to meet the desired standards of governance. And in this process state has vital role to play, so that the right kind of system of governance is established at the grassroots level. In the context of decentralisation, five fundamental challenges need attention.

- The *first* is the existing large social, economic and political disparities (see section 7.2), which are depriving people of certain sections from participating in local development and availing the advantages thereof. And how the policy interventions are to be introduced to bring equalities is of prime importance.
- The *second* is the low level of HRD, which has the effect of reducing opportunities for illiterates, which constitute a significant number at the village level. It is the single biggest factor in reducing the meaningful people's participation. It requires to be addressed through a concerted educational programme.
- The *third* is the weak institutions. The existing state of panchayats and of delivery system makes it difficult for them to deliver basic services to people. Also, they are not able to manage and keep pace with the increasing and complex forms of emerging socio-economic problems of varying scales at various levels. The panchayats need to be strengthened with administrative, infrastructural, manpower and logistics support, along with improved transparency, legal framework and accountability. Along with this, the efforts are required for improving the efficiency of delivery system. The administrative reform is an essential element of capacity building of institutions, and how it can be addressed is a challenge. The reform process should focus on responsiveness, efficiency, quality of services, transparency and accountability.
- The *fourth* is the socio-cultural and political values. There are certain values such as 'tendency to dominate others and of central-decision making', 'gender and caste biases', 'exerting political supremacy at the cost of development', that have detrimental affect on the process of decentralisation and keep a large section in the villages at the periphery of development. These deep-rooted attitudes, which are prevalent since centuries, cannot be merely addressed by statutes, though necessary. Sensitisation training programmes are required to break down the attitudes and bringing desired attitudinal changes. And the panchayat members and functionaries, especially the political leadership at each level needs to undergo such process of sensitisation.
- The *fifth* is the role of other village level institutions. How the local level institutions like CBOs, NGOs, cooperatives should be associated with panchayats is a big challenge. These organisations need to be recognised, supported and provided with enabling environment so that they can provide support and inputs to panchayats.

▸ *Governance and other Vital Issues*

- *Governance and People's Participation:* People's participation is going to hold key in providing good governance at the local level. The governance cannot be imposed, rather it needs to be evolved through a participative process, and ultimately good governance should be accomplished.
- *Governance and Capacity of Institutions:* The capacity of the panchayats is going to have impact on their abilities to deliver and sustain it in future. And in order to ensure

that people get basic services and in turn good governance at the village level, the capacity building programme for panchayats assumes high significance.

- *Governance and Natural Resources Management:* Over exploitation of forest and vegetative cover, unscientific practices and use of inputs for crop production have led to scarcity of fuel and fodder, loss of soil cover, loss of crop productivity in large parts of the country. Even in several cases, it has resulted into the state of drought, depletion of water table, and loss of soil fertility that is rendering land unfit for cultivation. And all this is affecting the rural economy considerably. It requires that the natural resources need to be managed efficiently. In this endeavour, good governance is going to add to better management of natural resources (as its success largely depends upon people's participation, which can be provided by good governance).
- *Governance and Values:* The value system has its impact on the way the people think and respond, and the way the institutions function and the decisions are taken. Or in a way, the prevailing values in the panchayat system will affect the output of panchayats. Therefore, it becomes crucial to promote the right set of value system that will enhance participatory approach, responsiveness for people's problems, transparency and accountability.
- *Governance and Law and Order:* The maintenance of law and order is crucial for instilling confidence in the people that the civil life is protected, that the law will prevail over wrongs, and that there will be peace. Though this particular issue is not the subject matter of panchayats, however, there should be coordination mechanism between panchayats on the one hand and police administration on the other, and the state needs to ensure a good environment of law and order.
- *Governance and Globalisation:* Globalisation is bringing new challenges for the economy at all the levels whether it is national or state or village. It has touched sectors ranging from agriculture to communication to technology to trade. At the village level, there are certain issues particularly concerning the agriculture and allied activities that are affecting the farmers (for example for the crops like coffee, rubber in Kerala; apple in Himachal Pradesh) and food processing industries (in the areas of dairy), which have direct impact on rural economy. Therefore, the panchayats will have to address these issues in the emerging globalised economy, which is directly impinging on the life of people in several parts of the country and is going to do so in many other parts in near future. Here, the state will have to provide necessary support to panchayats and to find balance between taking the advantage of globalisation and providing secured and stable socio-economic environment, also social security to the most vulnerable group.
- *Governance and Role of State:* The state has vital role in ensuring good governance. Though, under decentralisation, the management of local affairs is to be undertaken by panchayats, but the state has to provide requisite support for institution building and legal framework through policy and programme interventions.

▸ *Prerequisites for Good Governance*

In the backdrop of above discussions, for the good governance at the grassroots level, the following are pre-requisites, or, good governance will be evolved when we can achieve as given under:

- First, good capacity of local institutions to deliver;
- Second, higher level of HRD for meaningful participation;
- Third, sound policies and programmes for providing opportunities to people;
- Fourth, appropriate legal framework;
- Fifth, transparency in the panchayat functioning;
- Sixth, accountability of elected members to people; and
- Finally, proper law and order.

▸ *Specific Measures to enhance the Level of Governance*

In the context of above, the initiatives that need to be taken for enhancing governance at the grassroots level are:

- Setting the right vision for the role of panchayats.
- Enhancing HRD level — studies have shown that the improved education is a primemover in bridging the gap between the haves and the have-nots, or the rich and the poor.
- Good governance demands participation of all the people at every stage of development. For this, a dedicated educational programme with the required funds needs to be launched and the crucial areas to be addressed are:

  Sensitisation about — democratic values, sensitivity for the concerns of the poor and the weaker sections, appreciation for efficiency and quality of works, sense of belongingness for the village properties and to maintain and protect them, and respect for institutional norms. Also, there is a need for having code of conduct for social behaviour for respecting these values and bringing cultural sensitivity.
- Improving access to economic opportunities and reducing disparities — through appropriate development policy interventions.
- Institutional reforms — through simplification of procedure, improved transparency in the functioning, enhancing the functional capabilities of personnel, responsiveness towards people's grievances, system of accountability and so on.

▸ *What Good Governance will lead to*

Good governance is not an end, rather it is going to lead the virtuous cycle of participation, opportunities, improved democratic values, prosperity and sustainability of the process of development. And in nutshell, the following are going to be distinct outcomes of good governance:

- Improved opportunities;
- Efficient use of resources;

- Promoting democratic values;
- Sustainability.

7.5 Reform Agenda: Primacy of Fundamentals

In the backdrop of analysis about the present status of decentralisation, it is amply clear that the local (panchayat) institutions are not in a position to address the development needs and to meet the aspirations of people. It has been assumed that panchayat Acts, though vital, would automatically lead to decentralisation of development system. The findings in chapter five have categorically brought out that the focus has remained on the point that the panchayats will look after all the interest of villages, once they are constituted, while the empowerment of people and the capacity building of panchayats in real sense of terms have been neglected. In the last decade, conducting elections appears to be the only priority. Rather the focus should have been on improving capabilities of people and providing opportunities to them so that they can participate and contribute in the village development. The role of the panchayats should have been more of managing basic services and facilitating people for availing opportunities.

Lessons may be drawn from: how Kerala model has succeeded in the process of decentralisation. In all the states, except in Kerala, in spite of the Act, what have not been seriously attempted are: *first*, educational and awareness programmes for strengthening the people's participation; *second*, the necessity of establishing the transparency and accountability system; and *third*, the importance of institution building.

What Decentralisation should result into

In the backdrop of above, as illustrated by Fig. 7.3, good governance should be taken as the mission indicator for the success of the decentralisation, and it should aim at achieving the following fundamentals:

From the People's Perspective: Empowering People
- Opportunities for individuals; and
- Making basic services available to people.

From the Institutional Perspective: Panchayats as Units of Development
- Institution building at the panchayat level at the three tiers.

● ***From the People's Perspective***

▸ ***Opportunities for Individuals***

Creating opportunities for people should be taken as a key objective of the panchayati raj system. The opportunities are required in the political, social and economic areas, as given under (see table 7.1):

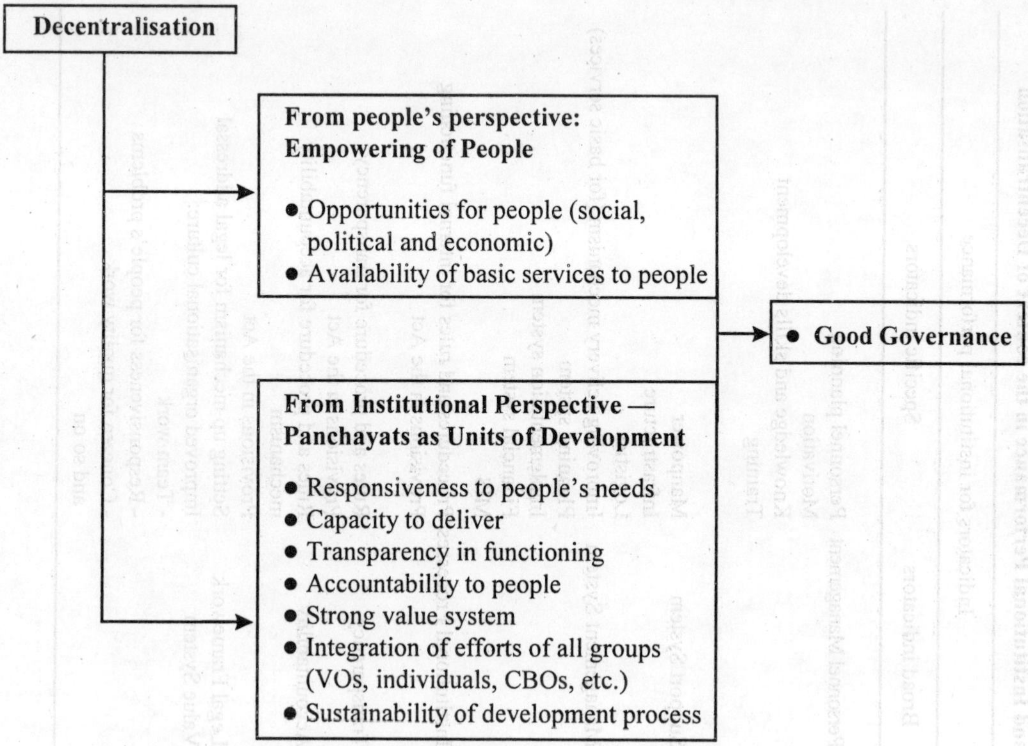

Fig. 7.3: **What Decentralisation should result into**

Political Opportunities

- Freedom to express views and form groups especially by marginalised groups;
- Equal opportunities for all in the elections;
- Free and fair elections;
- Participation in the village development (see table 7.2 for quality of participation).

Social Opportunities (Social Capital Formation)

- Access to social groups;
- Access to village meetings;
- Access to primary education;
- Access to health;
- Access to drinking water;

  and so on.

Economic Opportunities

- Skills development;
- Entrpreneurship;
- Access to economic information;

TABLE 7.1: **Indicators for Assessing Opportunities to People and Institutional Performance in the context of Decentralisation**

S.N.	Opportunities to people		Indicators for institutional performance	
	Broad indicators	**Specific indicators**	**Broad indicators**	**Specific indicators**
•	Political	Freedom to express views and form groups Equal opportunities for all in the elections Free and fair electoral process Participation in the village development	• Personnel Management	Personnel planning Motivation Knowledge and skills development Training
•	Social	Access to social groups Access to village meetings Access to primary education Access to health Access to drinking water	• Support System • Management System	Manpower Infrastructure Logistics Improving delivery mechanism (for basic services) Planning system Implementation system Financial system MIS
•	Economic	Skills development Entrepreneurship Access to economic information Access to infrastructure Access to income raising activities Access to marketing infrastructure	• Institutional Processes • Transparency • Accountability • Legal Framework • Value System	Procedures and rules for internal functioning Provisions in the Act Rules and procedure for transparency Provisions in the Act Rules and procedure for accountability mechanism Provisions in the Act Setting up mechanism for legal addressal Improved organisational culture: - Team work - Responsiveness for people's problems - Concern for quality work and so on

TABLE 7.2: **Indicators for Assessing the Quality of Participation**

S.N.	Indicators
First	Attendance in gram sabha
Second	Raising of development issues in the gram sabha
Third	Raising the problems of weaker sections
Fourth	Participation in planning process
Fifth	Participation in implementation process
Sixth	Participation in social audit and raising objections
Seventh	Registering complaints for non-functioning of utilities
Eighth	Participating in identifying solutions and contributing in the running of utilities
Ninth	Raising of public issues of importance
Tenth	Contribution in kind or money, or by *shramdan*

- Access to infrastructure;
- Access to income raising activities;
- Access to marketing infrastructure; and so on.

▶ *Need for Providing Basic Services to People*

In the context of decentralisation, providing basic services to people at the village level assumes high significance. And there cannot be two opinions about it. What constitute the basic services in the present context of socio-economic scenario in the rural areas are the availability of inputs and services under primary education, health, drinking water, social welfare in the social sector; and public distribution system, irrigation and agriculture in the economic sector, to name a few prominent ones.

• *From the Institutional Perspective*

The timely and efficient availability of basic services will demand setting up of credible institutions at local levels. It will require that the panchayats should function as 'units of development'. Rightly so, efforts are needed for improving the capacities of panchayats to deliver, which should be responsive to the needs of people, and for establishing sound transparency, accountability and value system (see indicators suggested in table 7.1 and refer tables 6.19 and 6.20). Improving delivery mechanism for various services needs urgent attention. Also, panchayats should try to integrate the efforts of all groups (VOs, individuals, CBOs, etc.) for creating synergies at the village level. And the panchayats should provide sustainability to the process of development.

Successful Conditions for Decentralisation

Based on the field study and the examination of various issues related to decentralisation, it can now be logically concluded as to what will constitute the successful conditions for decentralisation. And the reform process should facilitate the following :

- Security and peace to people especially during elections;
- Secured status for local bodies;
- Empowerment of people: Protecting the interests of weaker sections, improving individual's capabilities, and scope for opportunities to people (especially marginalised groups) for participation (in social, economic and political spheres) and utilising resources;
- Political will for providing autonomy to panchayats; and
- Improving capabilities of PR members and development functionaries to enable them to handle the development task of panchayats.

Reform Agenda

The past decade has witnessed some progress in the process of decentralisation, and yet where (giving opportunities to people and institution building) it mattered the most the achievements appear to have been quite dismal. If we draw comparison of the present pattern of functioning of panchayats (after the 73rd Amendment Act) with that of in the olden times and also before and after the independence (till 1993), similar observations are made. It is evident that functioning is and has been marked with influence of caste and class, control of elites over the decision-making, lack or almost no involvement of people in the decision-making, poor capacity of panchayats to deliver, lack of focus on development issues, poor financial resources and lack of transparency as well as accountability. In specific terms, before independence, the panchayats basically catered to the interests of elites; and after independence, emphasis has been more on elections, control and power, and lesser concern for development and institution building. And the same scenario is observed with varying degrees even after the new Amendment Act.

In the last five decades, the committees that were constituted to study the state of panchayats and to recommend measures (see chapter two) for strengthening panchayats also placed more focus on structure and regulatory aspect[11] (mainly issues concerning 'negative influence') such as conducting elections, reservations, and powers and control, while there has been a lack of clarity and thrust on issues of 'positive influence' like empowerment of people especially of marginalised groups through educational programmes, and improving the capacity of panchayats to deliver the basic services in the operational terms. Such approach, since independence till 73rd Constitution Amendment Act, has led to the evolution of panchayati raj under 'negative influence', and the measures initiated have proved to be too feeble to sustain in an atmosphere of stark socio-politico-economic disparities and institutional weaknesses. It has resulted into skewed focus with a definite tilt towards powers and control

[11] The amendment Act has provided structure to panchayati raj through creation of three tiers, constitution of gram sabha, conduct of elections and reservation of seats; and regulatory authorities like SEC and SFC.

than development in the panchayat Acts, as also in the panchayat functioning at the grassroots level.

If we examine carefully, what has lacked, though envisaged but not given proper focus, in the evolution of decentralisation process in India is: *first*, setting right the socio-political settings at the village level, which would provide equal opportunities to all; *second*, to make available the basic services to people at the panchayat level; *third*, to provide opportunities to people for socio-economic development; and *fourth*, strengthening of the local institutions. Such outcomes have not been clearly spelt-out in the reports of committees or panchayat Acts. Perhaps, it has been assumed that PR institutions, once set up, would lead to such a state. In a way, it has remained as a wishful thinking, but it has lacked the action needed for strengthening PRIs. The field studies indicate that in practice, the functioning of PR system revolves around statutory functions, and is still rooted in the historical tradition of central decision-making and control[12] by a few individuals than on the developmental and welfare role of the local institutions. It is the case in point that in terms of fundamentals of decentralisation, the present form of PR system even after Constitution Amendment Act is more or less an extension of previous system (see chapter five).

State of Vacuum: Absence of Addressal of Vital Issues

In the absence of institutions that can deliver at the local levels, people find that neither are their problems attended to nor is there possibility of addressing their basic socio-economic needs like primary education, health services, drinking water, etc. In the present set-up, the elections have become virtually the sole basis of the constitution of panchayats and the arbiter of their performance, which is not able to capture the vital issues that concern the people. Moreover, in the election process, the focus on winning the elections makes candidates to win elections somehow rather than concentrate on the issues of development, while people are more keen about development and absence of it is driving people to fringes. And even after winning the elections, the energies of the elected members are consumed more on making balances between different groups or protecting their positions rather than concentrating on development. As such there is very little attention given for addressing vital issues concerning people. For example: what about creating an environment for people to participate in the socio-economic development? What about making opportunities available to people? What about the addressal of important issues of development for a village? What about making basic services available to people? These issues, which matter for the people the most, are relegated to lower level of priority. Such a process of decentralisation is leading to a state of vacuum at the village level

[12] It is observed during field visits that invariably the panchayat members and elites are more concerned about the control over funds and control over departments. Often the panchayat members would express, 'Panchayats should control funds and they should be deciding the allocation for various projects'. But there is inadequate perspective as to how the funds should be utilised, how the people should be involved in development process, how the transparency and accountability should be observed and so on. It appears that the control is assumed to be an end in itself. They are not able to look beyond the control and regulation, as to how they can attend to local development.

for a large majority of people. And in fact, there are visible signs of alienation from the political and functional process at the village level and the existing measures under the Act are not sufficient to change such trend, to give voice to people and to make panchayats to address the needs of the people.

Action Needed

The upshot of above discussion categorically reflects that the present form of panchayat system is not able to meet the aspirations of people and a vast majority of people is marginalised in the process of functioning of panchayats. Here the important point remains as to how people should be meaningfully involved in the process of decentralisation so that they can contribute effectively, and also how their basic needs are met by the panchayats. They require to be given an environment that will be conducive for participation. It will require that the individuals must get opportunities in all the political, social and economic areas in the real sense of terms, not just merely by statutes but also by positive interventions and institutional support. If people have to be at the centre of the development and the local institutions should have the capacity to deliver, the social, political, institutional and policy reforms are very much needed.

Making critical assessment of the Amendment Act, Dreze and Sen (1995) have reflected though legislations are vital, but their actual success depends a great deal on other types of positive interventions. Further, they have stressed that the mandatory provisions are necessary, but it would be naive to expect too much, unless the measures for 'positive influence' such as improving capabilities and institutional support at the panchayat level are also taken. Presently, most measures like elections, giving some powers and functions under decentralisation have concentrated on short-term objectives of constituting panchayats. More emphasis must be put on longer-term issues like environment of equal opportunities, improving institutional capacity, if sustained improvement is to take place. The 'underlying need of the longer term approach' is the recognition that shorter-term measures must be supported by reforms.

Initiating Reforms

In the backdrop of underlying importance of primacy of fundamentals, as discussed in the beginning of this section, we need to bring paradigm shift in our approach of decentralisation and bring focus on making 'panchayats as units of development', ensuring 'good governance'. It will require bringing fundamental shift in socio-political life at the grassroots level, in mind-sets at the decision-making level, in policies, and in institutional approach. More specifically, issues such as how people have access to socio-political groups; how is the approach of the decision-makers for the addressal of problems i.e. the issues of responsiveness, transparency and accountability; how the policies are contributing towards improvement in quality of life, in bridging gaps or reducing disparities; and how institutions are able to attend to the people's basic problems and deliver services, are going to be vital in this process. In a way, it involves the whole gamut of issues and each one of them needs to be diagnosed and meaningfully addressed. It calls for initiating reforms, and the process should begin at the socio-political level. These reforms need to be underpinned by HRD, institution building and development policies.

Social and Political Reforms

Reform process must begin from the civil society. It must address the fundamental issue of disparity emanating mainly from caste, which is leading to marginalisation of socially disadvantaged groups. It calls for providing them enhanced space for socio-political activities. In this direction, attempts have been made to correct the imbalance by way of legislations (through reservation). But their actual success depends a great deal on other interventions. It requires attitudinal changes, breaking the deep-rooted biases based on caste, and having the campaign for improving literacy, for enhancing awareness among weaker sections about their rights, role and responsibilities, and for encouraging organisations that would take initiatives for reducing social inequalities and enhancing the socio-political access. There is a need of bringing new philosophy in social life that should be antithetical to higher archical system of caste. And a fresh thinking is needed that should recognise and respect human values.

From the political point of view, issue of equal opportunities to people, especially the weaker sections, to participate in political process assumes high importance. It will require the following political reforms:

First, the panchayats should be the institutions of development, rather than mere political entity (which is so perceived). They should be seen as units that will be in a position to provide basic services to people. These institutions should be developed on the underlying importance of development, with minimal political considerations. These should not be viewed by the political parties as a means of expanding their rank and files (though a difficult proposition, but highly desirable). Here, political parties will have to evolve consensus and give panchayats the role and status of people-centred-development units. *Second*, elections on non-party lines for panchayat elections: development requires the support of all groups and the integration of efforts of all. As elections on party lines divide the village on certain affiliations, therefore, the need of elections for panchayats on non-party lines is very crucial. *Third*, broadening the level of discussions during election campaign. It must make shift from narrow issues like personal stake in winning elections, petty group clashes to development issues that concern the people the most. The issues that deserve merit for being the part of election process are state of primary education, health and sanitation, drinking water; problems of landless and weaker sections; marketing of agricultural produce and so on. It will require change in mindset through mass awareness campaign programmes.

Fourth, attitudinal changes: Dominance by a few (village elites) in the gram sabha is an indicator of the perceived threat they feel from the people. Elites feel that their present authority or position is being questioned. Similarly, even the people hesitate to question their traditional authority due to cultural factor. So, what we indeed require is to make people first aware about their role and rights and instil confidence in them; and then create a conducive atmosphere through educational programmes, also to effect, by way of training programmes, attitudinal changes for bringing shift from the traditional socio-cultural values of dominance, central decision-making to people-centred participative approach. *Fifth*, electoral reforms are essential and are crucial part of political reforms. Among others, reforms should include measures such as educating people about their rights and village development needs, elections on non-party basis, state funding of elections, measures to check use of money and muscle power, and consumption of liquor; constitution of citizens committee (to work as ombudsman) to oversee the conduct of elections; and timely and simultaneous elections for all the tiers.

Kerala's experience - How Reforms have strengthened Grassroots Participation

In the context of reforms, the case of Kerala deserves mention. The education[13] and health programmes together with land reform movement and social reforms contributed a great deal in reducing disparities based on land, income, gender and caste (Dreze and Sen, 1999). The state government and many NGOs provided support for reforms. Education helped in reducing gender bias, made people conscious of both their rights and opportunities, and in building community institutions. These reforms facilitated in creating egalitarian structure in society and in generating public awareness to the extent of people demanding their rights and participating in the development process. It provided a good ground for launching people's campaign plan for decentralisation. It created conducive environment for participation by people cutting across caste or class or gender barrier or political groups. People can discuss their problems freely and meaningfully in the gram sabha and village development seminars,

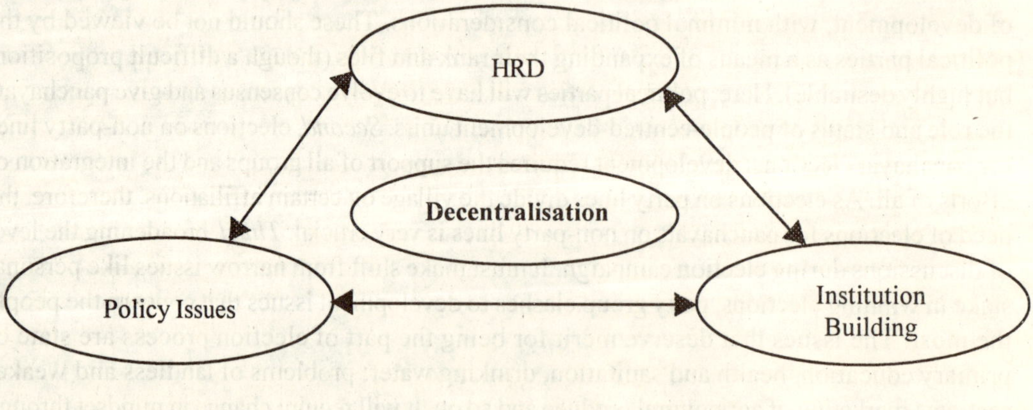

Fig 7.4 : **Fundamental Model of Decentralisation**

[13] Due to education and awareness, the enlightened public discussion in Kerala clearly has had a considerable role in creating cultural atmosphere that has acted against the gender bias in the family, and it also seems to have played an important part in spreading the use of birth control in Kerala and thus in the decline in fertility rate that has been so dramatic there in recent years (Dreze and Sen, 1999).

they can participate in their village development activities and can demand their rights. Political will and institution building added considerable strength to the process of decentralisation in the state. The reforms provided a very good foundation for inclusion of all segments, especially from marginalised groups in the socio-economic and political process at grassroots level.

Facilitating Reforms: Making Positive Interventions

The social and political reforms, that are envisaged above, need to be buttressed by positive interventions. It will require that people should be a□ dequately supported through capabilities improvement programmes, that institutional support should be provided for converting local plans into actions at the grassroots level, and that the policy initiatives be taken to create an environment of opportunities. In a way, what specific interventions (see fig. 7.4) are required are reflected below:

- Human Resources Development — enhancing access to opportunities;
- Institutional Reform; and
- Policy Reform.

• *HRD — for Enhancing People's Participation and Access to Opportunities*

Development means more than providing capital assistance with the aim of raising per capita incomes and the rate of growth of the economy. It involves investment in human resources, building skills, helping people to help themselves and promoting a self-sustaining momentum for development. In the context of decentralisation, lack of people's ability to participate cannot so much be seen only from the participation in the gram sabha functioning, as such an assessment will block the other criterion of need of providing access for opportunities (in other areas of village life) that are essential for people in future development. Participation has to be in all the opportunities. Participatory level should not be just judged only from the point of view attendance in gram sabha (a conventional criterion). It should also include participation by people in social, political and economic opportunities, with equal access. We require a conscious society with adequate capabilities, which is aware of its rights and has the capacity to avail opportunities. This will provide a person courage to put forth his grievance, confidence of getting his voice heard and can expect just response from the local panchayat, while accessing other socio-economic opportunities.

Human resources development is the key for enhancing the possibility of availing the opportunities, and its importance cannot be overlooked if the vital objectives of decentralisation viz., people's participation, collective action and improved opportunities to people are to be achieved. As a first step, we need to give thrust on HRD, putting people at the centre of decision-making and giving them opportunities and options through education and training for creative use of resources as per their local needs. In this backdrop, it will call for having a specific programme for human resources development that should include the following prominent measures:

First, environment building: The provisions in the Act are necessary for decentralisation, but not enough for ensuring people's involvement in the development process. Creating conducive environment is essential for people's participation, and, so, alongside every other initiative for decentralisation, an environment should be fostered so that public participation can be strengthened and they get opportunities in socio-economic development. *Second*, attitudinal changes are required for inculcating sound cultural values like importance of participatory development, sensitivity for people's problems, especially from the weaker sections, respect for institutional norms, sense of belongingness for the village property, respect for the *shramdan* and so on, so that good work culture is evolved for participatory development.

Third, information sharing: Information is going to empower the people for taking decisions and it is really going to provide opportunities for various socio-economic activities. People should have full access to information through a well-developed database and information system. *Fourth*, it demands that a dedicated programme of capacity building of all those associated, especially the weaker sections, directly or indirectly with the working of local bodies needs to be a part of decentralisation and should precede every other action that is taken for transfer of functions, or devolution of powers or funds. *Finally*, a comprehensive educational and health programme for hundred per cent coverage of the people in all the villages in the country.

- ***Institution Building — A Must for Decentralisation***

Institutional underpinnings are vital and without which the very purpose of the decentralisation would be defeated. Mere assumption that once the powers are given to people or to panchayats will do the necessary job for village development and will result into desired outcome is highly misplaced, and it needs to be looked from the following two illustrations:

Firstly, let us take the case of 'giving powers to people'. At the outset giving powers to people is more of a concept, as the 'people' as such are not a homogeneous group and may not represent the interest of all the constituents in a village. For instance, 'people' will include poor, rich, upper-caste, marginalised groups (SCs and STs), women, landlords, money-lenders and so on, and by experience and based on the field realities, more often, the interest of one group comes against the interest of others. *Secondly*, we take the case of 'giving powers to panchayat'. Here, in the typical village panchayat setting, the 'powers to panchayats' is normally construed as powers to chairperson or to ward members, and for all practical purposes they take all the decisions, which may sometimes be judicious, or in some cases be based on personal prejudices, or in some other cases be for political patronage. Presently, based on field studies, if we examine closely, due to a variety of reasons, the local institutions are run more by personal choices than by rational decision-making of panchayats.

It is in this context, what is crucial is setting up of appropriate institutions at local levels for handling powers and the utilisation of resources, and should include, *first*, what are the powers to be given, *second*, for whom and what purpose powers should be applied, *third*, who should apply these powers, and, *finally*, how these powers should be applied i.e. the norms, rules and procedures. And the good institutional structure is indispensable. The institutions that are to be built should have the capacity to generate natural resources capital, social capital, human capital, financial capital, and physical capital.

IB has to be looked from the point of view of shift that has taken place in the last two decades, in which the focus has shifted from law and order and revenue related matters to the development including economic and social welfare programmes. The previously performed functions required more of centralised and rule-based control, while the latter demands more of people-oriented-flexible approach. And, the need of attending to individual-based and village-specific needs and problems has got much higher priority. It is on which the very success of local institutions depends. Accordingly, the management practices of the local institutions have to be changed. It will require the change in mind-set. To be more specific, it will call for bringing attitudinal changes for a number of behavioural issues like appreciating the need of involving the people in the development process, listening their grievances and needs (rather than giving orders or command), facilitating them in utilising opportunities and so on. Also, in the backdrop of wide social disparities, what is needed is reforming the institutional thinking that should encourage and promote equality among caste, and values of human dignity, knowledge and work.

Also in present context of ever increasing needs of people arising due to a variety of technological, marketing, globalisation factors, a matching capacity is needed in the leadership that should be able to steer the institutions to meet the challenges. Panchayats should be able to inspire action and provide leadership from behind. Besides, good technical and management abilities, it will call for commitment for the work at very level and in everyone whether be elected members or be development functionaries.

> '...it will call for bringing attitudinal changes for a number of behavioural issues like appreciating the need of involving the people in the development process, listening their grievances and needs (rather than giving orders or command), facilitating them in utilising opportunities and so on. Also, in the backdrop of wide social disparities, what is needed is reforming the institutional thinking that should encourage and promote equality among caste, and values of human dignity, knowledge and work.'

In the light of establishing panchayats as institutions of development, rules or laws or policies should be framed in such a way that will help in meeting the local development needs and facilitate them (panchayats) in making availability of services to people, and that is where our focus should be. It needs certain institutional arrangements including:

- establishing arrangements for organic linkages among three tiers, and for coordination mechanism among panchayats;
- supporting various other institutions like CBOs, NGOs, cooperatives, private sector to participate in harmony for the development activities;
- promoting integration within regions to promote economic, social and political activities emphasising interaction among villages and urban areas; and
- evolving strong leadership within local institutions and higher structure of government that should facilitate reciprocal exchange of information, cooperation in development

areas, conflict management between local and upper tiers of government.

For setting local institutions, areas where the reforms are needed are personnel management, support system, management system, institutional processes, transparency, accountability, legal framework and value system in an integrated manner through participatory process. These measures including improved HRD level of people in the villages will contribute towards institution building, which should result into:

- *Capacity (Technical, Administrative and Behavioural) Building* — Improvement in the capabilities to undertake the task of village development planning and implementation;
- *Environmental Image* — To be seen as friendly organisations that will attend to the problems of people. People must have access to panchayats, which should be responsive to their needs;
- *Value System* — Through a process of attitudinal changes, bringing a set of values that will make the institutions efficient, effective and responsive. The values among others should include ability to respond to the problems of people, transparency, commitment for work, teamwork, respect for norms, and procedure and quality of work; and
- *Accountability* — The personnel whether elected or development functionaries should be accountable for their decisions and actions.

Policy Reform: Right Policies - Prerequisite for Development

Policies are required to give direction to the process of development, and the decentralisation is a means for facilitating the local institutions to achieve the development objectives. It has been evident during the field visits (also see section 7.3), the policies have direct impact on the ability of panchayats to function. And as such the ultimate success of programme outputs will depend upon how the policy measures are initiated.

It is the combination of three viz., education, social equalities and availability of economic opportunities that will determine the participatory level, especially the quality of participation. It will lead to increased representation of people in different stages of decentralisation and, in turn, towards the success of participatory democracy. It will facilitate in reducing disparities—whether be social or political or economic. Thus, if right policies are introduced, these can be useful instrument in meeting the twin-objectives of people's participation in development and socio-economic opportunities for them.

The policies are critical that will give panchayats the right options for formulating strategies and in designing programmes for village development, and will facilitate in meeting the aspirations and needs of people. Thus, if the right development policy measures are initiated, the process of decentralisation will find acceptance among people and facilitate in meeting the aspirations and needs of people.

In the context of existing state of narrow focus of policies on wage employment (see discussion in section 7.3) and the compartmentalised sectoral approach, we need to broaden our rural development policy. It needs a paradigm shift in the present approach of providing 'immediate relief' to a more sustained approach of 'creating opportunities' and 'expansion of village economies'. Policies should be such that would lead to improved 'quality of life' (in terms of access to education, health services, sanitation, safe drinking water and so on) and enhance 'purchasing power'. It requires calibrated shift in our policy. Efforts are needed for integrated policies rather than piece-meal changes, and we should not look agriculture, animal husbandry, rural-employment, etc. in isolation. Policies need to be such that will provide resource-matching and desired linkages among programmes of various sectors, and thereby, leading to integrated development. Also, it should address the development in a sector comprehensively and facilitate project approach. For giving boost to rural economy, sound policies are required on human capital development, natural resources management, trade, property rights, investment, infrastructural development and employment.

A Positive Focus

The careful analysis of the process of decentralisation reveals that it is marked with regulatory approach. It shows that much of the concern centres around issues such as regulation of resources and manpower. These issues have emerged more from the perceived regulatory or negative role of the government. On the other hand, there are certain functions like providing opportunities to people through educational and training programmes and creation of infrastructure for future social and economic activities, which have positive influence, are neglected while they have much bigger impact on the quality of life for people and are very fundamental for the village development.

In the process of decentralisation, much of the discussion is focused on how the power can be taken from the departments, how the control over resources can be exercised, how more functions can be brought under the panchayat control to exercise greater influence and powers and so on. A lot of time and energy is consumed in deliberating on these issues and sorting them out. We need to appreciate that this is just only one aspect of the decentralisation. There are certain issues like providing health services, especially at the village level, ensuring safe drinking water, creation of productive assets like irrigation structure, marketing infrastructure, soil and water conservation structures, etc. in villages that merit urgent attention. Besides, the local institutions are beset with an innumerable number of problems and require certain definite measures to bring them up to a level of delivering results. And without such efforts, the viability of implementation of projects in particular and sustainability of the development process in general will remain in question.

There is a scope for looking into much bigger aspect of decentralisation. From the people's perspective, it requires positive focus on providing basic services such as primary education, healthcare and drinking water, etc., and on responsiveness of the panchayats to the needs of people, especially the weaker sections; and from the institutional perspective, on strengthening delivery mechanism at local levels. So, instead of concentrating more on power and control, there is a need of bringing shift in the focus from the present approach of regulation to positive action. It will demand that we need to focus on fundamental issues (see beginning of section 7.5) and to widen the range of issues that merit attention.

7.6 Role of State

In operationalising the Panchayat Act, the state has vital role to play in providing support for building of local institutions, legal framework and in creating enabling environment for people to participate and take the advantage of opportunities. Dreze and Sen (1995) have also expressed that though the legislative reforms for decentralisation hold much promise, but the need for positive interventions by the state through policies for human resources development and institutional development are critical as these would strengthen the process of decentralisation.

Also, all over the world the changes in the economic and political systems have brought a number of advantages to people across the countries in both developed and developing worlds. The important question remains how these are to be distributed among the people through a proper policy framework, and it needs to be addressed by the government. And the right balance has to be struck between harnessing the technological advantages and meeting the basic needs of people, particularly of vulnerable sections. Enabling economic environment can be provided by the government, so here the policies of state on investment, trade, property rights, NRM and infrastructure development are going to play an important role.

Globalisation is another issue that is going to have its impact on the village life, and it may be difficult to visualise / determine its impact before hand. In the cases of emergent situations, the governments — Central as well as state — will have to provide critical support to local institutions. The states (governments) have to think strategically, analytically and globally, but work and support for the interest of people at the grassroots level. The state has to build institutional structures at the local levels and set standards to deal with challenges of global trade, communication system, environment, labour laws, etc., which have direct bearing on the lives of people in the villages, and simultaneously meet the standards of governance.

Implications of Decentralisation

Decentralisation in India assumes high significance in the present socio-political and economic scenario of the country, which is distinctly marked with four characteristics: *first*, vastness of the geographical area; *second*, plurality of society; *third*, regional disparities; and *fourth*, lack of availability of basic services at the village level. All these throw a big challenge for the functioning of panchayats at local levels. In this very context, once the reform process begins and the requisite interventions are introduced, it would lead to conducive socio-political environment for people's participation at the grassroots level and to capacity building of local institutions to enable them to come up to a position of delivering services. The implications of decentralisation would be:

- *An Environment of Opportunities:* Panchayats would be in a position to provide an environment for political, social and economic opportunities that would empower people and improve their socio-economic security.
- *Meeting Basic Services:* It would ensure making basic services viz., primary education,

health and sanitation, drinking water, inputs for agriculture, PDS, etc. available to people at the village level, so that the people are assured of quality of life.

- *Growth of Village Economy:* The enhanced capacity of panchayats would give boost to the growth of village economy through integrated development of various sectors.
- *Integration of Local, Regional and National Goals:* While addressing local aspirations of people, the regional and national goals would be integrated with that of local.
- *Sustainability through Institution Building:* The enhanced institutional capacity would lead to sustainability to the process of development in terms of social, political, economic and institutional dimensions.

7.7 Summing up

Panchayati raj has a very important part in the whole process of social and economic advancement of rural areas. Panchayats can play vital role in meeting the aspirations of people and in providing basic services to people. Yet a word of caution may be necessary, for there are those who look upon it as a *deus ex machina*, which will achieve remarkable results, not only in every field but also with great speed (Maddick, 1970). Panchayati raj should attempt to provide first the basic services to people in the rural areas, and then build upon the strength for bigger role in future. There must be cooperatives, voluntary associations, private organisations, individuals and government agencies dealing with different aspects of development, all of which have to contribute to the process of plan fulfilment. Panchayati raj should play the facilitating role in the system that can make an impact upon the individuals in terms of providing opportunities, and also provide a forum for redressal of problems and collective action for local development.

The development of local institutions, like the progress of any organisation, can only be a slow process, as changeover from one system to another can't change people and their varying attitudes in short time. It is important to examine critically at what is happening in the villages in terms of awareness among people and their participation, how the elected representatives are involving people in the process of development, and also how the development functionaries are responding to changes. But changes take time to firm up — a period of rumination, a time of careful investigation, a further period of watchfulness should begin while radical changes and reforms are introduced.

Changes cannot be brought about merely by regulations and legislations. While what is needed is greater understanding of the system and its objectives, and education and awareness building programmes among practitioners from villagers who would vote, participate and watch the development process to those who would have to operate it at every level and in every position, and to make them appreciate the philosophy behind the constitutional amendment.

Here, it needs to be stressed that people's participation can be achieved / will come about only when the right conditions are created. These conditions would entail both demand and supply side. The 'demand side' will be possible through higher capabilities on the part of people and if they are given right opportunities to participate in the decision-making process, which is possible through well-organised educational programmes. The 'supply side' can be created through well-structured development programmes that should provide both infrastructural base and the socio-economic opportunities on a sustained basis.

Though the 73rd Constitution Amendment Act is considered a landmark of sorts for strengthening the panchayati raj institutions, yet, neither from the point of view of people's participation, nor from the perspective of capacity of PR institutions to deliver in the rural areas, does the Act prove to be any effective. It has been assumed that the panchayat Acts, though vital, would automatically lead to greater institutional capability. Under the given state of panchayat functioning that is marked with lack of responsiveness, transparency and accountability, the elections have become the ultimate test of the performance of panchayats, which come every five years. On the other hand, people have to wait indefinitely for their problems and needs to be addressed by the panchayats. And the lack of capacity of panchayats to deliver basic services has raised questions about the governance at the grassroots level. Such a state of functioning of panchayats prompts us to re-examine the various provisions in the Act from the point of view of their effectiveness in improving the capacity of PR system. Though, keeping in view the spirit of the Constitution Amendment Act, the states should take initiatives, however, in order to provide a definite direction, there is a need of bringing the amendments in the Central Act in order to bring mandatory nature in the Act. Among others, the crucial aspects that need to be further addressed are: empowerment of people, transfer of functions and devolution of funds, transparency, accountability, planning unit and delivery system. And only when are these addressed by the Act in concrete terms, the PR system can be set up in right perspective.

The panchayats should address the bigger issue of development by making a definite shift from the present state of control and command of resources. It must make endeavour for addressing the development issues that matter people the most in every stage starting from election, to conduct of gram sabha, to planning, to implementation, to monitoring and to accountability. Panchayats must become the units of development. The panchayats have big potential in providing forum for people's participation, in convergence of resources and services, and synergy at the local level, and in improving the performance of delivery of basic services. And this needs to be recognised as an input for future strategy for decentralisation.

Now, in the backdrop of above, as a first step, what is needed is to give thrust on human resources development, placing people at the centre of decision-making, involving them in the creative use of resources, offering them more options, and giving them through education and training the freedom to generate for themselves economic and social opportunities best suited to their needs. It should result into enhanced space for socio-political participation especially by the weaker sections in a meaningful way. For ensuring that every person at village level participates positively and constructively in the development process, and is not swayed by popular programmes or dominated by rural elites; and for enabling the PR institutions to take the task of decentralised planning and implementation, a well-conceived capacitation programme assumes great significance. Without this support, the goal of decentralisation would not be achieved fully. And if Panchayati Raj system has to succeed, HRD must be central to the decentralisation process.

Secondly, of crucial importance is institution building that will call for having a design of interventions whose architecture is located in a multi-dimensional matrix featuring structural reforms, organisational development, devolution of funds, transfer of functions and capacity building of panchayats. It requires the creation of strong institutions that will be run by appropriate procedures and norms, and will have the capacity to deliver. Now with the advent of globalisation, the changes taking place at the national and international levels are directly impinging on the rural economy. It further necessitates that the capacity of local institutions needs to be enhanced in order to enable them to take up challenges of liberalisation, international trade and so on. It requires that the institution building and liberalisation should move in tandem so that the development at the grassroots level does not lag behind.

Thirdly, decentralisation by itself cannot be enough, and it is a process and not an end, and hence, for its success, sound policy initiatives are necessary in order to provide sustainability to the process of decentralisation and in turn to development. It needs to be particularly looked from the point of view of incongruity that exists between present policies and the socio-economic realities. It may require taking measures for human resources development, natural resources management, investment in infrastructure and creating production-led employment opportunities. And such initiatives are going to add to the creation of opportunities for people and in creating a conducive atmosphere for the growth of village economy.

In order to sustain the efforts for the process of decentralisation, State has vital role to play in having a definite programme of reform. That will require that each state should come out with clearly defined contours of action plan for bringing necessary reforms that will facilitate in evolving sound decentralised development system at the grassroots level. And the reforms should focus on fundamentals: how the decentralisation can contribute to achieving broad objective of mobilising the people in the development process; how the decentralisation can improve economic and managerial efficiency through institution building; and how the decentralisation can increase the government responsiveness to the needs and demands of various interest groups and can be a sustainable process to enable people in rural areas a good quality life. It will require that the necessary political, administrative and financial support, that is so vital, should be extended to PR institutions, and the necessary changes should be effected in the panchayat Acts to enhance operational efficacy of the local institutions.

Finally, under the given state of socio-economic and political disparities and the poor capacity of the panchayats to deliver, reforms are very critically required. Reforms must begin by creating enabling environment. It requires initiatives for reducing inequalities, making basic services available to people and enhancing the access for opportunities. In sum, from the people's perspective, this is what should be expected from decentralisation. In this pursuit, we require a conscious society, which is aware of its rights; institutions that will attend to the problems of people, have transparency in its functioning, and are accountable to people; and a comprehensive policy for socio-economic development. In a way, it calls for primacy of human resources development, institution building and initiating right development policies for successful decentralisation. It also necessitates introducing certain mandatory provisions in the Central as well as state Panchayat Acts in order to make panchayats as units of development. And, for good governance, reforms have to be a focal concern.

APPENDIX I

Recommendations about Global and Specific Revenue Sharing and other General Grants by SFCs

	State	Composition of suggested divisible pool / tax	Total share recommended to local bodies	Allocation to local bodies: Share of PRIs in total share (%)	Share of ULBs in total share (%)	Criteria of inter-se distribution
1	2	3	4	5	6	7
1.	Andhra Pradesh	**1. Global-Sharing** - States tax and non-tax revenue	39.24%	70%	30%	- Not specified
		2. Specific Tax Revenue-Sharing				
		- Land cess to be increased from 25% to 200%	100%	100%	-	- Existing basis
		- Profession tax revenue	95%	-	-	- Population basis
		- Surcharge on stamp duty to be increased from 5% to 10%.	95%	-	-	- Collection basis
2.	Assam	**1. Global -Sharing** - Total tax revenue	2%	-	-	- Population basis
		2. Specific revenue sharing - Addl. revenue of M.V. tax to be distributed to local bodies	10%			- No. of vehicles
		3. General - Local Finance Database: Registers and forms for proper accounts and records are to be maintained by each local body with effect from 1st April, 1997 in the	-	-	-	-

(Contd.)

APPENDIX I (Contd.)

1	2	3	4	5	6	7
		format prescribed. Cost of the registers and forms is to be borne by the State Government out of Plan Fund as grants to local bodies at the rate of Rs. 1000 per local body for 1997-98 and Rs. 500 per local body from 1998-99 to 2000-01 (para 8.1)				
		- Assessment of property tax should be made every five years for periodic revision. User levy should be imposed on the agricultural pumpset, user charges should be levied for services rendered by the local bodies on parks, public toilets, public health centres, etc. Fee for sale of animals being a village trade should also be imposed	-	-	-	-
3.	Goa	**1. Global-Sharing**				
		- State's own tax revenue and share in Central taxes for activities transferred under non-plan	36%	27%	9%	- To be distributed on the basis of actuals in the first year and in the same proportion as first year during subsequent years
		- Annual State Plan excluding ear-marked negotiated loan components and project specific central assistance	16%	13%	3%	- 40% on population 20% on geographical area 10% on backwardness 25% on performance 5% at discretion

(Contd.)

APPENDIX 1 (Contd.)

1	2	3	4	5	6	7
4.	Haryana	**1. No Global Sharing recommended**				
		2. Specific Tax Revenue Sharing				
		- Net royalty on minor minerals	20%	50%	50%	- Collection basis
		- Conversion charges / change of land use	10% net proceeds	100%	Nil	-do-
		- Stamp duty and Registration fee	7.5% of net proc.	100%	Nil	-do-
		- Motor Vehicle tax	20% of net proc.	Nil	100%	- Not specified
		- Entertainment tax	50% of net proc.	Nil	100%	- Collection basis
		- Show tax	100% of net proc	Nil	100%	- -do-
		- New levy on pumpsets	97% of net proc.	100%	Nil	- Not Specified
		- Tax on Tractors and harvesters combines	100%	100%	Nil	- Not Specified
		- Revenue from cattle fairs	100%	100%	Nil	- Collection basis
5.	Himachal Pradesh	**No Revenue Sharing Recommended**	-	-	-	-
6.	Karnataka	**Global Sharing**				
		- Non-loan gross own revenue of state government	36%	85%	15%	- Rural population-33.33% - Area - 33.33% - Illiteracy - 11.11% - Beds - 11.11% - Roads - 11.11%
		2. General				
		- Share of each tier : 25% Gram Panchayat; 35% Taluk Panchayat; and 40% Zilla Panchayat				

(Contd.)

APPENDIX 1 (Contd.)

1	2	3	4	5	6	7
7.	Kerala	**1. No global sharing recommended**				
		- Recommended 1% non-statutory non-plan grant				- Population basis
		2. Specific Revenue-Sharing				
		- Motor vehicle tax	25%			- Not specified
		- Building tax	100%			-do-
		- Income from sale of court fee stamps	Not specified			-do-
		3. General				
		- Allocation of state revenue between panchayats at the ratio of 15% to zilla panchayats, 15% to taluk panchayats and 70% to gram panchayats				
8.	Madhya Pradesh	**1. Global Sharing**				
		- Gross tax and non-tax revenue of the state government	2.91%	100%		- Population - 75%
		Or				
		Net tax and non-tax revenue of the state government (90%)	3.24%	100%		- To GPs only

(Contd.)

APPENDIX 1 (Contd.)

1	2	3	4	5	6	7
		2. General				
		- Devolution criteria: 15% in proportion to SC/ST population; 85% based on population area, no. of agricultural labour, per hectare gross value of agricultural output, number of workers in registered factories per lakh of population, per capita consumption of electricity and literacy rate				
9.	Maharashtra	**1. No Global Sharing recommended**	-	-	-	-
		2. Specific Tax Revenue-Sharing	-	-	-	-
		- 66.67% of the demand of land revenue and cess thereon, irrigation tax and local cess matching grant to be given to PRIs as advance grant. It is the minimum to be assured to PRIs. If collection exceeds this percentage the balance may be given to PRIs in the subsequent year		100%	-	- Existing basis
		- Forest revenue grants to be increased from 7% to 10% of total forest revenue collections	10%	100%	-	- Existing basis
		- 10% of the state administered profession tax to be earmarked to local bodies and 20% of this to be given to gram panchayats	10%	2%	8%	- Per capita basis

(Contd.)

APPENDIX 1 (Contd.)

1	2	3	4	5	6	7
10.	Manipur	**1. No revenue sharing recommended**				
11.	Orissa	**1. No Global Sharing recommended**				
		2. Specific Tax Revenue				
		- The existing surcharge on entertainment tax levied in rural areas of 25% to be increased to 50% and the entire amount transferred to gram panahcyats	100%	100%		- Collection basis
		- Surcharge on stamp duty at 3% to be levied on transfers of immovable property and the amount collected in rural areas to be given to gram panchayats	100%	100%		- Collection basis
		- Revenue collected from sairat (common property resources) in each district to be assigned to gram panchayats	100%	100%		- Population basis
		- Royalty on minor forest produce to be given to the panchayat *samitis* and gram panchayats under tribal sub-plan areas in the ratio of 60:40	100%	100%		- Population basis
12.	Punjab	**1. Global Sharing not recommended**				
		2. Specific Revenue Sharing				
		- Land revenue	100%	100%		- Not specified
		- Net proceeds of stamp duty MV tax, electricity duty and entertainment tax	20%	-		- Not specified

(Contd.)

APPENDIX 1 (Contd.)

1	2	3	4	5	6	7
13.	Rajasthan	**1. Global Sharing** - Total net proceeds of the state taxes	2.18%	77.29%	22.71%	- Population
		2. General - To set up a finance corporation in rural and urban areas - Government grant-in-aid to panchayats be raised from Rs. 5 to Rs. 11 per head (1995-96)				
14.	Tamil Nadu	**1. Global Sharing** Net tax revenue of the state government	8% per year to be increased progressively to 12% by 2001-02	60%	40%	- Population
		2. Specific Tax Revenue Sharing Entertainment tax	90%	-	-	- Collection basis
		3. General - Reserving 15% of resource devolution as 'equalisation and incentive fund' and sharing the same between panchayats and municipalities in the ratio of 60:40 - Criteria for distribution of funds: population (50%), SC/ST population (15%), per capita house tax collection (15%), core civil services / infrastructure deficiencies (20%)				

(Contd.)

APPENDIX 1 (Contd.)

1	2	3	4	5	6	7
15.	Tripura	- Share in central taxes received	20%	100%	-	- Formula basis
		- State government to pass on a reasonable portion of its total tax revenue	not specified	-	-	-
		- Share in sales tax, addl. sales tax, purchase tax and luxury tax	50%	100%	-	- Population basis
		- Profession tax	35%	100%	-	- Population basis
		- Agricultural income tax and land revenue	32%	100%	-	- 2% to each of the 16 panchayat samitis
		- Addl. stamp duty at 1%	100%	100%	-	- Population basis
		- Forest revenue	15%	100%	-	- Not specified
16.	Uttar Pradesh	**Global Sharing** - Net proceeds of state's total tax revenue	10%	30%	70%	- Population 80%, Area - 20%
17.	West Bengal	**1. Global Sharing** - Net proceeds of all state taxes	16%	Not specified		- ZPs - 30%, PSs - 20%, GPs - 50% - Population, backwardness, illiteracy, area, rural population, bank deposits, working capital allocation

Sources: NIRD (2000) and SFC reports of concerned states.

APPENDIX 2

Plan Outlay for Annual Plan 2000-2001 for the Schemes / Programmes of the Central Ministries Under the Subject mentioned in the Eleventh Schedule of Constitution

(Rs. in crores)

Sl. No.	Name of the Scheme / Programme	Outlay (Rs.)
1.	Crop husbandry	1380.22
2.	Soil and water conservation	63.42
3.	Animal husbandry	77.07
4.	Dairy development	36.45
5.	Fisheries	116.61
6.	Forestry & wildlife	281.65
7.	Plantations	169.35
8.	Agricultural research & education	550.00
9.	Agricultural fin. Institutions	28.76
10.	Other agricultural programmes	6.67
11.	Land reforms	67.50
12.	Minor irrigation	88.67
13.	Non-conventional sources of energy	858.46
14.	Village and small industries	1125.35
15.	Road & bridges	5548.15
16.	General education	4433.06
17.	Technical education	496.18
18.	Family welfare	3200.00
19.	Water supply and sanitation	2071.03
20.	Housing	3869.73
21.	Welfare of SCs, STs & OBCs	997.74
22.	Social security & welfare	2231.85
23.	Nutrition	2.90
24.	Other social services	1.20
25.	Special programmes for rural development	1075.45
26.	Rural employment	2798.40
	Total	31,575.87

Source : MORD (2001a).

APPENDIX 3

Plan Outlay for Annual Plan 2000-2001 for the Schemes / Programmes of the State Plan of the State Governments Under the Subject Mentioned in the Eleventh Schedule of Constitution

(Rs. in crores)

Sl. No.	Name of the Scheme / Programme	Outlay (Rs.)
1.	Crop husbandry	1268.77
2.	Soil and water conservation	643.50
3.	Animal husbandry	354.19
4.	Dairy development	49.87
5.	Fisheries	205.95
6.	Forestry & wildlife	1393.03
7.	Plantations	4.63
8.	Agricultural research & education	292.21
9.	Agricultural fin. Institutions	61.63
10.	Other agricultural programmes	98.18
11.	IRDP & allied programme	516.16
12.	NREP / JRY	1161.22
13.	Other programmes like EAS, etc.	1062.46
14.	Land reforms	294.08
15.	Minor irrigation	1907.93
16.	Non-conventional sources of energy	119.43
17.	Village and small industries	800.87
18.	Road & bridges	8128.44
19.	Road transport	1265.30
20.	Inland water transport	16.74
21.	Other transport services	614.50
22.	General education	4972.07
23.	Technical education	422.49
24.	Art & culture	171.07
25.	Medical & public health	3306.64
26.	Water supply and sanitation	6031.74
27.	Housing	1936.57
28.	Welfare of SCs, STs & OBCs	1972.99
29.	Social welfare	904.26
30.	Nutrition	721.79
31.	Other social services	119.86
	Total	40,818.65

Note : The outlay mentioned against each scheme / programme is the sum of outlay for all the state governments allocated against each of their scheme.

Source : MORD (2001a).

APPENDIX 4

Number of Panchayati Raj Institutions (As on Oct. 1997) in India

S.N.	State/UT	Gram panchayat level (gram panchayats) (Nos.)	Intermediate level (panchayat *samitis*) (Nos.)	District level (zilla parishad) (Nos.)	Rural population covered (lakhs)	Villages covered
1.	Andhra Pradesh	21943	1098	22	411.35	29293
2.	Arunachal Pradesh	2012	79	12	5.72	3737
3.	Assam	2489	202	21	171.83	20799
4.	Bihar	12181	725	55	611.96	76488
5.	Goa	183	-	2	9.69	406
6.	Gujarat	13316	184	19	234.84	18550
7.	Haryana	5958	110	16	100.96	7064
8.	Himachal Pradesh	2922	72	12	42.57	18850
9.	Jammu & Kashmir *	2683	0	0	47.27	6900
10.	Karnataka	5675	175	20	255.67	27024
11.	Kerala	991	152	14	201.63	1451
12.	Madhya Pradesh	30922	459	45	415.92	76603
13.	Maharashtra	27619	319	29	407.19	39354
14.	Manipur	166	-	3	6.06	672
15.	Meghalaya		(traditional council of village elders exist)			
16.	Mizoram		(traditional council of village elders exist)			
17.	Nagaland		(traditional council of village elders exist)			
18.	Orissa	5261	314	30	234.85	50744
19.	Punjab	11591	138	17	121.41	12795
20.	Rajasthan	9185	237	31	270.51	37124
21.	Sikkim	148	-	4	2.65	440
22.	Tamil Nadu	12584	384	28	324.56	16602
23.	Tripura	525	16	3	23.87	863
24.	Uttar Pradesh	58605	901	68	909.13	112566
25.	West Bengal	3314	341	17	394.78	38047
26.	A & N Islands	67	-	1	1.02	185
27.	D & N Haveli	11	-	1	1.03	72
28.	Daman & Diu	10	-	2	7.30	462
29.	Lakshadweep	10	-	1		-
30.	Pondicherry	10	-	1	-	334
	Total	230381	5906	474	5214.49	592495

* Election not held till 1997. * MORD (2001b).
Source: RDS (1999).

APPENDIX 5

Number of Elected Members of Panchayats in Different States in India

S.N.	State/UT	Number of Elected Members			Total
		DP	IP	VP	
1.	Andhra Pradesh	1093	14644	230529	246265
2	Arunachal Pradesh	77	1205	5733	7015
3	Assam	845	2564	30360	33769
4	Bihar	1585	15344	165452	182381
5	Goa	35	-	1281	1316
6	Gujarat	761	3814	123470	128045
7	Haryana	319	2528	60117	62964
8	Himachal Pradesh	252	1661	18625	20538
9	Jammu & Kashmir	NA	NA	NA	NA
10	Karnataka	919	3340	80627	84886
11	Kerala	300	1547	10270	12117
12	Madhya Pradesh	1036	9097	474351	281476
13	Maharashtra	1762	3524	276190	484484
14	Manipur	57	-	3714	3771
15	Meghalaya			(Traditional councils)	
16	Mizoram			(Traditional councils)	
17	Nagaland			(Traditional councils)	
18	Orissa	854	5260	81077	87191
19	Punjab	274	2441	78983	81698
20	Rajasthan	1028	5494	112897	119419
21	Sikkim	145	-	1827	1972
22	Tamil Nadu	648	6499	125852	132999
23	Tripura	76	228	6477	6781
24	Uttar Pradesh	2687	59991	799780	862458
25	West Bengal	664	9516	62139	72319
26	A & N Islands	30	-	667	697
27	D & N Haveli	16	-	135	151
28	Daman & Diu	15	-	63	78
29	Lakshadweep	15	-	129	144
30	Pondicherry	16	-	120	136
	Total	15509	148697	2750865	2915071

Source: RDS (1999)

DP: District Panchayat, IP: Intermediate Panchayat, VP: Village Panchayat

NA: Not applicable

APPENDIX 6

THE CONSTITUTION (SEVENTY-THIRD AMENDMENT) ACT,1992

AN ACT

Further to amend the Constitution of India

Be it enacted by Parliament in the Forty-third Year of the Republic of India as follows :

1. (1) This Act may be called the Constitution (Seventy-third Amendment) Act, 1992.
(2) It shall come into force on such date as the Central Government may, by notification in the Official Gazette, appoint.
2. After Part VIII of the Constitution, the following Part shall be inserted, namely :-

PART IX

THE PANCHAYATS

243 In this Part, unless the context otherwise requires, —

(a) "district" means a district in a State;
(b) "Gram Sabha" means a body consisting of persons registered in the electoral rolls relating to a village comprised within the area of Panchayat at the village level;
(c) "intermediate level" means a level between the village and district levels specified by the Governor of a State by public notification to be the intermediate level for the purposes of this Part;
(d) "Panchayat" means an institution (by whatever name called) of self-government constituted under Article 243B, for the rural areas;
(e) "Panchayat area" means the territorial area of a Panchayat;
(f) "population" means the population as ascertained at the last preceding census of which the relevant figures have been published;
(g) "village" means a village specified by the Governor by public notification to be a village for the purposes of this Part and includes a group of villages so specified.

243A. A Gram Sabha may exercise such powers and perform such functions at the village level as the Legislature of a State may by law, provide.

243B (1) There shall be constituted in every State, Panchayats at the village, intermediate and district levels in accordance with the provisions of this Part.

(2) Notwithstanding anything in clause (1), Panchayats at the intermediate level may not be constituted in a State having a population not exceeding twenty lakhs.

243C (1) Subject to the provisions of this Part, the Legislature of a State may, by law, make provisions with respect to the composition of Panchayats:

Provided that the ratio between the population of the territorial area of a Panchayat at any level and the number of seats in such Panchayat to be filled by election shall, so far as practicable, be the same throughout the State.

(2) All the seats in a Panchayat shall be filled by persons chosen by direct election from territorial constituencies in the Panchayat area and; for this purpose, each Panchayat area shall be divided into territorial constituencies in such manner that the ratio between the population of each constituency and the number of seats allotted to it shall, so far as practicable, be the same throughout the Panchay:. area.

(3) The Legislature of a State may, by law, provide for the representation

(a) of the Chairpersons of the Panchayats at the village level, in the Panchayats at the intermediate level or, in the case of a State not having Panchayats at the intermediate level, in the Panchayats at the district level;
(b) of the Chairpersons of the Panchayats at the intermediate level, in the Panchayats at the district level;
(c) of the members of the House of the People and the members of the Legislative Assembly of the State representing constituencies which comprise wholly or partly a Panchayat area at a level other than the village level, in such Panchayat;
(d) of the members of the Council of States and the members of the Legislative Council of the State, where they are registered as electors within -

(i) a Panchayat area at the intermediate level, in Panchayat at the intermediate level;
(ii) a Panchayat area at the district level, in Panchayat at the district level;

(4) The Chairperson of a Panchayat and other members of a Panchayat whether or not chosen by direct election from territorial constituencies in the Panchayat area shall have the right to vote in the meeting of the Panchayats.

(5) The Chairperson of—

(a) a Panchayat at the village level shall be elected in such manner as the Legislature of a State may, by law, provide; and

(b) a Panchayat at the intermediate level or district level shall be elected by, and from amongst, the elected members thereof.

243D (1) Seats shall be reserved for—
(a) the Scheduled Castes; and
(b) the Scheduled Tribes

in every Panchayat and the number of seats so reserved shall bear, as nearly as may be, the same proportion to the total number of seats to be filled by direct election in that Panchayat as the population of the Scheduled Castes in that Panchayat area or of the Scheduled Tribes in that Panchayat area bears to the total population of that area and such seats may be allotted by rotation to different constituencies in a Panchayat.

(2) Not less than one-third of the total number of seats reserved under clause (1) shall be reserved for women belonging to the Scheduled Castes or, as the case may be, the Scheduled Tribes.

(3) Not less than one-third (including the number of seats reserved for women belonging to the Scheduled Castes and the Scheduled Tribes) of the total number of seats to be filled by direct election in every Panchayat shall be reserved for women and such seats may be allotted by rotation to different constituencies in a Panchayat.

(4) The offices of the Chairpersons in the Panchayats at the village or any other level shall be reserved for the Scheduled Castes, the Scheduled Tribes and women in such manner as the Legislature of a State may, by law, provide:

Provided that the number of offices of Chairpersons reserved for the Scheduled Castes and the Scheduled Tribes in the Panchayats at each level in any State shall bear, as nearly as may be, the same proportion to the total number of such offices in the Panchayats at each level as the population of the Scheduled Castes in the State or of the Scheduled Tribes in the State bears to the total population of the State:

Provided further that not less than one-third of the total number of offices of Chairpersons in the Panchayats at each level shall be reserved for women:

Provided also that the number of offices reserved under this clause shall be allotted by rotation to different Panchayats at each level.

(5) The reservation of seats under clauses (1) and (2) and the reservation of offices of Chairpersons (other than the reservation for women) under clause (4) shall cease to have effect on the expiration of the period specified in Article 334.

(6) Nothing in this Part shall prevent the Legislature of a State from making any provision for reservation of seats in any Panchayat or offices of Chairpersons in the Panchayats

at any level in favour of backward class of citizens.

243E (1) Every Panchayat, unless sooner dissolved under any law for the time being in force, shall continue for five years from the date appointed for its first meeting and no longer.

(2) No amendment, of any law for the time being in force shall have the effect of causing dissolution of a Panchayat at any level, which is functioning immediately before such amendment, till the expiration of its duration specified in clause (1).

(3) An election to constitute a Panchayat shall be completed-

(a) before the expiry of its duration specified in clause(1):

(b) before the expiration of a period of six months from the date of its dissolution:

Provided that where the remainder of the period for which the dissolved Panchayat would have continued is less than six months, it shall not be necessary to hold any election under this clause for constituting the Panchayat for such period.

(4) A Panchayat constituted upon the dissolution of a Panchayat before the expiration of its duration shall continue only for the remainder of the period for which the dissolved Panchayat would have continued under clause (1) had it not been so dissolved.

243F (1) A person shall be disqualified for being chosen as, and for being, a member of a Panchayat—

(a) if he is so disqualified by or under any law for the time being in force for the purposes of elections to the legislature of the State concerned:

Provided that no person shall be disqualified on the ground that he is less than twenty-five years of age, if he has attained the age of twenty-one years;

(b) if he is so disqualified by or under any law made by the Legislature of the State.

(2) If any question arises as to whether a member of a Panchayat has become subject to any of the disqualifications mentioned in clause (1), the question shall be referred for the decision of such authority and in such manner as the Legislature of a State may, by law, provide.

243G Subject to the provisions of this Constitution, the Legislature of a State may, by laws, endow the Panchayats with such powers and authority as may be necessary to enable them to function as institutions of self-government and such law may contain provisions for the devolution of powers and responsibilities upon Panchayats at the appropriate level, subject to such conditions as may be specified therein, with respect to—

(a) the preparation of plans for economic development and social justice;

(b) the implementation of schemes for economic development and social justice as may be entrusted to them including those in relation to the matters listed in the Eleventh Schedule.

243H The Legislature of a State may, by law, —

(a) authorise a Panchayat to levy, collect and appropriate such taxes, duties, tolls and fees in accordance with such procedure and subject to such limits;

(b) assign to a Panchayat such taxes, duties, tolls and fees levied and collected by the State Government for such purposes and subject to such conditions and limits;

(c) provide for making such grants-in-aid to the Panchayats from the Consolidated Fund of the State; and

(d) provide for constitution of such Funds for crediting all moneys received, respectively, by or on behalf of the Panchayats and also for the withdrawal of such moneys therefrom as may be specified in the law.

243-I (1) The Governor of a State shall, as soon as may be within one year from the commencement of the Constitution (Seventy-third Amendment) Act, 1992, and thereafter at the expiration of every fifth years, constitute a Finance Commission to review the financial position of the Panchayats and to make recommendations to the Governor as to —

(a) the principles which should govern —

(i) the distribution between the State and the Panchayats of the net proceeds of the taxes, duties, tolls and fees leviable by the State, which may be divided between them under this Part and the allocation between the Panchayats at all levels of their respective shares of such proceeds;

(ii) the determination of the taxes, duties, tolls and fees which may be assigned to, or appropriated by, the Panchayats;

(iii) the grants-in-aid to the Panchayats from the Consolidated Fund of the State;

(b) the measures needed to improve the financial position of the Panchayats;

(c) any other matter referred to the Finance Commission by the Governor in the interests of sound finance of the Panchayats.

(2) The Legislature of a State may, by law, provide for the composition of the Commission, the qualifications which shall be requisite for appointment as members thereof and the manner in which they shall be selected.

(3) The Commission shall determine their procedure and shall have such powers in the performance of their functions as the Legislature of the State may, by law, confer on them.

(4) The Governor shall cause every recommendation made by the Commission under this Article together with an explanatory memorandum as to the action taken thereon to be laid before the Legislature of the State.

243J The Legislature of the State may, by law, make provisions with respect to the maintenance of accounts by the Panchayats and the auditing of such accounts.

243K (1) The superintendence, direction and control of the preparation of electoral rolls for, and the conduct of, all elections to the Panchayats shall be vested in a State Election Commission consisting of a State Election Commissioner to be appointed by the Governor.

(2) Subject to the provisions of any law made by the Legislature of a State, the conditions of service and tenure of office of the State Election Commissioner shall be such as the Governor may by rule determine:

Provided that the State Election Commissioner shall not be removed from his office except in like manner and on the like grounds as a Judge of a High Court and the conditions of service of the State Election Commissioner shall not be varied to his disadvantage after his appointment.

(3) The Governor of a State shall, when so requested by the State Election Commission make available to the State Election Commission such staff as may be necessary for the discharge of the functions conferred on the State Election Commission by clause (1).

(4) Subject to the provisions of this Constitution, the Legislature of a State may, by Law, make provision with respect to all matters relating to, or in connection with, elections to the Panchayats.

243L The provisions of this Part shall apply to the Union Territories and shall in their application to a Union Territory, have effect as if the references to the Governor of a State were references to the Administrator of the Union Territory appointed under Article 239 and references to the Legislature or the Legislative Assembly of a State were references, in relation to a Union Territory having a Legislative Assembly, to that Legislative Assembly:

Provided that the President may, by public notification, direct that the provisions of this Part shall apply to any Union Territory or part thereof subject to such exceptions and modifications as he may specify in the notification.

243M (1) Nothing in this Part shall apply to the Scheduled Areas referred to in clause (1), and the tribal areas referred to in clause (2) of Article 244.

(2) Nothing in this Part shall apply to —

(a) the States of Nagaland, Meghalaya and Mizoram;

(b) the hill areas in the State of Manipur for which District Councils exist under any law for the time being in force.

(3) Nothing in this Part—

(a) relating to Panchayats at the district level shall apply to the hill areas of the District of Darjeeling in the State of West Bengal for which Darjeeling Gorkha Hill Council exists under any law for the time being in force;

(b) shall be construed to affect the functions and powers of the Darjeeling Gorkha Hill Council constituted under such law.

(4) Notwithstanding anything in this Constitution,—

(a) the Legislature of a State referred to in sub-clause (a) of clause (2) may, by law, extend this Part to that State, except the areas, if any referred to in clause (1) if the Legislative Assembly of that State passes a resolution to that effect by a majority of the total membership of that House and by a majority of not less than two-thirds of the members of that House present and voting;

(b) Parliament may, by law, extend the provisions of this Part to the Scheduled Areas and the tribal areas referred to in clause (1) subject to such exceptions and modifications as may be specified in such law, and no such law shall be deemed to be an amendment of this Constitution for the purposes of Article 368.

243N Notwithstanding anything in this Part, any provision of any law relating to Panchayats in force in a State immediately before the commencement of the Constitution (Seventy-third Amendment) Act, 1992, which is inconsistent with the provisions of this Part, shall continue to be in force until amended or repealed by a competent Legislature or other competent authority or until the expiration of one year from such commencement, whichever is earlier:

Provided that all the Panchayats existing immediately before such commencement shall continue till the expiration of their duration, unless sooner dissolved by a resolution passed to that effect by the Legislative Assembly of that State or, in the case of a State having a Legislative Council, by each House of the Legislature of that State.

243-O. Notwithstanding anything in this Constitution, —

(a) the validity of any law relating to the delimitation of constituencies or the allotment of seats to such constituencies made or purporting to be made under Article 243K, shall not be called in question in any court;

(b) no election to any Panchayat shall be called in question except by an election petition presented to such authority and in such manner as is provided for by or under any law made by the Legislature of a State.

3. In clause (3) of Article 280 of the Constitution, after sub-clause (b), the following sub-clause shall be inserted, namely:

   "(bb) the measures needed to augment the Consolidated Fund of a State to supplement the resources of the Panchayats in the State on the basis of the recommendations made by the Finance Commission of the State;"

4. After the Tenth Schedule to the Constitution, the following Schedule shall be added, namely:—

"*ELEVENTH SCHEDULE*

(Article 243G)

1. Agriculture, including agricultural extension.
2. Land improvement, implementation of land reforms, land consolidation and soil conservation.
3. Minor irrigation, water management and watershed development.
4. Animal husbandry, dairying and poultry.
5. Fisheries.
6. Social forestry and farm forestry.
7. Minor forest produce.
8. Small scale industries, including food processing industries.
9. Khadi, village and cottage industries.
10. Rural housing.
11. Drinking water.
12. Fuel and fodder.
13. Roads, culverts, bridges, ferries, waterways and other means of communication.
14. Rural electrification, including distribution of electricity.
15. Non-conventional energy sources.
16. Poverty alleviation programme.
17. Education, including primary and secondary schools.
18. Technical training and vocational education.
19. Adult and non-formal education.
20. Libraries.
21. Cultural activities.
22. Markets and fairs.
23. Health and sanitation, including hospitals, primary health centres and dispensaries.
24. Family welfare.
25. Women and child development.

26. Social welfare, including welfare of the handicapped and mentally retarded.
27. Welfare of the weaker sections, and in particular of the Scheduled Castes and the Scheduled Tribes.
28. Public distribution system.
29. Maintenance of community assets."

APPENDIX 7

THE PROVISIONS OF THE PANCHAYATS (EXTENSION TO THE SCHEDULED AREAS) ACT, 1996

No. 40 of 1996 24th December, 1996

An Act to provide for the extension of the provisions of Part IX of the Constitution relating to the Panchayats to the Scheduled Areas.

Be it enacted by Parliament in the Forty-seventh Year of the Republic of India as follows:-

This Act may be called the Provisions of the Panchayats (Extension to the Scheduled Areas) Act, 1996.

In this Act, unless the context otherwise requires, 'Scheduled Areas' means Scheduled Areas as referred to in clause (1) of Article 244 of the Constitution.

The provisions of Part IX of the Constitution relating to Panchayats are hereby extended to the Scheduled Areas subject to such exceptions and modifications as are provided in section 4.

Notwithstanding anything contained under Part IX of the Constitution, the Legislature of a State shall not make any law under that Part which is inconsistent with any of the following features, namely :-

A State legislation on the Panchayats that may be made shall be in consonance with the customary law, social and religious practices and traditional management practices of community resources; a village shall ordinarily consist of a habitation or a group of habitations or a hamlet or a group of hamlets comprising a community and managing its affairs in accordance with traditions and customs; every village shall have a Gram Sabha consisting of persons whose names are included in the electoral rolls for the Panchayats at the village level; every Gram Sabha shall be competent to safeguard and preserve the traditions and customs of the people, their cultural identity, community resources and the customary mode of dispute resolution;

Every Gram Sabha shall approve the plans, programmes and projects for social and economic development before such plans, programmes and projects are taken up for implementation by the Panchayat at the village level; be responsible for the identification or selection of persons as beneficiaries under the poverty alleviation and other programmes;

(f) Every Panchayat at the village level shall be required to obtain from the Gram Sabha a certification of utilisation of funds by that Panchayat for the plans, programmes and projects referred to in clause (e); (g) The reservation of seats in the Scheduled Areas at every Panchayat shall be in proportion to the population of the communities in that Panchayat for whom reservation is sought to be given under Part IX of the Constitution.

Provided that the reservation for the Scheduled Tribes shall not be less than one-half of the total number of seats;

Provided further that all seats of Chairpersons of Panchayats at all levels shall be reserved for the Scheduled Tribes.

(h) The State Government may nominate persons belonging to such Scheduled Tribes as have no representation in the Panchayat at the intermediate level or the Panchayat at the district level;

Provided that such nomination shall not exceed one-tenth of the total members to be elected in that Panchayat;

(i) The Gram Sabha or the Panchayats at the appropriate level shall be consulted before making the acquisition of land in the Scheduled Areas for development projects and before re-settling or rehabilitating persons affected by such projects in the Scheduled Areas; the actual planning and implementation of the projects in the Scheduled Areas shall be coordinated at the State level.

(j) Planning and management of minor water bodies in the Scheduled Areas shall be entrusted to Panchayats at the appropriate level;

(k) The recommendations of the Gram Sabha or the Panchayats at the appropriate level shall be made mandatory prior to grant of prospecting license or mining lease for minor minerals in the Scheduled Areas;

(l) The prior recommendation of the Gram Sabha or the Panchayats at the appropriate level shall be made mandatory for grant of concession for the exploitation of minor minerals by auction;

(m) While endowing Panchayats in the Scheduled Areas with such powers and authority as many be necessary to enable them to function as institutions of self-government, a State Legislature shall ensure that the Panchayats at the appropriate level and the Gram Sabha are endowed specifically with:

(i) the power to enforce prohibition or to regulate or restrict the sale and consumption of any intoxicant;

(ii) the ownership of minor forest produce;

(iii) the power to prevent alienation of land in the Scheduled Areas and to take appropriate action to restore any unlawfully alienated land of a Scheduled Tribe;

(iv) the power to manage village markets by whatever name called;

(v) the power to exercise control over money lending to the Scheduled Tribes;

(vi) the power to exercise control over institutions and functionaries in all social sectors;

(vii) the power to control over local plans and resources for such plans including tribal sub-plans;

(n) The State legislation that may endow Panchayats with powers and authority as may be necessary to enable them to function as institutions of self-government shall contain safeguards to ensure that Panchayats at the higher level do not assume the powers and authority of any Panchayats at the lower level or of the Gram Sabha;

(o) The State Legislature shall endeavor to follow the pattern of the Sixth Schedule to the Constitution while designing the administrative arrangements in the Panchayats at the district levels in the Scheduled Area.

Notwithstanding anything in Part IX of the Constitution with exceptions and modifications made by this Act, any provision of any law relating to Panchayats in force in the Scheduled Areas immediately before the date on which this Act receives the assent of the President which is inconsistent with the provisions of Part IX with such exceptions and modifications shall continue to be in force until amended or repealed by a competent Legislature or other competent authority or until the expiration of one year from the date on which this Act receives the assent of the President.

APPENDIX 8

Agenda for Future Research Studies

The present study on decentralisation has focused on the state of panchayats after the 73rd Constitution Amendment Act. The main objectives of the study have been to study the present status of decentralisation and to examine the problems therein and to assess how decentralisation has helped in the socio-economic development of rural areas. It has made an attempt to explore the measures that are necessary to strengthen the process of decentralisation and in meeting the norms of good governance. Nonetheless, there are still several areas, which require to be further researched and studied, and the important ones are as under:

- First among all, the in-depth research is needed into socio-political and economic set-up at the village level, and how it is influencing the panchayat functioning in general and the ability of people to participate. In this context, it may also be studied how the present state institutions (political, executive and judicial) are able to ensure that the desired objectives of decentralisation are achieved. And what measures are further needed in the direction.
- At the micro-level, quality of people's participation in the development process needs to be examined. In this context the efficacy of gram sabha in ensuring people's participation needs special focus.
- Relationship between administrative officers and technical officers, and between officers and PR members is a subject of vital importance at the operational level. It requires to be studied elaborately. Also of importance is to study about attitudes of PR members about their perceived role, about development functionaries, about problems of people; and similarly, in case of development functionaries about elected members, about people's participation, about working with people. The perception of PR members and development functionaries about values such as responsiveness, transparency and accountability (social audit) needs to be examined. Here the study may concentrate on the nature of attitudes, causes of a particular attitude, which are the areas that would require attitudinal changes, and how training or administrative action can be useful in this regard and so on.
- Capacity Building: Identifying training needs is an another area that needs to be researched as a priority item. It must focus on functional skills and bahavioural aspects of training. The research study should also include the formulation of planning methodology for the preparation of plans at the three tiers and for suggesting the institutional mechanism; the criteria of transfer of functions and devolution of funds;

and the design of delivery mechanism for making basic services available to people at the village level.

- Other important area that merits specialised study is the role of PRIs vis-a-vis voluntary organisations, cooperatives and CBOs. Here, the study should deal with the issues like areas of functioning of each institution; areas that have overlaps and that require functional matching; and how the panchayats should involve other institutions in the village development programmes without impinging on their functional freedom.

The above areas are illustrative and many more issues can be added to but all the research studies must focus on: how the findings would add value to the framework of reforms that can facilitate people in availing opportunities and making basic services available to people at the village level.

Each area, that has been suggested for the research studies, should be studied as an individual subject, however, there is a need of having all these areas covered in totality in order to have comprehensive view about the process of decentralisation and the panchayat system. Here, it would be appropriate to organise the research work under one umbrella having research institutions of repute. And this umbrella organisation should be able to provide direction and coordinate the research and study, and then document the findings for future course of action.

DEFINITIONS

Decentralisation: It is a process through which authority and responsibilities for some substantial government functions are transferred from Central government to intermediate and local governments, and often also to communities. And lower-ranking decision-units acquire all powers and responsibilities and have also control over the determination of their goals and targets. The true decentralisation implies three things:

- Assigning of "responsibilities" (i.e. functions) with matching powers and requisite finances;
- Rendering the decentralised level fully accountable for its activities; and
- Ensuring participation of the local population in planning and implementation.

Literally, decentralisation means the action or fact of reducing or undoing 'centralisation' or 'concentration'. In the political sense, complete or total decentralisation would mean 'the withering away of the state'.

Decentralisation and its Variants

De-concentration: It implies handing over limited central government powers, functions and resources to its field units.

Delegation: It implies transferring responsibility for specifically defined functions to lower level organisations, but the accountability remains with the higher level that delegates the responsibility.

Devolution: It implies transfer of functions and authority with a greater autonomy in respect of certain defined functions, including decision-making authority. The authority handed over to local institutions through devolution can be taken back only after making amendments in the law.

Privatisation: It refers to a form of decentralisation in which the government may transfer functions to voluntary organisations or private enterprises, and allow them to perform certain functions.

Dimensions of Decentralisation

Political Decentralisation: It refers to transfer of policy, decision-making and legislative powers from Central governments to local bodies that are democratically elected by their constituencies.

Functional Decentralisation: It refers to transferring subjects to local bodies in order to enable them to plan and implement programmes as per their local needs.

Administrative Decentralisation: It refers to placing planning and implementation responsibilities with the local bodies and defining the roles and responsibilities of functionaries and elected members.

Financial Decentralisation: It refers to devolving taxation, funds and expenditure powers upon local bodies.

Self-government: It exists when a level of government has dominion over substantial, clearly defined functions and can pass / enact laws with regard to these functions within its area of jurisdiction — state, district, village, etc. For self-government to exist there must be unambiguous political, fiscal and administrative devolution of assigned subjects.

Institutional Development (ID): ID is the creation or reinforcement of the capacity of an organisation to generate, allocate and use human and financial resources effectively to attain development objectives, public or private. It includes not only the building and strengthening of institutions but also rationalisation of capacity (manpower, infrastructure and logistics) in the pursuit of enhancing efficiency and effectiveness of institutions.

Total Tax Collection (Own Income): The total tax collection is a sum of tax and non-tax revenue. In the context of panchayats, it is also referred as own income of a panchayat.

Tax Revenue: It includes tax collected from sources like property, vehicles, animals, trade, professions, theatre / shows, advertisements, boats, etc.

Non-tax Revenue: It includes tax collected from sources like rents from panchayat assets (including panchayat land), user charges, fee and fines, income from municipal investments, etc.

Shramdan: It refers to voluntary work done by people in their localities.

Natural Resources Capital: It refers to the quantum of water, forest, fodder and capability of land (including the quality of soil).

Social Capital: It refers to features of social organization, such as trust, norms, and networks that can improve the efficiency of society by facilitating coordinated actions.

Human Capital: The total sum of human potential in terms of capabilities is termed as human capital.

Financial Capital: It refers to the financial capacity of people and that of institutions.

Physical Capital: It refers to physical assets (roads, buildings, irrigation structures, etc.) created in an area.

Natural Resources Management: It refers to efficient and optimum utilisation of resources for meeting the human needs. Among others, it would include conservation of water, enhancing the forest cover and fodder availability, and raising the capability of land (including the quality of soil).

Conflicting Interests: It arises due to varying opinions or understanding of different clientele groups or decision-makers. The conflicts may be on account of personal or family or political or economic or caste factor, or combination of one or more.

Basic Services: Though the gambit of services will vary, but in the context of present scenario of rural development, it should include the availability of inputs and services under primary education, health, family welfare, drinking water in the social sector; and public distribution system, irrigation and agriculture in the economic sector.

People's Participation: It includes one or the combination of following activities:

- participation in the gram sabha;
- raising of development issues in the gram sabha;
- raising the problems of the weaker sections;
- participation in planning process;
- participation in implementation;
- participation in social audit and raising objections;
- registering complaints for non-functioning of utilities;
- participating in identifying solutions and contributing in the running of utilities;
- raising of public issues of importance; and
- contribution in kind or money, or by *shramdan*.

Meaningful People's Participation: When people have confidence to raise issues in gram sabha, mobilise public opinion on important issues; and when people will demand for quality of service and will contribute for the services to be provided.

Democratic Values: It includes, among others, meaningful people's participation, equal access to all sections in the socio-political life and respect for institutional norms.

Governance: The governance is a process encompassing decision-making and delivery of services with norms and values determining it. The norms and values, among others, will include responsiveness to people's needs, fairness and consistency, transparency, performance matching capacity and accountability to people.

Good Governance: It means achieving the desired goals and delivering through a system of adequate capacity to perform with sound norms and values. Good governance is in essence about being able to provide equal socio-economic and political opportunities to people, being responsive to people's needs, being able to provide basic services to people, and being fair and accountable in dealings.

Local Institutions: It refers to panchayats at the local levels viz., district, block and gram panchayats.

Gram Panchayat: It is the lowest tier of the panchayati raj (local institution) system. One gram panchayat may have one or group of villages.

Block Panchayat (Panchayat Samiti): It is the middle tier of the PR system, and generally has 10-12 gram panchayats.

District Panchayat (Zilla Parishad): It is the top tier of the PR system, and generally has 12-15 blocks.

Gram Sabha: It is the village meeting organised at the lowest level to discuss about village development planning, and is attended by the members of the concerned ward / village in a gram panchayat.

Marginalised Groups : SCs, STs, OBCs.

Weaker Section : Marginalised groups and women.

Negative Influence : Influence resulting from actions like control, regulation, etc.

Positive Influence : Influence resulting from actions like HRD, institution building, etc.

Sustainability *(in the context of decentralisation):* It refers to the abilities of panchayats in meeting the basic needs of people and providing opportunities to all in order to meet their aspirations and provide them quality of life, on a sustained basis. It has four dimensions:

Social Dimension: It refers to encouraging the social harmony and ensuring adequate and equal access to opportunities for all sections of society, so that it revitalises and strengthens sound social culture in a holistic manner.

Political Dimension: It refers to encouraging all the sections to participate with equal freedom in the political process.

Economic Dimension: It refers to generating efficiently the enough resources to meet the growing demands of people.

Institutional Dimension: It refers to delivering services to people at the village level and sustaining the development process.

Building Enabling Environment: It refers to creation of environment that would facilitate the panchayats to function efficiently. It would require taking certain measures such as providing security and peace at the village level; secured status for local bodies; empowerment of people; political will for providing autonomy to panchayats; and improving capabilities of PR members and development functionaries to enable them to handle the development task of panchayats.

Opportunities: In the context of decentralisation, it has three dimensions: *first*, social; *second*, political; and *third*, economic. Social dimension includes the freedom to form and join groups; political dimension entails the freedom to join and participate in political process; and economic dimension includes the freedom to avail services or economic activities for raising income. All will lead to raising the quality of life.

Equal Opportunities: It is a state when the opportunities are availed by people, without any prejudice.

Value System: It refers to the way people in any organisation think, respond and work. And, in the context of decentralisation, values would include transparency, responsiveness for people's concern, decision-making process, accountability, people's participation, working with people, commitment, team-work, and quality and efficiency of work.

Work Culture: It refers to values that are followed in an organisation. These values determine the work culture.

REFERENCES

1. Amatya, S.L., *Rural Development Through Decentralised Planning*, East West Centre Association, Honolulu, March 1988.

2. Aziz, Abdul and Arnold David. D., *Decentralised Governance in Asian Countries*, Sage Publications, New Delhi,1996.

3. Banerjee, Ajit M and Chandrasekaran, K.A., Editor, *Renewing Governance*, Tata McGraw-Hill Publishing Company Limited, New Delhi, 1996.

4. Bennett, Robert J.(ed)., Decentralisation, *Local Governments and Markets: Towards a Post-Welfare Agenda*, Oxford, U.K: Clarendon Press, 1990.

5. Carvajal, Eduardo P., "Decentralisation and Democracy : The New Latin American Municipality", Revista de la in Comisi 1995, *Decentralisation and Democracy Review*, 55 (April): 41-54, 1995.

6. Charles V. Kidd, *Manpower Policies for the Use of Science and Technology in Development*, Pergamon Press, New York, 1980.

7. Commonwealth Local Government Forum, *Good Local Government and Sustainable Development (Asia Region),* Islamabad, 1997.

8. Conyers, D., *Decentralisation of Development — A Review of Literature in Public Administration and Development*, 4, 1984.

9. Dayal, Rajeshwar, *Community Development, Panchayati Raj and Sahakari Samaj*, Metropolitan Book Co. Private Ltd., Delhi, 1965.

10. Dube, S.C., *India's Changing Villages*, Cornell University Press, Ithaca, N.Y. 1958.

11. Foote Whyte William, *Participatory Action Research*, Sage Publications, New Delhi, 1991.

12. Fox, Jonathan, "Latin America's Emerging Local Politics", *Journal of Democracy* (April) : 105-15,1994.

13. Gaventa, John, *Participation, Poverty and Social Exclusion in North and South*, Working Paper, Institute of Development Studies, University of Sussex, Brighton,1997.

14. Gideon Sjobergroger Nett, *A Methodology for Social Research, Rawat Publications*, New Delhi, 1997.

15. B.B. Goel, *Project Management*, Deep & Deep Publications, New Delhi, 1987.

16. Govt. of India Planning Commission and the Department of Rural Development, Ministry of Agriculture, New Delhi, *Report of the Committee to review the existing Administrative Arrangements for Rural Development and Poverty Alleviation Programmes*. (CAARD), New Delhi, December 1985.

17. Govt. of India, Department of Rural Development, *Report of the Committee on Panchayati Raj Institutions* (Ashok Mehta Committee), Ministry of Agriculture and Irrigation, New Delhi, 1978.

18. Govt. of India, Planning Commission, *Guidelines for Block-level Planning*, New Delhi, 1979.

19. Govt. of India, Planning Commission, *Report of the Working Group on District Planning*, New Delhi, May, 1984.

20. Gupta, D.N., *Rural Development System*, Books India International, New Delhi, 2001.

21. Gupta, D.N., *Integrated Development Planning*, Books India International, New Delhi, 2004.

22. Hanson, A.H., *The Process of Planning*, Oxford University Press, 1966.

23. Hicks, U.K., *Development from Below : Local Government and Finance in Developing Countries of the Commonwealth*, Oxford : Oxford University Press, 1961.

24. Hicks, U.K., *Development from Below*, Oxford University Press, 1961.

25. Isaac Thomas, T.M., *Local Democracy and Development*, Left Word, New Delhi, 2000.

26. Israel, Arturo, *Institutional Development*, World Bank Publication, The Johns Hopkins University Press, Baltimore and London, 1987.

27. Israel, Ligwe, *Local Government Journal Personal Management in Nigerian Local Government: A Review*, Local Government Studies, Volume- LXVII No.4 Oct-Dec 1996.

28. Israel, Ligwe, *Local Government Personal Management in Nigerian Local Government: A Review*, Local Government Studies, Volume- LXVII No.4 Oct-Dec, 1996.

29. ISS, *Status of Panchayati Raj in the States and Union Territories of India 2000*, Concept Publishing Company, New Delhi, 2000.

30. Jacob, G., (edited) *Readings on Panchayati Raj*, National Institute of Community Development, Hyderabad, 1967.

31. Jha, S.N. and Mathur, P.C., *Decentralisation and Local Politics*, Sage Publication, New Delhi, 1999.

32. John Van Leerdam, *Changes in Dutch Government Organisations*, Local Government Studies, Volume-21 Number -3, Autumn 1995.

33. John van, Leerdam, *Changes in Dutch Government Organisations*, Local Government Studies, Volume-21, No. 3, Autumn, 1995.

34. Kaufman, Roger A., *Educational System Planning*, Prentice Hall INC, New Jersey, 1972.

35. Khera, S.S., *District Administration in India*, Asia Publishing House, London, 1964.

36. Konrad Adenauer Foundation (KAF), *State-Local Fiscal Relations in India*, Manohar Publishers, New Delhi, 1998.

37. Kueck, Gert W., Mathur S.C. and Schindler Klaus, *Federalisam and Decentralisation*, Konrad Adenauer Foundation, New Delhi, 1998.

38. Leach, Melissa and Robin Mearns, *The Lie of the Land: Challenging Wisdom on the African Environment*, Oxford and Portsmouth, N.H.: James Currey and Heinemann, 1996.

39. Maddick, H., *Panchayati Raj - A Study of Rural Local Government in India*, Longman Group Ltd., London, 1970.

40. Maheshwari, B., *Studies in Panchayati Raj*, Metropolitan Book Co. Private Ltd., Delhi, 1963.

41. Mathur, H.M., *Administrating Development in the Third World*, Sage Publications, New Delhi, 1986.

42. Manor, James, *The Political Economy of Democratic Decentralisation*, The World Bank, Washington, 1999.

43. Meenakshisundaram, S.S., *Decentralisation in Developing Countries*, Concept Publishing Company, New Delhi, 1994.

44. Ministry of Rural Development (MORD), *Poverty Estimates*, New Delhi, 1996-97.

45. Ministry of Rural Development (MORD), *Report of the Task Force on Devolution of Powers & Functions upon Panchayati Raj Institutions*, New Delhi, 2001a.

46. Ministry of Rural Development (MORD), *Position Paper on Panchayati Raj in different States in India*, New Delhi, 2001b.

47. Misra, R.P. and Sundaram K.V., *Multi-level Planning and Integrated Rural Development in India*, Heritage Publishers, New Delhi, 1990.

48. Misra Sasi and Vijaya Sherry Chand P.G., *Institution Building, An International Perspective on Management Education*, Macmillan India limited, Delhi, 1999.

49. Montgomery, John D., *Public Administration Review*, Vol. 40. No.5, 1980.

50. Muthien, Yvonne and Meshack Khosa, "The Kingdom, the Volkstaat and the New South Africa: Drawing South Africa's New Regional Boundarie", *Journal of Southern African Studies* (June): 303-22, 1995, New Delhi, 1987.

51. NIRD, *Action Research Project — Strategy for Operationalising 73rd Constitutional Amendment*, Hyderabad, 1999a.

52. NIRD, *Research Study; Need for Restructuring Anti-Poverty Programmes and Strengthening Delivery System*, Hyderabad,1999b.

53. NIRD, *Report of State Finance Commission Cell*, Hyderabad, 2000.

54. Norman T. Uphoff and Milton J.Esman, *Local Organization for Rural Development: Analysis of Asian Experiences*, Cornell University, Ithaca, New York, 1974.

55. Ortrun Zuber Skerritt, *Action Research for Change and Development*, Avebury:Gower Publishing Company Limited, Hants Gull 3 H R, UK, 1991.

56. Ostrom, Elinor, Governing the Commons: The Evolution of Institutions for Collective Actions, Cambridge University Press, 1990.

57. Panganiban, Elena, *Democratic Decentralization in Contemporary Times: The New Local Government Code of the Philippines*, Conference paper, Institute of Commonwealth Studies, University of London, 1994.

58. Paul, Hirst, *Associative Democracy : New Forms of Economic and Social Governance*, Cambridge Polity Press, 1994.

59. Perry, James L., *Handbook of Public Administration*, Jossey-Bass Publisher, San Francisco, 1996.

60. Planning Commission: Report of the Task Force on Panchayati Raj Institutions, New Delhi, 2001.

61. Putnam, Robert D, Making Democracy Work — Civic Traditions in modern Italy, Princeton University Press, Princeton, 1993.

62. Rajiv Gandhi Foundation (a), *Revitalisation of Panchayati Raj in India*, New Delhi, 1997.

63. Rajiv Gandhi Foundation (b), *National Seminar on Panchayats*, New Delhi, 1997.

64. Rajiv Gandhi Foundation, *Dialogue on Panchayat*, New Delhi, 1999.

65. Reddy, Y. Venugopal, *Multilevel Planning in India*, Vikas Publishing House, New Delhi, 1979.

66. Richard Winter, *Research and the Nature of Social Inquiry Professional Innovation and Educational Work*, Avebury: Gower Publishing Company Limited, Hants, Gull 3H R, UK, 1987.

67. Robert Leach & Neil Barnett, *The New Public Management and the Local Government Review*, Local Government Studies, Volume-23, No. 3, Autumn, 1997.

68. Robinson, Marguerite S., *Local Politics: The Law of the Fishes: Development Through Political Change in Medak District*, Andhra Pradesh (South India), Delhi, Oxford University Press, New York, 1988.

69. *Rural Development Statistics* (RDS), NIRD, Hyderabad, 1999

70. Saich A.J., *Discos and Dictatorship: Party-State and Society Relations in the People's Republic of China*, Leiden: Rijks Universiteit Leiden, 1993.

71. Silverman, Jerry M., *Public Sector Decentralization — Economic Policy and Sector Investment Programms*, World Bank Technical Paper No.188, The World Bank, 1992.

72. Simon, David, *Third Regional Development : A Reappraisal*, Paul Chapman Publishing Ltd, London, 1990.

73. Smith, B.C., *Decentralisation, the Territorial Dimension of the State,* London Allen and Unwin, 1985.

74. Sundaram, K.V., *Decentralised Multilevel Planning*, Concept Publishing Company, New Delhi, 1997.

75. Tinker, H., *The Foundations of Local Self-Government in India, Pakistan and Burma*, Athlone Press, London, 1954

76. The Training Division (A brochure), New Delhi: Government of India Department of Personnel and Administrative Reforms, Training Division 1978.

77. Tilly, Charles, *Coercion, Capital and European States, AD 990 - 1992,* Cambridge, MA and Oxford: Blackwell, 1992.

78. Tordoff, William, "Decentralisation: Comparative Experience in Commonwealth Africa", *Journal of Modern African Studies*, 432 (December) : 555 - 80, 1994.

79. UNDP, *Governance for Sustainable Growth and Equity*, Report of International Conference (28-30 July), New York, 1997.

80. United Nations, *Decentralisation for National and Local Development,* New York, 1962.

81. UNDP, *National Workshop on Community Driven Management and Decentralisation, Strengthening Decentralisation*, Key Issues for Action, New Delhi, 2000.

82. Vajpeyi, Dhirendra, *Local Government in the Politics in the Third World*, Heritage Publishers, New Delhi, 1990.

83. World Bank, *Articles of the Agreement of the International Bank for Reconstruction and Development*, Washington, 1989.

84. World Bank, *Evaluation Results*, Operations Evaluation Department, Washington, 1995.

85. World Bank, *Overview of Rural Decentralisation in India*, Vol. I, New Delhi, 2000.

86. Yugandhar, B.N. and Mukherjee, A., *Readings in Decentralised Planning*, Concept Publishing Company, New Delhi, 1991.

87. Zafarullah Habib, *Local Government Reform and Accountability in Bangladesh*, Regional Development Dialogue, Volume 18, Number 2, Autumn 1997.

INDEX